To Jimmy !

May your labor
day not be
terribly laborious.
Best
Dr Harden

Done in a Day

100 years of great writing from The Chicago Daily News

Done in a Day
100 years of great writing from The Chicago Daily News

Edited by
Dick Griffin
Rob Warden

THE SWALLOW PRESS INC.
CHICAGO

Many members of the *Daily News* staff helped prepare this book. The editors particularly thank John Downs, Joe Cappo, John Fischetti, Henry Herr Gill, Martha Groves, Robert J. Herguth, John Justin Smith, and Lois Wille. The counsel and kindness of Joe Kamalick and June Rosner also were much appreciated.

First Edition
First Printing

Published by
The Swallow Press Incorporated
811 West Junior Terrace
Chicago, Illinois 60613

Library of Congress Catalog Card Number: 76-46675
ISBN O-8040-0755-1

Royalties from this work have been donated to the Albert P. Weisman Memorial Scholarship Fund at Columbia College, Chicago, Illinois.

Contents

Preface

Introduction   5

Openers   11

Metropolis   35

War   67

Learning   97

Catastrophe   123

Arts and Letters   147

Life and Death   182

Rights and Reform   231

Vietnam   269

Money   307

Sport   359

Crime   391

Challenges   425

Index to Reporters   472

Preface

We are delighted to present this collection of articles that have appeared in the *Chicago Daily News* in its century of existence as one of the world's most distinguished newspapers. The stories published here weren't chosen because they tell history as seen through the eyes of reporters, but rather to demonstrate fine newspaper writing as it is practiced by the staff of the *Daily News*. Thus, while some of the articles deal with such momentous subjects as war and assassination, many more concern small matters—a little girl's first day in school, an interview with a movie mogul, a school board meeting. Some of these articles are 10, 50 or 80 years old, but they are as alive today as when they were first inked on newsprint.

Marshall Field, Publisher
Chicago Daily News
December, 1976

Done in a Day

100 years of great writing from
The Chicago Daily News

Appendectomy below enemy waters. John Downs / Daily News.

Openers:
George Weller
George Ade
Robert J. Casey
Donald Zochert

Introduction

"There's a good reporter you ought to hire," the managing editor of the *Chicago Daily News* was told by one of his writers.

"We're overstaffed," replied the editor, Henry Justin Smith, hoping that would close the subject

"He writes good poetry," the staff member said.

Smith looked up. "What kind of poetry?"

"The new kind, wonderful stuff. Like Walt Whitman."

"Tell him to come around."

In due time the man came around. Smith hired him and turned him over to an exasperated city editor with orders not to burden the new reporter with trivial chores, like covering the day's news.

Smith had read the man's poetry and he was sure he was in the presence of genius. He was right. The man was Carl Sandburg, and the reporter who recommended him was Ben Hecht, who later became a world-famous playwright (co-author of *The Front Page*), novelist and movie writer. None of this impressed the city editor, who sniffed: "A good spotted terrier would round out the staff." But Smith, a sharp-eyed editor who cared as much about the day's news as did the city editor, cared too much about literature to pass up the chance to hire Carl Sandburg.

Smith was passionately in love with the *Daily News* and he saw the newspaper as a daily novel written by a score of Balzacs. More than any other single person, Smith helped create a literary tradition at the *Daily News* that is unparalleled in American journalism.

"Some of us, so long as we live, will never abandon the old-fashioned but thrilling idea that good writing for newspapers is worthwhile," Smith wrote in the 1930s, shortly before his death. "We shall wag our gray beards furiously at every fancied opponent. We shall break our lances against every windmill.

"We love fine, sincere, exceptional work, and we despise mediocrity. We hate with all our power of hatred every sort of easy, imitative, complacent, patented, bunk-filled pseudo-literature, and we loathe equally the conditions responsible and the men who teach that sort of writing."

Smith constantly searched for talent worthy of his standards and gave people whose talents attracted him compelling reasons to drop everything and come write for him.

On a dull day in Minneapolis during the Depression, a bored young editor invented a story about a local resident living to a prodigious age. Smith saw the story and was smitten by it. He telegraphed the editor, asking for the name of the writer. The young man, mortified at what he had done and terror-stricken at telling the revered Smith, wrote him a three-page confession. Smith wired the youth: "Accuracy can be taught, imagination cannot. We can use both. Offering you a job starting immediately. Confirm. Smith, C.D.N."

Overwhelmed, the youth accepted, then remembered money hadn't been mentioned and wired Smith about it. Back came the reply: "Salary inadequate, if that matters." Suddenly it didn't, and the young man flew to Chicago on winged feet.

His name was Robert Hardy Andrews, and he became famous for his extraordinary output—the fastest typewriter in the paper's history. Between Andrews' work for the paper and side work he wrote an average of 100,000 words a week—hardly literature but contributing something to our culture, for his side work as a radio writer brought into existence Jack Armstrong, the All-American Boy, and added thousands of episodes to the ethereal lives of Ma Perkins and Just Plain Bill.

Bob Andrews shared a tiny office with Carl Sandburg, already considered one of the five greatest living poets in the United States. For the newspaper Sandburg covered the early years of the labor movement, and wrote a pioneering series of articles in 1919 on the plight of America's blacks. But mostly, he was the newspaper's reviewer of "picture plays"; he could handle that job in a couple of days each week and spend the rest of the time working on his poetry and, later, his famous biography of Lincoln. That reviewing didn't capture his full attention is apparent from one review in which he failed to name the movie, but said it was based on a novel by a famous Polish author—then failed to name the novel.

Smith's endless search for talent included hiring copy boys who might someday blossom into fine writers. One man recalls writing an article about birds when he was 16 years old and being summoned to the *Daily News* to meet Smith.

"I liked your story about the herring gulls," said Smith. "I think you'd make a good newspaperman." The boy gulped and said he was planning to become a naturalist. Smith stiffened. "Any fool can be a naturalist. You've heard it said that the proper study of mankind is man. With your talent for writing, that's what you should be studying, man himself. Here on this newspaper we study men and women, their foibles, their idiosyncrasies, and we report them to the people."

What Smith built, in the first third of this century, was the most literary, talented staff any newspaper ever had—writers whose stories sparkled with style, elegance and wit.

"It was a reportorial staff half daft with literary dreams," said Ben Hecht, who went on to write such memorable movies as *Scarface* and *Spellbound*. Hecht continued: "But everybody was so busy being literary that nobody could produce a good murder story. Once I wrote a story involving a triple murder and forgot to mention until the third paragraph that somebody had been killed. This was difficult on the readers—and the city editor."

Meyer Levin, later author of the popular novel *Compulsion*, based on the infamous Loeb-Leopold murder case, said of the *Daily News* staff, of which he was a part in the 1920s: "In those days one didn't apply for a newspaper job in order to become a journalist. At least, not on the *Chicago Daily News*. One applied in order to become an author."

The paper's extraordinary literary tradition started in 1882, when publisher Victor F. Lawson hired a young man who became the nation's first daily newspaper columnist. The young man wrote a potpourri of topical items, witticisms and verse. His name was Eugene Field and among the verse he wrote for his column were two children's poems that will be favorites forever: *Wynken, Blinken and Nod* and *Little Boy Blue*. In 1895 Field died in his sleep at the age of 45. After him there were many others marked by genius. George Ade, later one of America's premier playwrights and humorists, wrote a daily column. Ray Stannard Baker, later the distinguished biographer of Woodrow Wilson, was a reporter and feature writer. Finley Peter Dunne, the famed humorist, was first a sports writer and editor. Lloyd Lewis was a theater critic, sports writer, war reporter and managing editor, and on the side he was renowned for his Civil War histories and a play he wrote with Sinclair Lewis.

Vincent Sheean, a reporter and foreign correspondent, later was a chum of Edna St. Vincent Millay and Ernest Hemingway and author of 20 books. Vincent Starrett, wounded in 1916 while covering a war in Mexico for the *Daily News*, later became a distinguished book critic and authority on Sherlock Holmes.

The *Daily News* Foreign Service, founded by Lawson, quickly became world famous. In one of Sir Arthur Conan Doyle's celebrated Professor Challenger stories, *When the World Screamed*, the professor was drilling through the Earth's crust to prove his theory that the world was a living organism. Reporters were hot on his trail: "Oh, they are buzzing round proper. Look at that," he said, pointing to a dot on the skyline. "See that glint. That's the telescope of the *Chicago Daily News*."

Sterling North, our book critic, went on to become the author of popular animal books, such as *Rascal*. Henry Blackman Sell created for the *Daily News* the first newspaper literary section in the country with signed reviews. (If he liked a book he reviewed it more than once. He gave Sherwood Anderson's *Winesburg, Ohio* seven reviews and something called *White Shadows in the South Seas* 26 reviews.)

In fact, the paper's critics probably have contributed almost as much as the fine writers to its literary tradition. The Christmas book section in 1940, for instance, included essays and reviews written, doubtlessly for free, by Mortimer J. Adler, Sinclair Lewis, Sherwood Anderson, James T. Farrell, Hemingway, Sandburg, Christopher Morley and Richard Wright. They obviously liked the company they kept in the newspaper.

The thousands of reporters and writers who have staffed the *Chicago Daily News* since its founding on Dec. 23, 1875, have taken their greatest pride in their work appearing in the columns of the newspaper. While many have written books on the side, their chief aim has been excellence in news reporting and writing.

Edwin A. Lahey wasn't known beyond the newspaper audience, but he did striking work as a crime and labor writer before World War II and as Washington correspondent and bureau chief afterwards. Robert J. Casey wrote 34 now-forgotten books in his spare time, but his local stories in the 1920s and 1930s and his vivid war reporting between 1939 and 1945 were eagerly read by Chicagoans.

Today there are others seeking excellence in newspaper work and finding it: our Pulitzer Prize-winning Mike Royko, widely considered the finest columnist in the nation; Peter Lisagor, chief of our Washington Bureau, a marvelous stylist considered by his peers one of the finest of all Washington reporters; Sydney J. Harris, for 32 years author of a dazzling daily column; John Fischetti, the incomparable editorial cartoonist and Pulitzer-winner.

There is Keyes Beech, a Pulitzer winner in Korea, who has been covering Asian wars for a generation; Lois Wille, also the winner of a Pulitzer, a sensitive writer about people, the city and their problems; science editor Arthur J. Snider, whose reporting experience embraces the discovery of the Salk polio vaccine, atomic research and moon shots; M. W. Newman, editor, critic, writer, reporter; Raymond R. Coffey, a versatile genius equally at home covering the civil rights struggle, the war in Vietnam and the diplomatic scene in London; William J. Eaton, a brilliant Washington correspondent who won a Pulitzer, and Philip J. O'Connor, a rewrite man with a typewriter like a machine gun and an incredible talent for getting stories by telephone.

A century of such men and women, writing tens of thousands of words every day about their city, their country, the world. Fifteen Pulitzers and five wars. More than 30,500 issues of the *Daily News*, from the shootout at the Little Big Horn to the flight from Saigon. Literature, done in a day.

Dick Griffin and Rob Warden

Weller of the News describes emergency surgery by a pharmacist's mate aboard a U.S. sub in enemy waters

An emergency appendectomy performed by a young pharmacist's mate aboard a U.S. submarine while Japanese destroyers passed above was grist for a popular World War II movie, Destination Tokyo. *But before it was a Hollywood production, it was a story in the* Chicago Daily News. *Correspondent George Weller's dramatic, exclusive account, published Dec. 14, 1942, won a Pulitzer Prize.*

SOMEWHERE IN AUSTRALIA—"They are giving him ether now," was what they said back in the aft torpedo rooms.

"He's gone under, and they're ready to cut him open," the crew whispered, sitting on their pipe bunks cramped between torpedos.

One man went forward and put his arm quietly around the shoulder of another man who was handling the bow diving planes.

"Keep her steady, Jake," he said. "They've just made the first cut. They're feeling around for it now."

"They" were a little group of anxious-faced men with their arms thrust into reversed white pajama coats. Gauze bandages hid all their expressions except the tensity in their eyes.

"It" was an acute appendix inside Dean Rector of Chautauqua, Kan. The stabbing pains had become unendurable the day before, which was Rector's first birthday at sea. He was 19 years old.

The big depth gauge that looks like a factory clock and stands beside the "Christmas tree" of red and green gauges regulating the flooding chambers showed where they were. They were below the surface. And above them were enemy waters crossed and recrossed by whirring propellers of Japanese destroyers and transports.

The nearest naval surgeon competent to operate on the 19-year-old seaman was thousands of miles and many days away. There was just one way to prevent the appendix from bursting, and that was for the crew to operate upon their shipmate themselves.

And that's what they did; they operated upon him. It was probably one of the largest operations in number of participants that ever occurred.

"He says he's ready to take his chance," the gobs whispered from bulkhead to bulkhead.

"That guy's regular"—the word traveled from bow planes to propeller and back again.

They "kept her steady."

The chief surgeon was a 23-year-old pharmacist's mate wearing a blue blouse with white-taped collar and squashy white duck cap. His name was Wheeler B. Lipes. He came from Newcastle near Roanoke, Va., and had taken the Navy hospital course in San Diego, thereafter serving three years in the naval hospital at Philadelphia, where his wife lives.

Lipes' specialty as laboratory technician was in operating a machine that registers heartbeats. He was classified as an electrocardiographer. But he had seen Navy doctors take out one or two appendixes and thought he could do it. Under the sea, he was given his first chance to operate.

There was difficulty about the ether. When below the surface, the pressure inside a boat is above the atmospheric pressure. More ether is absorbed under pressure. The submariners did not know how long their operation would last.

They did not know how long it would take to find the appendix. They did not know whether there would be enough ether to keep the patient under throughout the operation.

They didn't want the patient waking up before they were finished.

They decided to operate on the table in the officers' wardroom. In the newest and roomiest American submarine the wardroom is approximately the size of a Pullman-car drawing room. It is flanked by bench seats attached to the wall, and a table occupies the whole room—you enter with knees already crooked to sit down. The only way anyone can be upright in the wardrooms is by kneeling.

The operating room was just long enough so that the patient's head and feet reached the two ends without hanging over.

First they got out a medical book and read up on the appendix, while Rector, his face pale with pain, lay in the narrow bunk. It was probably the most democratic surgical operation ever performed. Everybody from box-plane man to the cook in the galley knew his role.

The cook provided the ether mask. It was an inverted tea strainer. They covered it with gauze.

The 23-year-old "surgeon" had as his staff of fellow "physicians" all men his senior in age and rank. His anesthetist was communications officer Lt. Franz Hoskins of Tacoma, Wash.

Before they carried Rector to the wardroom, the submarine captain, Lt. Comdr. W. B. Ferrall of Pittsburgh, asked Lipes as the "surgeon" to have a talk with the patient.

"Look, Dean, I never did anything like this before," Lipes said. "You don't have much chance to pull through, anyhow. What do you say?"

"I know just how it is, Doc."

It was the first time in his life that anybody had called Lipes "Doc." But there was in him, added to the steadiness that goes with a submariner's profession, a new calmness.

The operating staff adjusted gauze masks while members of the engine-room crew pulled tight their reversed pajama coats over their extended arms. The tools were laid out. They were far from perfect or complete for a major operation. The scalpel had no handle.

But submariners are used to "rigging" things. The medicine chest had plenty of hemostats, which are small pincers used for closing blood vessels. The machinists "rigged" a handle for the scalpel from a hemostat.

When you are going to have an operation, you must have some kind of antiseptic agent. Rummaging in the medicine chest, they found sulfanilamide tablets and ground them to powder. One thing was lacking: There was no means of holding open the incision after it had been made. Surgical tools used for this are called "muscular retractors." What would they use for retractors? There was nothing in the medicine chest that gave the answer, so they went as usual to the cook's galley.

In the galley they found tablespoons made of Monel metal. They bent these at right angles and had their retractors.

Sterilizers? They went to one of the greasy copper-colored torpedoes waiting beside the tubes. They milked alcohol from the torpedo mechanism and used it as well as boiling water.

The light in the wardroom seemed insufficient; operating rooms always have big lamps. So they brought one of the big floods used for night loadings and rigged it inside the wardroom's sloping ceiling.

The moment for the operation had come. Rector, very pale and stripped, stretched himself out on the wardroom table under the glare of the lamps.

Rubber gloves dipped in torpedo alcohol were drawn upon the youthful "doc's" hands. The fingers were too long. The rubber ends dribbled limply over.

"You look like Mickey Mouse, Doc," said one onlooker.

Lipes grinned behind the gauze.

Rector on the wardroom table wet his lips, glancing a side look at the tea-strainer ether mask.

With his superior officers as his subordinates, Lipes looked into their eyes, nodded, and Hoskins put the tea mask down over Rector's face. No words were spoken; Hoskins already knew from the book that he should watch Rector's pupils dilate.

The 23-year-old surgeon, following the ancient hand rule, put his little finger on Rector's subsiding umbilicus, his thumb on the point of the hipbone, and, by dropping his index finger straight down, found the point where he intended to cut. At his side stood Lt. Norvell Ward of Indian Head, Md., who was his assistant surgeon.

"I chose him for his coolness and dependability," said the

Doc afterward of his superior officer. "He acted as my third and fourth hands."

Lt. Ward's job was to place tablespoons in Rector's side as Lipes cut through successive layers of muscles.

Engineering officer Lt. S. Manning, of Cheraw, S.C., took the job which in a normal operating room is known as "circulating nurse." His job was to see that packets of sterile dressings kept coming and that the torpedo alcohol and boiling water arrived regularly from the galley.

They had what is called an "instrument passer" in Chief Yeoman H. F. Wieg, of Sheldon, N.D., whose job was to keep the tablespoons coming and coming clean. Submarine skipper Ferrall too had his part. They made him "recorder." It was his job to keep count of the sponges that went into Rector. A double count of the tablespoons used as retractors was kept: one by the skipper and one by the cook, who was himself passing them out from the galley.

It took Lipes in his flap-finger rubber gloves nearly 20 minutes to find the appendix.

"I have tried one side of the caecum," he whispered after the first minutes. "Now, I'm trying the other."

Whispered bulletins seeped back into the engine room and the crews' quarters.

"The doc has tried one side of something and now is trying the other side."

After more search, Lipes finally whispered, "I think I've got it. It's curled way into the blind gut."

Lipes was using the classical McBurney's incision. Now was the time when his shipmate's life was completely in his hands.

"Two more spoons." They passed the word to Lt. Ward.

"Two spoons at 14.45 hours (2:45 p.m.)," wrote Skipper Ferrall on his note pad.

"More flashlights. And another battle lantern," demanded Lipes.

The patient's face, lathered with white petrolatum, began to grimace.

"Give him more ether," ordered the doc.

Hoskins looked doubtfully at the original five pounds of

ether now shrunk to hardly three-quarters of one can, but once again the tea strainer was soaked in ether. The fumes mounted up, thickening the wardroom air and making the operating staff giddy.

"Want those blowers speeded up?" the captain asked the doc.

The blowers began to whir louder.

Suddenly came the moment when the doc reached out his hand, pointing toward the needle threaded with 20-day chromic catgut.

One by one the sponges came out. One by one the tablespoons bent into right angles were withdrawn and returned to the galley. At the end it was the skipper who nudged Lipes and pointed to the tally of bent tablespoons. One was missing. Lipes reached into the incision for the last time and withdrew the wishboned spoon and closed the incision.

They even had the tool ready to cut off the thread. It was a pair of fingernail scissors, well scalded in water and torpedo juice.

At that moment the last can of ether went dry. They lifted up Rector and carried him into the bunk of Lt. Charles K. Miller of Williamsport, Pa. Lt. Miller alone had had control of the ship as diving officer during the operation.

It was half an hour after the last tablespoon had been withdrawn that Rector opened his eyes. His first words were, "I'm still in there pitching."

By that time the sweat-drenched officers were hanging up their pajamas to dry. It had taken the amateurs about 2½ hours for an operation ordinarily requiring 45 minutes.

"It wasn't one of those 'snappy-valve' appendixes," murmured Lipes apologetically as he felt the first handclasps upon his shoulders.

Within a few hours, the bow and stern planesmen, who under Lt. Miller's direction, had kept the submarine from varying more than half a degree vertically in 150 minutes below the stormy sea, came around to receive Rector's winks of thanks. Rector's only remark was, "Gee, I wish Earl was here to see this job." His brother Earl, a seaman on the Navy submarine tender

Pigeon, is among the list of missing at Corregidor, probably captured.

When the submarine surfaced that night, the ether-drunk submarine crewmen found themselves grabbing the sides of the conning tower and swaying unsteadily on their feet. Thirteen days later Rector, fully recovered, was at his battle station, manning the phones. In a bottle vibrating on the submarine's shelves was the prize exhibit of surgeon Lipes—the first appendix ever known to have been removed below enemy waters.

George Ade tells how a New Orleans gentleman learned humility in Chicago

This story by the famed columnist and play-wright George Ade was published in the Daily News *in 1899.*

Pierre Deschaux awoke one morning in his luxurious bedroom in a North Side hotel, and as his eyes wandered lazily from the watercolors on the wall to the pattern of the paper, and then to the little patch of bright sunshine in the corner of the window shade, it suddenly occurred to him that he had very little money left. It was worthwhile to consider the situation seriously.

He jumped out of bed and, seating himself in a white and gilt chair, began to rummage in the pockets of his coat until he found a little morocco-leather case, from which he drew some neatly folded bills. He counted them and found that they amounted to $42. "La, la!" said Pierre. "That is very bad; I thought there was more than that."

He threw open the door of a wardrobe, disclosing a row of boots stretched on trees and garments of various patterns and cuts hanging above them. He regarded the array for a moment and then began to search.

Two silver dollars were in the waistcoat pocket of a dress suit and a pair of light tweed trousers yielded a $5 bill and a quarter of a dollar. "That is better than nothing," remarked the young man, cheerfully. "Come, then, there is yet another pair of trousers; let us shake them with vigor and see what there is of wealth inside of them."

He shook them, and a penknife and a small bunch of keys dropped onto the carpet. He shook them again and a coin tumbled out and rolled under the bureau. Pierre got down on his hands and knees and looked after it, but it was gone.

"Francis-with-the-blue-stockings!" exclaimed Pierre. That was about the strongest oath he permitted himself, for his aunt at Batignolles had brought him up very carefully. Then he continued in a self-communing fashion he had: "Shall I procure a stick and knock this money out from its retreat, or shall I leave it there for the good Clara? It may be a gold piece, and then it may be a little nickel. Well, I will leave it for Clara; it will encourage her all through the future to sweep under such places. It will be virtue rewarding her."

He knitted his brows thoughtfully and turned to count the money: $49.25. Fortunately he had paid for his apartments last week. Still, it would be necessary to practice economy. He would have to give up the hotel cafe, that said itself. What would that dearest little Emma think if she knew to what straits he was reduced? Would she believe that he was looking for her fortune? That would be a terrible thing. He must give up seeing Emma also. As this thought came to him, Pierre's face took on a tragic expression and he began to pace up and down the room.

Three months before, Pierre had arrived in New Orleans with 20,000 francs, a fair knowledge of English and of the routine of a bank. He had also a pocketful of letters of introduction. He had also a position in the house of Thibodeaux, Planchette et Cie. awaiting him; but in spite of all M. Planchette's arguments and a rather angry letter from his aunt, he had determined to accompany his friend Sabin to Chicago, where, Sabin told him, he could turn his francs into dollars inside of a year. Now Sabin was gone, nobody knew where, and some way— Pierre even now could hardly tell how—the francs had gone with him, saving and excepting the $49.25.

There was another deduction to be made from that total amount of his loss; that was the money he had spent for those little theater and supper parties where Emma was the guest of honor, and the thought of those evenings gave Pierre a glow of pleasure in the midst of his misfortune. Emma was a widow, not more than 25, however; Pierre must have been at least a year her senior. She was said to be rich and she lived with her mother in a house at Woodlawn. She had taken to the good-looking little Frenchman from the first, and up to the morning that Pierre had counted his money for the first time in his life they had seen each other constantly.

Two weeks went by and Pierre's capital was reduced to $20. He was eating meager and insufficient meals at a cheap restaurant now and lived in daily fear of detection. Once as he was coming out of this sordid place, where they soaked the things they called crackers in tomatoes and let verdigris accumulate on the lid of the mustard pot, the clerk of the hotel passed by. Pierre blushed to the tips of his ears and wondered whether he had been recognized. He brooded over this all day in the intervals of his unsuccessful applications for employment, and when he returned in the evening and the keen-eyed but suave personage behind the register greeted him as usual, and with no change in his manner, Pierre was wonderfully relieved. He would have liked to pay the rent of his apartments then and there, but that was of course impossible; instead he tipped the bellboy munificently and with some ostentation and then walked over to the cigar counter and bought an expensive cigar.

Within a week an unexpected laundry bill had reduced him to $5, and he polished his own shoes. He had already given up his morning boutonnieres, and the girl at the florist's stand looked at him so reproachfully that he dreaded to pass her. Then he got a note—his first note—from Emma, and she was reproachful, too. What had she and her mother done to offend him? she asked. Would he not call on them soon? She had some etchings concerning which she wanted his opinion.

Pierre expended $3 of his $5 for flowers and called and was received with a graciousness that first elated him and then depressed him. Emma's mother was very cordial, too, and proposed that Pierre stay and take them to the theater that evening. The young man thought of his last $2 and groaned in spirit as he pleaded an important business engagement as an excuse. He stayed as long as he decently could, however, for he had resolved that this should be the last time. He told Emma, when he said good-by, that he was about to leave Chicago. He thought she looked rather startled and anxious when he told her.

As he walked down the street he met an acquaintance, who airily remarked that he was "on the hog" and requested the loan of $1. Pierre did not understand the first remark exactly, but he acceded to the request and in a few minutes handed his last dollar to the streetcar conductor. That was on Saturday. On Monday he was genuinely, ravenously hungry, and on Tuesday when a man he detested invited him to dinner he accepted the invitation gratefully and ate until he felt that all the waiters must have been staring at him in wonder. The next day he regretted that he had not had the courage to pocket a roll, and was seized with a sudden dizziness as he undressed at night to go to bed. When he got up he suddenly remembered the coin that had rolled under the bureau, and pushing the piece of furniture to one side, found it. It was a quarter. Pierre blushed as he picked it up. "It is like stealing from the chambermaid, almost," he said to himself, "but then she can eat—and besides she did not sweep."

He bought bread with the quarter and was surprised when he found how little of it he could eat. He locked the rest of it in his trunk, and as he did so an idea flashed upon him. His clothes were worth money, surely. Why had he not thought of that before? He laughed. Then he shut down the lid of the trunk with a snap and shook his head. He pictured himself slouching through the streets with his hat battered and clothes frayed and threadbare. He resolved that he would at least die well dressed.

He found himself irresistibly attracted to the "dearest little Emma," and in spite of his brave resolution not to see her he was soon before her door. Yes, said the maid, Mrs. Graham was in.

"Why, Mr. Deschaux," cried Emma, "what have you been doing to yourself? Have you been sick? You are so thin and pale. Why ---"

Pierre had turned away and walked to the window. The tenderness and pity manifest in her voice were more than he could bear, weak as he was. He felt tears spring into his eyes and knew that if he did not manage to swallow the lump rising in his throat he would become hysterical. When he returned to where Emma had seated herself he owned that he had been sick and tried to talk in his usual gay fashion, but he was clearly forcing himself and Emma was puzzled and embarrassed.

Presently luncheon was served, and Pierre tried to keep his eyes from glistening and his mouth from watering when he saw the food. Then he tried to keep from revealing his wolfish appetite. Emma did not eat much, but she looked at the young man from time to time thoughtfully, and when the meal was over got up with an air of decision and asked him to follow her back to the parlor. Then she said, in a very businesslike and matter-of-fact sort of way: "Tell me all about it."

It was a hard thing to do, but brokenly and by degrees he did so, and then looked wistfully in her face. She was not looking at him, though, but was frowning at a ring that she was turning round and round on her finger.

Pierre arose. "Well," he said, "you now know all that is in my heart, and I must—I can, you understand, see you no more. I will say to you good-by."

He paused a moment, but Emma did not look up. Still frowning, she said: "Good-by, Mr. Deschaux."

Pierre walked to the door and out into the hall, and was fumbling blindly for his hat, when the widow called to him.

"Come back here, you little idiot," she said.

Two weeks after this Pierre's aunt at Batignolles received a bulky letter from her nephew. When she opened the envelope a small engraved card slipped out and fluttered to the floor. Picking it up and adjusting her glasses, the old lady read:

> Marriage ceremony at
> half-past seven o'clock

Another dive into the envelope brought out a sheet of note paper, also engraved. This was more explicit:

> Mrs. Albert Jones-Walsh
> Requests the pleasure of your company at
> the marriage reception of her daughter,
> Mrs. Emma Gertrude Graham,
> and
> Mr. Pierre Alphonse Deschaux,
> on Monday, August the sixth,
> Eighteen hundred ninety-eight,
> at half-past twelve o'clock,
> at 6631 Mozart Avenue.

A famous reporter awaits the end of Prohibition on Skid Row, where the last bathtub liquids are going cheap

Robert J. Casey was one of the most famous reporters of his time because of the unusual perspective he brought to a story. He began one piece about a sensational mass murder trial in 1938 this way: "Anna Marie Hahn's 11 husbands came to court today—10 of them in glass jars and 1 in a blue serge suit." The ones in the jars had been cremated. For the article reprinted here, Casey went to Skid Row on Chicago's Madison St. to localize a story that broke in Salt Lake City. Utah became the 36th state to ratify the 21st amendment, repealing Prohibition, on Dec. 4, 1933, and Casey's story made the front page of that day's Daily News.

In expectant and convincing attitudes the populace of Madison St. stood today awaiting the breaking of the great dike at Salt Lake City and speculating as to what might be the effect of a flood upon a territory already flooded— lo, these many years.

For, my children, this is the day on which alcohol comes back to a city theoretically parched and yearning. Gin, a beverage which our ancestors heard about from their fathers, will be on sale at all soda fountains where there are places for the customer to sit down. Whiskey, which is said to be highly intoxicating, will be introduced to palates which for 15 years have had to struggle with grape juice and lemonade. One can imagine the new public, to which cocktails, highballs and such are merely names, standing on a hundred thousand thresholds, eager to leap to the nearest hooch dispensary as soon as Utah proclaims the season open for the great experiment.

One can imagine the new public doing all this—and then again one can't.

The visiting firemen, anxious to determine the attitude of Chicago toward its alleged imagination, visited the laboratory of Louie Most at 513½ W. Madison St.

"I am not so sure about this repeal business," announced Most. "It is going to mean a lot of revision of policies and all of that—not to mention the fact that it is going to put a whole lot of men out of work."

Most leaned across his highly polished bar and surveyed a tavern, as the places are laughingly called, the like of which has seldom been seen. Joseph Urban had never been called in to decorate Most's walls in preparation for the approaching wet trade. On the other hand, Joseph Urban never saw a set of walls quite like them. From floor to the lofty ceiling, they were papered with beer labels hastily acquired and pasted since April 6. Somebody had recently painted a face on the barroom floor just to revive memories. Only the door was undecorated save for a little sliding panel, the reason for which everybody has forgotten.

"I have followed Prohibition very carefully," remarked Most. "For 15 years I looked out at the world through a slot and I collected the names of a lot of people on cards. A lot of the early ones are dead for one reason or another, but I still have 200 or 300 in the file here. I wonder if anybody wants to buy 'em for a mailing list."

He paused to look into a little book.

"It says here something about Italian vermouth," he announced. "Is that something the Capone mob made? We'll wash it out. . . . You know, Prohibition taught people to be careful about drinking. They got to like simple things like gin and alky with brown sugar in it and Jamaica ginger and lemon extract. All a bartender had to do was remember what the mugs of the Prohibition flat feet looked like. But now it's different.

"Only this morning a guy comes in and wants an old-fashioned. Whoever heard of that? The oldest-fashioned thing we got in the house is gin without too much ginger ale in it. And I suppose tonight when the lid is off there'll be a lot more of these eggs with notions. All night long I've been memorizing this book—and a lot of sense it makes.

"Here's a thing called a pouse cafe with 27 different things in it besides the spoon, and all I got to make it with so far is two kinds of bourbon and, of course, some gin."

Most sighed and closed his book.

"It's going to be very difficult," he said. "Me, I ain't had a drink in 15 years. . . . You couldn't drink and remember what the dicks looked like. But now I think things are going to be different. The customers are all going to be sober and the bartenders are all going to be drunk."

And with a wistful tear for the days that are gone he hung a sign on the door announcing bargain prices on the remaining stock of bathtub liquids with which repeal had found his shelves so plentifully stocked.

'It takes about 20 minutes to make up the breasts— 11 for the left, 9 for the right'

Donald Zochert broke a barrier of sorts in a family newspaper with this Dec. 19, 1969, essay on one source of fascination, frustration and occasional fixations from the Bronze Age to Myra Breckinridge.

The female breast is located between the second and sixth ribs, on the front of the body. It is a source of occasional nourishment and constant fascination.

It also is a highly modified sweat gland.

This, however, has not prevented its adoration and beautification—a custom borrowed from other cultures by Americans only recently.

The December issue of *Vogue*, for instance, features a two-page bare-breasted white goddess—a portrait that would have shocked previous generations of fashion-magazine readers. *Ladies Home Journal* featured a full section on the booming American breast this fall, and the bodice of modesty fell away this year even in *Time* and *Newsweek*.

In most cases, this spotlight on the breast shines under the guise of fashion. Some designers have suggested seriously that the bare breast is properly worn at cocktail parties or at the beach. Others have urged women to discard the strictures of the bra beneath see-through blouses.

The investment of cosmetics companies in the breast also has become substantial. Some fashionable ladies now make up their breasts with frosted blushers, gleamers, glosses, gels and fixatives. The breast makeup kit of New York hair stylist Kenneth Battelle is complete down to its small bottle of "tip rouge." It takes approximately 20 minutes to make up the breasts—11 for the left, which usually is larger, and 9 for the right.

The world of art never has been exempt from interest in the breast, but recently it has become more bold. Bare-breasted women appear in stage plays (*Hair* and *Oh! Calcutta!*) and New York artist Larry Rivers is filming a documentary on breasts.

Nor has high society been immune. Britain's Lord Snowdon, who is married to Princess Margaret, recently caused a stir with his film of a lady hatching a hen's egg between her breasts. The film induced Lady McGregor, who is married to British Air Marshal Sir Hector McGregor, to boast that she almost hatched a pheasant egg 10 years ago in the same manner.

The young also have their little manias, in which they are aided and abetted by adults. Girls now slip into their first bras at age 11 or 12, sometimes even earlier, more often for status than need.

Against this background, perhaps it is appropriate to examine the role of the breast in history, sociology, psychology and literature.

Each breast, according to the 27th edition of *Gray's Anatomy*, "forms a discoidal, hemispherical or conical eminence on the anterior chest wall.

"It protrudes 3 to 5 centimeters from the chest wall, and its average weight is 150 to 200 grams, increasing to 400 to 500 grams during lactation.

"The mammary gland is an accessory of the reproductive system in function, since it secretes milk for nourishment of the infant, but structurally and developmentally it is closely related to the integument.

"It reaches its typical exquisite development in women during the early child-bearing period."

The evolution of the breast is still a matter of contention among scientists, although Desmond Morris offered one view in his book *The Naked Ape*. He suggests that the breasts are the result of sexual, not maternal, development. They evolved, he contends, as a kind of sexual mimicry of the buttocks.

"Breasts are one part of the human body that has been selected for erotic elaboration" says famed anthropologist Margaret Mead. "Yet there are some societies where there is very little erotic emphasis on the breast.

"The more primitive societies place more emphasis on the lactation process, although the breast may be emphasized for erotic purposes by young girls before marriage.

"But here in a bottle-feeding culture the maternal function of the breast has become disassociated from the breast. The erotic function has been disproportionately increased."

There has been no substantial work done on cultural differences in the female breast, although it is worth noting that Negro and Caucasian bust measurements differ on mannekins.

Burt Kahn, president of Advance Mannekin Co. in Chicago, points out that the bust measurement of Negro mannekins in the big-selling Decter line is 34 inches. The corresponding white mannekin has a 33-inch bust.

"The much-publicized bosoms of Bali are praised as models of perfection," a medical journal observed some years ago, "but they quickly lose their shape and resiliency in the hot climate.

"By contrast, the breasts of women living at the extremely cold northern tip of Asia are reputed to retain their youthful characteristics longer than any others in the world."

Man has maintained a definite interest in the female breast, whatever its shape and resiliency. His changing taste, and woman's catering to it, may be traced in the world's great art.

The ancient Greeks and Minoans before them appreciated high, cultivated swaybacks with small breasts almost to the point of misogyny.

In literature, women's breasts have been compared to golden apples, oranges, roses, pomegranates and, by poet Edmund Spencer, to a "bowle of cream uncrudded." Such are the "fleshy principalities," to quote another poet, Robert Herrick.

In America, bigness often is the measure of breasts. Women with small breasts have attempted to build new figures with glass balls, plastic wood, ox cartilage, plastic sponges and fat from their own backsides, none of which have been notably successful and all of which are considered dangerous.

Dr. Milton T. Edgerton of Johns Hopkins Hospital in Baltimore estimates that no fewer than 40,000 American women have undergone breast implants of silicone.

As far back as 1897, Sears, Roebuck & Co. was offering American women a device that looked like a plumber's plunger, with the promise that for $1.46 it would "enlarge any lady's breast from two to three inches."

Women with large breasts also have problems, although lack of publicity is not one of them. Alexandra the Great, a Honolulu stripper, got her picture in the paper when she complained recently that she could not lead a "normal life" because of her 4-foot bust measurement.

A sweater girl named Francine Gottfried brought Wall Street to a standstill last year simply by walking up a flight of subway steps, an act that brought large-breasted girls up from the subways in other cities.

The American obsession with the breast has produced a creature known as a "breast man," in contrast to a "leg man." That breast men have certain personality traits was demonstrated in a study published last year by Dr. Jerry Wiggins, a psychologist at the University of Illinois, Urbana.

Men who like large-breasted women tend to view all parts of the body as strong and good, tend to smoke cigarets, tend to be independent in social relations, and relatively free from fears and worries, and tend to need to be the center of attention and say "witty" things, Wiggins observed.

Men who like small-breasted women tend to view breasts as weak and legs as neutral, tend to hold conservative religious beliefs, tend not to drink alcoholic beverages, tend to be helpful rather than independent and tend to be mildly depressed.

"The whole idea of a breast man is pretty oversimplified," Wiggins conceded in an interview, "because men tend to judge a woman's figure on the basis of configuration, on how the parts relate to the whole."

Women themselves have a curiously confused attitude toward the beautification of the breast.

"Women deserve much of the blame for allowing the breast to become the symbol of sexuality," one attractive young woman says. "Rather than refusing to co-operate with what obviously is a male-created fixation, women have gone to ridiculous extremes to go along with the idea.

29

"As long as the idea persists that a woman is merely an object, whose purpose is to stay at home and not bother her pretty head about the serious matters of the world, the emphasis on the breast will remain.

"But as women move out into the world, they will have to realize that success depends on more than what size cup they wear."

The objectification of women is a particularly sore point with modern suffragettes known as the Women's Liberation movement.

"In this society women are made into sex objects," one young activist observed, "and you don't even have to show all of them. You show parts: a breast, a face, a leg. Newspapers and television especially use parts of the woman's body as though women themselves don't exist."

One does not have to be an activist to hold these feelings about the breast boom.

"The breast today seems solely for decoration and sex," says Edwina Froehlich, although she herself holds a more functional view.

Mrs. Froehlich is executive secretary of La Leche League, a group headquartered in Melrose Park, Ill., and devoted to the "womanly art" of breast-feeding.

Mrs. Froehlich estimated that 700,000 U.S. mothers, or about 18 per cent, breast-feed their babies.

The impact of the breast on language does not seem to change. It goes back to the Frenchmen who named the Grand Tetons and is as modern as today's graffiti.

Americans have always been fickle in the frankness of their language. Webster substituted the word "breasts" for the biblical word "teats"; in the 19th Century such an inoffensive word as bull was changed to male cow, and leg to limb, as in "Pass me that chicken limb."

Graffiti offer an insight into the real role of the female breast in American life.

Dr. Ray B. Browne, director of the Center for the Study of Popular Culture at Bowling Green State University in Ohio, pointed out in an interview that most washroom graffiti are not the slightest bit concerned with the female breast.

"I conclude that when you get right down to brass tacks," Browne said, "we are not most aroused by the breast."

What goes on behind closed doors is one thing; what sells cars and fur coats and newspapers is another. The female breast is still queen of our anatomical, public life, the object of an adoration that seemingly knows no bounds.

It is a phenomenon that has been brilliantly analyzed in an unpublished study by a prominent Midwestern sociologist who shall be known here, in the interests of propriety, by the pseudonym Dr. Hugh B. Boylan.

Boylan's study has circulated in underground fashion throughout academia since it was written more than a decade ago. It is titled "Fashions in Female Breasts: An Attempt to Delineate and Explain Some American Variations."

The breast boom began, Boylan concludes, roughly around 1930. What emerged from the boy-meets-boy look was not the unified turn-of-the-century bust, but the plural breasts. Cleavage took on a new and important meaning.

There were several reasons for this renewed emphasis on breasts, the most important of which was the female need for sexual differentiation. Women had turned to short hair, cigarets, slacks and factory jobs in a man's world. The breast became their badge of femininity.

Aiding this emergence of breast emphasis was the decline of the Victorian and Puritan sexual codes.

These same forces can be seen today.

Instead of short hair, young women are wearing their hair long, but so are young men. The bell-bottom trouser, which originated with the Navy, was adopted by designers of women's clothes and then readopted by men.

Likewise, the moral code has loosened considerably.

Where does the breast go from here?

There is evidence that masculine interest is shifting from the female breast to the female buttocks.

Playboy magazine's "playmate of the month," possibly an accurate barometer of middle- and upper-class male fantasy, now frequently features beauties photographed from the back, with their breasts almost hidden.

Many television commercials also have shifted their emphasis away from the breast, in particular a number of commercials for tourism in the Caribbean.

And it is not only the breasts that are exposed in such dramatic productions as *Hair* and *Oh! Calcutta!*

If such a trend eventually does take place, it could produce a new and important impact on American culture. Boylan would have to perform another underground sociological study and Kenneth Battelle would have to come out with a new line of cosmetics.

But that would be another story.

Chicago's Loop. Henry Herr Gill / Daily News.

Metropolis:
M. W. Newman
Mike Royko
George Ade
Lois Wille
Dean Gysel
James Kloss
Diane Monk
John Justin Smith

M. W. Newman exposes the tragedy of wasted lives in Chicago's high-rise ghetto

M. W. Newman, distinguished reporter, editor and critic, was the first to disclose the horror and human destruction in the Robert R. Taylor Homes, a $70 million public-housing project. This article, published April 14, 1965, was part of a series by Newman.

Police seized a teen-aged gang boy living in Robert R. Taylor Homes and hauled him to the station.

He was suspected of murder—or at least some boy in Taylor was—and "they tried to get me to sign a confession."

First, he was made to open his shirt, and a knife point was jammed against his lean belly.

Then, as he tells it, he was handcuffed, knocked across the room, banged against a locker, slammed around.

He took it all grimly, living up to the code of the gangs, but he wasn't guilty and he didn't confess.

It was just another hard time in the life of a tough and bitter teen-ager living in Chicago's $70 million ghetto, the Taylor Homes.

This biggest low-rent housing project in the world occupies 95 acres between 39th and 54th streets along bleak S. State St.

Some 20,000 of the 28,000 Negroes packed into the 28 massive apartment houses are minors. Of all the tragedies of life in this superghetto, the tragedy of the youngsters is the greatest.

"Many are utterly doomed," said a sociologist who knows them well.

Their lives are wasted—both by themselves and by society—as though it didn't matter.

Early in life, they tend to become hard, cynical and explosive, or sink into silence and defeat. Only some of them manage to rise above the level of life at Taylor Homes.

It may well be that these kids, many of them from Jim Crow slums, were already that way before Taylor ever opened (in March, 1962). Taylor merely has added to their problems.

They come from big families (average 6.3 persons), half of whom are on relief. Many of the families are broken, without fathers.

These are the city's bottom-of-the-barrel poor, and the Chicago Housing Authority, Taylor's landlord, has crammed them into the huge buildings and hoped for the best.

There are hundreds of normal families at Taylor—creative, well disciplined.

But, in good part, Taylor is a woman's world and a children's world, without men—a place of overcrowded flats, no privacy, no place to go, little to do, isolated from the rest of the city, where the prevailing mood is resentment and suspicion.

The slum-bred despair here is so evident that you see teen-agers idling across State St., daring motorists to strike them.

"If you even brush against one of these boys, they'll gang up on you and overturn your car," said a social worker.

"And some care so little about life that they're virtually seeking death.

"They have no values—no belief in life. They figure that no one cares about them."

Sit in a room with some of these youngsters and you find they are either bursting with exploding energy, shouting and jumping—or just the reverse, they sit dully and never say a word.

A white face puts many of them on guard. This is a Jim Crow world.

One boy sat edgily and suspiciously while a reporter talked to a housewife in her cluttered flat.

"Just last week, he came at another fellow with a knife this long," the woman whispered when the boy drifted out of the room, "and for no reason at all.

"We got them separated and when I took the trouble to talk to him quietly about it, he was surprised and said, 'I thought no one cared.' "

Cut off from ordinary life, many of these youngsters bury

their desolation in cheap wine and gin—"but not much goof pills or dope," according to one lad.

They hang out in Taylor stairwells and on street corners, and there they dream up gang fights, car thefts, muggings, burglaries—amusements of the younger set at Taylor Homes.

Most have the same plaint:

"Nothing to do here except fight. We need more gyms—a clubhouse—someplace to play."

There is one gymnasium on the project site, for a community of 28,000, in the Park District fieldhouse at 47th St. The parks, housing authority and Firman settlement house at 47th St. all sponsor activity programs for youths.

The list is extensive—Boy Scouts, hobby groups, sports teams, reading programs, music clubs, camp committees, drill teams, dancing groups, Bible classes.

But available facilities are swamped. There simply are too many youngsters, with too many problems, at Taylor Homes.

Firman House, for example, operates a valuable preschool program. It can take only 60 or so children. There are thousands who need the same opportunity.

In the harsh world of Taylor Homes, sexual activity begins early. In one building, a boy gang leader got a girl pregnant. Seven other boys followed his lead. There were eight pregnant teen girls in that one building.

A reporter talked to an 18-year-old girl tenant who had borne two illegitimate children—the first when she was "15, going on 16."

So unrealistic was this lost, half-literate girl that she had dreams of becoming an airline stewardess.

Taylor has its dropouts, its jobless youngsters with low literacy and few skills.

They drift along, taking occasional work. But life has not taught them a reason for discipline or given them hope.

"They'll hold a job just long enough to get money to buy shoes or to spend on a girl," said a youth worker. "They won't stay with anything."

This human waste is enormous. And the smaller children may be even more pathetic. Kindergarten teachers are not surprised when some pupils don't even know their own names. No one at home ever bothered to call them by name—just Sis or Buddy.

The children often are not much good at talking, either, because often no one in these deprived homes talks to them. They lag in reading skills or in knowledge of colors.

Their feet may never have touched the ground—literally—before going to school. Some mothers, afraid to let their children into the barbaric atmosphere of the typical Taylor "playground," keep them upstairs where they can at least be supervised.

Thus, the youngsters grow up in a crowded TV world. The television set is blasting away all the time.

Their mother is overworked, tired and distracted. There is little privacy. People are everywhere.

In this world, you sink or swim on your own. It's not surprising to see children as young as 3 or 4 crossing State St.—where 15,000 vehicles whiz by daily—to go to the store for mother.

As dismal as this picture is, it is not all gray. Taylor has its brighter side.

"You can make it if you keep trying," said the teen-aged boy who refused to confess a murder he had not committed.

"I'm not giving up."

Taylor has its high achievers. Mrs. Dwayne Hampton, 4848 S. State, has six children in high school, three of them honor students.

Mrs. Hampton's husband is a letter carrier and the family moved to Taylor so that it could cut its rent. The extra money goes into such things as transportation or music lessons for the children.

The children take part in all available activity and Mrs. Hampton works with them devotedly. A poised, sensitive woman, she had plans to become a schoolteacher before motherhood took all her time.

There are all kinds of children, just as there are all kinds of families, at Taylor. You can go into some apartments and see youngsters studying quietly. They are extremely polite, take your coat, get you a chair or a glass of water.

The "leadership" families at Taylor are deeply concerned with giving these children a break. Most Taylor mothers, in fact, are eager to see their children get schooling, and deeply disappointed when they don't.

Mrs. M. E. Cowherd, vivacious and matronly, dreamed up the idea of a "coming-out" cotillion for the top teen-age girls of the project.

When the contestants were brought together for a briefing at Firman settlement house, they were as fresh-faced and attractive as North Shore debs.

Tenant leaders from a number of the buildings were on hand to plan fund raising for the formal gowns and the hundred other details of the cotillion. It was held in the Trianon ballroom March 5—a remarkable evidence of the pride of many people at Taylor.

"The young people here need help and sympathy, just as children do anywhere," said one tenant, Mrs. Dorothy Sykes Mason, 4037 S. Federal.

"They feel that no one cares, and that is the problem. For the most part, they are not exposed to life elsewhere and whatever opportunities that do exist.

"Their parents are up against it financially and even with the best will in the world, find it hard to pay for an education."

Here is a challenge for the community of Chicago—if it cares about the neglected youngsters of Taylor Homes and its citizens of tomorrow.

'When you are eatin' regular, what is a Great Lake or two?'

Pulitzer Prize winner, Mike Royko, author of the best-selling book Boss: Richard J. Daley of Chicago, *often is acclaimed as the nation's most outstanding daily columnist. This Royko column was published Dec. 16, 1966.*

When I was a kid, the best days of the summer were spent at the beach.

The cinder-covered schoolyard was too hot and dusty for softball. The alleys were so choked with flies and garbage smells that hunting bottles for their 2-cent deposits was no fun.

So we grabbed our itchy wool trunks, a fried-egg sandwich, rode a North Av. streetcar to the end of the line, and there it was—the big, blue, cool, clean lake.

You could smell it and taste it long before you saw it.

We threw our bony bodies at the waves, sprawled on the sand, stared in boyish awe at the older girls and went home exhausted, bleached and ready for 10 hours of deep sleep.

Sometimes we went to fish. I was lucky because the local tavern gentlemen didn't mind taking a kid along. Tiny the fat man, Chizel and Clem were good conversationalists as well as fine fishermen.

They sat for hours on the rocks, muzzling bottles of cold beer, talking about the Cubs' pennant chances (a long time ago) and pulling fat, needle-boned perch from the lake with their bamboo poles.

So I like the lake. I like knowing that Indians used it, city kids used it and hundreds of thousands of people still use it.

And I get sick and angry when I hear someone like Thomas H. Coulter, chief executive officer of the Chicago Assn. of Commerce and Industry, say:

40

"Our lakefront is not much more than a wasteland. Oh, it has some trees, but the only time I've been on the lakefront in the last 30 years has been to McCormick Place.

"I'm sure that is true of the 20 million other persons who have gone to McCormick Place, not so much for commercial or business meetings of various kinds, but for cultural programs, art, theater, ballet. . . . "

As a newspaperman, I've had to listen to some odd ideas—from Skid Row winos, aldermen, singing mice and editors—but I've heard nothing to compare with Coulter's blather.

He was making a pitch for further expansion of McCormick Place, the Tribune's grotesque Temple of $$$.

Coulter is paid to say things like that. He works for and with the city's commercial and business interests.

But even from a paid mouthpiece, it was in bad taste. His rich crowd has misused the beautiful lake. And a gentleman doesn't speak badly of a lady he has misused.

The lakefront is not yet a wasteland, despite what Coulter says. But it is on its way. And who has caused it?

When I went swimming, I took a shower in the bathhouse and left the lake as clean as I found it. When we caught fish, we took what we wanted to eat.

Ah, but what of Coulter's employers—the rich, smoke-belching industrial fat cats? They've poured enough slop into the lake to make a million pigs sick.

They've stunted and killed the fish and are rapidly making most of the shoreline unfit for humans. Beaches on the Far South Side and in Indiana have become sewers. Thank you, commerce and industry.

And the view from the shoreline? The swimmers, cyclists, fishermen, picnickers and golfers didn't blot it out. But the real-estate interests are crawling to the water's edge for their rich high-rise profits.

A wasteland? Not yet, but some day it will be. And it won't matter a bit to the commerce-and-industry crowd. They have their spacious suburban surroundings, their back-yard and country-club pools and their summer homes.

They don't use the lakefront except for yachting. So they dispatch a handsome, manicured, Canadian-born, Pennsylvania-educated suburbanite to inform us that it is a wasteland.

He probably thinks it is, because he doesn't go there to see the hundreds of thousands of ordinary yahoos using the beaches, parks and paths.

From the patio, one can't see that the lakefront is draped with humanity from Foster Av. to the Far South Side on warm weekends.

Oh, it is true that many of the users—especially south of McCormick Place—are Negroes. But even the most ignorant or the richest bigot shouldn't kill a lake because Negroes are dipping their toes in it. Yet a red-nosed politician once told me: "I don't care what happens to Jackson Park. Niggers have took it over."

The "lake-is-a-wasteland" people have wonderful arguments. Remember, they are doing something noble while pouring industrial wastes into the water and gobbling up the shoreline. They EMPLOY people. They put food in our mouths, clothes on our backs, roofs over our heads. So when you are eatin' regular, what is a Great Lake or two?

Spare me that soul talk. They employ people so their companies profit and they can make $70,000 a year plus stock options and early retirement plans.

And living the good life is worth the price of creating a concrete-walled septic tank bordered by four states.

Putting McCormick Place on the lake was a mistake. Expanding it is a mistake.

It should have been built in Cicero or on Rush St. That's where the action is. Conventioneers aren't looking for sunshine or moonlight glittering on the water. Ask the vice cops.

But it is there and the people who put it there are committed to it. And if they say the lakefront is a wasteland, they must be right. And they will do everything they can to prove they are right—including making it a wasteland.

George Ade, in 1895, describes that part of the city that is in the country

Turn-of-the-century playwright and Daily News *columnist George Ade was one of the most colorful writers of his era. This column about Chicago was published in 1895.*

The flat building with all modern improvements stands at the edge of the forest primeval of Chicago.

There are more acres of landscape within the city limits than would be needed for the ground space of a dozen average cities, and there are depths of tangled wildwood such as cannot be excelled in the timbered wildernesses of the Northwest.

An envious contemporary, in speaking of a recent murder mystery in Chicago, said that the body of the murdered man was found at a street corner that was miles from any habitation, and that the region was overrun by prairie wolves.

Apparently the people of Chicago are undecided whether to be ashamed or proud of the city's vast area.

There are 186 square miles within the city limits. This area is equal to 119,129 acres. The distance from the north line to the south line of the city is 25½ miles. The greatest distance east and west is 14 miles, and the distance from the southeast corner to the northwest corner is 28 miles.

In the gentle springtime, when the rains descend, the southern end of the town has more water than Venice ever claimed. The garden-truck belt compares in area and productiveness with the State of New Jersey.

Is it to be regretted that within four weeks the wild flowers will be blooming within a stone's throw of the elevated railway stations?

As a matter of fact, everyone who lives in Chicago knows that Chicago people do not make a practice of boasting about the immense area of the city. All the visitors who come have heard that the larger part of northern Illinois has been annexed and, as a rule, they know the area of the city and can give information to the natives.

The Chicago man knows that the shore of Lake Michigan and the Indiana state line mark the eastern boundary, but when he is going south, north or west he is seldom able to point out to his car mate where the city leaves off and the country begins.

He is so far out into the country before he leaves the city that the imaginary line has no artificial landmarks to show its course.

As long as he sees the city policemen at the railway stations he knows he is in town.

Admitting that one-half of Chicago is farm and garden land, open prairie untouched by scythe or plow, or timber country that has been allowed to remain unaltered from the earliest days of Fort Dearborn, what does it mean except that the city may grow up to and beyond all expectations during the next half a century and still have elbow room for all the inhabitants and a patch of front yard for nearly every house? When the 186 square miles are built up, every resident will still be within an hour's ride of that dense little spot by the lake—that business center from which all distances must be reckoned.

Paul Bourget, on the occasion of his recent visit to Chicago, said that when the satisfying effects of age were added to Michigan Avenue it would be the most magnificent thoroughfare in the world, because, in addition to massive and graceful architecture, varied in a pleasing way, it had open space, trees and lawns.

The "unbuilded part of Chicago," an imaginative real-estate man calls the new city that is to spread across the reserve prairies and put boulevards through the cool, cheerful woods to the north.

"In 20 years," said he, "Chicago as seen from a balloon will be three-fourths grove, dotted with rows of housetops. Because of our immense area we shall always have room for trees, and the name 'Garden City' will be revived."

Lois Wille reports: 'Whites fade away when the lights go on along State Street'

Pulitzer Prize-winning reporter Lois Wille writes fondly about the city she loves. This article was published Dec. 1, 1973.

A few weeks ago I met with some high-school students from Elk Grove Village, and as we talked about their interests, their after-school activities, what they thought about Chicago, I learned something startling:

Not one of them—and there were 45—had ever been "to the Loop."

None of them had strolled down Michigan Avenue to the Art Institute. None of them had seen the great, gleaming skyscrapers sitting in new grass west of the riverbank and Wacker Drive.

None of them had wandered around State Street, basked in the golden splendor of Marshall Field's at Christmastime, seen the Civic Center Picasso gazing placidly at Free-the-Captive-Nations pickets, admired the Chinese jade in the black marble-and-gold-lined windows of Lebolt & Co., heard Carmen Fanzone blow his trumpet in the sunshine of the First National Plaza, listened to the sandy-haired, saffron-robed kids chant in strange Eastern tongues at State and Madison, gulped a frothy Orange Julius and marveled at the wardrobes of the exuberant young blacks crowded into the little yellow-and-orange plastic shop.

I remembered when I was their age, growing up in Arlington Heights. One of the rewards of starting high school, besides wearing lipstick, was going "to the Loop" without parents.

It had been familiar to us through years of being taken to State Street to shop, to museums on summer Sundays, to stage shows (Perry Como! Live!) at the Chicago Theater, to Old Heidelberg to hear the singing waiters.

But it wasn't until that first trip alone, that first long,

45

windy, unchaperoned hike from the North Western Railway Station to State Street, that the Loop really was ours. After that, for special gifts, for the best movies, for the greatest window-shopping and gawking—there was only one place to go: the Loop!

What has happened to the Loop—or to Chicago-area families—in the decades between then and now? How can teen-agers grow up 20 miles from the heart of a great city and not be drawn to it, enthralled by it?

They're not coming downtown any more, these children of new suburbia, and neither are their parents. (And not enough are coming from old Chicago, either.)

"Our biggest area of concern today," says Jack Cornelius, executive director of the Chicago Central Area Committee, "is that this will become a 5-day-a-week, 10-hour-a-day downtown. We've got to get people who work here to stay down after work, bring their wives here. And we've got to attract more people down here who don't work here."

When the Central Area Committee is worried, that means Chicago's commercial power structure is worried, because the committee is made up of the heads of the top 100 downtown-area business and financial firms.

(In their nightmares, of course, the ghost-like downtowns of Detroit and Cleveland and the terror-ridden streets of Manhattan haunt them. That hasn't happened here, but is it coming? Young people who never come downtown—isn't that a deadly symptom?)

"What the Loop needs is people-generating activities," says Dorothy Rubel, director of the Metropolitan Housing and Planning Council. "Attractions that will bring families to the Loop at night as well as day—good restaurants, good movies, book and music and art shops that are open at night; taking advantage of all the cultural and educational resources that only a downtown can offer.

"Our Loop, even though we're putting up a lot of very expensive structures, has become a 9-to-5 place, and it has pockets of such intense drabness."

Pierre de Vise, an urbanologist who is a specialist in Chicago's population trends, estimates that the after-work population of the Loop, the people who shop and eat and see shows on its streets after dark, has dropped from 70,000 a day in the 1950s to 23,000.

De Vise, Cornelius and Rubel attribute this to a variety of factors. First, people don't live in the Loop. One thing that makes European central cities so exciting, so healthy, so safe, they believe, is the families who live right in the heart of "downtown."

Second, downtown Chicago has had a spectacular surge of immense new office buildings that have gobbled up little retail stores and restaurants—inviting, drop-in, people places—and replaced them with stark, sterile, granite-and-marble lobbies. The great shining giants are impressive to walk past in daytime, but dead and ominous at night.

Have you walked to the Loop recently after an evening at Lyric Opera? (You may have to walk, with Chicago's disgraceful shortage of taxis and dwindling CTA [Chicago Transit Authority] night service.) Or have you walked to one of the west-of-the-Loop parking lots after a late dinner at Le Bordeaux on State and Madison? Dark stretches, only a few lone straggling souls, iron gates over shop doors, lunch-hour-only restaurants shuttered.

West of Dearborn, downtown is ghost town. Remember the crowds that used to line up outside the Blue Note and the College Inn? Or flock to Henrici's for after-theater pastries? If you do, you're getting a bit gray, old chum. And up there on the Mid-North Side, they're squeezing into R. J. Grunts and waiting in line at midnight at Mel Markon's.

The years between 1968 and 1972, when many of the monolithic office buildings were rising, were rough on the downtown area, according to a study by the Chicago Central Area Committee. About 13 per cent of the retail stores were demolished to make way for the new giants or went out of business for other reasons; 15 per cent of the entertainment spots and 8 per cent of the restaurants also were lost.

The year 1968 was a turning point for the Loop for another reason, according to Don Roth, owner of the Blackhawk restaurant at Wabash and Randolph, and an astute Loop historian.

"It all started in April, 1968," he says. "Two things hap-pened—the West Side riots after Dr. Martin Luther King, Jr. was murdered and the fire that sabotaged Carson's [Carson Pi-rie Scott & Co.]. Middle-class people were afraid. Saturdays in the Loop haven't come back."

In addition to chewing up stores, the huge new office struc-tures have produced other ominous statistics: Chicago now has a glut of downtown office space. About 13 per cent of it is vacant; in 1969, the vacancy rate was less than 2 per cent. Today, more than 6 million square feet of downtown office space is unused; by the end of 1975, another 6 million square feet of office space will be added as the new giants now under construction are completed.

That means the downtown could face the ugly prospect of vacant and abandoned old office buildings, potentially as deadly as the vacant and abandoned old tenements were to Woodlawn and the West Side.

("Why couldn't some of those buildings have been living space, instead of office space?" I asked one big real-estate devel-oper. He replied, "A large law firm makes a far better tenant than, say, the 50 families who might occupy that space. There's more money and less bother.")

The third reason for the trouble downtown is more com-plex, rooted in the sickness of our society—and the failures of Chicago government. As the old city neighborhoods fell apart, as schools decayed and city services deteriorated and only crime thrived, whites fled to the suburbs. Developers and businessmen responded by giving them everything they needed out in the country: luxury stores; elegant shopping malls; good, live thea-ter; quality movies; attractive restaurants. So they stopped com-ing to the Loop.

(Arlington Park Theater in Arlington Heights offers *The Skin of Our Teeth*, with Sarah Miles, while the Shubert on Monroe St. is dark all fall. The McVickers on Madison St. has switched to movies and the Selwyn and the Harris are forgotten, known today only as the Cinestage and the Todd, the soft-porn twins.)

The old, crumbling neighborhoods continue to crumble; shops and movies were wiped out by expressways and urban renewal, and by crime. So where do the new residents of these areas—the blacks and the Latins—go for shopping and entertainment? To the Loop, of course.

"I'll tell you what's wrong with the Loop," says Arthur Rubloff, the blunt and enormously successful real-estate developer. "It's people's conception of it. And the conception they have about it is one word—black. B-L-A-C-K. Black.

"We have a racial problem we haven't been able to solve. The ghetto areas—47th and King Drive, the West Side, the Near Northwest Side—have nothing there but rotten slum buildings, nothing at all, and businessmen are afraid to move in, so the blacks come downtown for stores and restaurants."

And they come downtown for movies. To the business leaders of State Street and Wabash Av., there seems to be a single villain in the Loop, and his name is Henry Plitt.

Plitt, as president of ABC Great States theaters, controls five Loop movie houses—the Roosevelt, United Artists, Chicago, Michael Todd and State-Lake. When the violent movies with bad-black heroes began to appear, he booked them into the Roosevelt. Young blacks and money poured in. The Oriental and the Woods also began booking them. Then a year ago, at Christmastime, Plitt beefed up sagging business by switching his other four theaters to films about blacks shafting whites, with the Chicago booking them intermittently.

Today the big theaters in the Loop, which once had live stage shows as well as the best of the first-run movies, rarely show anything but violence (kung fu is very big now) and the gaudiest of the horror films.

Quick-food restaurants thrive while places like Fritzel's and the Wabash Berghoff have folded; other good restaurants have been forced to close early in the evening for want of business. The west side of State Street, which always did have trouble attracting good stores, grew into a strip of Super-Fly clothes shops blaring loud rock from doorways.

And in the evenings, State and Randolph became the focal point of the new Black Promenade.

Today, whites fade away when the lights go on along State Street. Young blacks in big Aussie hats; enormous berets with huge flopping pompons; coats of pink suede, checkerboard fur and silver lame, and four-inch heels gather under marquees that blare, "*The Black Six*—See the Biggest and Baddest Waste 150 Dudes" (the Woods); or "*The Chinese Professionals*—Meet the Kung-fu Beast, the Karate Killer, the Siamese Devils!" (the Oriental); *Super Fly* and *Cleopatra Jones* (the Chicago), and "*Coffy*—Never a One-Chick Hit Squad Like Her" with "*Mack*—The Big Dealer Man for Soft Goods" (the State-Lake).

The gaudy display windows of Sun Discount store, at Randolph and Dearborn, offer marijuana paraphernalia under a big "For Heads" sign, and the junk-food shops—18-cent hamburgers and hot dogs full of bone and gristle—are packed.

Three police cars cruise slowly around State and Randolph, and more police patrol the sidewalk. They are there to make people feel secure, of course, but somehow it has the opposite effect. Why so many police? What happened? What's going to happen?

(Actually, the Loop is one of the safest places in the city. The number of violent crimes has dropped steadily in recent years. In 1964 there were 167 assaults; last year there were 97. To further reduce crime, 60 additional policemen were assigned to the Loop area in April, many of them foot patrolmen.)

West of Dearborn and south of Washington, the streets are dark and empty.

Over on Michigan Avenue, whites hurry out of Orchestra Hall and the Studebaker and Goodman theaters, heading quickly to the Grant Park garage, to their cars and out of downtown. If they stop for a snack, it probably won't be in the Loop.

The next morning the State-Randolph promenade looks hung over. Orange Julius cups blow around the sidewalk—State Street always was so neat!—and the "For Rent" and "Space Available" signs on the old office buildings seem to have multiplied overnight.

What came first, the desertion of the Loop-after-dark by whites or the outpouring of the blacks? And why can't both races enjoy it? That's the absurdity of nighttime downtown.

"When the seven downtown movie theaters went all black, that was the horrible thing," says Rubloff. "Attribute that to avariciousness."

"It's those black theaters, that's what's killing us," says an executive of a State Street department store. (He adds, though, that his store and the rest of the big ones on State Street are having a good year, with the dollar volume of sales running 4 to 5 per cent ahead of last year. That means the increase hasn't quite kept up with inflation, but the big retailers—who have poured millions into remodeling their State Street stores in the last few years—are thankful they're holding their own.)

"We have too many porno and black-power movies downtown, that's a big part of the problem," says Jack Cornelius of the Chicago Central Area Committee.

"I took my family downtown one Saturday night," says an Elk Grove Village father, "and with all those movies it looked like a black-power meeting. Never again."

"Talk to Henry Plitt," says Don Roth of the Blackhawk. "The mayor, I know, is furious about those movies. He thinks they're attracting an element that is really unsavory."

Is Henry Plitt destroying the Loop?

He says he's too busy expanding his theater chain to discuss such "nonsense." His assistant says, "They're so goddamn wrong to blame Hank and the movie industry. What have they ever done for State Street, the businessmen and City Hall? Not a damn thing. They don't want to do anything that's going to cost money."

OK. She was defending her boss. But her assessment probably isn't too far off target. "This is the only major city in the country that hasn't used urban renewal to rebuild its downtown area," says Cornelius.

But to admit that the Loop needed that kind of major surgery—even as a preventive—was too difficult for City Hall. After all, wasn't Chicago "the one big city that works," the place "where things get done"?

So, Minneapolis, which is hardly falling apart, creates a lovely multilevel, garden-like mall in its downtown to separate pedestrians and auto traffic. And in Chicago's Loop the intersections are clogged, a tangle of cars and people, crammed with illegal (and unpunished) parkers and jaywalkers.

State Street merchants moan about the total absence of housing in the Loop. "You walk into Bloomingdale's in New York, and every day is like Christmas at Field's, because people are living right there," says Arthur Osborne, president of the State Street Council and general manager of Field's. And when new housing does rise close to the Loop, as in Illinois Center east of the Outer Drive, it is high-priced condominiums that will fill with people who much prefer the elite shops of N. Michigan Avenue to those of State Street.

(Expensive condominiums are the only type of housing that developers can afford to put up in the downtown area, according to Rubloff. He blames "confiscatory" real-estate taxes. What is needed, he says, is legislation that gives breaks to developers who build rental units, "as some 36 other cities and states throughout America already have done.")

The downtown merchants also are upset about the steady deterioration of mass transportation to the Loop. Several commuter railroads have cut services in the last decade, and the CTA eliminated a number of downtown bus routes in its last round of cutbacks.

At the same time, Loop-area parking garages were raising rates, so that it now may cost a downtown shopper or theater-goer $4 or $4.50 to park for a few hours.

To see how far our mass-transit system has sunk, look at the Loop about 60 years ago, when it thrived under one of the finest transportation networks in the world.

Cable cars powered by below-ground steam engines, running on wire ropes on rollers, fed into the central business district from the North, West and South sides. Their tracks, completed in the 1880s, formed a "loop" around the downtown area—one version of how the name was born.

A second "Loop" formed in the 1890s, when steam-powered railroads built elevated lines downtown. That elevated loop, with little more than periodic repairs, is the one that rattles and clatters around the downtown area today.

It's going to be around, shrieking, spraying muddy snow

and dirt and snarling traffic, for at least another eight years. Federal funds for the subway extension that will replace it probably won't be available until 1975, if then. Work, once it starts, would take at least six years.

About 40 feet underground was an ingenious third "loop." Little freight cars zoomed through more than 60 miles of tunnels, hauling goods and fuel from the major railway terminals to the downtown stores and offices.

At its peak, this efficient little rail system delivered 650,000 tons of freight annually.

Electric railroads from the suburbs fortified the transit system; by 1910, seven interurban lines either ran into the Loop or connected with streetcars at the edge of the city.

Today, that great transportation system has crumbled. The cable cars are gone. The network of freight tunnels no longer is used, and trucks clog the downtown streets. The interurban lines are dead or dying, and more automobiles cram into the city.

And, according to Osborne of the State Street Council, we are now at the point where a Regional Transit Authority to shore up dwindling services "is so important it's scary." Pressure from Osborne and other downtown powers is one reason the feuding factions of the Legislature finally are working together on a Regional Transit Authority bill.

The business leaders' growing concern over the Loop has a second thrust: Chicago's City Hall. After more than a year of quiet pushing and prodding, the Chicago Central Area Committee and the State Street Council finally succeeded in ending the official silence on the downtown area and its problems. Mayor Richard J. Daley and his planning chief, Lewis Hill, announced two proposals in City Hall.

One was the ambitious "Chicago 21" plan created by the Central Area Committee. It calls for partial pedestrian malls on State Street and Wabash Av., a web of underground and second-floor-level walkways throughout downtown, expansion of the proposed distributor subway to Lincoln Park on the north and 31st St. on the south, and family-styled, mixed-income housing for 120,000 on the idle railroad yards and fallow fields south of the Loop.

It is an excellent plan. The housing, in particular, could pump new vitality into the Loop. "But so far the city hasn't even tried to get prices from the railroad people on that land," says one prominent Michigan Avenue businessman. "Yet we've been talking about doing something with it for 20 years. Well, I know I won't be around to see it happen."

The second plan, pushed by the State Street Council, asks the city to designate a six-block North Loop area as urban-renewal land, giving it the power to condemn the property, purchase it and demolish it. A "feasibility" study of the plan is under way in City Hall, and a decision probably will be announced early next year.

Rubloff's development company designed the plan, with $70,000 from the State Street Council. It, too, features housing—two high-rise condominiums—and pedestrian walkways and malls.

But it has a catch, one not likely to go unnoticed by Chicago's black community: It would level the black entertainment area around State and Randolph.

Doesn't that smack of racism? "That area was selected because it contains so many older facilities on undeveloped land, not because it's black at night," says Cornelius. But to people who have seen their neighborhoods leveled in Woodlawn, Kenwood, Oakland, Lawndale and now the Near Northwest Side, that may not be very convincing.

The State Street Council hopes that demolition in the area can begin next spring. But this plan, like "Chicago 21," probably is a decade away.

"The thing I always find discouraging," says Julian Levi, the tough-minded new head of the Chicago Plan Commission, "is that people talk in glowing terms of these plans, without specifying how we get from here to there. What is a realistic price tag? Where will the financing come from? These things need a hard look."

In the meantime, Dorothy Rubel's plea for more "people attractions" in the Loop must be heard. Some did begin this summer, when the Civic Center Plaza, the First National Plaza and little Quincy St. were alive with noontime and after-work bands, jugglers, tumblers, Cubs and Sox signing autographs, animal acts and accordion players, and office workers enjoying it all. The bank and the State Street Council financed most of the activities.

The new First Chicago Center at the bank is promising, too, with its package plans for good theater, dinner at The Presidents and free parking—patterned after the successful dinner-theaters in the suburbs and the Ivanhoe.

The pity of it is that those kids from Elk Grove Village—and their parents—may not even know this is happening.

And if they did, could the presence of exuberant young blacks in fancy clothes—and sedate black families shopping in Carson's and Field's—really keep them out in the suburbs? That would be tragic; not just for the Loop, but for all of us.

Dean Gysel interviews a new police chief in Al Capone's suburb

Cicero, a suburb of Chicago, long bore the reputation of a wide-open town where everything went. It earned it. When a reform mayor was elected in Chicago, Al Capone moved his gang's headquarters to Cicero. Capone hoods ruled Cicero's police department, politics and businesses. Elections were won in Cicero with brass knuckles and machine guns. When Chicago's reform mayor lost his bid for re-election to a politician friendly to Capone, Big Al and his gang returned to Chicago. But Cicero retained its reputation for gambling, whoring and dangerous saloons. This interview by reporter Dean Gysel with a Cicero police chief a generation after Capone moved out shows what the town was like as late as 1964.

There's going to be a new era in law enforcement in Cicero. Just be a little patient, says the new police chief, Joseph Barloga.

"I have a program that I will install that I haven't decided on yet," Barloga disclosed.

In what passes in Cicero as a candid interview, Barloga, 53, said he is moving cautiously into his new, sensitive role.

"I can't decide what I'm going to do until I get acclimated to the police department," said the white-haired, department veteran of 26 years.

Until then, "We're going to move slow."

Tuesday was Barloga's first day on the job after replacing Erwin Konovsk, who resigned because of ill health. The fact that the police chief could be found at all was something new in Cicero.

Like his predecessor, Barloga promised to enforce all laws, even those relating to gambling and vice, which have been to Cicero what beer is to Milwaukee.

Asked about his policy toward gamblers and B-girls, Barloga was wary, possibly so he wouldn't tip off the syndicate.

"We'll cross that bridge when we get to it. I'll formulate my policy after I acclimate myself to conditions of the police force."

He was asked, "In view of the publicity, do you think there has been any gambling and vice in Cicero?"

"Not necessarily. I don't think so. In what way?"

As for the town's reputation as a Suburban Sodom, he said, "I think we're rattling a lot of skeletons in the closet."

"Do you like being police chief?"

"That's a question that I have to foresee," he said, cagily.

"Will you wear a uniform?" (Barloga wore a blue suit and blue bowtie.)

"I haven't gone into (the policy of) wearing a uniform yet. It's not compulsory."

After the interview, Barloga smiled and said he wants to be co-operative with the press.

On the wall next to his chair were two signs that read:

"Be sure brain is in gear before putting mouth into motion" and "If I look confused it's because I'm thinking."

The doctors told Lena, 15, to come back if she had trouble, but she didn't go back

James Kloss spent the night of Nov. 8, 1967, in the waiting room at the world's largest charity hospital, and wrote this story for the next day's Daily News.

It was a slow night Wednesday at Cook County Hospital, according to the clerk in the patients' waiting room.

A *Daily News* reporter had walked into the large room that resembles a railroad-station waiting room.

The clerk said everyone—including those who are seriously ill—waits for an examination. She didn't know exactly how long it would take. She couldn't say how many doctors were on duty.

"But it shouldn't be very long tonight," she said, as she took a handful of cards and papers from an elderly man.

Most of the hundred or so persons who sat quietly in the room were Negroes. Some slumped half asleep in the wooden benches lining the walls. Others sat on the edge of folding chairs. Most stared ahead blankly.

They looked as if they had been waiting a long time.

Men and women patients sat in separate areas—alone. Each patient sat alone because he had obeyed one of the many signs decorating the room:

"ATTENTION. Only patients wait here. All visitors or relatives wait in main waiting lobby."

A tall Negro man looked anxiously into the women's waiting area. He said his wife was there. She almost had a miscarriage Tuesday, but the doctors had sent her home, he said.

She was back today because of the pain, he said. He and his wife had arrived at 6:30 p.m. It was now 11 p.m.

In the men's section, a stout man said he was back with pain in his shoulder.

"I don't know what it is. They didn't tell me last time. You wait for hours, then they see you for a few minutes and send you home. They don't look at you like you're human."

But he didn't have time to say any more. A man in a business suit, flanked by two security guards, was leading the reporter away into the hall.

The man said his name was Smith, that he was night warden and that he was angry.

"You can't just come in here and bother the staff. If your intentions were honest you would have gone to the public-relations department to get the facts. Get out," Smith said.

Smith turned and stalked past a sign that said, "Send all patients with suspicious VD lesions . . . to social hygiene unit."

He turned and called back: "After what we've had here recently we don't want you in the building."

It was recently that Lena Fulwiley, 15, of 1537 N. Mohawk, had waited.

She saw two doctors Saturday and they gave her a shot of penicillin, for what they diagnosed as venereal disease, and sent her home.

They told her to come back if she had trouble. She won't come back.

Lena will be buried Friday. She died Sunday of a gangrenous appendix.

Diane Monk tells how children in an unheated apartment sleep in a sink to be near the kitchen stove

Diane Monk, a white reporter, was escorted by members of the Black P Stone Nation street gang through the apartment where she got this story, published Jan. 18, 1972.

Baby Sister can tell it's getting warmer outside because the inch-thick ice on her bathroom floor is starting to melt.

But it's still very cold in the unheated apartment, and so Baby Sister and four of her children slept in the kitchen by the stove again Monday night.

They've been living in that kitchen since Thursday when it got so cold. The little ones have been sleeping in the sink and on the sink counters to be closer to the heat of the stove.

Baby Sister, who is in her early 30s, didn't want the photographer to take pictures at first because the kitchen is crowded and untidy and the kids aren't dressed up. She also doesn't want her real name in the newspaper.

"I don't want people to see the kitchen and think I'm a bad housewife," she says. "I'm not a bad housewife."

And so she leads the reporter through the ice-and-slush-covered hallway to the living room. That room and the bedroom are neat and clean, but they are so cold.

Two floors above Baby Sister's apartment at 1449-51 E. 65th Pl., a 35-year-old mother died Saturday night. Friday, she had been to Billings Hospital, where she was told she had pneumonia and then sent home with a prescription.

Baby Sister pays $155-a-month rent for her six-room apartment in the building some Woodlawn residents call "Big Red." She has 10 children, but sent 6 of them to stay with her mother.

The Chicago Dwellings Assn. (CDA) took over the building 3½ years ago, according to residents, to "rehabilitate" it.

Baby Sister says she can't remember when the heat worked right, and now there's no running water, either. In the basement, the water pipes are split in pieces, and the water gushes out on the floor.

Baby Sister says she has called the CDA and City Hall, but nobody will come out to look at "Big Red."

A *Daily News* reporter tried to call the CDA Monday night, but found that both its executive director, Terry Goldberg, and public-relations official, Barbara Howar, apparently have unlisted phone numbers.

Members of the Woodlawn Sisterhood, a group of dedicated black women who work out of a storefront at 6521 S. Blackstone, called the Red Cross, too.

"But they told us this building isn't a disaster, that the Red Cross has fires to take care of," said Annie Fort, director of the sisterhood.

The sisterhood has been on Blackstone for more than a year. A sign on the door of the storefront reads: "It is said that a black woman can make a way out of no way."

The sisters do believe that, but with so much suffering all around, it's hard to keep believing.

Mae Rose Shelton, founder and co-ordinator of the sisterhood, asks: "Why do little babies have to suffer like that? They haven't done anything wrong, haven't done anything but just get born."

Back on the fourth floor of 1449–51 E. 65th Pl., relatives and friends were gathered to mourn the woman who died Saturday.

Porter Johnson, 18, was trying to figure out how he would care for his mentally retarded sister and brother now that his mother is gone.

There really isn't much you can say to this young man after he thanks you very much for stopping by, except "Good luck." And those words have a hollow ring.

"I'll need that, thank you," says Johnson. "But I don't see how things can get worse, so I guess they'll get better."

For 10 kids, bread was
all there was to eat,
John Justin Smith reports

The Daily News *touched off a long and success-*
ful crusade against slum owners with this story
by John Justin Smith on June 10, 1953.

In Chicago in the 20th Century, the 10 Lee kids had bread for lunch.

Bread and what? Bread and nothing . . . just bread.

"That's right, just bread. There's nothing else," said one of the kids.

This is but one of the things that doesn't make sense in the life of a Chicago slum family.

Visit the Lee family in their home at 633 N. Wells and see for yourself the things that don't add up.

Push through the front door, and push through the wall of foul smell.

First count the kids. One, two, three, four, five, six, seven, eight, nine, ten. Ten.

Then there's the father, Standard; the mother, Annie, 29, and her mother, Lucinda Grant. That makes 13 in the family.

Now count the beds. One, two, three. Three beds and 13 people.

"Where do you sleep?"

"Me and the kids sleep in two beds," said Grandma Grant.

"Sure it's crowded. But we got to sleep somewhere, don't we?"

Walk around the cardboard partition, past the stenciled beer ad that shows this was once a saloon. Now you're in the kitchen.

Count the dishes. A cockroach scurries away at your first touch. Six plates and 13 people.

How do they eat? The kids gave a demonstration at a later meal that consisted only of potatoes baked in their jackets.

The youngsters held the potatoes in one hand and used a spoon with the other.

It is well that there are few dirty dishes. The kitchen sink has water, but the drain doesn't work.

Ten kids, and the bathtub doesn't work, either. And the toilet has been flushing for seven months straight.

Ten kids, and there is no place to do laundry. A photographer took a picture of Geraldine, 6, in a blue dress.

Two weeks later a reporter visited the Lees. Geraldine was wearing the same dress.

"I 'most always wear it," she said.

Ten kids, and the only toy in the four-room flat is an old bicycle tire, just a tire.

The kids don't seem to mind. They are quiet as they stand around the dark flat—too quiet for kids.

Mrs. Lee's greatest worry is that one of her children will be bitten by rats.

"They come up from the basement all the time," she said. "All we can do is chase them."

Lee earns $56 a week as a punch-press operator. This doesn't seem to add up, either. With that much money, why not spend more for food?

"We can't," Mrs. Lee said. "Our rent here is $75 a month. That leaves us with very little."

Who gets the $75? Owner of the building is Jack Winkler, who lives with his wife in a 14-room apartment at 2355 N. Commonwealth.

THE ROAD BACK?

1937 Pulitzer Prize cartoon.
Vaughn Shoemaker / Daily News.

War:
Raymond Swing
A. T. Steele
Leland Stowe
Robert J. Casey
Keyes Beech
John Justin Smith
Ellen Warren

Raymond Swing
in World War I:
'America would wake up
to war soon enough'

*Dozens of men and at least one woman covered
World War I for the* Daily News *Foreign Service, an organization started in the Spanish-
American War to provide accurate war reports
instead of the propaganda produced by overly
patriotic news organizations. Among the correspondents were John Gunther, later author of*
Inside Europe *and other books; playwright-
novelist Ben Hecht; Edward Scott Bell, later
nominated for a Nobel Peace Prize; Paul Scott
Mowrer and his brother Edgar, whose reporting
for the Foreign Service won Pulitzer Prizes.
This dispatch, published April 27, 1917, was
written by Raymond Swing, later one of the
world's most famous radio commentators.*

The emotions that stir this writing elude the clumsy tentacles of
words. They are the emotions of an American come home after
three years of war, come home to the fresh air of undistressed
pleasantness and to begin a new war that lays its hands of
death, not on cousins of another language and another psychology, but on its own kin, the brothers of his own fraternity of ide-
alism, the comrades of his own state.

The story begins and ends with the same grave thoughts,
the same grieving feelings, though it starts with a conversation,
mostly of unuttered communion with a Frenchman at the rail of
a Spanish steamer in New York harbor, and ends with a Chicago
audience at a symphony concert.

The Frenchman had been my cabin mate and in the intima-
cy of the unsought informality I had seen the wound where a

bullet had entered his breast and emerged just beside the spine. He had fought two years and now had been sent on some mission or other by his government. During the voyage, when I brought him the news of Haig's victory and the capture of 10,000 prisoners, he had gripped my arm and shaken his head spasmodically, as though he would shake unwelcome thoughts from his mind.

"I'm not ungrateful for the victory," he said at last. "Understand, I can't be but thinking what it cost us, of the inexpressible suffering it means to my friends and my friends' friends. I am very sad." He loosed his grip on my arm and stared long into the uncomforting hold of the sea.

And so we heard together the week-old news of America's declaration of war. Neither of us spoke for many minutes. But I know his thoughts were always in the trenches, and mine, too, were saturated with the lifeblood of the world, growing unchecked on the desolate, shot-burned fields of Europe. We had become allies in those silent minutes, but we could not rejoice. Finally he spoke:

"It is a terrible punishment to belong to this generation. The lights are out. Happiness, ah no! We can't have that. It must suffice to be right."

For two hours in New York I was searching to find the difference between America and Europe. Not the traditonal distinctions in velocity and appearance; I was not surprised by the skyscrapers, the rush, the maze of co-operating vehicles; I was not even astonished to see so many men, so few cripples, for I had been prepared for streets black with men who were not soldiers. But there was a difference. I felt it, breathed it, bathed in it, tasted it. It was indefinable, but it was real, comforting good.

The customs inspectors at the dock were courteous. I was shown to my taxicab by a porter who revealed something welcoming in his minor, perfunctory service. My driver threaded his way through the hazardous traffic without losing his temper when some other driver, by doing the unexpected, suddenly forced him to a quick, unhesitating pulling of levers and application of brakes. At the telephone I had prompt service. And the operator's voice rang with a vague tone of interest and geniality.

And the corner policeman was calling out to a brood of dodging pedestrians, scurrying like chickens between the automobiles:

"Well, well! What does this mean? What does this mean?"

His ruddy, large face was smiling, his hands were busy cautioning the advancing drivers and pointing out the fleeting paths of safety.

At last I laid a mental finger on the difference. America, the nation of peace, was vibrating with unworried kindness. The customs official had no relatives at the front in the great drive; the porter had not lost his son; the chauffeur was not on furlough from the trenches; the telephone operator knew where she could buy food; the corner policeman was not haunted by disquieting presentiments of hunger riots. And all the faces of the good, gentle, courteous folk I had marveled at in the streets of "selfish" New York were the faces of folk who had not looked over a trench parapet at the million hostile daggers of wire entanglements.

It was sweet, this taste of peace. I was suddenly reminded of the life Europe had lived, must have lived, before the eternity that set in on Aug. 1, 1914. I had forgotten that Europe ever had been unconcerned, devoted to making the insignificant commerce of life tolerable and cheerful. I had come to believe life was only endless, relentless, pitiless waste. In Europe no one expects more than cruel abstraction, nervousness, fatigue, irritability. They are taken for granted. It cannot be otherwise. Death does not stalk merrily.

The canyons of New York's streets were gala with flags, though it was no holiday. Recruiting posters, Wilson pictures, vendors of patriotic badges gave the city the appearance of a metropolis playing at an afternoon of war. The curb newspapers, all headlines, tried with inky profligacy to tell the story, which can never be told, of the Western offensive.

"Washington is worried about the country's apathy," a friend told me. "The nation isn't awake to the war."

"Dear friends," I said hotly, "you can't wake up a nation with flags and posters. It takes funerals, cripples, deprivations. This kindergarten war is a criminal travesty."

Generals were throwing out the first ball at baseball games, the players were giving exhibition drills before the contests, but they played ball just the same. New York and Chicago were busy proving that the other city was the more apathetic, while neither was giving the war enough recruits a day to hold a mile of trenches. Summit, N.J., where I was stopping, had bought a municipal machine gun. Think of it!

"America, why did you go to war at all?" I could not help thinking. "And now you are in it, why not give up this tinsel, this superficiality, this flag waving, pacifist hating, hurrahing, and go to war, in earnest; solemnly, desperately, grimly, as war must be made! Why pursue the pacifists? Do you know not that pacifism in Europe rises in the trenches? Should our pacifists be persecuted because they have the imagination to know a little what war is and costs? Once get into the war and you will be like all the rest — a great majority of inspired pacifists bossed by a small group of militarists!"

And then I began finding friends missing—off at camp drilling. Or this man or that could not see me next week because he was going into training. My cousin, in his study the other night, was making out not his notes on carbon electrons but his application for the officers' corps. And my good friend H., who had been in the Berlin embassy, one of the precious men of this generation, stopped over to say he was enlisting next week.

"Why?" I asked. "For you know what it means."

"I hate to do it. I hate war. But we are in it, and the young men have to go first because they can be spared first."

I was sitting at my typewriter when a friend of my cousin came in, very sober and nervous.

"I've had an awful experience," he said. "A man tried to board the I. C. [Illinois Central] train and fell between the car and the platform. I think he was killed, but I couldn't wait to see." He fell on the bed, worn out.

And I thought of the corpses I had stepped over on the Polish battlefields, with their sienna, parchment faces and their grinning, yellow teeth, grimacing at the unsympathetic sky. And I remembered that my French cabin mate said the one thing he never could get used to was to step on his dead comrades in a charge.

America would wake up to war soon enough.

The parlor talks to which I was admitted were of war, nothing else, be it in terms of politics, principles, potatoes. Not unlike the talks we in Europe had heard for three years, only fresher, less frightened, less desperate.

"America is not after anything selfish. We are fighting for democracy. Wilson was patient. The country is with him." How often these sentiments are the pith of the discussions! And every day I hear of more friends volunteering or arranging their affairs to volunteer. And soon we shall have selective draft, and to all of us the war will begin to come home, to our homes as it is coming to all European homes. The American jingoes need not worry about American apathy, nor I about kindergarten war.

I knew this before I went to the symphony concert. It happened the program was all German music. Beethoven, Brahms, Strauss and Wagner. The flag hung behind the orchestra as though to serve as a sounding board to these foreign strains that have emanated from the Germany no one hates and fights. And when the program ended something unutterably wonderful happened.

With a quick sweep over the orchestra with his baton, conductor Frederick Stock started the national hymn and turned to us. We were all standing and we began singing. The orchestra and organ gave their full, vibrant force, gave to it a harmonization of the familiar tune that raised it to the imposing, inspiring eminence of great music, changed it from shallow drivel to something moving and magnificent, an anthem great enough for a hundred million souls. And we sang it; we were a little doubtful of all the words of that one verse, but we repeated the last phrase with roused security and profound feelings:

Oh, say, does that star-spangled banner yet wave
O'er the land of the free and the home of the brave?

I sang it too, but I was seeing trenches, blood-blackened earth and the unburied, unpitied dead. Not dead Germans, Russians, Frenchmen, but my own friends, my cousin, my brother perhaps. So while the others cheered conductor Stock at the close I concealed my emotions by leaving quickly.

But I knew I had faced a great and awful truth. They were worthwhile, the trenches, the dead, the desolation, if they could secure freedom, a world of the free.

The politics of war are the expression of man's frailty, the frank registration of human weakness. The most appalling fact of the war is that nearly all the men who are killing each other do it in the name of identical ideals, for soldiers are not content to die for petty achievements. But if they are sowing for the same fine harvest of peace and justice, the potential brotherhood is there. There is no hostility among the dead: there must be none, at last, among the living. The way of life is inscrutable, the price of human progress infinite. But if man is to be more free, no price is too high, not even for us of this stricken, unwise, brave generation.

A. T. Steele
witnesses the infamous
'Rape of Nanking'

A. T. Steele stunned the Western World with this exclusive eyewitness report on Dec. 18, 1937, of the Japanese army's "rape of Nanking."

NANKING (via the *USS Oahu*) — "Four days in hell" would be the most fitting way to describe the siege and capture of Nanking.

I have just boarded the gunboat *Oahu* with the first group of foreigners to leave the capital since the attack began. The last thing we saw as we left the city was a band of 300 Chinese being methodically executed before the wall near the waterfront, where already corpses were piled knee-deep.

It was a characteristic picture of the mad Nanking scene of the last few days.

The story of Nanking's fall is a story of indescribable panic and confusion among the entrapped Chinese defenders, followed by a reign of terror by the conquering army that cost thousands of lives, many of them innocent ones.

While the behavior of the Chinese before the city's abandonment was deplorable in many ways, it was mild compared with the excesses of the invading force.

All foreigners in Nanking are safe.

Japanese brutality at Nanking is costing them a golden opportunity to win the sympathy of the Chinese population, whose friendship they claim to be seeking.

After the complete collapse of Chinese morale and the blind panic that followed, Nanking experienced a distant sense of release when the Japanese entered, feeling that the behavior of the Japanese could not possibly be worse than that of their own defeated army. They were quickly disillusioned.

The Japanese could have completed the occupation of the remainder of the city almost without firing a shot, by offering mercy to the trapped Chinese soldiers, most of whom had discarded their arms and would surrender. However, they chose the course of systematic extermination.

It was like killing sheep. How many troops were trapped and killed it is difficult to estimate, but it may be anywhere between 5,000 and 20,000.

With the overland routes cut off, the Chinese swarmed to the river through the Ksiakwan gate, which became quickly choked. Emerging through this gate today I found it necessary to drive my car over heaps of bodies 5 feet high, over which hundreds of Japanese trucks and guns had already passed.

Streets throughout the city were littered with the bodies of civilians and abandoned Chinese equipment and uniforms. Many troops who were unable to obtain boats across the river leaped into the river to almost certain death.

Japanese looting made the Chinese looting, which had preceded it, look like a Sunday-school picnic. They invaded foreign properties, among them the residence of the American ambassador, Nelson T. Johnson.

In the American-operated University Hospital they relieved the nurses of watches and money. They stole at least two American-owned cars, ripping off the flags. They even invaded the camps of refugees, stripping many poor of the few dollars they owned.

This account is based on the observations of myself and other foreigners remaining in Nanking throughout the siege.

I saw Chinese troops needlessly applying the torch to whole blocks of homes and shops around the city walls, dispossessing thousands in a futile attempt to impede the Japanese attack.

I saw a terrific two-day bombardment of Nanking's defenses, which finally softened and shattered Chinese resistance.

I heard the din of cannonading and machine-gunning accompanying the final Japanese assault on the strongly held south gate, where towering torches of flame lit up the battlefield.

Later I saw a scene of butchery outside that gate where the corpses of at least 1,000 soldiers lay in every conceivable posture of death, amid a confusion of fallen telephone and power lines and charred ruins—apparently trapped by the closing of the gates.

I saw Chinese troops looting shop windows, but later I saw the Japanese troops outdo them in a campaign of pillage that the Japanese carried out not only in the shops but in homes, hospitals, and refugee camps.

I saw hundreds of Chinese tear off their uniforms in the street, some donning civilian clothes, others running away in their underwear. Many came to me and to other foreigners, imploring protection and offering guns and money in exchange.

I saw fear-crazed troops attempt to force their entry into the headquarters of the international committee and, when refused, begin to toss guns, revolvers and machine guns over the walls into the hands of the startled missionaries, who gingerly stowed them away for surrender to the Japanese.

These things, too, I saw:

A frightened soldier crawling under a German flag; hundreds of wounded crawling and limping through the streets, beseeching every passer-by for assistance; Japanese soldiers impressing coolies and donkeys into service to carry their loot; Japanese machine gunners moving through the streets in the moonlight, killing anyone who ran and some who did not; Japanese systematically searching houses and seizing many plain-clothes suspects, scores of these bound men being shot one by one while their condemned fellows sat stolidly by, awaiting their turn.

I saw the Japanese beating and jabbing helpless civilians, and in the hospitals I saw many civilians suffering from bayonet wounds.

I saw the dead scattered along every street including some old men who could not possibly have harmed anyone; also mounds of the bodies of executed men.

I saw a grisly mess at the north gate, where what once had been 200 men was a smoldering mass of flesh and bones.

Outside the gate I saw rope ladders, strips of clothing and blankets hanging from the wall, where many escaped from the city after finding the gate choked, only to fall into a deadlier trap.

The safety zone created in the heart of fortified Nanking by the committee of foreigners was built on a foundation of colossal nerve, for from the first it was evident that neither side would respect it fully. Nevertheless, while a score of shells fell inside the zone and the area was occasionally sprayed by stray bullets and shrapnel, it was probably safer than other parts of the country.

The pathetic aspect of the picture was the way the Chinese of this once intensely nationalistic capital flocked to foreigners for protection. Ten years ago, when Generalissimo Chiang Kai-shek's nationalist army marched into Nanking, shouting anti-foreign slogans, a display of the American flag would have been an invitation to death. Now thousands of Chinese would give anything short of their lives to get under the protection of a foreign flag.

For those four chaotic days between the collapse of their defense and the occupation of Nanking, the Chinese submitted themselves meekly and eagerly to the orders and suggestions of the few foreign missionaries and merchants running the international committee, which then was the sole administrative organ in the city.

Even trapped soldiers, hysterical with fear, besieged the committee headquarters with abject supplications for foreign protection against the approaching enemy.

It is noticeable that, despite the complete demoralization of the Chinese soldiers, they did not turn on the foreigners who would have been easy prey for looting. The same cannot be said for the Japanese, who flouted foreign rights and repeatedly raided foreign properties plainly marked with embassy notices and flags.

All of us did some service in carrying wounded to the hospitals. The streets were full of them, and the piteous pleading for assistance was difficult to resist.

Leland Stowe tells
of the 'Snowbound Forest
of the Dead'

Early in World War II, Leland Stowe visited a tragic battlefield where a short time earlier Russian and Finnish soldiers killed one another in the silent, frozen forests. This dispatch was published Jan. 2, 1940.

TOLVAJARVI, Finland—In this sad solitude lie the dead; uncounted thousands of Russian dead. They lie as they fell—twisted, gesticulating and tortured. But they lie beneath a kindly mask of two inches of new-fallen snow. Now they are one with the cold, white shapes of the illimitable pine and spruce trees. An unknown legion of fallen, they have been covered over with winter's spotless sheet.

But even this profuse, virginal coverlet cannot quite conceal the anguish of their last movement or the catastrophic suddenness of their end. Here all the pain and all the cruelty of their betrayal have been preserved. It is as if Mme. Tussaud of the famous London wax-works museum had decided to preserve one of war's final horrors—as if she had created this scene of false peace and inexpressible tragedy and with appropriate simplicity had called it the "Field of Battle."

Every winter deep solitude hovers above the snows of Tolvajarvi. But today it is infinitely deeper than in other years, for it is heavy with the loneliness of death; and thousands of the dead may be as lonely as a single one. In this place we have heard of a magnificent victory. In this place the silence speaks of things that man may destroy but never more restore.

When we rode out upon the narrow finger of Lake Tolva's peninsula, we were not prepared for this. It is a thin and twisting road with trees standing high on either side and the white, frozen bosom of the lake just beyond. All along this central artery of the battlefield we saw the shattered tanks and broken supply trucks and heaped debris of the Red Army's annihilated divisions.

All along the roadway we saw strange shapes bulging beneath the snow among the trees, shapes that might have been logs. Sometimes they looked like crooked limbs cast into discard by the woodsman's ax. Sometimes heavy felt boots, bared of snow by the stumbling contact of some passing Finnish soldier, protruded suddenly and revealed the naked truth. Sometimes, too, we saw soldiers dragging frozen shapes, like pieces of cordwood, from the forest—and here and there bodies lay in crude, contorted piles, waiting for a final nameless common grave.

December's last snowfall had cloaked these forms in immaculate anonymity. Nature had done her charitable best. It did not seem possible that these could have been human beings only a few days before.

Then our white-painted army bus stopped on the crest of the ridge. We climbed out and followed our guide into the forest.

"There are many of them here," he said. "They were all wiped out by our machine-gun fire." It was true; there were very many of them here.

All about us they lay—featureless human shapes, their masks of snow making them more anonymous than death itself. Some lay straight on the ground, but mostly the arms were drawn convulsively upward to project stiffly above the shoulder. Mostly their legs were bent or doubled. The grotesque bodies were curiously oversized with their two-inch coating of snow.

Who did not wonder what these men looked like and what might be written on their faces? Slowly I brushed the snow away from one. An unshaven face with an alabaster forehead emerged first, and then the stubble of close-cut, black hair. This face was peaceful, as if its owner had fallen asleep here in the blizzard. It was the face of a man of 30—still and frozen and lifeless.

But there were other faces on which was written such suffering as can scarcely bear contemplation. One of these belonged to a young soldier who had been shot in the right knee. He lay with both hands clutched desperately against the wound. This had been the young Russian's last action and the terrible frost of 35 degrees below zero had mummified him in the precise attitude in which he had died.

We could not look for long. Never has any battlefield been more deeply saturated with the imploring silence of the dead.

Steel helmets with a slender red stripe painted on them lay where they had fallen. From some of the pockets protruded letters or newspaper clippings or membership cards in the Bolshevik Comsomol organization. These had spaces for dues to be paid up to the year 1946. Oddly enough beside one soldier we found the photograph of a young man lying in a coffin. It would be impossible even to dig a grave for his brother here until spring.

Someone picked up a packet of letters written by a soldier's wife in Leningrad. Although they were written by an almost illiterate woman, he was able later to translate them. They told how she had written letter after letter, but still had received no answer since he had been taken by the Red Army in October; how she had sent 5 rubles this time and 20 rubles another; how she had sent a picture of their little boy, Loonja; how the bills could not be paid and how they waited for him to come home.

"I spent the holiday (Nov. 7) very badly," she wrote. "I cried all the time. Loonja keeps asking when is Daddy coming home. He asked Uncle Pete, 'Haven't you seen my papa?' Uncle Pete said no but that you were coming home soon. Loonja said, 'Well, tell Mother that Daddy is coming home and that if he comes at night she must wake me up as soon as he comes.' "

I hope that I did not see this Russian soldier's face. We left him there, with countless hundreds of other proletarians of the Soviet Union, in Tolvajarvi's snowbound forest of dead. On almost all these rigid, frozen bodies there must have been similar letters. But they will never be read again. In this vast solitude, all will return to the earth, when another spring burgeons the pine and spruce forests of eastern Finland.

British in Norway: 'Too little and too late'

On April 25, 1940, the Daily News *published this exclusive report by Leland Stowe on a disastrous British attack on Norway.*

GÄDDEDE, Norwegian-Swedish Frontier—Here is the first and only eyewitness report on the opening chapter of the British expeditionary troops' advance in Norway north of Trondheim. It is a bitterly disillusioning and almost unbelievable story.

The British force that was supposed to sweep down from Namsos consisted of one battalion of Territorials and one battalion of the King's Own Royal Light Infantry. These totaled fewer than 1,500 men. They were dumped into Norway's deep snows and quagmires of April slush without a single antiaircraft gun, without one squadron of supporting airplanes, without a single piece of field artillery.

They were thrown into the snows and mud of 63 degrees north latitude to fight crack German regulars—most of them veterans of the Polish invasion—and to face the most destructive of modern weapons. The great majority of these young Britishers averaged only one year of military service. They have already paid a heavy price for a major military blunder that was not committed by their immediate command, but in London.

Unless they receive large supplies of antiaircraft guns and adequate reinforcements within a very few days, the remains of these two British battalions will be cut to ribbons.

Here is the astonishing story of what has happened to the gallant little handful of British expeditionaries above Trondheim:

After only four days of fighting, nearly half of this initial BEF [British Expeditionary Force] contingent has been knocked out—either killed, wounded or captured. On Monday, these comparatively inexperienced and incredibly underarmed

80

British troops were decisively defeated. They were driven back in precipitate disorder from Vist, three miles south of the bomb-ravaged town of Steinkjer.

As I write, it is probable that the British field headquarters has been withdrawn northward and that the British vanguard has been compelled to evacuate one or several villages. Steinkjer was occupied by the Germans Tuesday.

I was in Steinkjer Monday evening just before the British lines were blasted to pieces. I was the only newspaper corre-spondent to enter the burning town and the only correspondent to visit British advance headquarters and to pass beyond to the edge of the front's heavy firing zone.

A score of buildings were flaming fiercely on the town's waterfront from a bombing two hours earlier. In the midst of the smoky ruins I heard machine-guns cracking at high tempo in the hills just beyond the town. Shell explosions rapped the val-ley regularly with angry echoes. This was the first sustained bat-tle between German and British troops on Norwegian soil. Al-ready the conflict was snarling hot.

A battalion of 600 Territorials was fighting desperately to hold Vist, the point of their farthest southwest advance toward Trondheim. As Monday's twilight closed they were completely done in. For hours they had been torn and broken under the ter-rible triple onslaught of German infantry, trimotored bombers and naval firing from destroyers at the head of Breitstadfjord.

Within two hours the British troops were in flight. They had no chance whatever of standing off bombs and three-or six-inch shells with nothing but Bren machine guns and rifles. Be-fore 11 that night I talked with the nerve-shattered survivors of the British battalion. We found two truckloads of them several miles above their headquarters and on their way north away from the front.

One of the officers told me that more than 200 in the bat-talion had been killed and that one entire company had been captured. He could not estimate the number of missing but said that perhaps 150 of the battalion's 600 might be rallied later on.

"We have simply been massacred," he declared. "It is the planes. We have no planes to fight back with, and we have no antiaircraft guns. It is just like Russians against the Finns, only worse—and we are the Finns."

A subofficer greeted me gratefully when he learned that I was a reporter.

"For God's sake, tell them we have got to have airplanes and antiaircraft guns," he pleaded.

"We were completely at the mercy of the Jerries. Their bombers flew low over us, at 500 feet. They scattered us. We were up to our hips in snow.

"Then they dropped signal flares so their artillery knew our positions. Last night our wounded were crying in the woods, but we couldn't get to them or do anything. We had not even got proper clothes to fight with in the snow. Without white capes the Jerries just spotted us and mowed us down every time the bombers drove us out."

Paul Melander, a Swedish photographer, and I saw these things together. We were the only newsmen to spend nearly 24 hours in the British sector and to reach the edge of the firing zone on that front.

Although almost exhausted from lack of sleep, the British officers maintained remarkable calm. But this was a small military machine with vital cogs missing. Able to bomb at will, the Germans had seriously disrupted the organization of the little British expeditionary vanguard in their first four days at the front.

Forty British fighting planes at present could probably clear the skies over the entire Allied Norwegian fighting zones and all vital sections of their rear guard north of Trondheim. The British troops are praying that these fighters will arrive soon before it is too late.

Following the British defeat near Vist, we were told that Norwegian troops had been compelled to take over virtually all the north front above Trondheim. North of Trondheim the military initiative is now held by alert, aggressive and first-class German troops. It is guaranteed by Nazi warplanes that are flying constantly at less than 1,000 feet over the Allies' Norwegian sector and that bomb their objectives as easily as a marksman picks off clay pigeons.

Three times in one day German planes roared over my head at only 500 or 600 feet, and twice I was in buildings where key Norwegian commands were located. I thought the Nazis' espionage service—with its formidable network throughout Scandinavia—had already betrayed these locations. Providentially, this had not happened and no bombs were dropped. So these two Norwegian control centers escaped. But without the Allies' aircraft and antiaircraft guns such miracles cannot endure for long.

This is merely an illustration of the tremendous initiative that has been handed to the Germans north of Trondheim by one of the costliest and most inexplicable military bungles in modern British history.

It has been handed to them by those high British authorities who thrust 1,500 young Territorials into the snow and mud below Namsos 10 days ago without a single antiaircraft gun or a single piece of artillery.

Robert J. Casey finds heroism in a man nobody noticed

Robert J. Casey gained fame as a chronicler of crime in Chicago in the Capone era. When Hitler invaded Poland in 1939, Casey became a war correspondent at the "old" age of 49 and covered World War II in Europe, Africa and the Pacific. This dispatch was published Sept. 17, 1940.

HOTSPOT, Southeast England—In the larger matters of threatened invasion by aerial bombs and artillery fire people have given little thought to Jock Evans, upon whose thin breast nobody will ever pin any medals, even posthumously.

He will never have a public funeral with muffled drums, muted trumpets and suchlike tokens of civic gratitude. It is most unlikely he will ever have any funeral at all.

In the years before the war he had done nothing to distinguish himself. He had some sort of dock job where the dust hadn't been too good for his lungs. Because of bad eyes and other deficiencies, he had been rejected for military service even at the end of the last war, when medical examiners hadn't been too particular.

In other words, though nobody noticed it at the time, he was made of the stuff heroes are made of.

So far as concerns the elements that have made England to date, he was an architect's model for the spirit of the British Empire.

Evans, to get on with it, was in his most recent career an air raid-precautions warden. In a year's drill on how to put on the gas mask, how to revive fainting women, how to direct people to the nearest shelter, he had never shown more than ordinary aptitude.

Evans was on duty that night. He had been on duty most nights in the last month, as he would be now with warnings on all the time and never an all-clear. He had phoned to the central control at 11 p.m. that he had seen a bright light somewhere— his superiors, remembering Jock, suspected it might be somebody with a too bright cigar.

He had stationed himself near the telephone kiosk near the edge of an outlying suburb where the artillery shells still land each day when the town is shelled. He had had no occasion to move from his post at midnight when the big crump fell.

The big crump was a dud. For a moment Jock felt glad of that. The shriek of it had been pretty nerve-racking. But after a while, when he remembered he had better go run over and look at it, he wasn't reassured. It wasn't a dud. He had looked at enough diagrams and sketches to know. It was a time bomb— and a big one.

He told all this to his chief in his report a minute later.

"Where is it?" inquired his chief.

"In the garden," said Jock.

Then the same order:

"Get people out, empty nearby houses, and keep people away!"

"Yes, sir," said Jock.

Maybe it might be as well to mention here something of the nature of a time bomb, especially for Americans, who so far haven't had much experience with such things.

In the first place, it is not like the old-type torpedo with nose fuse that could be unscrewed by a handy man with a monkey wrench. This is more complicated. The timing device is a simple interior arrangement of acid working on metal.

By varying the thickness of the metal density, the acid rate of corrosion may be set for anything between one minute and one month. Eventually the acid reaches the fulminating charge and the neighborhood goes to pieces.

There have been some hints that in what followed after his report Jock didn't show any great judgment, but the same might have been said of Dewey if he had run into a mine at Manila Bay. He followed out his orders. In less than an hour he had evacuated the few homes in the immediate vicinity. Then he stationed himself to warn off traffic.

There wasn't much to do until about 7 in the morning, when workers and sightseers began to pass afoot, on bicycles and in automobiles.

The odd feature of a community that is being continuously bombed is the inquisitive interest in lethal hazards. Evans suddenly found himself alone in a two-man job. The bomb lay almost at the junction of two lanes, giving access to it from four directions.

Evans solved this problem as best he could. He roped off the street a hundred yards behind the bomb, then took up his post at the middle of the crossing.

Dozens of persons heard and heeded his call during the next two hours. "Time bomb here. Keep away, keep away."

One of those who passed was the priest of the neighborhood Anglican church, to whom is owing the best description of Evans' last stand.

"He hardly needed to point out the bomb," said the padre. "It was lying there in a grass plot right behind him, and it was evident he knew all about it. His face was white and drawn, but there wasn't any tremor in his voice. I couldn't get it out of my head, as he sang out the warning and blew his whistle, that he was the psychological equivalent of the medieval leper, ringing his bell and shouting, 'Unclean! unclean!' "

"I had told him to get away from the corner, block off the streets with ropes. But he said, 'My duty is to stay here. Please go on, sir; don't set a bad example.' I went to telephone for help."

The bomb went off at 9:10, blowing a crater 40 feet wide. No trace has been found of Evans.

Keyes Beech in Korea: 'This was no retreat,' the colonel said

Keyes Beech has been attending wars since the 1940s and he has seen, he said, altogether too many men of too many nationalities and races lying dead on battlefields. His reporting during the Korean War won a Pulitzer Prize. The following dispatch was published Dec. 11, 1950.

YONPO AIRSTRIP, Korea—"Remember," drawled Col. Lewis B. (Chesty) Puller, "whatever you write, that this was no retreat. All that happened was we found more Chinese behind us than in front of us. So we about-faced and attacked."

I said "So long" to Puller after three snowbound days with 1st Marine Division, 4,000 feet above sea level in the subzero weather of Changjin Reservoir. I climbed aboard a waiting C-47 at Koto Airstrip and looked around.

Sixteen shivering Marine casualties—noses and eyes dripping from cold—huddled in their bucket seats. They were the last of more than 2,500 Marine casualties to be evacuated by the U.S. Air Force under conditions considered flatly impossible.

Whatever this campaign was—retreat, withdrawal or defeat—one thing can be said with certainty. Not in the Marine Corps' long and bloody history has there been anything like it. And if you'll pardon a personal recollection, not at Tarawa or Iwo Jima, where casualties were much greater, did I see men suffer as much.

The wonder isn't that they fought their way out against overwhelming odds but that they were able to survive the cold and fight at all. So far as the marines themselves are concerned, they ask that two things be recorded:

1. They didn't break. They came out of Changjin Reservoir as an organized unit with most of their equipment.

2. They brought out all their wounded. They brought out many of their dead. And most of those they didn't bring out they buried.

It was not always easy to separate dead from wounded among the frozen figures that lay strapped to radiators of jeeps and trucks. I know because I watched them come in from Yudam to Hagaru, 18 miles of icy hell, five days ago.

That same day I stood in the darkened corner of a wind-whipped tent and listened to a Marine officer brief his men for the march to Koto the following day. I have known him for a long time but in the semidarkness, with my face half covered by my parka, he didn't recognize me. When he did the meeting broke up. When we were alone, he cried. After that he was all right.

I hope he won't mind my reporting he cried, because he's a very large marine and a very tough guy.

He cried because he had to have some sort of emotional release; because all his men were heroes and wonderful people; because the next day he was going to have to submit them to another phase in the trial by blood and ice. Besides, he wasn't the only one who cried.

In the Marines' 12-day, 40-mile trek from Yudam to the "bottom of the hill," strange and terrible things happened.

Thousands of Chinese troops—the marines identified at least six divisions totaling 60,000 men—boiled from every canyon and rained fire from every ridge. Sometimes they came close enough to throw grenades into trucks, jeeps and ambulances.

Whistles sounded and Chinese ran up to throw grenades into Marine foxholes. Another whistle and the Chinese ran back.

Then mortar shells began to fall. The 3d Battalion of the 5th Marine Regiment was reduced to less than two companies but still was ordered to attack "regardless of cost."

"We had to do it," said Lt. Col. Joe Stewart, of Montgomery, Ala. "It was the only way out."

Fox Company, 7th Regiment, was isolated for three or four days—nobody seems to remember dates or days—but held at terrible cost.

One company killed so many Chinese the marines used their frozen bodies as a parapet. But for every Chinese they killed there were 5, 10 or 20 to take his place.

"What 'n hell's the use in killing them?" said one marine. "They breed faster 'n we can knock 'em off."

The Chinese had blown bridges and culverts behind the Americans. The marines rebuilt them or established bypasses under fire.

No part of a division escaped, including headquarters sections composed of file clerks, cooks and bakers. Bullets plowed through a Korean house in Hagaru occupied by Gen. O. H. P. Smith.

Always the infantry had to take high ground on each side of the road to protect the train of vehicles that sometimes stretched 10 miles.

When the Chinese attacked a train, the artillerymen unhooked their guns from their vehicles and fired muzzle bursts from between trucks at the onrushing foe. This was effective, but rather rough on Marine machine gunners who had set up their guns on the railroad tracks 15 or 20 yards in front of the artillery.

If there was an occasional respite from the enemy there was none from the cold. It numbed fingers, froze feet, sifted through layers of clothing and crept into the marrow of your bones. Feet sweated by day and froze in their socks by night. Men peeled off their socks—and the soles of their feet with them.

Among the men of the 5th Marines, Lt. Comdr. Chester M. Lessenden Jr., of Lawrence, Kan., a Navy doctor, became a hero.

"Lessenden is the most saintly, godlike man I've ever known," said Stewart. "He never seemed to sleep. He was always on his feet. He never said it can't be done. And yet he was suffering from frostbite worse than most of the men he treated."

In their struggle to keep from freezing, the marines wrapped their feet in gunnysacks or pieces of old cloth scrounged from the countryside. When they could, they built fires, but this wasn't often, because fire gave away their positions.

When they came to Koto before the final breakthrough to the sea, they made tents of varicolored parachutes used by the Air Force to drop supplies. The red, white and green chute tents looked like Indian wigwams.

Some covered themselves with Japanese quilts dropped from the air. But they were warmest when they were fighting. Combat was almost welcome because they forgot about the cold.

The cold did strange things to their equipment. Because of subzero temperatures, artillery rounds landed as much as 2,000 yards short. Machine guns froze up. Men tugged frantically at their frozen bolts. The M-1 rifle generally held up but the marines cursed the lighter carbine.

Communications gear broke down because equipment, like men, can stand only so much. Canteens burst as water froze inside them.

Despite all these things, the marines who walked down from Changjin Reservoir still could laugh.

"It was impossible for us to get out, because we were surrounded, encircled and cut off," said one lieutenant. "But we never got the word, so we came on out. That's us—we never get the word."

Some of the boys
come home from Korea:
'He always did like trains'

Reporters are accustomed to writing a story, forgetting about it and moving on to the next assignment. But John Justin Smith remembers this story a quarter of a century after he wrote it, because 200 readers took the time to write him letters thanking him for his words. The article was published May 14, 1953.

The bodies of 136 soldiers killed in Korea passed through Chicago Thursday.

They were in three Army mortuary cars that arrived at the North Western Station during the morning rush hour.

Who were the 136? Where did they come from?

"They could be anybody," a captain said. "They could be from Chicago—or any place east of the Mississippi.

"We take 'em all to Brooklyn and ship them home from there."

(Home? That's a good one—home. How can they take them there? Home is the place where he had a mother, a father, brothers and sisters.)

Thousands of commuters walked near the cars in the station. Not one paid any attention, or even slowed down.

"Want to take a look?" the captain said.

He led the way into the dark car and struck a match. On steel racks the caskets, covered with long, drab crates, were piled three deep.

The first was numbered 33.

(He always did like trains. When he was 4 he got a windup train for his birthday. It ran fine. But there were no mortuary cars. Just pretty yellow ones.)

The match burned out. As he lit another, the captain said:

"They all died within the last two months. Old Baldy."

(When he was 9 and studied geography, the teacher called Korea "Chosen." She said the people were mostly farmers. She didn't say anything about death or a hill called Old Baldy.)

"This used to be a Pullman car," the captain said. "Then it was a hospital car."

(Hospital? Had he ever been in one before? Yes, when he was 11. He fell from a tree and broke an arm. In the hospital the doctor set the broken arm and Pop said he was brave, brave not to cry.)

Back on the platform a pretty girl walked past the mortuary cars without looking. She had brown hair and brown eyes.

(When he was 14 he sort of fell in love with a girl with brown hair and brown eyes. Nancy. She was pretty. And she walked right past his life, too. Gee, that was only five years ago.)

A young mother walked down the platform, bumping her 5-year-old son on the back of the head to make him walk faster. She didn't notice the mortuary cars.

(Stop pushing him, Mom. Take his hand and hold it tight. It's such a short time.)

Beirut's tragedy:
'Good evening, sir.
If she died or still alive?'

Ellen Warren, a local reporter and rewrite person, filed this dispatch from Lebanon on her first foreign assignment. It was published Dec. 31, 1975.

BEIRUT—For those who wonder how the year ended in Beirut, a city torn by months of fighting, the answer came Wednesday in a brief exchange of messages between two Teletype operators.

One sat at his machine in a nearly empty second-class Beirut hotel. The other sat at his machine in a hotel in Amman, Jordan, more than 100 miles away.

They spoke to each other on this last day of 1975 by Teletype, because the telephone lines don't work between the two cities.

Here is what they said:

"Good evening, sir, this Amman Intercontinental Hotel. Please, can you help me again to call 338270 or 248502, asking about my sister, Mrs. Angeal Bahbah. If she died or still alive? I am Yousef Bahbah, her brother.

"Please, please, dear?"

BEIRUT: "Moment, please. The first there is no answer. I am trying the second. Moment. Sorry, also there is no answer."

AMMAN: "Please, I have a third number—283353."

BEIRUT: "OK. Moment, sir." (There is a pause and then):

"Sorry to tell you about your sister as she was shot by a sniper and she passed away after the operation and her husband does not know what to do. Please can you tell us what to do?"

AMMAN: "About my sister. Burn it (the body) in Beirut and if all you can come to Amman, please come."

BEIRUT: "OK, will pass your message. Sorry again. Byby."

1971 editorial cartoon.
John Fischetti / Daily News.

Learning:

Robert G. Schultz
Joseph Haas
Ed Eulenberg
Thomas E. Sellers
Mike Royko
Robert J. Herguth
Bob Schenet
Sydney J. Harris

Robert G. Schultz:
'Little Janet didn't
touch her breakfast'

Reporters often grouse about the assignments they get and Robert G. Schultz was no exception. He thought his editor was losing his mind when he told Schultz to do a story about a 5-year-old girl starting to school. It was a small assignment and resulted in a little story, but 20 years later Schultz recalled it as one of his most pleasant experiences. This article was published Sept. 4, 1957.

It was 7 a.m. when Janet Kelen first stirred uneasily and rubbed a night's sleep from her blue-gray eyes.

Her mother Lee had gently talked her awake.

In her nearly five years, this was to be Janet's biggest of big days: She was starting to school.

And like thousands of other Chicago-area youngsters who face the same prospect this week or next, Janet was excited and just a little apprehensive.

She didn't say much, but you could tell.

You could tell when she sat down to breakfast with her three sisters in the kitchen of the Kelen home at 1173 S. Ridgeland in Oak Park.

She didn't touch her breakfast—just sipped a little milk.

Janet laughed, perhaps a little more than usual. It was an excited laugh, a little tense, a little nervous.

Her older sister Linda, 7, was calm by comparison. After all, Linda was going into second grade. This was old stuff.

Sally, 3½, the family cutup, was taking it in stride. But she kind of wished she could go to school, too.

Nancy, 11 months, just sat in her high chair gurgling little approvals from time to time. She didn't care whether school kept or not.

Janet really looked scrubbed and shiny when her mother gave a last minute whisk of the hairbrush to Janet's light-brown hair.

Her shoes were glistening and every fold in her glazed cotton dress was in place.

It was a nice dress with pink and white candy stripes.

Her daddy John held her hand as she walked up the steps of the big, red-brick Washington Irving School, 1101 S. Cuyler.

The hallways echoed with the voices of other children and other parents as they walked toward the kindergarten.

Some of the parents looked as nervous and sad as some of the children.

The kindergarten was a bright and cheery room with a little fish pond and little tables and little chairs and a piano and blocks and toys.

Laura Boose, the teacher, was bright and cheery, too. But Janet mostly snuggled close to her daddy. She was still excited but now she was frightened.

Her eyes said so. Especially when the tears squeezed out and trickled down her cheeks.

It wasn't until her daddy left the room that Janet felt assured enough to join the other children, who were seated on a big rug in the center of the room.

She looked down at the floor and her eyes were still red-rimmed when Miss Boose led the children in singing such songs as *Ba Ba, Black Sheep, Mary Had a Little Lamb, Jack and Jill.*

Janet was silent.

But later Janet glanced up at the teacher from time to time.

And if you looked real close, she seemed to be singing, too.

Joseph Haas explores the etymology of a sophisticated sublanguage

Joseph Haas, a crack reporter and writer who became a distinguished book editor of the Daily News, *wrote this article, published Feb. 28, 1959.*

"Baboy! Appo ogone couts . . . duty. Nonono!"

This isn't gibberish or a foreign tongue. It is a perfectly literate sentence in Jaimese. It means:

"I am a bad boy. I dropped my apple on the couch and stained the couch cover ('duty' means 'dirty'). I had best not do it again."

Jaimese is a sublanguage in the general grouping of tongues known as Babytalk. It is spoken only by Jaime Haas, age 19 months.

It can be interpreted only by his mother, myself and, to some extent, by his grandparents, who speak a sort of tourist Jaimese.

This is intended to be a guide to Jaimetalk. Perhaps it will help you understand Bobbietalk or Billiesque, other baby tongues.

First, there are so far, as well as I can determine, 144 vocables in Jaimese, falling into three general categories—recognition, demand and condition words.

Roughly, recognition words are nouns, condition words are adjectives and demand words, nouns or verbs. But the classification is not binding.

A good example of this is the vocable "bub," meaning "bib," a recognition-demand-condition word, depending on its context.

It can mean Jaime sees a bib (recognition), he wants his bib removed (demand) or that the bib is dirty, torn, wet, absent or some other parentally undesirable state (condition).

Among the more colorful recognition words are peetsiz (peaches), ornjoots (orange juice), couts (couch), eck (egg) and wingwing (what the "tefone," or "telephone," does).

Some demand words are horshie (put me on the rocking horse), teekoteeko (tickle me), waykiki (find the cat), tootbus (lift me up so I can brush my teeth) and icize (tune in Paul Fogarty).

Condition words include Jaimewet, poopoo, putee (pretty), hot (hot, and not to be confused with "hot," meaning "hat") and seepy (sleepy).

An interesting aspect of Jaimese is the number of borrowed words. Just as English has accepted verbatim words such as chemise and battalion from French, Jaimese has vocables on loan from English.

These include meat, bone, cooky, box, sox, teeths (sic), button, book, bite, bell, buggy, car, sweeper (pronounced SWEEP-uh) and teabag (with a Boston A, as in Bar Harbor).

There are also vulgate loan words from English, easily recognizable to their originals, including apane (airplane), boodie (birdie), titoktitok (the sound of a clock), wass (wash), poon (spoon) and cose (close).

Most of these vulgarized loan words result from the mere change of a letter or two or the dropping of a syllable.

This is a symptom of the highly sophisticated language, the gradual simplification that indicates an extremely civilized society or, in the extreme, an effete society.

Perhaps this is a clue to indicate that in the dim past a race of ultrarefined babies inhabited the Earth and degenerated through easy living into sniveling infants.

But that is a question for sociologists or anthropologists, not for us etymologists.

Ed Eulenberg:
'He gots twouble'

Veteran reporter Ed Eulenberg wrote this delightful article Aug. 4, 1960.

There's nothing like giving your vacation an extra purpose.

Like offering the younger generation a few tips on rearing kids, the way I decided to do it when we accepted an invitation to visit our niece and nephew in East Lansing, Mich.

Let it be clear that Anita and Marty—the niece and nephew—are intelligent young people, both college graduates, whose home is loaded with books, records and art objects. And Marty teaches at Michigan State University.

Generally, they're rearing our grandniece—their 2-year-old Janise—in modern fashion: proper feeding, restrained discipline, educational toys.

But what they're doing to that child's language—baby talk!

"Nisey," they call her, imitating her own speech. Sure, it's cute, but must they encourage this nonsense?

So Uncle Eddie quietly resolved to give Janise the benefit of his language skill as a newspaperman. He'd squelch this baby talk.

The first evening he subtly offered to read to Janise at bedtime. We started with her favorite book, *The Happy Appa*—I mean *Happy Apple*.

Well, the first night it was too soon to do much. She does have a cute way of talking. Besides, her linguistically deficient parents were present. So we looked at pictas while Nisey sitted on Unca Eddie's wap.

But next morning, after bweakfast—I mean breakfast—we taked—took—a walk. This was the big chance. Nisey and Uncle Eddie alone.

We saw birdies and wabbits. We walked on the gwass and under the twees. We stopped to make bow-wow to a nice doggie. Then we say by-by to the doggie.

We frowed stones and we smelled flowas. And Nisey holded Unca Eddie's hand when cars come. Nisey wan fast and Unca Eddie huffed and puffed and catched up. Den we goed home for lunchy and Nisey eated real nice and dwank up all her milky.

Then she gave Unca Eddie a big kiss before going to beddy for nappy.

Next day and next day we had more walks, more picta books and Unca Eddie push Nisey in glida.

And when Unca Eddie say by-by to go way on choo-choo, he fink maybe he let Mommy and Daddy-o teach Nisey talk like they want, because she's such a cutems.

(Please, Mista Edita, maybe you let Unca Eddie sharpen pencils and fill stickum bottles till he learn English again.)

The school board:
So much ado
about almost nothing

Conflicts and crises make news stories, but lit-
tle things can make good stories, too, if an alert
reporter spots them. Thomas E. Sellers wrote
this perceptive report, which was published
April 7, 1973.

The Chicago Board of Education always seems to have an abun-
dance of big crises to work on when it meets. Sometimes, however, it's the little things that consume the time.

Take a recent decision to hold public hearings on school issues.

It's usually no big deal. Every year about this time the
board gives parents and community groups a chance to sound
off. So routine approval seemed assured when board member
Gerald L. Sbarboro announced: "I have this short motion . . . regarding public hearings on school issues and problems."

Sbarboro then proposed the board hold hearings on April
17 and 19. After that, things began to get complicated.

First the board debated whether to hold hearings at all.
Then members began arguing WHEN to hold the hearings and
this is how it went:

BOARD MEMBER CAREY B. PRESTON: And the other
thing I want to say, I cannot be present on the 17th, or the dates
that have been allotted. I made (other plans) quite some time
ago.

BOARD MEMBER LOUISE MALIS: Mr. President, can I
be recognized at some point today? I mean, I have heard
everybody.

BOARD PRESIDENT JOHN D. CAREY: Yes, be patient,
madam.

MALIS: Well, I had my hand up. Before we debate April

17, I do want to point out, according to my calendar, that is the Passover holiday . . . It would be discriminating toward many people. The 17th would not be acceptable to me.

BOARD MEMBER MRS. W. LYNDON WILD: Good Friday would be very bad. (Laughter.)

MALIS: I do not think that we should eliminate the public hearings that we usually hold in April until we have evaluated the others, so that we have some basis for comparison as to which we feel we may want to eliminate.

WILD: Good point.

MALIS: Or which one should be eliminated.

WILD: Good point

MALIS: As opposed to the other.

WILD: Good point. I mean it. I am saying it.

PRESTON: We said last fall that we would have the public hearings and we did say the first week in April. So I think we ought to have them this year and then evaluate—

WILD: Good point.

MALIS: How about April 4? I move we hold them April 4.

BOARD MEMBER MRS. WILLIAM L. ROHTER: One day?

MALIS: How about the 3rd?

ROHTER: No, April 5 is the Science Fair (for Chicago students).

PRESTON: Can't we make it the 3d and 4th?

MALIS: The 3d is not good. Could we have some order, please? If it is necessary, I will stay until 9 o'clock and wait until they (the audience) are quiet.

WILD: But you will get hungry.

CAREY: They are quiet now. Proceed.

MALIS: Mr. (Lloyd) Waterloo (board secretary) has raised a point, that the first week in April will not give the people in the community an opportunity to get their statements together (for the public hearings). So he is suggesting that . . . we move it into the following week.

WILD: The 10th and 11th.

PRESTON: The 11th is a regular board meeting.

WILD: All right, the 9th and 10th.

CAREY: The week of the 16th through the 20th. What's wrong with that?

WILD: The 9th and 10th.

MALIS: How is April 9th and 10th? I move for April the 9th and 10th.

BOARD MEMBER BERNARD S. FRIEDMAN: What date? I will be out of town.

WILD: That's all right, Bernie, you're lucky. Go ahead and be out of town.

BOARD MEMBER MARIA CERDA: That isn't fair.

WILD: We can't have it the 16th and 17th. We can't have it the 3d and 4th, and now you are telling me this is bad?

CERDA: I said we can go back to the 3d and 4th.

WILD (TO MRS. MALIS): But you can't be here.

MALIS: The 4th and 5th?

WILD: I can't be here the 5th, but go ahead. That's too bad. Go ahead, that's fine.

FRIEDMAN: Let's vote on one day at a time.

CERDA: The 2d and 9th.

FRIEDMAN: Bingo.

SBARBORO: Let's go into executive (closed) session.

MALIS: How is April 23 and 24?

PRESTON: I can't come on the 24th. I have a meeting to go to.

WILD (TO MRS. MALIS): How about April the 2d and April the—no. April the 9th and 16th, Louise?

PRESTON: What happened to the 2d and 9th?

MALIS (TO MRS. WILD): What did you say, Marge, the 9th and 16th?

WILD: I gave you a couple of choices. The 2d and the 9th, or the 9th and 16th.

PRESTON: I still would like to remind you that last October we said . . . we were going to have hearings the first two weeks in April.

WILD: Now, could we adjourn?

MALIS: Did we decide the date? What was wrong with the 4th and 5th?

WILD: Nothing. I can't come on the 5th.

MALIS: Oh. the 4th and 6th?

SBARBORO: Let's just do it the 4th and 5th.

WILD: I can come then. The 4th and 6th. No. I might be missing for part of the 4th.

SBARBORO: All we need is a majority. We don't need 11.

MALIS: All right, the 4th and the 5th.

CAREY: All in favor of the 4th and 5th say "aye."

SCHOOL SUPERINTENDENT JAMES F. REDMOND: The 5th is the opening of the Science Fair.

PRESTON: I move we have it the 3d and 4th.

WILD: So move! Second. Aye, aye, aye!

MALIS: I object to this. We have gone through every day in April because somebody couldn't come. And I have been here at almost every meeting since we started. I have been here for nine years. I object that I do not have considerations for a date. . . . (Pause) Have it any time you want.

(The board discussed another topic for a while. But the issue of public hearings refused to die.)

MALIS: I want to go back to something, Mr. Carey. Mr. Waterloo indicated that the first week in April for those hearings would not be acceptable.

WILD: You are quite right. I think we ought to reconsider those dates again.

PRESTON: What was wrong with the 9th and 10th? I move that we have them on the 9th and 10th.

MALIS: Fine. Second.

(The board approved the motion.)

WILD: I move we adjourn.

(The meeting was adjourned.)

Board members later were polled by telephone and decided to hold the hearings April 26—a day that never was mentioned during the discussion.

'What could be dumber than Turkey Gobbler?' Mike Royko asks

This Mike Royko column was first published on Thanksgiving, 1970, and has been reprinted each Thanksgiving since.

There was a funny story in the paper a few days ago about how incredibly stupid the turkey can be.

Until I read it, I didn't realize that the turkey is just about the dumbest thing there is.

But a turkey farmer was quoted as saying: "Man and boy, I've been growing turkeys for upwards of 50 years, and I never saw one I had any use for."

I was still chuckling about that when I flipped a few pages and noticed an item about a store security guard who spotted a shoplifter, and when the shoplifter ran, the guard shot him dead, which seemed an odd thing to do.

But to get back to turkeys. The breeders say they are capable of committing suicide through their eagerness to follow each other blindly and without thought. The story said:

"They have been known to flap, one after another, into a barrel, with the last one who is able to cram himself inside suffocating to death just as the first ones have."

That struck me as being so amazingly dumb, even for turkeys, that I thought about it all the way home, which was a long trip in bumper-to-bumper expressway traffic.

Actually, I didn't think about it all the way, because we all stopped miles behind a jackknifed truck that had mashed a couple of cars and the expressway fumes gave me such a headache and coughing fit I couldn't think about anything else.

When I finally reached an exit, I got off and stopped at a place for a drink and happened to run into a friend.

I started telling him about the turkey story, and read him the part that said:

"A turkey has to be taught how to stop drinking. Left on his own, he will quite happily drink and drink and drink until he drowns."

My friend smiled, then fell off the stool and went right to sleep. The bartender said he had been there all day, but you can't blame him because he is worried about his older kids, who have developed an insatiable taste for drugs.

Later that evening, another friend of mine dropped in. Because he seemed morose, I tried to cheer him up by telling him about how dumb the turkeys are. I read him the part about how they have to be taught to eat:

"A turkey has to be taught to eat. Farmers put marbles into the feed; the bird pecks a marble, his bill slides off into the corn, and after a dozen repetitions he learns."

But that didn't cheer him up, which is understandable because only that day his doctor put him on a diet. He's 50 pounds overweight and his heart sounds like a bathtub draining. It seems unfair, because the last time the doctor told him to lose only 40 pounds.

So I drifted over to a neighbor's house and while we were talking, I told him what modern feeding habits have done to the turkey. According to the story:

"The turkey is front heavy these days. . . to the extent that males can't even breed any more. Artificial insemination is the only thing that keeps the species going."

My neighbor thought that was pretty funny and laughed so hard his belly jiggled. He yelled to his wife to come in and hear it, but she had already gone to bed after fixing him a frozen pizza for a snack while we watched the late-late show.

I was still chuckling over the turkey story the next morning when I got to work, especially a quote from a farmer who said: "Turkeys are beautiful to look at, fragile as an orchid and stupid beyond belief."

One of the young secretaries came in, and I quoted it to her, but she had lost her sense of humor while walking eight blocks into the cold, howling wind wearing a miniskirt.

Anyway, if you want to read for yourself how stupid turkeys are, just get a copy of that paper. I don't remember the exact

date, but it was the day the paper had a story about how we are
still arguing, after 20 years, whether Red China should be in the
UN; and a story about a debate over whether factories should
pay a surcharge for polluting the streams; and something about
the My Lai trials; a couple of bombings, a Senate filibuster, and
a plot to poison a city's water supply.

Read about the turkeys, though, the dumbest creatures on
two legs.

Robert J. Herguth:
'Any wife who can
organize a house
can run General Motors'

*Robert J. Herguth writes a popular daily col-
umn, Herguth's People, for the* Daily News.
*Once he tried his wife's job for two weeks—and
lived to tell about it in this April 14, 1975, article.*

My beautiful wife has thrown her back out. She has been in the
hospital two weeks, as a result.

I have stayed home, caring for the house, 62, and our three
kids, ages 4, 5 and 6.

I have some observations about those two weeks.

I wrote them down during the only 30 minutes of spare time
I had in a fortnight. Here they are:

I spent 48 hours at home last Tuesday.

The proper training for the mother of young kids is not
home ec in college, but lion taming at circus school.

I have met a whole new class of citizens: moms of small
kids. They seem to have a good sense of humor. They need it.

I do things early and read the newspapers early, since the
haze of fatigue that sets in after 10 p.m. prevents my compre-
hending words in type.

Dishwashers are more work than doing them by hand. God
bless paper cups and plates. Why not paper frying pans and
pots?

Any wife who can organize a house can run General Motors.

Where does the household money go that I give you? I used
to ask. I will never again ask where the money goes, after spending it at the rate of 150 per cent a week. Nursery school is a
great invention and very educational. It gives me two hours
alone to do things in. The other 22 hours are spent meeting

emergencies, breaking up fights, fixing meals, washing dishes and getting a little sleep.

Suddenly the dog wants to lick my hand. I feel it is not affection, but the detergent I am using.

Any mother who can work an automatic washer and dryer properly, without turning white clothes red, can run Ford Motor Co.

I am teaching the kids a few new words. I hope they forget those new words.

I love the kids to pieces, but I wish they would like the food today that they liked yesterday. Dammit, you LOVED grapefruit Wednesday. What do you mean, you hate it Thursday?

I get up half an hour before they do and shower and shave and put on clean clothes. If I don't feel like a bum and look like a bum, maybe it will be a good day.

Good baby-sitters and good neighbors are pearls beyond price. Ours are pearls beyond price.

I thought I could run everything better. I'm not so sure now, and I damn well don't want to try.

Cleaning one room a day is like cleaning up the San Francisco quake with a whisk broom.

I started keeping a record, and I still don't know where the money goes.

I lost five pounds in 10 days. This is not a sedentary job. Would you rather lift weights at the health club once a week or lift your kids six times a day?

You put your socks on. That's great. What do you mean, you lost all your shoes?

I can't force you to eat. But Popeye is on TV soon and will you be there to watch him? God forgive me. I'm resorting to blackmail.

Any mother who can make all her kids eat all the food on their plates at one meal can run Chrysler. Even Fritz Chrysler.

OK, I just washed and dried all your dirty clothes. They're here on the sofa. Pick out what is yours. Wait a minute! Stop that! That blouse can't belong to both of you!

If all you have clean is one blue sock and one brown sock, wear one blue sock and one brown sock. So wear boots with one blue sock and one brown sock. Nobody will ever know.

You want your mama? I want your mama. In fact, I want MY mama.

There are circumstances when the simple act of getting a newspaper at the local drugstore presents logistical problems that are worthy of a clamber up the Matterhorn.

Alps. Alpo. When's the last time I fed the dog?

I figured it out. I'm climbing to the top of the John Hancock each day, using the stairs in my own house.

Let's see, I came into this room to get something. What is that something I came into this room to get? While I'm here, trying to think of that something I came in to get, I'd better pick this trash off the floor. There's the doorbell and the phone, both ringing at once. I will never remember what I came into this room to get. And it seemed important 10 seconds ago.

I must be doing something right. The kids seem to like me at the end of the day.

You say you have a great idea? You want to go out in the back yard and make quicksand?

Tomorrow I will not shout. Not even once. Bellowing doesn't count.

There's a strange smell in the refrigerator. An ant appeared in the bathroom. Another was in the living room.

She's coming home! I think I'll raise the U.S. flag in front of the house. The one we use for national holidays.

'To' and 'two' make functional illiterates

Reporter Bob Schenet, a recent college gradu-
ate, wrote this article Nov. 5, 1975.

Colleges and universities are turning out "experts" who are functional illiterates.

They can't write. They can't write when they enter college, and they are no better off when they graduate. Not only are a high percentage of freshmen poor writers, but they also have been getting progressively worse over the last several years.

Nobody is sure how this came about, although there are a lot of theories. And nobody is sure just what to do about it.

Here are some of the reasons college officials are worried:

• Average verbal scores on the Scholastic Aptitude Test dropped 10 points between 1974 and 1975. Scores have dropped 23 points since 1966.

• About 80 per cent of the freshmen entering the University of Illinois at Urbana-Champaign have "serious" writing problems, according to the English department.

• Scores on a special proficiency test used by the University of Illinois from 1968 to 1974 dropped every year.

• About 60 per cent of sophomore journalism students at the University of Wisconsin flunked a required English-usage test this fall. About 30 per cent could not pass the test a year ago.

• Graduate schools are screaming that although their applicants are technically proficient, they are "functional illiterates," one university official said.

When instructors complain that students can't write, they really are talking about two different problems. Sometimes they go together, sometimes not.

The most blatant writing problem—and the most difficult to deal with—is constant "glaring mechanical errors," according to Dorothy Matthews, director of undergraduate studies for the University of Illinois' English department.

"They confuse 'to' and 'two.' They don't know the difference between 'its' and 'it's.' 'There,' 'their' and 'they're' are confused. For some reason, many students write 'a lot' as one word. They just don't know these things.

"In terms of grammar, it is very difficult to explain what's wrong with the writing if they don't know what you're talking about. They don't even have the nomenclature to discuss the problems. They say they never had teachers who told them to clean it up," Mrs. Matthews said.

"We don't see our function as teaching spelling and punctuation, but it's a shame if the kids never learned this earlier."

But what most bothers officials such as Mrs. Matthews is students' "inability to write a clear, expository theme."

"If they are asked to answer an essay question, they simply can't get it all together," Mrs. Matthews said. "There has been a lot of emphasis on creativity in recent years, and that has taken the center of the stage. But the kids need to learn how to give clear, concise sentences."

These are verbally talented kids having problems. They are very bright kids, but they just haven't had enough practice. The only way to learn how to do it is through practice."

School administrators are unanimous in agreeing there is a problem, but what do students themselves think?

Generally, they agree.

Most Big Ten schools now have organized writing laboratories where students may go on their own—or to which they may be assigned—if their writing needs work.

"They are well used. The students realize their shortcomings," according to Robin Wilson, associate director of the Committee on Institutional Co-operation, which deals with Big Ten schools.

Ten years ago, when "relevant" was the big word, students thought of ideas as being important. How those ideas were expressed—the form—was considered to be of secondary importance. "The kids themselves have done an about-face on this," Mrs. Matthews said. "Now it means their bread and butter.

"Now that we have hard times, they realize they have to write letters to get jobs and to carry on a professional career. They have to persuade, to communicate. Now they come in and say, 'I wasn't prepared. I never had a chance to write.' "

How did it happen that students were not prepared? Why didn't they have a chance to write?

The obvious answer is to blame the high schools.

"Deteriorating quality in high school is one possibility, admittedly speculative," according to Robert Rogers, dean of the University of Illinois College of Liberal Arts and Sciences. "There are larger classes and less formal training in writing in high school. English teachers sometimes have intolerable loads."

"I don't want to blame the high-school teachers," Mrs. Matthews said. "They are overburdened. The best writing teaching is on a one-to-one basis. The maximum class size should be about 15—and you know how often you find that. You get what you pay for."

English courses in high school have been changing, and that might be part of the cause, some officials believe. "There are more and more elective courses, a lot of options," Mrs. Matthews said. "This does tend to make them enjoy English more, and it gets them reading, but there often is not a lot of theme writing."

Roger Applebee, chairman of a faculty committee attempting to deal with the problem at the University of Illinois, agrees. "There is some evidence English (as taught in high schools) is not what it used to be, not so comprehensive. It now tends to be broken down. It may be interesting, but it isn't teaching students to communicate," Applebee said.

But Wilson believes the teachers must share at least part of the blame. "I think the change must come in teaching writing to those intent on teaching writing themselves.

"How can you expect a teacher, with no experience in writing, to teach it? The fact that some manage to do so is remarkable. Let's face it—most people in English departments are not good writers," Wilson said.

The influence of television on declining writing abilities also is debated, with no clear-cut decision rendered.

"TV has to be considered, but I don't personally feel this is such a strong cause," Applebee said.

"TV is an easy cop-out," according to Wilson.

But the role of television is considered an important factor by William Lenehan, professor of English at the University of Wisconsin. He believes television has led students away from both reading and writing by it's "de-emphasis on writing skills."

Lenehan believes another factor is that "our hero models are not masters at using language." Instead of a Churchill or a Roosevelt as a model, college-age students have the words of Johnson, Nixon, Agnew and Ford, Lenehan pointed out.

"As for their use of language, they've murdered it."

The new faculty committee at the University of Illinois first wants to define the problem before deciding how to deal with it. But university officials already have decided the problem is not one simply for the English department. The committee includes faculty from chemistry, history, sociology and microbiology as well as English and communications.

"To relegate the solution to the English department would be to deny the responsibility of the entire college in solving the problem," Dean Rogers said.

"All we have now is the tip of the iceberg. We want to see its dimensions," committee chairman Applebee said.

Adding or restoring basic writing courses at the college level might be part of the answer, Wilson believes.

"There has been a general tendency, pioneered by the elite schools such as Yale and Harvard, to eliminate freshman writing courses. You might see them come back.

"Another way of dealing with this is to get back in bed with the high schools, to see what they're doing," Wilson added.

"The University of Wisconsin at Milwaukee is working on a pilot program, fostering close articulation with the university and feeder schools and having frequent meetings."

At the Madison campus of the University of Wisconsin, students now are required to obtain a special certificate, in effect saying they can write, before they are allowed to graduate.

At Iowa, whenever a faculty member found a student who could not write, he was supposed to give the student a slip to take to the English department for remedial work. The program was dropped because the faculty wasn't co-operating, Wilson said.

Dean Rogers said that "faculties generally, whether historians or scientists, should insist on higher standards."

All of these are possible solutions, but Rogers believes the root of the problem is something not easily overcome. "There is little in contemporary society that encourages either literacy or skill in written communications among the college-age group."

Like the musician, the writer must have an ear, according to Sydney J. Harris

One of the problems with much collegiate writing was identified by Sydney J. Harris in this column that appeared on the Daily News *editorial page.*

While reading the entries, as one of the judges in a collegiate writing contest, I was reminded of Mark Twain's annoyed remark that "the difference between the right word and the almost right word is the difference between lightning and the lightning bug."

Most persons—and this includes aspiring writers—simply fail to recognize that there are very few true synonyms in the language, no matter what the dictionary may insist.

The dictionary, for instance, gives "devour" as a synonym for "eat." But no woman would care to have it said of her that she "devoured her dinner," which sounds more like an animal than a human. (Indeed, German has "essen" for human eating, and "fressen" for animal eating.)

Again, a woman's eyes may "glow" with affection, but they do not "glitter," although the two words are roughly synonymous. Eyes "glitter" with greed or contempt, but they "glow" with love or compassion.

Distinguishing between two words that seem to mean the same, but have different colors and shapes and suggestions—this is essential to the art of writing, and also of speaking. The dictionary can tell you only what a word points to; it cannot tell you what it feels like.

An interesting example is the word "fat." The unabridged

dictionary gives as synonyms: fleshy, plump, corpulent, obese, stocky, portly, tubby and thick, among others.

Obviously, different people are fat in different ways—a woman may be "fleshy," but a man is "portly." "Obese" carries the connotation of a glandular sickness. "Stocky" involves size as well as shape. We speak of a "plump" or "tubby" baby, but nobody would call him "corpulent."

The same is true of hundreds of words, which only superficially resemble one another. "Unspeakable" in the dictionary means the same as "unutterable"—but the former is always used to mean something base or vile, while the latter usually means some rapturous or divine thought or emotion.

The right word is as important to the writer as the right note to the composer or the right color to the painter.

Hemingway's prose is so compelling (despite his defects of mind) precisely because he always knows the right word to capture the essence of a situation or the feel of a person. A writer needs an "ear" as much as a musician does.

And without his ear, he is lost and groping in a forest of words, where all the trees look much alike.

Gutted Our Lady of the Angels classroom. Edward DeLuga / Daily News.

Catastrophe:
Nicholas Shuman
M. W. Newman
Long Hwa-shu

To the school, rectory, hospitals, police—and then to County Morgue: 'Is my child here?'

Fire swept through Our Lady of the Angels Catholic elementary school in Chicago Dec. 1, 1958, killing 95 children and teachers. Nicholas Shuman, one of the dozens of reporters and writers covering the tragedy, wrote this moving sidebar for the next day's paper, based on telephoned reports from the various locations by reporters Robert G. Schultz, Arthur J. Snider, Edmund J. Rooney and others.

In screaming hysteria and in horrified silence—far into the night the parents made their bitter rounds.

First the school. . .then Red Cross headquarters in the rectory . . .then to each of seven hospitals. . .then to Austin district police headquarters.

There were hundreds of them, but all with the same question:

"Is my child here?"

Each carried the hell of uncertainty in his heart, and almost invariably each saved until the last the feared and rarely named place—the County Morgue, the end of the line.

Singly and in pairs they trooped into the rectory, red of eye and ashen of face.

Lists were being compiled there by the Red Cross, but they were pitiably incomplete.

"I'm sorry. We just don't know. Leave your name and phone number and we will call you when we do."

In a steady procession, they trooped next door into Our Lady of Angels Church. Their children were not there, but hope was.

The nave of the church was black because fire had doused the lights. But two portable floodlamps operated by a fire-department generator threw an eerie, harshly white light on the altar.

At any given time hours after the fire, about 50 persons knelt in the shadows. They made no sound. The silence was broken only by the punkety-punkety of the generator.

There was pandemonium at the hospitals.

About 200 came to Walther Memorial. "Is my child here?" It was shouted. It was sobbed out. It was whispered. "Is my child here?"

Hundreds jammed the corridors, the lobby, the entrance to the emergency receiving room.

Many mothers were there in house slippers, surprised by disaster. There was a carpenter in overalls, his hammer still dangling in its sling.

There were screams when charred bodies were brought in. Eager straining when a living tyke with a smudged face went by.

"Who has a list? Why don't you have a list? Where is my child?"

Antonia Patraiso, 35, of 1129 N. Lawndale, broke into tears and wailed: "We found Tommy, but we can't find Antoinette."

Maybe she was lucky. Some found what they prayed they wouldn't and feared they would.

"Oh, my God. It can't be. It can't be," sobbed Rosemarie Chambers, of 3818 Huron. At St. Anne's hospital her husband, Jasper, had just looked at four small bodies, seeking their daughter, Margaret, 9.

The fifth was too badly charred to be recognized. But there was a familiar dime-store ring with a red stone, bought just last Saturday.

"It can't be," Mrs Chambers said. But she recognized the shoes. Then she collapsed.

The searching hundreds at Walther besieged the receptionist, Irene King, of 1060 N. Spaulding, who had been a British war bride.

"I saw the blitz at Coventry, in London and in Birmingham," she said. "But this is the most horrifying experience I ever had."

Mr. and Mrs. Louis Secco, of 3922 Augusta Blvd., came with four relatives, seeking their daughter Antoinette, 10.

"We have been to the other hospitals. What can I do now?" Secco asked. His wife slumped on Mrs. King's desk and twisted her babushka.

In the background others suggested to the relatives that there was only one place left—the morgue. Louis told his wife: "You go home now. I'm going to make one more check."

The mother knew. "She's gone. Oh, my God, she's gone."

There were young searchers, too. Joanne Pettanon, 12, of 903 Trumbull, came with a 10-year-old cousin, seeking Joanne's sister Mary Ellen, 9.

She was not on Mrs. King's list, and the girls fell to weeping.

Two nuns comforted them and said: "Please go home now. Pray. You can't do anything more."

Austin police headquarters, at 5327 Chicago, had a constant stream. In spite of the rapid flow, there were always at least 30 anxious persons about, asking, asking, asking.

Occasionally detectives in the squad room would read the lists of the injured. Parents strained forward with each name, hoping for injury rather than worse. Many swept away tears. Many mouthed prayers inaudibly as the names came.

At one reading, only two heard the names they wanted to hear. The others heard the cruel words from the detectives: "The morgue."

One man was called to the telephone. He came out of the booth weeping: "Oh, no. Please, God, no."

It was a kinsman calling from the morgue.

When the lists of the living were over, each man and each woman stood momentarily in dazed silence. Then all filed out for the long, long trip to the end of the line.

As they walked, one mother shrieked, "I want my baby."

Many others Tuesday wanted with her—and wanted in vain.

M. W. Newman tells how
75 million tons of snow
brought strangers together

*When a record-breaking 23 inches of snow fell
on Chicago in 1967, dozens of staff members
were assigned to write about various aspects of
the event. Veteran reporter M. W. Newman
was told to pull all the pieces of the vast story
together and write a wrapup. This article was
published Jan. 30, 1967, three days after the
event, while the city was still digging out from
the Big Snow.*

It came walloping over the plains like a swollen fist,
scooped up all of Chicago and casually tangled it in knots.

The stricken metropolis lay gasping, barely able to move.
The storm swatted it, slugged it, smashed it, crushed it in 75
million tons of snow.

But, in the end, the metropolis did not break. Like a dazed
giant, it shuddered under the monstrous weight and began
stumbling to its knees. . .then regained its feet.

Its boulevards and byways had become ghostly wrecking
grounds, strewn with 30,000 derelict cars, trucks and buses buried in ice-cold storage.

Its auto civilization, its multimillion-dollar expressways lay
prostrate and useless—mocked by a superstorm.

Its millions of people, once they were safely in their homes,
peered in wonder through snow-packed windows.

Those who went forth during the storm's height were staggered by 60-m.p.h. winds and flailed by blinding snowflakes.
Heavy drifts clutched at their boots and their waists, and each
step was an effort.

But they did go forth. Tens of thousands of Chicagoans
fought the storm, from the first.

They met a superstorm with superresistance and the storm

could not break the city. In fact, it brought strangers together, uniting them in missions of kindness and mercy.

It hit with unbelievable speed and power, this great invader of '67. While Chicago basked in disarming 65-degree weather early last week, a low-pressure air mass roared out of the Pacific and across the Rockies, gathering disastrous strength.

By Wednesday, the city's private weather forecasting service, Murray & Trettle, knew a storm was speeding in. The U.S. Weather Bureau also began flashing warnings.

"But no one in his right mind would have predicted 23 inches (the eventual record snow total)," said meteorologist Charles Feris.

At 1 a.m. Thursday, the bureau issued a heavy storm warning. At 3 a.m. it predicted 4 inches or more.

Great blobs of snow began hitting about 5 a.m. The wind hurled it through open windows, and many Chicagoans awoke to find snow in their living rooms.

By 9:45 a.m., the bureau warned we would get 5 to 8 inches more, but foresaw a tapering off by night.

City and CTA [Chicago Transit Authority] officials even went on television as late as 10:30 p.m. to assure listeners that the worst was over and that the roads would be open the next morning.

Instead, the tons of snow (24 million tons in Chicago alone) kept falling, falling—and didn't stop until 29 hours and 8 minutes had passed, and Chicago had experienced its worst snowstorm in history.

Why was it such a surprise? The forecasters ruefully explained the storm moved slower than they had foreseen (25 miles an hour over the city, instead of 35).

As it slowed it intensified and began swirling like water in a bathtub when the plug is pulled out. The plug was pulled out right over Chicago.

By Thursday afternoon, the city and its dependent ring of suburbs were in terrible shape.

Traffic choked. Motor buses by the scores coughed and died in crests of snow, waiting to be plucked out one by one, like broken toys.

The wind piled up drifts as high as 15 feet.

Tens of thousands of suburbanites struggled home, soon to find themselves snowbound—particularly in the south suburbs.

Inevitably, some people died from the effects of fighting the killer storm. The toll was to top 40.

Commuter trains ran erratically. Thousands of marooned Loop workers checked into hotels, overloading phone circuits, bars and liquor supplies, lobbies and restaurants. It took more than three minutes of steady ringing to reach the switchboards of most hotels.

The great rush-hour route, Lake Shore Dr., was closed early for its entire length. Other expressways soon became impassable. The battle to get home that night produced thousands of anecdotes, most of which began:

"Would you believe it took me five hours?"

As the storm grew fiercer, so did the people's will to resist. At Chicago Wesley Memorial Hospital, on the Near North Side, said administrator Kenath Hartman, some dedicated employees arrived from as far as 10800 south.

Student nurses at St. Francis Hospital in Evanston walked the 10 blocks from the Howard St. L.

The subway-L system somehow kept going, although it was badly slowed by drifting snow on the tracks.

Most hospitals weathered the storm well, despite runs on their bread and milk supplies. Some played emergency host to tens and hundreds of marooned visitors and motorists.

Many hospital staffs were depleted 50 per cent. It took one physician eight hours to get to Michael Reese Hospital, but he got there. Another skied over gaily from nearby Prairie Shores apartments.

At Northwest Hospital, 5645 Addison, one emergency patient had to be carried 300 feet from a fire-department ambulance, because 6-foot snow drifts blocked the way.

Babies were delivered "by telephone," with physicians giving instructions.

Nearly 1,400 students, forced to spend the night at suburban schools, learned the lesson of the Good Samaritan. Sea

Scouts trudged through the snow to bring them food-laden sleds. Civil Defense and Red Cross workers rushed in aid.

Fire-department helicopters dropped insulin supplies to diabetics stranded in schools, police and firehouses, gas stations. More than 1,000 persons found refuge in a fire station at 127th St. and Doty.

O'Hare Airport was closed down and resembled a gigantic snowbound ski lodge.

All schools shut down and 1 million children stayed home Friday. Most of the city's business firms took a holiday, too.

The Loop became a snowy wasteland, with muffled walkers trudging in streets where traffic once flowed unceasingly. By Friday, the city's polluted air had become amazingly washed and refreshed, free of its usual overload of gasoline exhaust and industrial fumes.

Nervous shoppers jammed into groceries and supermarkets—those that managed to stay open—and grabbed up milk, bread and meat.

There were ugly episodes—looting of stalled trucks and deserted shops on the West Side—and more than 100 persons were arrested. Ten-year-old Delores Miller of 2450 W. 12th Pl. was fatally wounded when caught in crossfire between policemen and vandals.

No one could measure the financial loss to the community caused by the great storm. One figure, possibly low, was $150 million.

The bill to the CTA alone for damage, repairs, snow clearance and lost revenues probably will exceed $1 million.

The massive battle against the storm actually began even before it hit. The results, of course, were not visible at first—as any stranded or traffic-blocked motorist could attest.

A telephone call at 2:50 a.m. Thursday to the city's snow office—on the lower level at 50 E. Wacker Dr.—touched off the enormous battle.

The call came from the Murray & Trettel forecasting service, warning that 2 to 4 inches of snow was on the way.

Theodore C. Eppig, deputy commissioner of streets and sanitation, is the city's "storm general." He pulled in street-sweeper drivers and 89 trucks with salt spreaders. At 4 a.m. snowplows were out.

But it was too little and too late. Rush-hour traffic piled in, and so did the overpowering snow. By noon, 389 plows were on the street—just about the maximum available.

By 8 p.m., 2,500 men and 600 pieces of equipment toiled to turn the tide. Many men worked steadily for more than 24 hours until and beyond exhaustion.

Some plows cleared out drifts 20 times, only to have the snow pile up on the same spot 21 times. But they kept plowing.

County highway officials also dispatched plows over 600 miles of roads. But they never mustered more than 45 trucks with plows, 11 power graders and 8 front-end loaders, a tiny contingent by the city's standards.

Snow-fighting equipment rumbled in from Downstate Illinois, Iowa and Wisconsin, at the request of Gov. Otto Kerner.

Giant plows were driven from the Rock Island area, 150 miles away, and even greater distances.

In the suburbs, which suffered even more than the city, improvised emergency ambulances rolled on toboggans and treads when necessary.

Fortunately, there were few disastrous fires.

Gradually, the staggered metropolis began to lift its head. Over the weekend, nearly all tollways and expressways were reopened, at least in part, and public transportation struggled to return to some semblance of itself.

The Loop was cleared, and so were many streets in the richer, better-equipped suburbs—Winnetka, Glencoe, Kenilworth among them. All over the great metropolis, people dug at the packed snow with shovels.

But thousands of streets in city and suburbs remained blocked—and will stay that way for days. It will take Chicago a long time to recover.

Black Friday—April 21,1967
—the day the sky fell in

*Three months after he wrote about the effects
of Chicago's worst snowstorm, M. W. Newman
was assigned to cover the city's worst tornado
disaster —54 dead, 1075 injured and $50 mil-
lion property damage—on April 21, 1967. This
story was published four days later.*

On a perfect day for tornadoes, the sky fell in.

Death came dancing and skipping, whistling and screaming, strangely still one second and whooshing and bouncing the next.

For some in the Chicago area, death was a black cloud funnel, toeing the earth and crushing the skulls of children.

"It was the most terrible black I ever have seen," shuddered Minnie Jasinski of south suburban Hometown.

But in leafy Lake Zurich on that same Black Friday of April 21, death came hooded in "an eerie green and white," as Dorothy Schultz saw it.

And along the 75-mile arc from northwest Belvidere to southwest suburban Oak Lawn, there was a strange smell in the air and it was cold and warm at the same time.

And always death came with monstrous force, and those who survived could thank their stars.

Riding three monstrous twisters, the worst in the Chicago area's history, death sounded like a frontlines bombardment to Mayor Clair M. Hetland of Belvidere, a World War II veteran.

In Oak Lawn, worst hit of all, death roared like two locomotives running wild.

And yet it could explode a house—and it exploded many—and seemingly made no sound at all.

It slammed people, furniture, autos and trees through the shattered air and shook homes into splinters.

"My God, we've been thrown into our driveway—how did we get here?" gasped Mrs. Jasinski seconds after the storm bumped her house at 8906 S. Crawford. Moments before, she and her family had been sitting in the kitchen, drinking coffee.

It ran wild, this cosmic delinquent of a windstorm—without pattern, without meaning, touching down on an eastward path along Chicago's 87th St. like a berserk giant.

Along a crazy route the storm heaped death and injury, wrecking almost everything it touched.

The toll included scores of smashed homes and buildings and whole streets wiped out. Sometimes the path of destruction was no more than half a block wide on a day when life and death were measured in fractions of an inch and tenths of a second.

And after two awful hours, the storm tiptoed away. Only now is the full story of suffering and heroism, martyrdom and miraculous survival being stitched together.

The death-laden twisters boiled out of the sky on a spring day when it was a comfortable 72 degrees at Midway Airport and a chilly 58 downtown.

With warm-wet and cold-dry air masses on a collision course, it was a classic time for tornadoes to form. Nineteen of them did, along a 500-mile front from Madison, Wis., to Kansas City, Mo.

By 1:35 p.m., the first official warning in the Chicago area was sounded—two hours in advance, as it turned out, and yet not nearly enough time.

At 3:40 p.m., an alert patrolman, Harry Faris, spotted a gray funnel, bouncing and jigging in wanton abandon, racing toward Belvidere at 45 miles an hour. It had popped out of the southwest. The two hours of terror had begun.

Frantically, Faris radioed to Capt. Francis Whalen. The farming community of 13,000 had only 12 minutes to brace.

The first of 1,200 youngsters were just pouring out of the doors of Belvidere High School, ready for a carefree weekend. Many of them were grammar-school children who had gathered at the school for busing home.

"Get back! Get back!" Whalen shouted. He set his squad-car siren howling.

Some of the children, already in the buses, were scrambling off when the giant twister hit, bouncing like a rubber ball over the building and scattering buses and cars like toys.

"It just upped and snatched them around and flipped them all over the place," said the horrified Capt. Whalen.

Policemen, teachers and students rushed to the upended buses, trying to lift them. Screaming children lay pinned under the wreckage and 16 were dead or dying.

"When you see a kid partly scalped, Christ!" said Police Chief Kenneth Richardson, in a cry of prayerful anguish.

In a few seconds, Belvidere lay stricken.

The winds clawed at houses and business firms, destroying many homes and leaving 2,000 persons homeless.

Perhaps most grievous of all was the anguish suffered by survivors who hunted the missing in the rubble of homes and in the open fields.

One boy was found with a spearlike, 8-foot board driven through his leg. A girl of 11, missing for hours, was rescued from the basement of a ravaged home—so shocked she was unable to call for help.

In Belvidere and wherever else the storm brought death, most of the victims suffered skull injuries or other violent fractures.

"I don't think most of them knew what hit them," said Coroner Andrew Toman of Cook County.

Gilbert Julin, 68, a bus driver killed at the Belvidere school, was pinned down when his vehicle rolled over.

Julin was a well-to-do, retired farmer who drove the school bus because he wanted to keep busy and because he liked children. He died with the youngsters he loved.

But there were also remarkable accounts of survival— which some might interpret as blind luck and others as the results of modern science or unusual powers of decision.

One 10-year-old boy in Belvidere was found with a severe arterial wound. He had no pulse or heart beat.

"But we gave him plasma and he snapped out of it," said Paul Dommers, one of many physicians who hurried to the aid of the injured.

The one-story Immanuel Lutheran School was virtually wiped out—but its 80 young pupils were saved when principal

Joel Schumacher rushed them into the basement.

The children bravely sang "Jesus Loves Me" as the winds tore away the roof.

While the tornado pounded Belvidere and rushed on to tear up Woodstock farms, two other twisters cut paths to the south. One left broken trees and buildings at Fox River Grove, North Barrington and Lake Zurich.

All over the Chicago area, the sky darkened and thunderstorms drenched the city and suburbs. People hurried indoors and many remained there for hours, until an all-clear was signaled.

In Stone Park, about halfway between Arlington Heights and Oak Lawn, 5-year-old Deborah Pruim was killed when she was blown into the path of an auto.

That was about 5:25 p.m. Meanwhile, the third tornado had begun hitting southwest Cook County, rising and spinning to earth like a whirling top gone out of control.

Fate had placed the communities of Oak Lawn, Evergreen Park and Hometown in the third twister's path. Fate—plus warm, moist air from the Gulf of Mexico, on the one hand, and colder, drier air from the northwest, on the other.

The warmer air began rising and the colder air began dropping, a fact that could have been of little interest to most people earlier on that Friday afternoon.

As the two atmospheric masses came together, air closer to the ground rushed in to fill the void. The winds were "just right" and the inrushing air started spinning.

A tornado was born—and with it, upward-whipping winds surging around at 300 miles an hour or faster, creating a vacuum powerful enough to suck the roofs off houses.

It was this monster of the skies, with its speeding winds, deadly vacuum and contrasts in air pressure, that zigzagged into Oak Lawn, a busy, prospering village of 54,000.

And with it came the same kind of horror that had crushed Belvidere.

At 5:29 p.m., the twister sliced from 103d St. and Roberts through 97th St. and Ridgeland and on to 95th St. and Southwest Hwy. From there it leapfrogged to 91st St. and Cicero.

Over a two-square-mile area, houses were crushed, autos hurled into buildings, big signs smashed.

The tornado rampaged through an entire block of a trailer park, where frightened people huddled inside mobile homes never designed for this kind of an emergency. More than 200 trailers were destroyed.

"It was terrible," said shaken Art Bleau, owner of the trailer park at 9001 S. Cicero. "Bodies were sticking out of the wreckage. My God! My God!"

The south end of Oak Lawn Community High School was twisted into a tangled mass of brick, concrete and steel. Fortunately, only a few boys were in the school when the storm hit, and they were not hurt.

To Arthur Sluis, 40, the tornado roared "like a pair of locomotives."

He and his father Jacob, 71, ran into their seed store at 6161 W. 95th St. and lay on the floor.

"There was no basement, so that was the best we could do," Sluis said. "We didn't have time to pray."

Passing only a few feet behind the store, the howling funnel smashed garages, houses and other buildings and twisted chain-link fences like nylon netting.

And at 95th St. and Southwest Hwy., Mr. and Mrs. George Heinzel were driving to dinner in a new car.

They had stopped for a red light when the tornado touched down, showering bricks, stones and glass onto the auto. Only 25 feet away was a food store where several persons were killed, but the Heinzels escaped serious injury.

At Christ Community hospital, severely injured youngsters were brought in from the Oak Lawn Roller Skating Club. Some of the boys and girls still were wearing their skates. The skating club had become a death house, with only the front of the building still standing.

At St. Gerald's Church, 94th St. and Cicero, 21 of 25 parochial classrooms were destroyed. Classes were canceled at St. Gerald and in Oak Lawn Community High School.

Crazily, the big twister bounced down on its wrecking path, touching lightly at Kedzie, Damen, Ashland, Cottage Grove and

South Shore Dr. along 87th St., and racing 20 miles to Lake Michigan.

And yet its funnel of death was less than a block wide in Oak Lawn. Fractions of an inch separated the living and the dead.

"I thank God that there was nothing really personal about this tornado," said Fire Chief Allen Hulett of Oak Lawn.

"The edge of this thing touched down two doors from my house. My children had just gotten in. This is something I can be thankful for."

Mrs. Thomas Carmode, of 9401 Massassoit, may have echoed his thoughts. Seconds before the twister hit Oak Lawn, she grabbed up her two small children from a second-floor bedroom and rushed to the basement. Almost immediately, the upper floor was carried away in a violent gust. Mrs. Carmode hugged her children.

By 6:30 p.m., the U.S. Weather Bureau announced that the tornado danger in Cook County had ended.

There had been only one death in Chicago itself. Grant Miller, 32, of 8220 S. Langley, was electrocuted when his auto became entangled in downed wires near 82d St. and Cottage Grove.

When the terrible clouds went and the winds began to ease, the city and its stricken satellite towns began to take stock.

Rescue workers rushed in, feverishly pawing through debris and mud for bodies. Many stricken parents hunted—and found—their children in hospitals or morgues.

Hundreds of homeowners found that they owned nothing but a heap of rubble. Swarms of volunteers poured in to provide emergency food, clothing and shelter.

National Guardsmen and sheriff's deputies joined in Operation Dig Out—and Sheriff Joseph Woods of Cook County ordered his men to shoot looters on sight. The order kept "a lot of rotten people" out of the disaster areas, Woods said.

Bravely, Belvidere, Oak Lawn and other hard-hit communities began burying their dead and picking themselves up. Oak Lawn's indomitable president, polio-stricken Fred Dumke, symbolized his town's chins-up spirit by announcing with no flourishes: "We can handle it."

But others helped. From as far away as Rock Island, Ill., came food and blankets. As always, people rallied to each other's aid—just as they had done in the great Chicago snowstorm of Jan. 26–27.

Said one man boarding up a massive hole in the roof of his house on S. Moody St.:

"If I can just get this wood on we'll be all right."

And there was something inspiring about the wedding of Ethel Marie Harmston and Clyde F. Mansfell Saturday.

Volunteers cleared rubble outside Garden Methodist Church at 100th St. and Central while the ceremony went on.

"We just closed the door to the sanctuary and the wedding went on," said a rescue worker. "It was lovely."

'There was blood
in the water'
—men vanished at a rate
of 100 a day for five days

When the USS Indianapolis *was torpedoed and
sank in the last days of World War II, one of
the most horrifying disasters of the century began. Thirty years later reporter Long Hwa-shu
was assigned to talk to local survivors. He
wrote about their recollections in this article,
published Aug. 2, 1975.*

Dawn was yet hours away and the *USS Indianapolis* sliced
steadily through mist that rose from the gently rolling seas of
the South Pacific.

She had just completed a supersecret mission, moving at
high speed from San Francisco to Tinian to deliver a cargo that
Capt. Charles B. McVay III, the skipper, learned later to be critical parts of the atomic bomb that leveled Hiroshima.

Now, in the predawn hours of July 30, 1945, the 10,000-ton
heavy cruiser, proud former flagship of the 5th fleet, was heading for Leyte in the Philippines at a steady 15 knots. It was a
beautiful, calm night. The moon peeped now and then from behind clouds.

Six miles away, Lt. Hiromu Tanaka, the duty officer of the
Japanese submarine I–58, alerted his skipper, Lt. Comdr. Mich-
itsuki Hashimoto, that he had spotted "a dark mass" through
the mist.

"Possible enemy ship," he reported. Hashimoto ordered his
sub, which was in the process of surfacing, to dive and sent the
crewmen to battle stations ready for the kill. When the target
was about a mile away, Hashimoto gave the order to fire. Six
torpedoes were launched. Three blasted through the four-inch-
thick armor plating of the *Indianapolis'* hull.

Within minutes, the 1,196 men aboard the *Indianapolis* were plunged into one of the most horrifying ordeals in the Navy's annals. It was an ordeal of terror, of fire, of endless seas ready to swallow them up, of deprivation and exhaustion.

But most of all, for the more than 800 men drifting in the water, it was an ordeal of sharks.

The sharks began swarming around the survivors of the *Indianapolis* soon after she sank. For the nearly five days during which the men drifted helplessly, the sharks attacked them continuously.

About 300 of the *Indianapolis'* crew were killed in the explosions of the torpedoes, in the blasts and fires they triggered aboard the ship or below decks as it sank in flames. No one knows how many—thirsty, hungry and exhausted during the five days—drowned. And no one to this day can be certain of how many were killed by sharks.

Many kinds of sharks feed mainly at night. Their attacks on some of the helpless survivors went unseen in the darkness and mist.

But some of the sunken ship's crew told of the howls they heard through the nights. Distant cries of terror and agony would pierce the darkness. Then there would be silence. At dawn, more men would be missing.

From sharks and other causes, they vanished at the rate of 100 a day for each of the five days. Not all of the shark attacks were fatal. Coxswain Cozel L. Smith's hand was torn away. Other men lost flesh on their buttocks, legs, backs and arms.

Gus Kay, a 48-year-old insurance salesman from Elmwood Park, was an 18-year-old seaman on the *Indianapolis* when it was sunk.

He recalls what happened to the group he found himself clustered with in the waters:

"It was about our third day out. It was a calm sea, like a mirror. I was one of those clinging to a floater net: We didn't have a life raft.

"We saw a wake in the water—it was bubbling. We thought it (the bubbling) was rescue boats. Then, someone yelled, 'Sharks!' and said for everybody to make a lot of noise.

"The ones able to swim away from the floater did. But the wounded men were inside the floater. It was a school of sharks. I felt them brush against me as I swam away.

"It was like a massacre that lasted about 8 to 10 minutes. When we came back the bodies were there. There was blood in the water. We formed a barricade with life jackets and paddled the blood away.

"If they (the sharks) came back, they would smell the blood. The bodies were mutilated . . . ," Kay said, his voice trailing off momentarily.

"We had to take the life jackets off (the men who had been attacked). We washed off the blood and put them (the jackets) on the floater to dry in the sun during the day. At night we put them on.

"We lost about 85 men to the sharks," Kay said. "When my group started out, there were about 250 men. When they picked us up, there were only 17 left.

"The ones bitten just died from their wounds. There wasn't anybody in our group that got bitten and survived," Kay said.

Others, he said, died of heat, exhaustion, lack of food or from drinking seawater. The sharks didn't return to molest his group.

"Only God knows why they didn't return," he said. "They must have got their belly full."

Robert M. McGuiggan, 53, of 3643 N. Oakley, is one of the 316 who survived, drifting in his life jacket with nothing to eat or drink, all but abandoning hope for rescue. Now in the construction business, he is on the executive board of the USS Indianapolis Survivors' Assn.

The tropical sun baked the men during the day and the chilly temperatures sent them shivering to their bones at night. Their life jackets, which held the men's heads above water, had become so waterlogged that they began to lose their bouyancy. McGuiggan watched many of his exhausted shipmates vanish beneath the sea.

Then 23 and a gunner's mate, he had just come off the 4-to-midnight watch from his station and was sleeping on the open deck when he was shaken by a thunderous explosion from the forward area of the ship.

He dashed to his battle station as he had been conditioned to do. He saw smoke and fire coming out of portholes.

"The gunnery officer told me to get my life jacket and abandon ship," he recalls.

McGuiggan jumped overboard and swam away—as fast as he could.

"I turned around and saw the ship going under head first in a roaring fire."

After the torpedoes hit, the *Indianapolis* sank fast—some say within 12 minutes. An "abandon-ship" alarm never was sounded.

Before Herbert J. Miner II, an electronic technician's mate, "slipped into the water," he took time to put on his socks and shoes.

"I just didn't want to be running around in my bare feet," said Miner, then only 19. Miner, now president of the Great Lakes Paper Co., 308 W. Erie, credited this formality with saving his toes from the snapping jaws of the swarms of sharks.

Miner said that at first he did not appreciate the seriousness of the situation, but recalled that right after the explosion, a chief warrant officer raced to the radio shack and shouted, "We've been hit; let's send a message."

"I was standing there when the officer himself sent out an SOS," Miner recalls.

But the message somehow was never received. Miner swore that the message was sent out. "The communication gear was not damaged," he insists.

In the water, the men figured that rescue ships and planes would arrive when dawn broke. They didn't come, and none arrived on the days that followed. During the agonizing wait, the men saw planes, but the pilots never saw them.

Although the ship was overdue at Leyte, for some strange reason no one on shore missed her. The Navy simply didn't know the *Indianapolis* had been sunk.

After the second day of drifting, many found the thirst irresistible and began to drink seawater. Some hallucinated and went berserk. "They began to lose their minds and fight over life jackets," said Norman Galbraith, then 23 and a machinist 2d class, and now a machinist with Continental Can Co.

In one such fight, the men clawed and tore at each other.

After it was over, 25 lost their lives either from drowning, exhaustion or injuries.

Others talked about an island full of beautiful native girls, then removed their life jackets and started to swim toward their "dream island." Still others tried to dive down to the graveyard of the *Indianapolis* to get drink or food from their lockers.

"They never came back," Galbraith, of 9005 S. 49th Av., Oak Lawn, remembers.

And through it all, the men were sitting ducks for the man-eating sharks. They would see the dorsal fins, triangular sails that barely broke the surface, moving—constantly moving— around them, drawing tightening circles before the ominous forms slipped into the depths.

Some of the men told of waiting for terrifying moments after a shark's fin would submerge. Some said they felt the sandpaper skin of a shark brush against their bodies. Then there would be nothing. They were the lucky ones.

Fear still etches McGuiggan's face as he talks about how a man three feet away from him suddenly gave out a loud yell and went under. "Moments later, a pool of blood rose to the surface," said McGuiggan.

Until a year ago, McGuiggan said, he had an aversion to large bodies of water and boats because of the experience. "I just kind of stayed away from them."

Miner, who still had his socks and shoes on in the water, said he saw a lot of shark fins, sometimes a horde of them, sticking out of the water. "I just kicked and yelled whenever they got too close."

But the sharks were not the only danger menacing those still alive. Miner strongly believes that the diesel oil from the ship that covered his head saved him from being scorched to death by the tropical sun. "It worked as suntan lotion."

Ray A. Kinzle, of 8100 W. Addison, then 35 and a baker 2d class, was luckier. He sustained himself with malt tablets that men in his group had picked up from floating ration cans.

"I just waited, hoped and prayed," he said. He is now a retired commercial baker.

During the nearly five days that must have seemed like an eternity to the men, the cruel sea and its sharks claimed more than 500 lives. Of the bodies that were recovered, 88 had been mutilated by sharks or other carnivorous fish.

The men still afloat finally were spotted, almost by accident, by the pilot of a Navy plane on a routine reconnaissance flight. A giant rescue operation of ships and planes then got under way.

The Navy, embarrassed by its failure to detect the loss of the ship sooner, filed charges against Capt. McVay and ordered a court-martial that was held after the bomb the *Indianapolis* delivered was dropped and the Japanese surrendered. He was found guilty of negligence in failing to chart an evasive zigzag course for his ship before the submarine attack.

McVay, who had pleaded innocent, testified that zigzag action was not necessary because of the misty weather conditions.

Hashimoto, the Japanese submarine skipper, was brought over to testify during the trial over the protest of many Americans. But Hashimoto, ironically, came to McVay's defense, pointing out that a zigzag course would have made little difference.

Five of the six torpedoes launched on that night were equipped with magnetic warheads, which had a way of hunting down their targets anyway.

The Navy later remitted McVay's sentence because of his excellent previous record. He was awarded the Silver Star for "conspicuous gallantry and intrepidity" for his role in the bombardment of the Solomons. Four other officers, blamed for the delay in searching for the survivors, also got off with little more than a reprimand.

But for the survivors—who are holding a reunion this weekend in Indianapolis—the ordeal is as real today as it was 30 years ago when they struggled against the sea and its insatiable sharks.

Erika Goodman and Glenn White of the Joffrey Ballet.
Don Bierman / Daily News.

Arts and letters:

Henry Hanson
Richard Christiansen
Sydney J. Harris
Jay McMullen
Henry Kisor
Jack Schnedler
Dan Miller
Eugene Field

Victor Skrebneski's world: A silver Mercedes under a dappled sycamore in a prize-winning yard

Henry Hanson is a versatile local reporter who writes about politics one day and avant-garde art the next. This story by Hanson was published Nov. 29, 1975.

High-fashion photography is a moist lip, a quicksilver mood—and maybe a navel. It is languorous beauty—captured in a flash. And gone.

It is Victor Skrebneski's world. Chicago's most successful fashion photographer, he's making international waves. And he creates in an incongruous setting.

Skrebneski's handsome studio-home on the Near North Side is sandwiched between a three-story walk-up home for ex-drug addicts who shave their heads, and a Lutheran home for women with handicaps and emotional problems. Everyone seems to get along fine.

Skrebneski's life-style may be a cut above his neighbors'. But you'd expect that of a prominent photographer of long-stemmed beauties.

What is Skrebneski's world? It is . . .

A silver Mercedes parked under dappled sycamore trees lighted at night by floodlamps nestled amid ivy ground coverings in a prize-winning front yard.

"A sensuous celebration" of nudes—including actress Vanessa Redgrave ("wow, what a woman") and ballet's Dennis Wayne ("a friend of mine")—published in a book with Skrebneski's blank-verse prolog:

> *People, timeless.*
> *They will last my time.*
> *Designed as sculpture.*

147

> *I have left them alone.*
> *In the human contact they live in reality.*
> *I live with them.*

A magazine review trumpeted: "Cerebral as well as electric. Should end puritanism once and for all, but probably won't."

Photographing Orson Welles, Bette Davis, Andy Warhol and Liv Ullmann dressed in the same prop—a big, black turtleneck sweater. "I must have bought it a hundred years ago at Brooks Brothers."

Jet travel to the West Coast to talk with literary agent Irving Lazar (who also is Richard M. Nixon's agent) about snapping Liza Minnelli, Katharine Hepburn, Dominique Sanda, Bette Midler and Barbra Streisand for a new Skrebneski book of photos.

Food: Chicago's Maxim's de Paris, New York's Veau d'Or, London's Guinea and Paris' Le Petit Montmorency.

Skrebneski is trying to set up a photo session with Jackie Onassis, who recently wrote for the New Yorker's Talk of the Town about the opening of the International Center for Photographs. No Jackie nudes. "She's an absolutely beautiful woman. That's how she should be photographed," said Skrebneski.

Chicago magazine wants Skrebneski to shoot Mayor Richard J. Daley for an issue on the city in the year 2000. Skrebneski has been warned that Daley "is very conscious about his jowls."

A small TV security camera peers down to screen callers buzzing the doorbell at the renovated Jalka family coachhouse, which is Skrebneski's studio-home.

With soft FM rock filtering Simon and Garfunkel's *My Little Town* from a speaker high in his white brick box studio, Skrebneski was finishing work on a sexy nude shot to publicize a new Broadway show—*Le Belly Button.*

The model, and one of the show's stars, is Marilyn Chambers, who went from cuddling a baby on Ivory Snow soapboxes to box-office boffo in the X-rated fim, *Behind the Green Door.* Chicagoan Gail Davis is director and co-producer of *Le Belly Button,* opening Dec. 26.

On Skrebneski's studio wall is a large surrealist painting by Valkus. The painting depicts a blue golliwog man with a big green pea pod scaling his neck while he glares at a crater-pocked moon hovering above two red pyramids and a palm tree.

During an interview, Skrebneski served white wine on the rocks in Polish wine goblets. He chain-smoked Viceroy cigarets, which he stashes in the refrigerator near a dinner dish for his dog—a Shin-Tzu named "Shih-Tzu"—who likes pigs and has pig-of-the-month photographs taped on the wall over his bowl.

Green feathery leaves of a black aralia plant climb up past a ceramic elephant in a mirror-encased nook. On the walls are photos for ads that have sold millions of dollars worth of clothes (Marshall Field & Co.), cosmetics (Estee Lauder), cigarets (Virginia Slims), hair permanents (Toni) and LP record albums (Muddy Waters, Burt Bacharach, Lana Cantrell and Upchurch-Tennyson).

Skrebneski—dressed in Italian jeans, navy-blue sweater and soft leather moccasins—confided:

His portraits cost $1,500: "People who want to be photographed nude should get it over with before they're 30. And first they must have a point of view about life."

He grew up at the foot of Rush St., son of a tool and die maker for International Harvester Co.

French films of Jean Cocteau at the old World Playhouse theater were a major childhood influence: "My father used to take me."

He buys his suits ($325 to $375) at New York's Denoyer Inc., which does not advertise.

His photos of Sen. George McGovern were auctioned for $2,500 each at a 1972 political fund raiser. He also has photographed Sheriff Richard Elrod.

Chef Louis Szathmary of the Bakery "sends over a bottle of Dom Perignon to my table when he sees me in a restaurant. And I send him a bottle back—Dom Perignon."

He takes color with a Nikon camera, black and white with a Hasselblad and packs a pocket Canon 110 ED on vacations.

His woman models: "You've seen pictures in magazines of

girls running, looking surprised, hair all blowing. My woman is not that wild, insane kind. She is . . . ladylike."

Nudes: "I photograph, design, make happen what I want to see: A statement—pure, simple, no tricks."

He dislikes photographing children and animals.

He admires Richard Avedon's work but felt Avedon's recent show at New York's Marlborough Gallery was badly designed. "Everything was white." He also likes Irving Penn, Helmut Newton and Horst, the Paris photographer who photographed Skrebneski's home for *House & Garden* last February.

He studied art at Roosevelt University and the Institute of Design of Illinois Institute of Technology, but is a self-taught photographer.

His pictures have been displayed at the Arts Club, Deson-Zaks Gallery and the now-shuttered Center for Photographic Arts on W. Erie, and he was honored in a multimedia event at the Museum of Contemporary Art.

Above his studio is a spacious apartment designed by interior designer Bruce Gregga. It is furnished with cubist art, 18th Century French furniture, a bronze by Max Ernst, sculpture by Man Ray, paintings by Gleizes, a Bombois nude and a Domela collage over the fireplace. "I like art of the '20s and '30s," said Skrebneski, who collects mostly in Paris and New York.

In the living room are three Lalanne fleece-lined sculptures of sheep—two headless and one with a head—that double for chairs.

In a parlor is a spindly floor lamp by Diego Giacometti. Under the parchment shade is a sculptured iron head resembling the heads of Skrebneski and his models—gaunt, unsmiling, world weary—but flattered by soft light from above.

Joe Levine—'too old, too fat, too tired'—meets the press in Chicago

Richard Christiansen is a modern Renaissance man equally at home at the movies and the opera. This story by Christiansen was published June 26, 1965.

We are on the 17th floor of the Ambassador East Hotel (in the same suite Richard Burton and Elizabeth Taylor use when they are in town) and the scene is a small dinner party given by Joseph E. Levine, motion-picture producer.

At the moment, Joseph E. Levine is not here, because he is running a little late and had to change suits for the occasion, but the big dinner table is all set, tablecloth gleaming and crystal shining, and the hesitant waiters are tiptoeing around getting orders for drinks and offering hot and cold hors d'oeuvres to everyone.

The talk at the moment is about *Harlow*, the expensive movie Levine has produced for Paramount Pictures, and which he had screened in Chicago earlier in the day. There is some chatter about a big luncheon for exhibitors held after the screening, and the studio representative says, "It was a very successful luncheon. Only three fights, and only two people fell asleep."

But here at last is Joseph E. Levine himself—Joseph E. Levine, 59, who has put his name on everything from Fellini's *8 1/2* to *The Carpetbaggers* and *Jesse James Meets Frankenstein's Daughter.*

There's a smile on Levine's moon face, his eyes beam through heavy dark-rimmed glasses, and as he sinks his round 5 feet 4 inches into a chair, everybody asks Joe how he is.

He slowly rasps out a reply.

"Too old, too fat, too tired. Look at me. I lost and gained

151

2,789½ pounds in the last two years. I figured it out. What a life. I stole one line from Mike Todd, the only thing I ever stole from him, 'It's a hard way to make an easy living.' Everybody got a drink? Where's the kid with the sandwiches? Give me one of those little sausages. I like the little sausages. Look at this waiter, he's a cute kid, isn't he? If I had a television station, I'd put him on a TV show."

More small talk. Then someone asks him about his star, Carroll Baker. Is it true he has become disenchanted with her?

"We have a very wonderful relationship. We kiss by cable every day. She's in the south of France now, with her husband. He got her a present when they got there, a boat. I think it's the same boat we used in *Hercules*."

He smiles a little at that, reaches over for a big napkin from the table and wipes his face a couple of times.

Another question, this one about the other film of *Harlow*, a quickie version made by producer Bill Sargent that was released before Levine's production and stole some of his publicity.

Levine scowls, and his voice becomes more hoarse.

"This is not a question of two pictures. This could be a body blow to the whole motion-picture industry. I know I'll never make a picture that's in the public domain again. Look what could happen. George Stevens spends three years making *The Greatest Story Ever Told,* and this guy Sargent can come around and make *The Bible* in eight days.

"This *Harlow* thing Sargent made is gonna cost us. It'll cut into our profits. We're spending $1,250,000 on publicity, and it would've been a lot less. Don't get me wrong. I'm not sore. I wish he'd drop dead. He's a bum. But I'm not sore.

"We bought this book, a salacious, dirty piece of junk. We threw everything away except the title and made our own high-class picture. Tonight is the first, and maybe the last, time people will actually pay money to see it."

Dinner is ready, and we all sit down at the big round table. Levine chops at his steak and Caesar salad, and he reminisces about his early successes as a showman.

"I used to have 86 offices, every one of them in my suit

pockets. I was running around everywhere, catching planes with a can of film under my arm and a bunch of papers in my pockets. Then I found this Japanese movie called *Godzilla*, one of the greatest pictures ever made. It must've won 70 or 80 awards. (He leans over to the lady on his right and gives her a wink.)

"I bought it for $12,000, spent a lot more to Americanize it and made $850,000 on it. Then I bought another Japanese picture, *The Mysterions*, another all-time great movie. I got that because the Japanese producer had seen my card trick, said he wanted to know how I did my tricks, so he gave me the option on the picture.

"I was sitting in the office of MGM one day, and they tell me, 'Joe, we saw a picture that's got your name all over it.' So I asked what it was, and they said, *Hercules*, with a guy named Steve Reeves. I like that name, *Hercules*. I'm always great for good titles. So I buy it. It says in my biography the movie made $20 million. It's a bunch of lies. If I made that much, where's my money? My wife looks in my pockets and there's nothing there.

"I made five pictures last year that lost $6 million. Of course, I made two pictures that took in $8 million. I got 39 pictures going, low-budget things and very expensive ones. Some of them I'm going to use for television. . . ."

A telephone rings in the bedroom, and the call is for Levine. He answers it, returns a few minutes later and says, "That was Sammy Davis Jr. He just saw *Harlow* and thought it was great. I told him, 'Aw, you just say that because you're Jewish.' "

The meal is over now, we are on coffee and cigars, and Levine is entertaining us with his magic. He takes a spoon and sticks it on his forehead. He balances a toothpick, fork and spoon on the edge of a water glass, and for his finale, just before we leave for the theater to see his movie, he tells us this story:

"Now, ladies and gentlemen, when I was 16, and thin, and had all my hair, I went on a safari and saved a man's life by shooting a tiger that was going to eat him. He was so grateful that he promised me anything I wanted. So I thought and thought and finally I said, 'Oh sir, if you will give me $100 a day for the rest of my life, I will always be happy and never ask for anything else. And so, ladies and gentlemen. . . ."

At this point, Levine borrows a cigaret, he touches the lighted end to a paper napkin in front of him, there is a brief burst of flame, and from the ashes Levine picks a crumpled piece of green paper. He unfolds it slowly and, guess what, it is a $100 bill. Applause, applause. Joseph E. Levine smiles broadly and invites us to see his movie.

Sydney J. Harris argues that 'infancy' is no excuse for television

This article was written by Sydney J. Harris, a modern philosopher and popular syndicated columnist of the Daily News.

One defensive comment of the television addicts that I fail to understand is the argument that television is still in its "infancy" and that it is unjust to compare it to the other arts.

"Give television some time," they mutter. "Think of the other arts in their infancy!"

All right, let's. Think of the drama in its infancy— Aeschylus, Sophocles, Euripides, Aristophanes, still the greatest of playwrights.

Think of sculpture in its infancy—Praxiteles and Phidias, whose work has not yet been excelled.

Think of architecture in its infancy—the magnificent pyramids of Egypt, the temples and public buildings of Greece.

Think of literature and poetry in their infancy— the unrivaled Songs of Solomon, the *Odyssey* and *Iliad* of Homer, the *Aeneid* of Virgil, the odes of Horace—which moderns are still translating into inferior versions.

An art form does not develop with time—if it did, our playwrights would be 300 years better than Shakespeare, and we know that they are 300 million light-years behind him.

Movies are not conspicuously better than they were 30 years ago; they were not helped by sound, by color nor by technical improvement. Radio programs are not more adult and civilized than they were in the days of battery sets—at least then there were no soap operas on the air.

The difference between these two latter forms (and television) and the other arts that came to fulfillment from their beginnings is a difference in purpose, not in time or technique.

The great art of the past wanted to express something about life—about the nature of man and the universe. It asked real questions, and tried to answer them in terms of truth and goodness and beauty.

The latter-day arts want merely to please as large an audience as possible—either to lull them into a false complacency, or to make them responsive to a sales pitch. With these ends, you can wait an eternity for movies and radio and television, and they will not grow up. Artistic maturity, like emotional maturity, means giving, and they are interested only in getting.

Back from Broadway,
The Gimp
confided to Jay McMullen:
'I started voting at 15'

Jay McMullen, on his beat in Mayor Richard J.
Daley's City Hall, encountered some of Chica-
go's most incredible characters. On May 22,
1965, he told the story of just one of them.

Once he was toasted as "the mayor of Randolph St."

As the husband of blond Ruth Etting, romantic songstress of the '20s and '30s, he was one of the nation's most sought-after booking agents.

He packed a heater in the Old Chicago tradition and was feared as a "tough guy."

The confidant of the greats of Broadway, he rubbed elbows with Jolson, Eddie Cantor and Jimmy Walker during his palmy New York days.

Today, Col. Martin (The Gimp) Snyder, lonely and almost forgotten, is a broken-down horse-player running out his string on a city payroll, living in a small room in a third-rate Loop hotel.

As a politically sponsored jobholder, he works a precinct on his native West Side in contrast to the day when he could pick up the telephone and reach Mayor Jimmy Walker in New York.

You see The Gimp often these days, limping around City Hall, always friendly and cheerful, running errands for the city clerk's office where he works for $520 a month, a sum that wouldn't even have been walkin'-around money in the old days.

He emerged briefly from obscurity a decade ago when his ill-fated marriage with Ruth Etting and the dramatic Hollywood shooting scrape that climaxed it were portrayed in a movie, *Love Me or Leave Me.*

James Cagney portrayed The Gimp as ruthless promoter of

157

young Ruth Etting's career in show business, a career that brought the winsome, onetime Nebraska farm girl fame and fortune as one of America's best-loved singers. It brought heartbreak and ruin to The Gimp.

Snyder sketched the details of his colorful life, including his stormy marriage to the woman who was once America's sweetheart. Although he is in his 70s his memory is keen and his mind alert.

The Gimp was born Moses Snyder at 14th and Solin in the heart of the West Side. The neighborhood was a breeding ground of tough guys.

In infancy, in a manner unknown, he received the injury to his left leg that was to give him the name "The Gimp."

"I think I got through the sixth grade," he recalls. "We were poor and everything like that so I went to hustling papers."

The Gimp's neighborhood was hemmed in by clashing nationality youth gangs, tough Polish, Italians and Irish.

"I had to change my name from Moses to Martin," he said. "In school when I got up to read I got hit with everything—rubber bands, spit balls. That's how I got to be a tough guy. I came home bleeding many days."

One of the greatest fights he ever got into was when six kids set fire to the beard of an elderly Jewish man and The Gimp waded into all of them.

As a kid, he frequently slept, as did other boys, in the alley behind the old *Daily News* building on Wells St.

In his middle teens he got into politics—as a floating voter in the old 19th Ward of John (Johnny DePow) Powers.

"I guess I voted over 100 times in some elections," The Gimp recalls. "We'd get beer money, eatin' money. I started voting at 15."

The Gimp's voting finesse brought him almost naturally into the old "bloody 20th" Ward of Denny Egan, a Democratic ward boss. Egan put him in a clerical job in the election commissioner's office, where The Gimp was able to exercise the franchise with even less restraint. At one point he was on three payrolls in the careless tradition of Chicago politics in the Capone era.

"And they think they got vote frauds now," he exclaimed.

Along the way, The Gimp picked up friends, big shots some of them. His pals called him "Colonel Moe." He got the title in World War I when Doughboys who wanted to send home banned articles would address them to Col. Moses Snyder." Apparently they went through because they were addressed to an "officer," The Gimp.

One of The Gimp's big breaks came through his friendship with Rocco Vocco, a music publisher who knew Al Jolson. Jolson was playing the Garrick Theater in *Honeymoon Express* and Vocco took The Gimp over to introduce him.

En route they met Timothy (Big Tim) Murphy, a Democratic ward boss, and "Mike de Pike" Heitler, a vice lord and gambler. Jolson, it seems, had read news stories about Heitler's activities and was using them on stage in his gags. Mike de Pike was seething. His pal, Big Tim, was going back to Jolson's dressing room after the show to work him over.

Backstage, The Gimp drew the pistol he always carried, showed it to Jolson and informed him of Murphy's intentions. At Jolson's request, The Gimp interceded. From then on, when the famous *Mammy* singer was in Chicago, The Gimp was his bodyguard.

"I met Eddie Cantor, Sophie Tucker, Blossom Seely, Fanny Brice, all the great headliners," Snyder recalls. "That's how I got to be friendly with people in show business."

It was through Vocco that The Gimp also met a long-legged chorine at Marigold Gardens who had come from a Nebraska farm to study dress designing. Her name was Ruth Etting.

"I was picked to take Ruth in for an introduction to Blossom Seely, who was famous for the clothes she wore. Ruth stood and sketched them from the wings. Later, she, Benny Fields, Blossom and I went to the Bismarck for supper."

That was the beginning of The Gimp's one-sided love affair with the girl he made famous.

The Gimp knew the manager of the chorus at Marigold Gardens and applied one of the unscrupulous tactics he was to use so successfully in promoting Ruth Etting's career.

"They had a certain number where the curtain wasn't fire-proof," Snyder recalled. "Ald. Dorsey Crowe fixed it for me with the fire department and in return they took Ruth out of the chorus and put her up in front.

"She thought I was really mayor of the Loop, as a Chicago newspaper writer had christened me.

"Now I used Jolson through Rocco," said Snyder. "I talked to Jolson about getting Ruth to play in a show. Jolson arranged it through an editor of *Variety* magazine. Three weeks later Ruth was doing a single number in the College Inn with Ben Bernie, who was Jolson's buddy.

"The town was talking about her. Then along came Columbia Records. She started making records.

"It wasn't long before she was on the stage at the Palace Theater and that was tops in Chicago. She was kept over and stayed two weeks. Show business had a new name."

A grateful Ruth Etting and The Gimp were married in 1922.

The breaks kept coming. Flo Ziegfeld took her to New York for the Follies, the biggest break in show business. Ruth insisted that The Gimp come along as her manager. She revived the song *Shine On, Harvest Moon* and made it a nationwide hit.

"Then along came radio and Walter Winchell went on the radio for Jergens lotion and he insisted on Ruth as his first guest," The Gimp recalled. "From then on it's history what Ruth did for Chesterfield and other great sponsors. She was one of the greatest singers of all time."

She broke all records at the Roxy. She worked six weeks at $15,000 a week. At one point with Paul Whiteman at the Paramount in New York she played 12 weeks at $27,500 a week.

The Gimp was by this time "the mayor of Broadway," living high. Everybody knew him at Lindy's restaurant. The money kept rolling in and then . . . and then the bottom fell out.

"Ruth came to me and said, 'I don't love you any more. I want to live alone,' " he recalled.

The Gimp said they split her fortune on a 50–50 basis. He wound up with almost $500,000 in the divorce settlement in 1938.

"Ruth was an obsession with me," said Snyder. "Eating,

drinking, breathing and loving Ruth Etting all those years."

The Gimp went on a prolonged spree with his money. He blew it big on booze, broads and slow horses.

Then came the biggest blow. Ruth Etting, it seemed, was involved in a love affair with her pianist, Merle Alderman, according to news reports.

In a fit of jealous rage, The Gimp flew to Hollywood, invaded the singer's home and shot her lover when he arrived on the scene. Alderman survived his wounds to elope with the singer while The Gimp went on trial for assault to commit murder, a charge on which he was found guilty.

The famed Hollywood defense lawyer, Jerry Giesler, won freedom for The Gimp but with that victory went his last $80,000.

The great free-spending, glamor days were over. Back in Chicago, the late Artie Elrod, stogie-chomping boss of the 24th Ward on the West Side, gave The Gimp a lift and got him a city job as city license investigator.

Miss Etting is now retired and lives in Las Vegas, Nev.

"I work every day," said The Gimp. "I don't bother anybody. I don't go with women. I don't drink much."

His only luxury is the racetrack, where on every holiday and weekend The Gimp may be seen at the $2 window.

"What else can I do to get out in the air, talk to a few old-timers still around and punch the bag with them. I bet my deuce and have a drink and it's sort of a tonic—an expensive tonic.

"I've had a good life. I can't beef. I'm ready to meet my Maker."

Then The Gimp hobbles down the cool marble-lined corridors of City Hall, swinging his left leg stiffly, haunted by the memories.

The Sage of Moberly, Mo., grants an interview

This story, published Aug. 18, 1973, was written by book editor Henry Kisor.

At 74, the writer-editor-yarnspinner-folk hero Jack Conroy enjoys a reputation, practically worldwide, as the Sage of Moberly, Mo.

It was almost with a sense of pilgrimage that I went there to see him recently. For in 1966 this antic Irishman left Chicago—"after 28 years of standing in the alien corn, often with a sad heart sick for home"—to return to the town of 12,000 where he was born.

Conroy from early on has been up and down and all over this country, as working stiff and writer, editor and fund-raising bagman for angry little magazines, and friend of man, common and uncommon. His 1933 novel, *The Disinherited*, now is a certified Depression classic. In fact, so is Conroy.

He is still large, bluff and hearty, and he still favors his correspondents with fistfuls of fundamentalist religious tracts, exhorting them to spread God's word where it will do the most good. The Sage of Moberly, son of a former Jesuit priest who turned coal miner, is a do-gooder in his own way.

Moberly, in the mining country of northern Missouri, is about as far from the Loop as you can get. It is so nondescript, according to some authorities, that it is classically so.

On the other hand, it makes few class distinctions. Gen. Omar Bradley of World War II glory is its most famous son, a roadside historical marker proclaims. Just below the general's name is that of Jack Conroy, grand old man of the literature of America's left and a writer who has been compared with Jack London and Maxim Gorky.

When I got to Moberly, Conroy was waiting patiently in the study of his brownstone house, where he is writing his memoirs. His flop-eared hound nuzzled my knee.

I was exhausted from the seven-hour trip from Chicago, with missed airline connections and a hot, dusty, 40-mile drive in a rented car up from Columbia. "Let's talk about Chicago yesterday and today," I suggested, as much to catch my breath as anything else. "How did you happen to get there? And what happened?"

"Ah," Conroy said, leaning back in his chair with an expression of relish. Here was a storyteller in his element, someone having dropped the hat.

And he drifted back to 1938, when the now-celebrated Chicago novelist Nelson Algren was a young author around town and Conroy was having trouble rounding up three meals a day in Moberly.

"Nelson had been on the federal Illinois Writers' Project," Conroy recalled, "and had been suggesting that we revive the *Anvil* (a left-wing literary magazine Conroy had edited in Moberly and which had merged three years before with the *Partisan Review*). Nelson told me that if I'd come up to Chicago, he thought he could get me into the project.

"Here in Moberly, my wife was working at the shoe factory for $4 a week, and I was getting $4.16 a week after taxes from the *St. Louis Post-Dispatch* for book reviews. So on a cold, windy March day we arrived by bus in Chicago. Nelson took me out to his pad, which was in an arcade of storefronts, built for the World's Columbian Exposition, on Cottage Grove Av. We called it 'Rat Alley,' because of the ferocious rats that lived there.

"Nelson fought them tooth and nail. Even flattened tin cans over their holes didn't faze their powerful teeth. One day Nelson told the rent collector, 'Say, you sure have big rats.' 'Yeah,' the collector replied, 'and our mice ain't nothing to sneeze at, neither.'

"I stayed there while waiting for my acceptance on the writers' project. In the meantime we began raising funds to get out the *New Anvil* with a series of lectures and things of that sort—

however you could snag a little money from Depression-ridden people.

"Our main source of revenue was a melodrama called *The Drunkard's Warning, or Chicago by Gaslight*, which we staged at several Chicago locations. It recounted the misfortunes of a man we called James T. Barrelhouse and his troubles with both strong drink and his wife, Phyllis.

"I myself essayed the role of Behemoth Frittertitter, a temperance crank who had long been enamored of Phyllis. At one point the girl who was playing Phyllis got temperamental on us, and Algren took over the role. The long gray wig he borrowed for it gave him a woebegone air of injured innocence that was both pathetic and appealing.

"It brought us quite a lot of money. Much more than the fund-raising lectures by the writers Peter De Vries, Langston Hughes, Richard Wright and others. That gives you an idea of the taste of Chicago audiences." Conroy's rich, booming laugh rattled the windows of his study.

"And then there were the parties for Maxwell Bodenheim, the famous poet of the Chicago Renaissance. It became our custom to throw parties for his benefit; we took a little out for the *New Anvil*.

"The expectation was that Bodenheim would arrive blind drunk, unable to recite his poetry. It made everybody feel so great to say 'Look at that drunken bum, and here I am, sober as a judge.'

"On one memorable occasion a very prim schoolteacher who had long admired his poetry was waiting to meet him. Bodenheim appeared, his hair dyed a horrible red with Mercurochrome, his long greasy overcoat pinned at the breast with a single large brass safety pin.

" 'Mr. Bodenheim,' the teacher said, stretching out her hand to greet him. The besodden Bodenheim lunged toward her, missed her hand and broke wind loudly as he fell flat on his face."

As I wiped the tears from my eyes, Conroy continued, "We did get the magazine started. Algren and I rented office space in a place called the Institute for Mortuary Research, a public-relations service for undertakers. We had access to the outfit's letterheads. It was of good quality, but of a ghastly blue hue, like that of a corpse whose embalming had been delayed too long. Partly to save money, we wrote amiable rejection notes on it, making some sort of genial comment to soften the blow.

"Just as the *New Anvil* was about to fold in 1941, a young fellow wrote to thank us for our amiable rejection letter—it'd taken the chill off, he said. 'I'm feeling kind of high now,' he said, 'for I've just sold a story to *Esquire*.' It must have been the first thing he ever sold.

" 'Let me know if the magazine ever starts up again,' he added, 'but I'll be damned if I ever send any more manuscripts to the Institute for Mortuary Research.' It didn't sound right, somehow, I guess. He was Jerry Salinger—who later became famous as J. D., and wrote *Catcher in the Rye*.

"And we had some marvelous literary parties when I lived in an old house with thick brick walls on Green St. If you had been outside when the revelry of 300 people was going on, all you'd hear was a dull hum, like summer bees.

"One of the pilgrims Algren brought over to the house—he was always bringing somebody—was a young fellow named Norman Mailer. His *The Naked and the Dead* hadn't yet been published. Mailer had just been to the peep shows on S. State St. and announced with great satisfaction, 'You've got better dirty movies here than they've got on Coney Island.' "

There was a long pause. "Today's little magazines are always in financial trouble," I ventured. "But you always were able to keep your magazines going, even if only for a short time, without federal and state grants and university subsidies."

"In the early '30s," Conroy mused, "I was president of a loosely organized club called the Rebel Poets. Ben Hagglund, a printer up in the wild muskeg country of Minnesota, had a patched old press, and suggested we get out a magazine called *The Rebel Poet*. He would take whatever he could get to buy a little paper and ink, and if there wasn't any money he'd go out and work on a railroad section gang or bale a little hay to get some cash. Show me where there's a printer like that nowadays!

"And later there was a group of zealots who believed in the

New Anvil so much that each would hawk 8 or 10 copies at union meetings, and send all the money to us. They asked nothing for themselves. The profit motive wasn't important to these people in those days.

"As for today? One of my old contributors recently told me that she went to a Hollywood bookstore to ask for a certain book. It wasn't in stock, so she asked the store to order it for her. 'We would have to order it by computer,' they told her, 'and it would have to go through our computer in Milwaukee, and it would take at least eight weeks to arrive. Do you really want the book that badly?' See, they were discouraging her from ordering it!

"ITT has taken over six old publishing houses and computerized them, including the venerable Putnam," Conroy added. "You're familiar with the remaindering process—that's when a book no longer selling is put out at a reduced price and sold by some cut-rate bookstore, with no profit to the author. A friend recently told me he'd heard that one publisher's computer had ordered a book remaindered even before it was published!

"The personal kind of bookshops, like my dear departed friend Max Siegel had in Chicago—that sort of thing is going by the board. They market books like they do potatoes in chain stores.

"We no longer have the devoted sort of people who went out of their way to help because they believed in books and magazines. Now, I'm not against federal and state funds for literary magazines and other aspects of culture, but I think the present administration's attitude toward culture is similar to that of the Nazi official who said, 'When I hear the word "culture," I reach for my gun.'

"There's some kind of deep, morally rotten cynicism that has descended on this country. It's a very distressing thing—for the arts, for politics and every aspect of American life."

We ruminated for a while over that. Then I asked: "Jack, what have you been doing since you left Chicago?"

"I came back to Moberly mainly to look back over where I had been, and to arrive at some sort of meaning about what I had seen and done, and more particularly to try to set down some of them. I have always liked Moberly, but it was impossible for me to make a living here.

"Many of my friends and relatives are dead and gone, of course. But something remains—I'll come across a building on Main St. that hasn't burned down, with '1894' still on its cast-iron facade. It all evokes something that will come out in my autobiography. I think because I'm away from the turmoils of the city and have, I hope, achieved a sort of serenity here, I'll be able to look at the past with a more judicious, a more praising eye."

I interrupted: " 'You can't go home again,' Thomas Wolfe said. How could you, a firebrand of the proletarian left, come back to little Moberly?"

"Oh, the attitudes of the townspeople have changed," Conroy replied, smiling. "Although I wasn't exactly chased out of Moberly, I wasn't very welcome here either. But now, since I'm quiescent, they don't think there's much danger in me any more. There's a Kipling story about an aged cobra guarding a sacred elephant goad or something in a ruined temple. When people came near, he'd hiss fearsomely, but then someone discovered he had no teeth and was harmless.

"I feel that the good citizens here regard me much like that ancient cobra—that my teeth have been drawn and whatever potential I had for damage is gone." He chuckled ruefully.

It was growing late in the afternoon. Conroy suggested that we drive to the outskirts of Moberly to see the scenes he made famous in *The Disinherited*. We visited the site of the Monkey Nest coal camp, where Conroy's father and two brothers were killed in mining accidents. Only a cornfield and a few farm homes stand there now.

A brief stop at Sugar Creek graveyard, resting place of the Conroys and other Moberly miners, and there was just time for dinner at the Conroys'. His wife, Gladys, laid a trencherman's spread of two kinds of meat, half a dozen vegetables, a huge salad and dessert.

Then it was time to go. "Do you have any messages for Chicago?" I asked.

"Yes. Give my regards to Rush St. And I'll see all my

friends there in October at the publication party for *Writers in Revolt* (a collection of pieces from the *Anvil* and the *New Anvil*, to be published by Lawrence Hill Inc.).

"But no drinking, though. I've quit. Had to—I'm a diabetic. They'll all be surprised to hear I haven't had a drop for three years. That'll be astonishing to those who knew me in the old days!" He threw his head back and laughed uproariously.

'With good wishes to you— and, of course, to me too. Joseph Heller'

Jack Schnedler of the Daily News *interviewed Joseph Heller upon the occasion of the publication of Heller's second novel. Schnedler's story was published Oct. 5, 1974.*

Tell us, Joe, why do you write so slow?

"Because I can't do it any quicker," says Joseph Heller, in a voice that unmistakably grew up around New York's Coney Island.

"I don't think that slowness in writing is a virtue. I just can't write faster. I'm slow. If I got back to New York and had to write you a business letter complaining that I had been misquoted, I would probably have to do three or four drafts to get it right."

Joseph Heller needed seven years to get his first book just right, but what a book *Catch-22* turned out to be. With more than 8 million copies now in print, this highly satirical story of a World War II bomber squadron is the most celebrated American novel of the 1960s. And Yossarian, the life-loving bombardier of *Catch-22*, has become fictional talisman to an entire generation.

Having made it as a literary saint on his first try, Heller began his second book. In 1962, the year after *Catch-22* appeared, his publisher ran an ad with this optimistic message:

"And the best news of all. Joseph Heller is now working on his second novel, *Something Happened*. Publication date not set yet, of course—but look for it some time before we get to the moon."

As it happened, the astronauts landed five years ahead of *Something Happened*. But now Heller has touched down, after 13 years, and by early critical accounts his second novel is entirely worth the wait. It certainly looks like the novel of 1974.

"From what I've heard, the reviews are going to be almost uniformly favorable," Heller says. "I hope I don't sound too smug, because it's hard for an author to sound otherwise when things are going so well."

We're talking in Heller's corner suite on the sixth floor of the Drake Hotel, in a room only slightly smaller than Pianosa, that mythical Mediterranean island of *Catch-22* from which Yossarian and his comrades kept getting sent to fly more missions.

Heller, who looks younger than his 51 years, partly because he has brought his weight down 50 pounds to a trim 160 in the last few years, is making Chicago one of his stops on a very short promotional tour.

One reason for stopping in Chicago, he explains, is that Shirley, his wife of 29 years, has a cousin here and wanted to make the visit. The Hellers took the train from New York, and it seems fair to ask why an old World War II bombardier (as Heller was in real life) wouldn't be flying in.

"Actually, like a number of guys in my Air Corps squadron, I swore that if I got through the war alive, I would never fly again," he answers, while *Daily News* photographer Henry Herr Gill circles in close for pictures.

"For a number of years after the war, I would travel only by train. But a train can get so long and boring that I finally decided to risk flying again rather than take the chance of being bored to death. Taking the overnight from New York to Chicago isn't so bad—and besides, I'm not flying until after the reviews are out."

Heller doesn't laugh at his own jokes, and he is also kind to photographers. "Here let me take off my jacket," he tells Gill. "The *Tribune* took their pictures with my jacket on, and you'll want something different."

Jacketed again after the photographs are done, but tieless, Heller leads us down to the Drake's Camellia House for lunch and the main course of our interview. Heller is a martini man, and after he toasts our success and we toast his, book editor Henry Kisor and I begin the questioning in earnest. Our subject turns out to be a consummate conversationalist.

Yes, it's true that he originally thought of having some connections between *Catch-22* and *Something Happened.* Bob Slocum, the melancholy middle-aged executive who is the new novel's main character, was to have been in Yossarian's squadron during the war and, as Heller at first planned, would occasionally reflect on their military days together.

"I discarded that idea fairly early," Heller says. "I also had the idea at one point of writing the entire book in children's language, like a Dick and Jane reader. It would have read the way the chapter on Slocum's office now begins: 'In the office in which I work there are five people of whom I am afraid. . . .' But I decided it would get pretty tiresome for a whole book."

The vast audience for *Catch-22* has been mainly a young audience, many of whom saw Yossarian's struggles to stay alive as a dry run for the murderous foolishness of Vietnam. Some critics are suggesting that a lot of these *Catch-22* cultists will not appreciate *Something Happened,* which is certainly a very different kind of book.

Heller disagrees. "I believe young people will relate to *Something Happened,*" he says, dipping into a cup of Bookbinder soup. "Many young people today are alienated from the work experience, but they know that they have to work. They know older people like Bob Slocum, and already they're envisioning the same kind of fate for themselves."

Bob Slocum suffers in a corporate world, but Heller believes the same fears and anxieties apply to colleges and universities, where so many young people find themselves these days.

Heller knows the campus. This is his fifth year on the faculty of City College of New York, where he teaches creative writing; he also has ventured forth on the college lecture circuit, doing readings from *Catch-22.*

"I enjoy the teaching and the readings very much," Heller says. "One of my favorite questions from the audience after the readings used to be which character from *Catch-22* I'd identify most closely with Richard Nixon."

For a while, says Heller, his choice for a Nixon double was Major Major Major, the squadron commander who was always in hiding, from real and imagined troubles. "Then Lt. Scheisskopf seemed just right" (here Heller laughs), "but since Nixon has gone into the hospital, I guess he's most like Chief White Halfoat" (who had made up his mind to die of pneumonia).

The income from teaching and readings, along with *Catch-22* royalties, has left Heller free in the last few years to concentrate all his writing energies on *Something Happened.*

Heller says his income from *Catch-22* was never very great until 1970, the year that the Mike Nichols-directed movie version starring Alan Arkin came out. That year, his royalties added up to $80,000. Now, with *Something Happened* already sold to a paperback publisher and with glowing reviews in the offing, he has hopes of the new novel bringing in something like $500,000 in fairly short order.

Heller does not pretend that money matters are beneath his artistic sensitivities. "I wouldn't ever want to be forced to go back," he says. "Do you know what I mean?

"Well, in the early '30s, there were a lot of suicides by people who had seen their income drop in the Depression from, say, $150,000 a year to $40,000. They weren't broke by any means, but they couldn't stand going back to a lesser standard of living. It may have been the humiliation that killed them."

Over the years, the Hellers have moved up from a four-room apartment to a seven-room apartment in the same Manhattan building, along with acquiring a Long Island summer home. "We have a very comfortable life-style," Heller says, "and I wouldn't want to change it."

One thing Heller has never changed is his liking for New York City. He was born in Brooklyn and grew up in that borough's Coney Island neighborhood. He worked as a file clerk after graduation from Abraham Lincoln High School, then enlisted in the Air Corps at age 19. He flew 60 combat missions over Italy and France and was discharged a first lieutenant.

Then Heller went to college, graduating Phi Beta Kappa from New York University, getting a master's degree from Columbia, and studying one year at Oxford on a Fulbright scholarship. For two years, he taught freshman English at a state college in Pennsylvania, and he was writing advertising and promotion copy in New York at the time he started *Catch-22.*

Heller says he had pretty much the entire story for *Catch-22,* and later for the new novel, in mind before he began writing them.

"I don't think I could begin working on a book if I didn't know how I was going to end it," he adds. "It's funny, though—I didn't think either story was going to be long enough for a novel. I thought *Catch-22* might make 200 pages, and I originally thought *Something Happened* would be a novelette, maybe 60 to 80 pages."

Catch-22, of course, turned out so full and rich that the movie makers were unable to digest more than a small part of it. Surprisingly, looking back, it was not an instant smash as a book, either critically or commercially. In fact, the original working title, *Catch-18,* had to be changed because a better-known author named Leon Uris was coming out with *Mila 18* at the same time.

The *New York Times* reviewer wrote that *Catch-22* was a failure "because half its incidents are farcical and fantastic." But a second wave of reviews was highly favorable, including an influential paean in the *Daily News* by novelist Nelson Algren, who called it "the best American novel in years."

Many readers have wondered over the years how much of Yossarian's character is based on Heller's own experience, particularly since both were bombardiers. Since *Something Happened* is written in the first person, it raises even more strongly the question of autobiographical content.

"Actually, there is very little of myself in either book," answers Heller. "Of course, the Air Force setting of *Catch-22* is drawn from my World War II background, and much in *Something Happened* comes out of my observations.

"But neither novel is autobiographical, certainly not *Something Happened.* I have always enjoyed my work; I liked writing advertising copy at the time. I even enjoyed my assignment in the war, until the last 15 or 20 missions, when I realized I might be killed.

"The sensibilities of Yossarian were not my own during the war. I went through that later, and the book is more a reaction to the '50s, to the McCarthy era. In *Catch-22*, I set down what I felt about a country in turmoil, a turmoil from which we are still suffering. The temporary national unity of World War II had broken down; you'll notice that *Catch-22* takes place in the final months of the war, when that breakdown has already started."

So, if *Catch-22* is in the third person, why is *Something Happened* written in the first person?

"In *Catch-22*, the threats to Yossarian are external," Heller replies. "There actually are people out there trying to get him, not so much the Germans any more, but the Cathcarts and Dreedles and Peckems on his own side.

"In *Something Happened*, all the threats to Bob Slocum are internal. His enemy is his own fear, his own anxiety. The story is his.

"Yossarian, at the end of *Catch-22*, realizes he can't sell out. So he deserts and has a kind of rebirth through that desertion. He is happy for the first time.

"Slocum is also brought to the point of decision near the end of his book by the loss of the only thing in life that really mattered to him. He pulls himself together and begins to function in the last section. But this new energy is not going to sustain him long."

There is little hope for Slocum, as Heller sees it: "If death was the overriding presence in *Catch-22*, perhaps memories are the overriding presence in *Something Happened*. Slocum's trouble is that he carries everything one stage too far in his mind. He thinks too far ahead. For example, when he's thinking about getting divorced—which incidentally is one of the funniest parts of the book—he's not sure who'll get his undershorts home from the laundry."

Heller pauses over his sole when asked whether there is any note of optimism in his new novel.

"Well, perhaps that Bob Slocum is only Bob Slocum. He is not Everyman. The book is a novel. Its primary intention is not to convey truths. Its objective is to be a good novel. Of course, a good novel has to contain much that is recognizable to readers as truth. But the attitude of *Something Happened* is not my attitude to life."

Part of the reason Heller needed 13 years to finish this novel of middle-aged anxiety is that he took two years off in 1967–68 to write a play, *We Bombed in New Haven*. The antiwar drama didn't exactly bomb in New York, but it ran only 12 weeks on Broadway. There's a hint that Heller still carries some pain from the experience, when he says, "An unkind review hurts you. It's a public insult, particularly with a play."

In January, 1969, Heller went back to work on the novel, rewriting his earlier notes. "It was good that I took two years off," he says. "The texture of the book changed when I resumed. Otherwise, it would have been a shorter, less substantial book. It wouldn't have been as good."

Heller guesses he must have rewritten every sentence of *Something Happened* at least four or five times. "There were days of agony," he says, "when I'd sweat to produce even a couple of handwritten pages on the legal pads I use." Finally, last January, he delivered the completed manuscript to his publisher, Alfred A. Knopf.

Heller does most of his writing in the mornings, but first he jogs. "I jog three miles a day," he says. "If I tried to jog six miles, I'd drop dead—not from exhaustion, but from boredom. Jogging is the most boring activity I know. So while I'm jogging, I write in my mind."

Then Heller puts it on paper at an office he rents. He normally doesn't write at home, which he and his wife share with a Bedlington terrier named Sweeny. Daughter Erica, 22, and son Ted, 18, are away at school.

With a host of favorable reviews about to be unfurled, Heller has reason to be smug about *Something Happened*. It's also a book-club selection by the Literary Guild.

Movie rights for *Something Happened* have not yet been offered, but Heller says the book has been read by four actors—Alan Arkin, Richard Benjamin, Jack Lemmon and Dustin Hoffman. They all liked it, he reports, with an enthusiastic Benjamin commenting, "I feel like I'm reading about myself."

Heller believes his new novel is better suited for movie adaptation than *Catch-22* (which he had no part in adapting, but still maintains was an excellent film).

"In *Catch-22,* there was a very large number of scenes spelled out in great detail," he explains. "There was little a screenwriter could do beyond selecting and arranging. In *Something Happened,* scenes are indicated rather than spelled out. The book is in the nature of an illusion, which gives the screenwriter a chance to do the fleshing out."

Meanwhile, what about Joseph Heller's next novel?

"I do want to write another one," he assures us. "But I don't have any specific ideas now. I may think about the Dunbar (Yossarian's sidekick in *Catch-22*) book."

The interview is winding up, although Heller appears capable of talking on, because he has appointments with the student papers at Northwestern and the University of Chicago.

There's time for a half-serious question about what Heller thinks happened to Yossarian after *Catch-22* ended. ("He's still on the loose; he has not been caught.") And Heller has a bit of advice while he autographs his book for us: "Don't write before you're ready. A lot of people make that mistake. I was past 30 before I started *Catch-22.*"

Heller's inscription on the first page of my *Something Happened* copy is worthy of the mind that created Yossarian:

"With good wishes to you—and, of course, to me too. Joseph Heller."

J.R.R. Tolkien, with help from a bored copyboy, put Hobbiton on Page 9B

Dan Miller, a J.R.R. Tolkien devotee and ex-
Minneapolis Tribune *copyboy, paid this tribute*
to the author of the LOTR trilogy on Sept. 8,
1973.

Outwardly, the *Minneapolis Tribune* for Sunday, April 3, 1966, looked like most other Sunday newspapers, stuffed with news, comics and features. But deep inside, on Page 9B, in the tiny type that summarized the weather and temperatures in foreign cities, there was one curious listing. Placed in the proper alphabetical order between Copenhagen and London was a place called Hobbiton.

No matter where Hobbiton fit alphabetically, it most decidedly didn't fit in a listing of foreign temperatures. Hobbiton, it turns out, is a mythical village situated in The Shire, a small, out-of-the-way section of Middle Earth, a place that grew from the stunning imagination of one John Ronald Reuel Tolkien, an Oxford scholar, linguist and author of *The Lord of the Rings,* certainly the greatest fantasy epic of modern times.

Tolkien died last Sunday in his home in Bournemouth, England, 81 years after his birthday Jan. 3, 1892.

It's ironic that a particularly American holiday like Labor Day, with its preoccupations of picnics and traveling, should have obscured Tolkien's death, for it was American students who pushed the recalcitrant professor into the fore of an immense cult in the United States in the mid-1960s, a cult that Tolkien himself tried unsuccessfully to repudiate.

The listing of Hobbiton in the Minneapolis paper by a bored copyboy is only one example of how pervasive the cult was that surrounded *The Lord of the Rings.* Tolkien Societies sprouted through the United States, and members met regularly

177

to discuss the Rings story. With nearly 3 million sales backing it, the LOTR trilogy topped the U.S. paperback best-seller list in 1966, and booksellers everywhere agreed that LOTR had replaced *Catcher in the Rye* and *Lord of the Flies* as the ultimate literature of the American campus.

The Lord of the Rings epic is told in four books, the first of which, *The Hobbit,* was published in 1937 at the urging of Tolkien's friends, among them C. S. Lewis.

Hobbits, Tolkien explained, are little people, about a yard high, peace loving and affable, who flourished during the Third Age of Middle Earth, long before the memory of man. The hobbit in question is Bilbo Baggins, a wanderer who discovered by accident the One Ring of Power and brought it with him back to Hobbiton in The Shire.

The next three books became *The Lord of the Rings* trilogy, which was published in successive years in 1954–1956. The trilogy chronicles the War of the Ring, which brought an end to Middle Earth. It begins with the discovery of the true nature of Bilbo's bauble: The One Ring that gave its wearer power over every living thing but which by its nature corrupted all who attempted to use it. LOTR continues with the struggle to possess and control the Ring and the quest to destroy it.

No plot outline can possibly do justice to Tolkien's work, capturing the sweep of the narrative, the beauty of his prose and his inimitable power to evoke terror, joy, happiness, sorrow and satisfaction from reading. Most who have read the books have done so more than once, usually devouring the final volume nonstop so the entire trilogy can be started over again immediately.

But its popularity wasn't always so strong.

Popular legend in the mid-1960s held that Tolkien wrote *The Hobbit* as an amusement for his four children, but Tolkien late in life denied that story. He didn't dispute it earlier, he said, because "if you're a youngish man and you don't want to be made fun of, you say you're writing for children." He didn't particularly like *The Hobbit* with its condescending, childlike tone, as if a child's literary standards were somehow deficient compared with an adult's tastes. If *The Hobbit* is childlike—as it certainly is—Tolkien said it was the fault of his style at the time, "as if one were talking down to children. There's nothing my children loathed more."

The purpose of any fairy tale, Tolkien wrote in an essay on the subject, is not pretentiousness or imparting of a moral but to offer "a catch to the breath, a beat and lifting of the heart."

By Tolkien's own version, *The Hobbit* had its beginning on a blank page in a student's rather dull term paper that the professor was correcting at Oxford. Grateful for the break provided by the page, Tolkien penned the opening lines of the book, "In a hole in the ground there lived a hobbit." He said he never heard the word before.

Writing *The Lord of the Rings* took a little longer, 14 years all told before the first edition appeared.

A linguist of international repute, Tolkien enjoyed playing with words, creating them and, he said, the background to go with them. "The invention of language is the foundation" for LOTR, he said. "The stories were made rather to provide a world for the language than the reverse."

In the first of the LOTR trilogy, *The Fellowship of the Rings,* Tolkien switched his prose style from the condescending tone of *The Hobbit* to the grandeur of epic narrative that he would sustain throughout the trilogy, creating along the way in hundreds of pages of glossaries and appendices a geography of Middle Earth, history, lineages, languages, calendars and customs. The second and third volumes, respectively, are *The Two Towers* and *The Return of the King.*

Houghton Mifflin published the trilogy in England and sent a few copies to the United States, thinking the book to be something less than a commercial success. With no promotion by the publisher, the trilogy steadily grew in popularity among college students.

By the time Houghton Mifflin realized what it had, LOTR had lost its copyright and was pirated by Ace paperback books for a 1965 printing. Ian Ballantine, head of his own paperback publishing house, contacted Tolkien and offered to pay royalties if Tolkien would authorize and designate an official edition.

Tolkien gratefully agreed and in October, 1965, Ballantine

published its special edition with Tolkien's plea to readers: "Those who approve of courtesy (at least) to living authors will purchase it and no other." Although the Ace edition sold for 20 cents less than the Ballantine volumes, the Ballantine books outsold Ace, forcing Ace to negotiate royalty payments with Tolkien and to make up back payments.

Together, the two editions sold hundreds of thousands of copies in a few months.

Reviewers generally were favorable to LOTR, although some, notably Edmund Wilson, were less than enchanted. Wilson called LOTR "essentially a children's book . . . which has somehow got out of hand."

Still others objected to losing their cherished epic from a close intimate circle to the mass of hippies and others who scrawled clever little sayings like "Frodo Lives" on bathroom walls.

But despite the setbacks, the books survived and continue to be among the best-selling paperbacks.

Tolkien, however, resented the allegorical interpretations to which enthusiasts subjected the trilogy. In a letter to his publishers, he complained that the book is not about World War I or II or the Christ story. "It is not about anything but itself. Certainly it has no allegorical intentions, general, particular or topical, moral, religious or political."

A friend complained to a newspaper before Tolkien's death, "He hates the cult, and people who have absolutely nothing in common with him cashing in."

But the books had long passed from Tolkien's circle of friends to the public domain.

Science-fiction fans were among the first to appreciate Tolkien's feat, and at the World SF Convention in Toronto last week, author Lester del Rey praised Tolkien as "a man who enriched literature as very few men could do in their lifetime."

Isaac Asimov, author of what is perhaps the finest science-fiction trilogy ever written, the *Foundation* series, praised Tolkien as among the greatest writers of fantasy.

"He created a world so rich in detail," Asimov said, "so self-consistent that while reading it, it's difficult not to believe that

Middle Earth was the real world and that our own history was fiction."

Eugene Field eulogizes his dying contemporary, Victor Hugo, in 1885

Nearly 90 years before the death of Tolkien, the famed Eugene Field, first daily newspaper columnist in America, paid this tribute to Victor Hugo, who died shortly after Field's brief piece appeared in the May 19, 1885, Daily News.

"Hush," said they, "make no noise—the Poet is dying." And they stood reverentially and watched the coming of the death angel. Even the winds were hushed; they had stolen in softly and asked the morning sunbeams what it all meant, and the sunbeams had told the winds that the death angel was coming to take the Poet away, and so the winds stood still in great wonderment and sadness. But the death angel did not come. His grim shadow did not steal athwart the morning sunbeams nor chill the gentle winds that hovered round the Poet's couch. Withal the Poet was dying and there was sadness everywhere. Suddenly a thousand voices filled the chamber with sweetest music.

"How strange and yet how beautiful," thought the people. And the dying Poet thought so too, for a smile came and rested on his venerable face, and his lips moved as if they would echo that sweet music. They were the songs the Poet had sung; all over the world had they been and every human heart had they touched, and now they had come back to bear the Poet's soul away. What could be more beautiful than that?

And the Poet went with his songs, the hoary father with his children, and entered into his rest. From that still chamber was the weary soul borne away upon the thousand singing voices, and the clouds stopped in the sky to hear the wondrous music.

So shall they come to thee—thy songs, O Master Poet—and lulling thy a-wearied soul to sleep, shall bear thee with sweet music to eternity.

Derelict who lived in Chicago's subterranean expressway system in 1972, nick-named Lawrence of the Lower Level. Don Bierman / Daily News.

Life and death:
Lois Wille
Howard Vincent O'Brien
Charles Nicodemus
William F. Mooney
Arthur J. Snider
Arthur Gorlick
David Jackson
Saundra Saperstein
Harry Schaudt
Edan Wright
Dick Griffin

A lonely girl reaches for fame, tra-la-la-la, but it's unlikely lightning will strike Franceen

This article by Lois Wille in the May 26, 1970, Daily News *caused Mangam's Chateau temporarily to withdraw its advertising from the newspaper.*

There she goes, striding through the forest preserve, across the Des Plaines River, past trailer park and dry cleaner, long dark hair flying, strapless bra and hair spray in her shoulder bag— looking for fame and fortune in Lyons, Ill.

She's Franceen Devon, once Francine Goldstein, and some people have told her that when she hits certain notes she sounds like Barbra Streisand.

It's a long road from Sheepshead Bay in Brooklyn to a two-week singing engagement at Mangam's Chateau in Lyons, and it will be a lot longer before Franceen gets where she wants to go.

Where is that, Franceen? "I'd like to do Vegas, and TV— like the Johnny Carson show, and the really exclusive clubs, you know, the ones with little lamps on the tables and where the people aren't all bowling-league parties," she says, words rushing out in a soft whispery voice.

"And California. Have you ever been to California? I'd like to live there someday, like the Big Sur, or someplace."

So far, Franceen has never been west of 7850 Ogden, where hundreds of young singers, most of them forever unknown, have tried to shout down the noisy crowds at Mangam's supper club.

It's likely Franceen won't do any better than the rest. But then who can say she won't be one in a thousand? Couldn't lightning strike Franceen Devon?

After all, last year she had her hand read and the woman said in five years she'd be very well-known.

"And she didn't even know I was in show business," Franceen says, although the long black hair, made longer and fuller by a black fall; the big green eyes with the blue-shadowed lids; the white lipstick, and something about the eager, whispery voice may have hinted that she was trying.

It's 11 a.m. and she has just awakened in the bare beige room at Chicagoland Motel, a mile east of Mangam's, the room she can't stand.

"I'm going crazy with boredom; there's nothing to do here," she says. Just David Frost on TV, and a grilled-cheese sandwich and french fries at the coffee shop. Franceen won't eat meat because she loves animals too much ("I just couldn't pick up a chicken leg; I'd get sick"), and she can't afford the lobster tail at Mangam's. In fact, she can barely afford the 40 cents Mangam's charges her for tea in her dressing room.

On her bed is a paperback, *Crime and Punishment*. She just finished *Wuthering Heights*.

"I got this list at Brooklyn College that said, 'The 50 Great Novels,' " she explains. "I'm trying to go through them all."

Her manager, Carmine Scotti, comes in with coffee. A slight, mild-mannered man with nervous brown eyes, Scotti has had a number of failures trying to launch singers and dancers.

He doesn't really know why he's managing Franceen, except that he's so softhearted. "People in the business told me not to bother, but she had called me so often, and was trying so hard, and I didn't have the heart to say 'No.' "

They're both a little edgy today because an agent from William Morris might come out to hear Franceen. A few days ago they took a train to Chicago and made the rounds of all the theatrical booking agents, pleading with them to come.

"They ask what I do, and I say, 'All kinds—pop, rock, ballads, up tunes,' " says Franceen. "But it's hard, very hard. I'm 20. I'm nowhere.

"What agent wants to see Franceen Devon at Mangam's when he can hear Vikki Carr downtown?"

Carmine tries to soothe her. "That man from William Morris was very nice; it's just that he has to catch Liza Minnelli first at the Auditorium."

But it's hard to soothe Franceen today because last night was so awful. "It was a horrible audience—so crude, so vulgar.

One man ran up and tried to give me some money—tried to shove it in my hand. I turned my back and kept on singing, but I wanted to run off to the mountains somewhere.

"The audience? They didn't even notice. No one was watching. They couldn't have cared less if I was a singer or a juggler or a dancing poodle."

Neither Franceen nor Carmine is making money. The $700 she gets for two weeks at Mangam's, the most she has earned in her year of rather sporadic work, will go for voice lessons, musical arrangements and satin-and-sequined jumpsuits.

"I have a few other things going for me in New York. I get by," Carmine says. "And I've got no family to support. No ex-wives or illegitimate children or anything like that."

Franceen gets by because she lives at home in Brooklyn with her parents, Shirley and Max Goldstein, who call her every afternoon.

She really misses home, where her mother keeps her well rounded with pizza and knishes and she can cuddle Pixie, the little white poodle she misses desperately. "I love her more than anyone," she says. "She's like a person, only better. When I come home she sobs and cries, she's so happy."

Her father is in real estate, but when she was a little girl he had a stand on Coney Island and once sold custard to Cary Grant.

"The ghost rides, the scooter rides, the merry-go-round— they were all like next to my father's custard stand and I used to get on for nothing," Franceen says.

"They were run by old people, mostly ex-vaudeville, kooky, weird people. I loved them. The man made of alligator skin used to buy custard from my father all the time."

She and her friends saw all the Debbie Reynolds movies. "Debbie was so beautiful—her makeup, her gowns—so glamorous. The places she lived. I wanted to be part of that world.

"When we left the theater my friends would be back in Brooklyn but I was off dreaming in that Debbie Reynolds world."

In grade school Franceen was the best in her class at reciting poems, especially *If* by Rudyard Kipling.

A teacher suggested she audition for Manhattan's High School of the Performing Arts. She did one of Frankie's monologs from *Member of the Wedding*, and was accepted.

She gave herself new names—like Tiffany Griffin and Felicity Scott, with an accent mark over the "c" in Felicity until someone told her that didn't make sense.

On her lunch hour she would go to producers' offices. "I'd knock on doors, very timidly, and run away before anyone answered."

When she was 15 she had an enormous crush on a well-known actor-singer-composer, and after school she would hang around his stage door. "I thought he was such a genius," she says. "A true genius."

Then one day he invited her in to see his dressing room and said something lewd. Horrified, Franceen fled home to Brooklyn. "I was only 15," she says, still shocked.

She doesn't get crushes on actors anymore. "They're not all perverted, but they all have their hang-ups." Instead, she gets crushes on television newsmen, who she thinks must be the wisest, most witty men in the world. "And noble. I like the idea of a noble man." She especially likes Sander Vanocur and Frank Reynolds. She hasn't met them, but she has a girl friend who once met Peter Jennings at a party.

Her 19th year was spent waiting in line for auditions, sometimes getting called back, sometimes "getting looked over like cattle at an auction," but never getting a job. She did earn $8.32 for two weeks in a play where the hat was passed during intermission. She can't remember the name of the show, but she played a statue and wore a white sheet.

Finally came the Big Break: An agent paid her $25 to sing in a military hospital in Queens. The boys liked her, so the agent got her two weeks at a motel cocktail lounge in Shrewsbury, Mass., and at the Parakeet Club in Brooklyn.

After pleading with dozens of agents and prospective managers to come to hear her, she finally got a "yes" from Carmine.

"I thought she was bad, to be honest with you," he says. "But she was trying so hard, and she looked good up there."

Franceen does look good: a romantically pretty face, with

high cheekbones and big green eyes, and a bountiful body. Her voice is small but it is sometimes dramatic, and her eagerness is appealing.

After dates at half a dozen clubs in New Jersey and Massachusetts, Carmine arranged an audition with comedian Rodney Dangerfield, whose new Manhattan club is a good showcase for new talent. He liked her *Spinning Wheel* and *Light My Fire*, and Franceen calls that evening "the most fantastic moment of my life."

Dangerfield signed her for a week—joy! But it turned out to be the last week in December—heartbreak! Agents don't work during holidays, and Carmine couldn't get anyone to hear Franceen.

Every so often through the afternoon Franceen stretches her mouth around a big plastic bottle. Her voice coach says that keeps her face limber.

"And I blow," she says "Listen." The sound that comes out is something like a Bronx cheer or a raspberry. "It cleans you out," she explains. "Try it, it looks easy, but it isn't."

She insists, so it is necessary to try. Sure enough, the peculiar sound is hard to duplicate.

Carmine smiles. "She's so serious about this. She works very hard. Any little suggestion, she'll take it up right away."

"She's a good kid, a very nice kid. No temperament."

The long afternoon won't end. Franceen is nervous, nibbling on a silver-nailed finger, blowing the raspberry, brushing her long hair, asking for the correct time.

Finally, about 7 p.m., it's time to spread the dark makeup over her fine olive skin, and pin on the long fall. Carmine goes to the motel office to ask Mildred, the receptionist, if anyone is heading to Mangam's. "Sorry, honey," Mildred says. "Not tonight."

That means walking a mile along Ogden Av. and past the forest preserve and across the river, because a cab is so much money. But Franceen doesn't mind because the first blocks border Riverside, and she loves looking down the winding streets at the tall trees and "the very fine homes in there."

Mangam's is already packed with celebrating diners as

Franceen squeezes her way through to her dressing room, with its worn rug and the yellowed sheet hanging over the windows. Next door is a bigger room where the chorus line puts on feathers and sequins.

Franceen doesn't associate with them. The first night she was there one of the girls mentioned that the chorus has to work in the bar until 2:30 a.m., and Franceen was shocked.

"I said I was going to report to AGVA [American Guild of Variety Artists], our union, that they had to hustle drinks. But then they all got on me and said I better not, and besides I had it all wrong—they like staying in the bar until 2:30."

At 8:30 p.m., in her black satin jumpsuit with the tight halter top, Franceen bounces out into the spotlight. The audience is momentarily intrigued. But the music is so loud her opening *So Good to See You* is lost.

By the time she begins *Spinning Wheel* the diners are shouting and laughing again, the band plays louder to drown them out and poor Franceen is overwhelmed.

Then comes *Those Were the Days, My Friend*. Finally, when she gets to the tra-la-la-la part, the audience joins in and she has their attention.

That's all. She runs off the stage, tight-lipped, near tears.

"See what I mean?" she says. "Listen to them." She pulls a ring on and off, pulls a blue brush through her hair. "See, what I did was all surface. I didn't perform. I just made motions. I have a beautiful, beautiful ballad, but it would have been butchered.

"All those idiots want is that stupid tra-la-la-la song. If I had done *Bye-bye Blackbird*, they'd have been out of their minds."

To calm her down, Carmine takes her to a small table near her dressing room where they watch the comedian, the star of the show.

His routine is mainly about homosexuality and the thrills of going for an Army physical. It goes on and on. The audience adores it. Especially the women, who shriek and whoop at every sexual euphemism.

Franceen is revolted. "The Great Silent Majority, that's what they are," she says. "I'll bet they all love Agnew. And they think the college kids are terrible. Listen to them. It really turns my stomach, it really does."

Wait till the second show, Franceen keeps saying. Then the prom kids come, and they're really sweet. They listen. "The little darlings; wait till you see them. I'll do my ballad for them."

Sure enough, about 11 p.m. the boys in white jackets and girls in corsages arrive. But just then the lights go out. And stay out. A power failure in Lyons. The microphones won't work, so Franceen's second show is canceled.

And, in the dark, she tears the filmy brown-and-white chiffon gown she wears for the prom kids. Her best gown.

And she wants to leave, but so far the hatcheck girl hasn't found anyone to give them a lift back to the motel.

And the agent didn't come.

Howard Vincent O'Brien shares his family's personal tragedy with readers of the Daily News

Howard Vincent O'Brien was a famous Daily News *columnist who joined the staff shortly after World War I and continued until his death in 1947. He shared a deep personal tragedy with readers with this group of columns, which spanned three years and four days of his life.*

Jan. 8, 1942—There was no band, no flags, no ceremonial. It wasn't even dramatic. A car honked outside and he said, "Well, I guess that's for me." He picked up his little bag, and his mother said, "You haven't forgotten your gloves?"

He kissed his mother and held out his hand to me. "Well, so long," he said. I took his hand but all I could say was "Good luck!"

The door slammed and that was that—another boy gone to war.

I had advised waiting for the draft—waiting at least until he was required to register. I had pointed out that he was not yet of age. He had smiled at that, and assured me that his mind was made up. He wanted peace, he said. Without peace, what good was living?

There was finality in the way he said this—a finality at once grim and gentle. I said no more about waiting.

After the door closed behind him I went upstairs. I went to what had been his room. It was in worse chaos than usual. His bureau was littered—an incredible collection of things, letters, keys, invitations to parties he would not attend.

Clothing was scattered about—dancing pumps, a tennis racquet, his collection of phonograph records, his trumpet gleaming in its case.

192

I went then to my room. On the wall was a picture of a little boy, his toothless grin framed in tawny curls—the same boy who had just taken my hand and said, "Well, so long."

Not much time, I thought, between the making of that picture and the slamming of the front door. Not much more than a decade.

Suddenly a queer thing happened. Objects came alive, whispered to me. The house was full of soft voices. They led me up to the attic—to a box of toy soldiers, a broken music rack, a football helmet, a homemade guitar, schoolbooks, class pictures, a stamp album, a penny bank with the lid pried off—ancient history, long hidden under dust.

The voices led me on to a filing case and a folder stuffed with papers—report cards, letters (among them the wail of an exasperated teacher: "Though he looks like an angel ... "), telegrams, passports, a baptismal certificate, a ribbon won in a track meet, faded photographs (one taken on the memorable first day of long pants), a bit of golden hair.

I sat down and thought how time had flown. Why, it was only yesterday when I had held him in my arms! That, somehow, made me remember all the scoldings I had given him, the preachments, the exhortation to a virtue and wisdom I did not myself possess. . . .

I thought, too, of that last inarticulate "good luck," that last perfunctory handclasp; and I wished that I had somehow been able to tell him how much I really loved him. Had he perhaps penetrated my brusque reserve? Had he perhaps guessed what was in my heart?

And then I thought, What fools we are with our children—always plotting what we shall make of them, always planning for a future that never comes, always intent on what they may be, never accepting what they are!

Well, curlyhead, you're a man now, bearing your bright new shield and spear. I hated to see you go out of my house and close the door behind you, but I think I would not have halted you if I could. I salute you, sir. I cannot pretend that I am not sad; but I am proud, too. So long.

Nov. 2, 1943—It was a bright October morning. Nature

smiled through her veil of green and gold and scarlet.

I had no appointments—nothing exciting on the day's calendar. The infant was being readied for school. The cook was dressing for her day out. Grandma was starting for the grocery.

Then the phone rang—four times before anybody answered it.

There was a choking silence at the dear, familiar voice. "Only an hour between trains, Mom. Yes, it was sudden. These things always are. Yes, I'm committed. No, I can't tell you. England, I think."

There was a mad scramble into city clothes, a race for the train, a ride that never seemed to end.

He was waiting for us at the office—so straight, so gravely gentle. The navigator's wings gleamed on his tunic and there was a droll little wisp of a mustache under his nose, hardly visible against his clear skin.

In one respect he hadn't changed. He was broke. He grinned when he told us.

He kissed his mother and patted her on the shoulder. Her lip trembled, but she caught herself quickly. "Your face needs washing," she said, just as if time had stood still.

Furtively he glanced at the watch on his slender wrist. "It wouldn't do to be late," he said. "The Army might call it desertion."

The hands on the station clock seemed to be spinning. We talked against time, pressing out the words. There was so much to be said, so many questions to be asked. But one forgot what one wanted to know. Or perhaps one really didn't want to know. My fingers shook a little as I wrote down his serial number.

We skirted the reefs on which our thoughts were. We wandered off to other waters—aimless but safer. We talked about the new gyro compass, the accuracy of flak, the merits of the B-17 against the Liberator, the cold at 30,000 feet, the chance of a broken leg when bailing out.

One listening might have thought we were really interested.

The silence grew longer. We just looked at him and he looked away—not at us, not at the restaurant walls. He looked far away and I do not know what he saw.

He was close to us, then—and oh, so very far away! I thought of Noel Coward's poem about the bombers droning in the night—I could remember only one line—something about "we'll never know."

I asked him if he would be glad to find it was England. He said he'd rather go to the Pacific. "I don't think I like Japs," he said.

That was all he said. I think his mind was on his school days in Germany—on his classmates, especially the blond, blue-eyed boy who led the Boy Scout troop with which he went camping in the Alps . . . the boy who held him when he slipped on the edge of a crevasse.

There was a long silence. He looked at the clock. "You have all the dope—about the insurance, I mean?"

"Yes," I said. "I have it all."

"Then I think I'd better be going," he said.

He kissed his mother as he got into the taxi. Then he did a strange thing. He turned and touched his lips lightly to my cheek. And with a faint little smile he said to his mother, "Don't let the Ancient One worry too much, will you, Mom?"

That was all. For a minute I felt a little sick and my eyes hurt. Then I went back to the day's work.

March 23, 1944—There is a line of Walt Whitman's—something about life being a matter of surmounting one hill, only to find another in the way. I have found this true. But I have found also that with each hill climbed there is a new vista, a broader horizon.

One who gets that red-starred telegram: THE SECRE-TARY OF WAR DESIRES TO EXPRESS HIS DEEP REGRET. . .is plunged into the Valley of the Shadow.

You can brace yourself for that message. You can, in a way, be ready. But it rocks you. It takes you off your feet, no matter how firmly they have been planted against it.

But there is work to be done. The show has to go on. You have to laugh—and be laughed at. The boy who joined the clouds would scorn you if your altered your course or turned your back. He didn't.

So you carry on. You start climbing the next hill. And then

you find something you weren't prepared for. Your pain eases. You see a strange brightness in the sky. Warmth creeps through your chilled heart. It is not the numbness of resignation. It is an active sense of well-being.

Suddenly you realize what has happened. It is the letters. They come from close friends and from old but distant ones; from those you had thought indifferent or hostile; from strangers and from people who signed no names; from the great and, from the humble.

This fragrant bloom of sympathy—and you recall the Greek root of this word: "suffering with"—fills you with awe.

In one letter was a phrase to remember: "God knows no accidents." As earthlings, it is hard for us to grasp this. Wailing, we plead with the empty heavens to answer a querulous, self-pitying "Why?"

It is not for us to know the plan and purpose of things. We cannot measure what we get in exchange for our blood and tears. We can only "wonder what the vintners buy one half so precious as the stuff they sell."

We cannot balance the sweet against the bitter, but those outstretched hands of compassion are proof that there is a balance. If war reveals the beast in man, it also reveals the angel. In the depths of the valley one can best see the sun on the hilltop. Under the thorns of hate one finds the blossom of love. In the last grim climax of strife, one achieves peace. Tangled with brutality and chaos one comes upon kindness and affection.

You pay high for what you learn from that War Department telegram. The new light hurts your eyes. But the letters that come afterward—they are worth their cost.

Telegrams are coming to German homes, too—letters afterward. German boys are melting into mist and those who loved them search the flaming skies for an answer to the riddle.

Is there an answer? Well, there is faith and hope and perhaps, in the centuries yet unborn, more charity. And there is that flood of gentle sympathy, sign and portent man is climbing slowly toward the stars. In the hot fire of sorrow shared, the dross of despair is burned away.

More boys will grow to strength and beauty, only to wink

out like sparks in the night. More bubbles form and glow and vanish whence they came.

Their memorial is the deep-buried spring of goodness uncovered by their passing.

Jan. 12, 1945—The box came by express the day after Christmas. The children thought it was a belated gift from Santa Claus and jumped up and down, clapping their hands. They thought it was a doll.

The carton was the right size for a doll, but I knew it wasn't a doll. Dolls don't come from the Army Effects Bureau, Kansas City Quartermaster Depot. Besides, I had a letter.

Nobody but the children wanted to open the carton; so it was taken to the attic and for days stayed out of sight if not out of mind. Then, Sunday afternoon, when I was alone in the house, I got a pair of metal shears and snipped the steel tape with which the carton was bound.

It was packed just as he might have done it himself—the coats and trousers neatly folded, the socks and handkerchiefs and underwear all helter-skelter.

On top was the made-to-order dress uniform, as fresh as the day it had come from the tailor. He had been so proud of this extravagance, admiring himself in the close-fitting tunic; and he had looked so smart when he stood with long fingers around his wasp waist, buttons gleaming like fire against the dark green. He had so little time to be proud.

In the corner was a pair of officer's shoes, almost like new. Even less worn were his summer things. He saw no summers in Britain. His work was done before he could hear the skylark or see the meadows "knee-deep in June."

At the bottom of the carton was a tattered envelope, stuffed with orders and a diploma of graduation from a Louisiana training school.

Beside it was a leather-bound diary, given him by his mother, with her name on the flyleaf. Eagerly I leafed through its pages. They were blank!

The only other record of his life was a couple of flashlight pictures of himself and comrades—all laughing—snapped in New York "spots."

Under them was a small paper bag, torn in the corner. In it were the following:

A jeweler's ring box—with no ring.

The silver wings of a navigator.

A wristwatch, minus crystal, which had stopped at 23 minutes to 9.

A pair of sunglasses.

A Yellow Cab identification tag, No. 3233.

Three coins—a nickel, a dime and a threepenny piece.

The winter twilight was settling as I finished the inventory, and my nostrils ached with the sick-sweetish odor of disinfectant. Methodically I unpinned the gold lieutenant's bars and the navigator's wings and snipped off the buttons.

Then I sat staring at the box in which these things had come. It was such a small box to hold all the laughter and tears, all the hope and apprehension, which had been packed into it. So much gaiety and tenderness, so much generosity and fun, such talent and eager inquiry, such virile beauty. . . . It was hard to believe it had all vanished like the song of a bird at dusk, leaving only a little heap of clothes and a torn paper bag.

It was incredible that of high adventure in a far land nothing was left but a threepence and a watch that had stopped ticking.

'It would kill her if she had to stay back with the younger children'

A veteran reporter, Charles Nicodemus, was working the 4 p.m.-to-midnight shift when he developed this exclusive story, published May 22, 1976.

Last September, when 13-year-old Gloria Covington's brother Willie, 15, shot himself to death in their home at 5642 S. Emerald, it left Gloria profoundly shaken.

Willie had had learning problems, and had been sent to a special boarding school. He hated it. And when he learned last fall that he'd have to go back, he took a .32-caliber pistol to the basement and put a bullet through his left temple.

Gloria was just starting seventh grade at St. Martin's School, 5838 S. Princeton, at the time of Willie's death. She'd been having academic problems since her transfer from public school the year before. Willie's death just made the situation worse.

A tall, high-strung, combative girl, she had been very close to Willie. His death left her depressed, distracted, unable to concentrate.

Her seventh-grade teacher, Emanuel Williams, worked hard with her—on math and reading in particular. Finally, in the spring her grades starting picking up.

But it was still slow going, and she was still very far behind.

As the end of the spring term approached, school officials pondered whether to keep her back for further seventh-grade work or promote her to eighth grade, and hope that the pace of improvement would quicken.

Gloria was almost the biggest in her class. That was a strain —standing out, feeling different. And holding her back in seventh grade—that would make the height problem even worse.

After grappling with the question for days, Williams finally decided to visit the Covington home and take up the problem with Gloria's parents. He talked to Gloria's mother, Addie, and to Gloria, too.

Gloria was almost frantic at the prospect of having to stay behind, while her classmates moved ahead.

"I'll go to summer school," she volunteered, desperately. "I'll work extra hard. I'll catch up, honest I will," she pleaded.

Williams warned that passing her when she wasn't ready really would be doing Gloria no favor. St. Martin's is very conscientious, he explained. The school cares about each child. No student is passed just for the sake of passing.

But summer school would be the answer, Gloria repeated. "Just give me a chance," she implored. "You'll see."

Mrs. Covington told Williams she would talk it over carefully with her husband.

When Martlee Covington got home from work, the parents sent Gloria up to her room and talked the situation over. Finally, they agreed.

With the strong support St. Martin's was providing, if they, too, pushed Gloria hard, she'd have a chance to pull even with her classmates.

So they would call the school Friday and say, "Yes, promote Gloria."

"You know," Gloria's mother told Covington, "it would kill her if she had to stay back with the younger children, big as she is."

She called upstairs to Gloria, to tell her the good news. There was no answer. She called again. Silence.

Anxiously, the Covingtons hurried upstairs. Gloria's bedroom was empty. But the closet door was slightly ajar.

Inside was Gloria, crumpled on the floor. In her hand was a tiny, two-shot, .22-caliber pistol her mother kept. The girl had wrapped it in a towel— apparently to deaden the sound.

Then she had shot herself in the head.

"She thought we'd say, 'No,' and she couldn't stand it," the dazed Covington told homicide investigators.

Said a red-eyed Mrs. Covington, "I guess she's gone to join Willie."

Reporter William F. Mooney answered the telephone and heard James Lee's last words

In March, 1968, the Daily News *had covered the tragic death of 9-year-old Shirley Ellen Lee. On April 17, reporter William F. Mooney talked on the telephone for the last time with the dead girl's father.*

James Lee, the Chicagoan who gave away all his money and possessions in memory of his 9-year-old daughter, Tuesday gave his life.

Lee committed suicide by shooting himself in the head in a phone booth of a Wilson Av. tavern while talking to me.

"If I don't finish this up, I'll be a bum," he said.

"If I don't do this with dignity, I'll have to bum dimes to buy drinks. That would not be fair to the memory of my little girl."

Those were his last words. There was a sob, then a shot.

Police, who had been alerted by another reporter who had traced the call, entered the booth and found Lee dying of a single wound.

Only a few hours earlier Lee had visited St. Lucas Cemetery where his only child, Shirley Ellen, is buried. Fifty dozen red and white gladiolus, the last gift he could give her, blanket the grave.

Then Lee gave away his white Thunderbird auto to a friend, and went to a bar, where, as he expressed it, "I thought things over."

Shirley Ellen died in a fire March 4 that struck the Lee apartment at 4400 N. Racine.

Since then Lee had stripped himself of all his possessions, seeking to make a lasting memorial for her.

His wife died when Shirley Ellen was only 2 years old, and

Lee's entire life was wrapped up in her.

He gave to the Lutheran Church of St. Philip, where Shirley Ellen attended school; the 19-apartment building, and another two-flat he owned.

A plaque in memory of Shirley Ellen was placed on each building and at seven charitable institutions to which Lee made contributions.

Lee called the *Daily News* to speak to reporter Richard Stout, whose story about Lee's gift was picked up by the national wire services and given nationwide publicity. Stout was on an assignment, so I took the call on the city desk.

When Lee almost casually mentioned that he planned to kill himself, I had another reporter start checking the telephone call. The reporter alerted police, who sent two squads to the tavern at 1018 W. Wilson.

I kept talking to him trying to stall and at the same time talk him out of his plan.

He frequently sobbed as he told how he planned to kill himself.

"I planned to carry out my plan last night at the cemetery," he told me. "But things pile up. I'm real flighty, and it's hard for me to co-ordinate."

At another point he said:

"I've got to get a real good sleep."

Then he said:

"It looks like it's getting dark."

He sobbed, and continued:

"I'll wind it up tonight. I want peace. I haven't got a penny, not a penny. I haven't eaten all day, but I've had a couple of shots.

"If I don't finish this up, I'll be a bum.

"If I don't do this with dignity, I'll have to bum dimes to buy drinks. That would not be fair to the memory of my little girl."

There was a sob, then a shot.

The phone receiver banged and echoed several times against the side of the phone booth.

There was some unidentified noise, probably as someone pushed open the phone-booth door.

Then a policeman was heard to say:

"He shot himself."

James Lee was dead.

Arthur J. Snider reveals 'a tragic case of human error' at Pontiac Osteopathic Hospital

When Daily News *science editor Arthur J. Snider called the Oakland County (Mich.) prosecutor about the surgical deaths at Pontiac Osteopathic Hospital, the prosecutor said: "It is incredible these deaths were not reported to me or the police." This story, published Dec. 4, 1965, won a National Headliner Award.*

PONTIAC, Mich.—There are three other children in the William Ketchum family, but 12-year-old Michael, the oldest, was especially close to his father, a 33-year-old decorator.

Both had a love for scouting, Ketchum as a scoutmaster, Michael as a Life Scout, only two merit badges away from Eagle.

Father and son also shared an interest in sports. They swam and hunted together and rooted for the Detroit Tigers.

They shared something else—a double hernia, a family characteristic. Dad had his repaired and Michael wanted the operation so he could continue his favorite sport of tumbling.

"Sure, Mike," consented E. T. Hunter, osteopathic physician and the family's longtime medical counselor.

The operation was scheduled to take advantage of the Thanksgiving holiday.

"Mike didn't want to miss school," said Ketchum. "He was a good student. . . . "

All evening long, Kimberly Anne Bruneel, a robust 8-year-old with dark hair and blue eyes, had been in distress. Her usual gay manner had given way to repeated cringes of pain:

"Mommy, my tummy hurts bad."

M. M. Jaffee, the family's osteopathic physician, told Mrs. Oscar Bruneel: "It looks like appendicitis. Let's put her in the hospital. . . . "

About 10 miles away, in a quiet residential area of Pontiac,

Laurea Covington, 24, was also having abdominal pains. They had been recurring over several weeks.

Russell Erwin, osteopathic physician, had advised a laparotomy (exploratory operation). Mrs. Covington didn't want to leave her two small children. But the pain was becoming unbearable. She agreed to surgery. . . .

Within a matter of hours, Mike Ketchum, Kimberly Bruneel and Laurea Covington entered Pontiac Osteopathic Hospital for routine surgery. They had never met but they were destined to be joined in a fateful chain of circumstances that ended in tragedy.

Pontiac Osteopathic Hospital, a block-long, concrete, brick-and-glass-walled building, is on the edge of the city's thriving business district.

Its growth has been phenomenal. Starting 12 years ago with 26 beds, it is now the largest osteopathic hospital in the nation with 406 beds, 28 departments, a medical staff of 120, a nursing staff of 300, including 50 registered nurses and a corps of 30 residents and interns.

Last year the hospital admitted 10,992 patients. Of the 212 who died in the hospital, 123 were autopsied, a rate double that of the national average. The medical staff operated on 4,960 patients, administered anesthetic 5,612 times, delivered 935 babies.

Typical of a large hospital, it performs sophisticated procedures such as radioactive scanning, electroencephalography, exchange transfusions and arteriograms. Sixteen people staff the inhalation-therapy department. Closed-circuit television soon will permit patients to talk to their families in the lobby.

There are seven operating rooms, a recovery room and a special service unit for intensive nursing care.

A nonprofit enterprise with a $5.4 million investment, the hospital is managed by a board consisting of two doctors and seven laymen, including D. C. Pence, former president of the Michigan Bar Assn. and the hospital's attorney.

But autocratic control is exerted by a veteran of several hospital administrative positions, Harry H. Whitlow, the ramrod-erect, neatly dressed hospital founder.

The assistant administrator is his son, Jack H. Whitlow. Another son, F. F. Whitlow, has just completed osteopathic training and in the first two months of practice has been averaging about 15 patients a day.

Largely because of the hospital's influence, osteopathy has flourished in this area. Land has been purchased on the edge of the city for a $60 million osteopathic college to be financed by contributions of osteopaths.

Pontiac Osteopathic Hospital is seldom in the newspapers because it conducts no fund-raising drives or research of the type that makes headlines.

But it hit the front pages on Feb. 7, 1963, when a mother of six died in an anesthetic explosion in the operating room. A volatile gas, cyclopropane, was administered while a cautery procedure was taking place.

The disaster did not destroy the community's faith in the hospital. Occupancy rate is 90 per cent and there is frequently a waiting list for elective surgery.

Perhaps if Margaret Lauringer hadn't received word of a death in her family, Michael, Kimberly and Mrs. Covington would be alive today.

The case history of a triple tragedy must begin with that telephone call Wednesday, Nov. 17.

Mrs. Lauringer, a nurse anesthetist, determined that before departing she could keep her promise to Dr. I. B. Posner to anesthetize his young patient for a tonsillectomy.

Having a preference for ether, she poured the liquid into the inhalation machine in operating room No. 1 and applied the mask to the 15-year-old patient. The tonsils were snipped out and an uneventful recovery followed.

Mrs. Lauringer quickly changed into street clothes and left the hospital after asking Stanley Abrams, 42-year-old assistant chief anesthesiologist, to cover.

For the next patient, 2-year-old Michael Hutton, who was to have not only a tonsillectomy but also an impacted tooth extracted, Abrams decided to use Fluoromar, a volatile liquid with a potency similar to that of ether.

Looking about for a container in which to drain the ether

from the anesthetic machine, he grabbed a near-empty flask of Surital, a popular injectable anesthetic administered 2,150 times by the hospital last year.

The used jar, to be thrown out with the day's discard, contained 20 cubic centimeters of Surital dissolved in distilled water.

After distilling the ether into it, Abrams replaced the rubber seal to prevent the pungent odor of ether from permeating the operating room. The bottle was returned to a shelf for his later disposal.

On Thursday, Nov. 18, at 7:30 a.m., Ruby Brantley, 46, was wheeled into operating room No. 1 for a gall-bladder operation. Awaiting her were Lloyd Goodwin, chief anesthesiologist, and L. J. Huddle, surgeon.

Goodwin shook the bottle of Surital he spotted on the shelf. There seemed to be plenty for the operation. He tipped it, inserted the needle through the rubber seal, withdrew several c.c.s of yellowish fluid and injected it into the vein.

Mrs. Brantley escaped death by a quirk of ether's physical characteristic. Lighter than water, it quickly rises to the surface. When the Surital bottle was tipped, the ether raced away from the rubber seal. The syringe withdrew only Surital.

The next patient, Patricia Thomas, 39, was doubly fortunate. A suspected malignancy in the left breast turned out to be only a cyst. And once again, the anesthetic syringe picked up the Surital.

However, a brief siege of coughing and labored breathing on the operating table temporarily interrupted the surgery. It was a harbinger of ill events to come.

A few drops of ether had apparently entered the syringe. Still unsuspecting, Goodwin and B. F. Dickensen, the surgeon, were relieved when the untoward reaction suddenly ended.

But luck had run out for Kimberly Anne Bruneel, patient No. 3.

When nurse anesthetist Joan Booth withdrew the anesthetic from the fateful bottle, the remaining yellowish fluid was mostly ether.

As the abdomen was closed, Kimberly developed a violent

attack of coughing. Her breathing rate fell rapidly. Her face turned blue.

Doctors recognized a major emergency on their hands. Cardiac massage was instituted. A tracheal tube made certain of no windpipe obstruction. A bronchoscope was introduced. The child continued to sink.

Dr. Jaffee, assisting in the operation, was dispatched to tell Mrs. Bruneel to summon the other children. He was ashen white.

"Kim's in trouble . . . " he blurted, and then broke down.

Kimberly died at 1:30 p.m. She never made it off the operating table.

Dr. Jaffee again was sent to request permission for a postmortem. "They can't understand what happened," he tried to explain to the stunned family.

Joseph Maxwell, a gentle pathologist with deep-set eyes and thinning hair, caught the acrid odor of ether on entering the autopsy room, but he quickly dismissed it from his mind. Ether is a familiar smell in a hospital.

Several days later, he was to say in self-reproach: "I feel foolish."

A meticulous dissection revealed nothing except that the lungs were filled with fluid.

"Pulmonary edema. Etiology (cause) unknown," he concluded.

Late that night, Kimberly's body was taken to the mortuary and the cleaning crew prepared operating room No. 1 for Friday's schedule.

Dr. Goodwin arrived early for Mike Ketchum's 7:30 hernia operation. He prepared a fresh bottle of Surital by dissolving five grams of powder in a pint of distilled water and placed it on the shelf next to the ether-laden solution.

Mike was wheeled in and Goodwin reached for the nearest bottle. It was the fateful flask.

Only minutes after injection, Mike began to squirm. But Dr. Paul W. Trimmer managed the hernia repair and sent him on to the recovery room.

As Laurea Covington was rolled in, Goodwin stood deep in

thought. He had now seen a succession of strange reactions on the operating table. Could it be the anesthetic? Could a bad batch have come from the pharmaceutical house?

He decided to proceed with caution, introducing only a minimal amount into Mrs. Covington's vein. Almost immediately, she began coughing. Her lungs began to fill with fluid.

Abruptly he swept up the two Surital bottles, one of them the untouched fresh batch, dumped them in a wastebasket and proceeded to mix a new solution.

As Trimmer was placing the final sutures in the abdomen of Mrs. Covington, whose laparotomy had revealed a diseased appendix, he was urgently summoned to the recovery room. Michael Ketchum was sinking.

The father, puzzled over the delay in Michael's return, found his way to the recovery room and looked through the glass. Michael saw him and smiled weakly. Minutes later, he died.

Mrs. Covington was failing fast, too. Trimmer rushed to her side. Resuscitative attempts were futile.

The surgical suite was in near panic. Goodwin revealed his belief the Surital was faulty. Trimmer, his nerves frayed, turned to Goodwin unbelievingly and exploded:

"You suspect Surital and you dispose of it?" He retrieved the bottles from the basket.

Administrator Whitlow ordered the operating room locked and all drugs, including the discarded Surital, brought to his office.

Meanwhile, pathologist Maxwell telephoned Dr. Bernard Berman, county health officer who doubles as county coroner. Berman listened briefly, called the deaths a "therapeutic misadventure" and told the hospital to proceed with its own autopsies.

Again the findings: Pulmonary edema, cause unknown.

No mention of the staggering ether smell was made on the autopsy report.

By now it was clear to Whitlow the hospital was in deep trouble. Summoning a malpractice-insurance agent, he was instructed to say nothing and leave town for the weekend.

As a new week dawned Monday, new patients entered surgery at Pontiac Osteopathic Hospital and returned to their rooms without incident. There was no longer ether-contaminated Surital on the premises. The nightmare in the operating room was over. It was back to business as usual.

At midafternoon Monday, prosecutor S. Jerry Bronson was thumbing through some briefs in his fifth-floor suite of the multimillion-dollar Oakland County courthouse.

His secretary put through a long-distance call. It was a *Chicago Daily News* reporter relaying a tip. Did he know there were three mysterious deaths the previous Thursday and Friday in Pontiac Osteopathic Hospital? Bronson was stunned.

"It is incredible these deaths were not reported to me or the police," he said later. "The hospital is two miles from my office, and I have to learn of this from a newspaper 300 miles away. It is doubtful we would ever have learned of the matter had not the *Daily News* told us."

Bronson, a brisk 35-year-old elected official, has been in office less than a year. His name became known throughout the state in his first weeks as prosecutor when he succeeded in convicting a husband of murder after the wife had officially been declared a suicide 14 months earlier. An exhumation of the body revealed she had been strangled and then strung up.

The occurrence prompted him to demand of the state legislature a medical examiner's system.

The first Democratic prosecutor in Republican Oakland County in 36 years and the second in a century, Bronson, by his vigor, has attracted a group of 15 assistant prosecutors to fight crime in this fastest-growing county in Michigan. Its 750,000 population is second only to Wayne's (Detroit).

Two of the assistants were ideally suited to conduct the investigation into the hospital tragedy. They are Walter Schmier, a disarming veteran of many court battles and skilled as an interrogator, and Timothy Dineen, a specialist in hospital affairs and a former troubleshooter for Blue Cross.

Bronson's announcement that an investigation was to be launched forced the first comment from Pontiac Osteopathic Hospital.

"We were intending to come in on Tuesday to talk to Mr. Bronson," said Pence, the hospital's lawyer. "There was no intention to conceal the facts. When you call in a prosecutor, it indicates you agree someone was guilty of a crime."

After a two-week probe, Bronson announced Friday that no criminal prosecution would be undertaken.

"It was a case of human error," he concluded, "but an error made possible by deplorable neglect of proper safeguards for the lives of patients."

He ticked off a series of failures. Elimination of any one could have prevented the tragedy or nipped it along the way:

• Failure to adopt strict procedures in emptying an anesthetic machine.

• Failure to discard the contents of a used anesthetic bottle.

• Failure to determine the contents of an anesthetic bottle or under what circumstances it was placed in the operating room.

(New rules adopted by the hospital forbid any further batch mixing of Surital. Individual quantities will be prepared.)

• Failure in communication between surgeon and anesthesiologist on type of anesthetic used.

• Failure to raise questions about ether smell in autopsy room after the first death.

• Failure of coroner to investigate the deaths. Permitting a hospital to perform its own autopsy in questionable deaths makes it a judge of its own actions.

Bronson also had some advice for hospitals who seek to cover up a calamity:

"Public confidence is fostered by thoroughness and honesty in bringing all facts out into the open, and not trying to cover up or mystify in the mistaken notion that a quick burial will prevent criticism."

Five men were dead, and
none of them had last names

*Reporter Arthur Gorlick covered this tragedy
in a Chicago flophouse on Christmas Day,
1965.*

A trickle of yellow wine dripped through the two-day beard of
Eddie Talkowski's scarred chin.

He held a pint bottle in one hand, a scrawny cat called Pepe
in the other and sat on the edge of his sagging cot in the Grange
Hotel at 1016 W. Madison.

"Big Nick was my best friend," Talkowski said. "He was my
best friend—and I didn't even know his last name."

Big Nick was Nicholas Davis, 49, one of five men who died
mysteriously in the Skid Row hotel Christmas Day.

For all that seemed to matter, none of the five had last
names.

"They were drinkers. That's all you know about anybody
down here," said William Rundy, a room clerk.

For about two hours, Davis had lain sprawled on the floor
of the $1-a-night flophouse lobby, where faded brown paint
curls away from the walls, exposing spots of gray plaster.

There were 35 or so other men in the lobby. They sat drinking on hardwood chairs lined in rows facing a blaring television
set and slightly bent, sadly blinking Christmas tree. None of
them noticed Davis.

Or, if they did notice, they didn't care.

"He was drinking," one of the men said. "He was celebrating Christmas. We all thought he was just drunk. Guys fall down
all the time here."

Seated a row behind Davis, his glassy eyes still fixed on the
television screen, was Stanley Gonzola, 58. He was dead, too.

It was later, after a search, that the bodies of three other
men were found.

Two of them were on cots in their 6-by-4-foot cubicles,

where a single light bulb sways from the chicken wire that serves as a ceiling.

Nobody knows how long Nelson Stanton, 60, or James Dorlain, 55, had been dead.

A fifth man, Walter Kramer, 65, was found lying near a case of empty pint wine bottles in a washroom.

Pepe, the cat, spotted a skinny cockroach marching across a wall of Eddie Talkowski's cubicle and leaped from his lap to chase it.

Talkowski wiped the muscatel from his chin and shook his head.

"I didn't even know Big Nick's last name," he repeated.

"He was a big guy. He'd share his last bottle with you—even if you wasn't too hard up and he had the shakes.

"They were all good guys, though. Nobody knew Jimmy too well. He was a loner, but the other guys, they were good guys. They'd give you a drink if you asked them. Every time, almost.

"It wasn't no muscatel that got Big Nick. I drink muscatel and it didn't get me.

"I saw what they was drinking. It wasn't muscatel because I took a swallow of it. It looked like muscatel, but it wasn't."

Bundy, the off-duty room clerk who was the first to realize that Davis and Gonzola were dead, said that he knew nothing about the five men—where they came from, who they were or what they had been drinking.

"Gonzola talked to me about an hour before he died," Bundy said.

"He said, 'Ain't you working tonight?' and I said, 'It's Christmas and I got a night off.' Then he walked over to sit down and I could see he was pretty high. Everybody was high, because it was Christmas."

A toothless old man shuffled across the floor, shook his head, muttered, "Wine, wine," and moved slowly down a narrow corridor.

"He doesn't know what he's saying," Bundy said, pointing a thumb at the old man.

"I found three of those bodies—Davis and Gonzola and Kramer—and I went to bed. I didn't want to find any more."

A coroner's pathologist, James Henry, said that autopsies on the five men failed to reveal a cause of death. He said that chemical analyses will be made on the contents of four wine bottle found near the rooms of the dead men.

But outside the hotel, in a shadowy store vestibule where a man can suck on a bottle of cheap wine and not be seen by cruising police cars, a faceless figure will tell you how the men died.

The figure—hardly more than a moving bulk in grimy clothes squatting on its heels, its back resting against an old brick wall—drank from a bottle hidden to its neck in a brown paper sack.

"The word on the street," the voice from the shadow confided, "is that these guys got hard up for dough because they were celebrating Christmas and they mixed a batch themselves."

"A batch," he explained, "is furniture polish mixed with grapefruit juice."

'I still got a lot to learn,' said 17-year-old Celeste, 'only I'm learning it the hard way'

David Jackson was a new reporter on the midnight police beat when he wrote this story for the Dec. 14, 1974, Daily News.

She stands a little over 5 feet 4 inches tall, has her brown hair cut in a shag and wears a sweater, a turtleneck and bellbottom blue jeans that scuff the ground.

Her name is Celeste. She's 17 years old, has hazel eyes and looks like many girls her age in high school.

Except Celeste is a prostitute and a heroin addict.

When asked what she wanted for her life, she says resignedly, "For somebody to put a contract out on me."

She buries her face in her arms and sobs. Behind her a few feet sitting at a desk in the vice-control division offices at police headquarters is investigator Andrew Murcia, who arrested her hours earlier.

"Those people who talk about prostitution being a victimless crime," he says, "take a look at her."

Murcia has made many arrests and seen a lot of prostitutes. He isn't easily surprised by hard-luck tales or wasted lives, but Celeste's story moved even him.

Minutes earlier, he listened while Celeste tried to call her mother in Pennsylvania. Although it was after 3 a.m., her mother wasn't home and the man who answered refused to accept the charges.

Celeste called her boy friend, Sam, but he wasn't home either. Investigator Murcia knows Sam. After spending 11 years in California's San Quentin prison for murder, Sam came to Chicago. He is now out on $26,000 bond charged with kidnaping, armed robbery and home invasion. He is also a heroin addict.

Celeste says Sam doesn't work but lies around their apartment.

"He's been a dope fiend almost all his life," she says without any emotion. "I got him to kick (the habit). We kicked together but I went back."

Sam, who introduced Celeste to heroin, also taught her to walk the streets when her heroin habit became too financially demanding.

"I didn't know anything about that game (prostitution)," she says, when queried. "Sam just schooled me. He didn't want money. We'd just use it for food. I just come down there to get my fix money, you know."

"Fix money" has become expensive for Celeste. So expensive, in fact, that she turns three or four tricks a day, every day of the week.

Murcia says she waved his car down at 850 N. State early Tuesday morning and offered to perform a sex act for $20. She had $15 in her purse from an earlier, less profitable customer.

At 17, Celeste has developed a fundamental fear of men that conflicts with her dependence on them. She wasn't surprised that Sam was unavailable when she needed $1,000 bond to bail her out for her prostitution arrest.

Of her father, she says, "I wouldn't ask him for nothing."

"My father used to beat us (Celeste, a brother and sister) real bad," she says.

When Celeste was 11, her father was arrested for incest with his young daughter. She was taken from him and made a ward of the state.

The last time she saw her mother was last Christmas in Harrisburg, Pa. But she does not want to visit her again because "I don't want to bother them. I don't feel welcome."

She spent two months in the Audy Home last year on a theft charge ("The judge didn't want to keep me there") and was released to the custody of a minister and his family who lived on E. 50th Pl.

While living there—two months after her release—she was

arrested for possession of hypodermic needles.

Later she moved into a Near North Side apartment hotel with Sam.

She has been hoping that Sam would be better to her than Tony, her last boy friend. He disappeared last year when she was arrested for attempting to cash a stolen $289 check for him.

Celeste fishes into her purse for a tissue as her eyes fill with tears. Inside her purse is her grade-school diploma, but she cannot give a good reason why she carries it.

"I still got a lot to learn," she says quietly, "only I'm learning it the hard way."

Mr. Michaels was legally dead, but he was still collecting Social Security

Saundra Saperstein began as a copygirl at the Daily News *but soon worked herself into a reporting job. Her first regular beat was the state courts, where she found this story, published Oct. 24, 1975.*

Is Helen Michaels a wife or a widow?

She wants to know.

The courts say her husband, Edward Michaels, is dead.

The federal government says he's alive.

Mrs. Michaels, of 115 LaVergne, Northlake, wants the truth. She has been living with uncertainty for more than seven years.

It was on the night of April 11, 1968, that Michaels, 68, finished a chop suey dinner with his family and walked out the front door, saying he was going for a walk.

He never came back.

"I'm confused, at the end of my rope," Mrs. Michaels said Thursday.

"I'd just be relieved to know what happened."

After a futile search, which Mrs. Michaels said involved detectives and newspaper ads she could barely afford, she sat back to wait and hope. So did her five children, two of them still at home.

When seven years had passed she petitioned the court to declare her husband legally dead.

The decree was issued last June by Circuit Court Judge Daniel A. Covelli.

Then Mrs. Michaels, who was laid off her job recently, filed to collect Social Security retirement benefits she believed had been accumulating in her husband's name for seven years.

Suddenly Michaels came to life—at least in the files of the Social Security Administration.

"I'd been in touch with Social Security for years and even was receiving benefits as Edward's wife," Mrs. Michaels said.

"They never said anything about knowing his whereabouts.

"Then suddenly, I file for the widow's benefits and they say he's alive.

"If that's true, let them bring him forward and prove it."

But Social Security officials in Chicago say they can't because it would be an invasion of Michaels' privacy.

The Privacy Act that went into effect Sept. 27 and Section 1106 of the Social Security Act prohibit them from saying anything about Michaels' whereabouts or even discussing their evidence that he is alive, Social Security spokesman David Kading said.

"My heart goes out to her, but our hands are tied," he added. The decree filed in Circuit Court says that Edward Michaels "departed this life April 1, 1975."

A letter from Social Security officials tells Mrs. Michaels "evidence indicates that he is alive."

Mrs. Michaels says she and her daughter, Doreen, 14, don't know where to turn.

And David Kading says: "We're sorry, but we have a law to administer."

Harry Schaudt tells how an overextended man was driven to despair—and rat poison

This story by Harry Schaudt, published Feb. 8, 1960, touched off a successful drive for consumer-credit reform in Illinois.

William Rodriquez died of an overdose of credit.

The 24-year-old native Puerto Rican was a trusting soul with a taste for good things for his family.

But trusting William Rodriquez trusted too much.

"He would always take anybody's word for anything when buying things," a friend said. " He wouldn't read anything."

And his taste for good things for his wife and four children boomeranged. It drove him to despair. . . . and rat poison.

"Why should I work for nothing," he told his wife, Nilda, 26, when he left home at 807 S. Spaulding for work Friday morning.

He didn't come home until 2:30 a.m. Saturday. He was sick, having convulsions.

He told his wife he had bought rat poison in a drug store and had eaten it while walking along the street.

From his bed in Bethany Hospital, he told police he was debt ridden and being "hounded by creditors." At 6:15 a.m. William Rodriquez died. It was a second-hand TV set he bought for $200 that drove him to kill himself.

He still owed $167 when he made a payment Jan. 18 and had refused to pay any more because the set kept konking out.

The set was worth about $25, said a friend who had warned Rodriquez about clip joints.

The credit company had stopped his $60 weekly check at Sears, Roebuck & Co., where he was an order filler.

He was also under pressure to pay $34 for a bedspread he never wanted.

Mrs. Rodriquez said the bedspread was left in their apartment by a man who said it was for someone else. He asked her to hold it for him until he returned, she said.

But this man never reappeared. Instead another man did, demanding that the family pay. Rodriquez protested to the company that he never ordered it, much less signed any contract.

But the company persisted and threatened to tap his wages.

His $60-a-week-salary had managed to pay the $87.50-a-month rent on the drab, five-room apartment with linoleum-covered floors and with walls in need of paint.

It also paid for a handsome $32 clock and a $79.48 electric fan. And a pastel-colored telephone.

A neighbor said Rodriquez was a "nice, quiet guy and a hard worker" who was devoted to his wife and children, Marian, 7; William Jr., 5; Jose, 4, and the baby, Raymond, born Dec. 30. He came to this country 10 years ago.

Mrs. Rodriquez, a short woman with thick curly black hair, sat on her bed and sobbed.

"I just don't know what I'll do."

But William Rodriquez was a good provider, even in death. He had a $7,000 life-insurance policy with Sears.

Edan Wright writes the inside story of a state mental hospital

Edan Wright was one of the first reporters who specialized in "living" stories, and writing of her experiences in first-person articles. These included being confined as an inmate at the Dwight (Ill.) Prison for Women and being "rescued" by a helicopter from a rubber dinghy afloat in the Gulf of Mexico—a dramatic demonstration staged by a Navy air-sea rescue team. A woman of many tastes, Miss Wright had written a regular movie column from Hollywood and later a syndicated column for teenagers; she also did articles on antique furniture, a field in which she was considered an expert. The following story from Elgin State Hospital was published Oct. 26, 1949.

ELGIN, Ill.—It was shock-treatment day.

In the upstairs ward I had helped prepare beds with rubber sheets and pillows for the insulin patients. Insulin, in large enough doses to produce a coma, was given to younger women who had delusions of persecution.

A typical case was a mother in her early 30s. She had "broken" after the birth of a second child.

"I was all right when I only had my boy," she said. "But when the girl came I suddenly didn't feel capable of raising her.

"I thought of my own childhood and I asked myself 'How could I show her how to live? What would I teach her to make it come out right?' "

It appeared from the rest of her conversation that her parents had sheltered her too much and marriage had been a shock. In her parents' fears for her virtue they had made her feel that

222

sex was bad. She married and suddenly sex was supposed to be something good.

She hadn't worried about her son because she felt he could take care of himself. But the daughter was identified with herself.

As her anxiety increased she got so she couldn't even look after the house properly. Then she began to escape through delusions about her husband.

While I was eating breakfast one of the insulin patients was forcibly rushed to the treatment dormitory. An attendant and another patient propelled her along by hooking their arms in hers as she resisted.

The insulin patient had had some angry words with an attendant the previous night. She became wrought-up when smoking was forbidden after someone was found doing it in bed.

She had stewed about it all night long—tossing in her bed (I had the one next to her). By morning her resentment had grown to a stay-in-the-toilet strike against taking her treatment.

When I got downstairs, Anna Wooster, head nurse in Female Diagnostic, asked me to help with electric shock treatments.

In preparation, all the beds in one dormitory were stripped of spreads. A bunch of arm ties were brought in and slung over a screen in front of the beds.

The ties—6 or 8 feet long—were strips of stout cloth. They had a wristband center of extra thickness—with a slot opening.

A black box—about the size of a diathermy machine—was set up on a tall stand near a long, sheeted table. Then one of the dormitory beds was wheeled near the table. Now we were ready.

Charles Wahl, a staff psychiatrist, stood in front of the black box. Besides Mrs. Wooster, there were three or four attendants and three patients to assist. My eyes seemed glued to the woman receiving the treatment.

"Don't be frightened," Wahl told her. I could have used some of that reassurance myself. Goose pimples were popping out all over.

The woman got on the table. One attendant took off the woman's shoes and tucked them under the mattress of the bed.

Another squeezed out a jelly from a tube, placing a gob on the top of the woman's head and one on her temples. She placed a cotton bit in her mouth and a metal band around her head.

Wahl turned on the black box, then switched off the current in a fraction of a second.

Immediately, the woman began a convulsive jerking. Even her toes cramped grotesquely and shook in spasms. To keep her from thrashing about and falling off, six assistants held her to the table.

A bubbling sound—with a bit of foam—came from the woman's mouth. The convulsion was over. It had lasted only 40 seconds in all but it seemed much longer. The woman was hoisted from the table to the bed on a sheet.

Then another patient and I hurried to tie her wrists to the bed before she began thrashing with returning consciousness.

We scooted the bed over behind the screen and grabbed a couple of ties. The other patient showed me how to slot one end through the wristband, double it around and knot it, then anchor it to the bedspring with another knot.

My fingers were numb and clumsy, but there was no time to think about it. Another patient had come in and there was another bed to be hustled over to the table.

Somewhat stunned, I counted close to 15 patients. As soon as the first ones stopped struggling on the beds, we untied them and walked them to the dormitory across the hall to make room for more. Most of them were dazed and unsteady on their feet.

One woman began to cry hysterically, grabbing my hands. I tried to soothe her, telling her over and over, "You'll be all right." She clutched my hands each time and said: "Honey, you're so good."

When the treatments were over and all the patients had been moved, we made up the beds with fresh linen.

Mrs. Wooster interrupted me with: "If you'd like some explanations of what you saw I'll be glad to answer any questions. We don't usually have new patients help with these treatments. So perhaps it would be good to understand what they're for."

She pointed out, then, that the patients were largely older women with lots of anxiety and depression.

Some of them were going through change of life. Others were schizophrenic (split personalities) or suffering from delusions of persecution.

After the bed–making I helped with a spinal puncture in the doctor's office. The patient was a huge Negro woman, who made no sound as I steadied her on the table. She just looked at me—rolling her big eyes.

It was lunchtime then. I had no stomach for eating. But the shock patients were all at the tables, consuming their food eagerly.

They told me they didn't feel anything. They had "blanked out" as soon as the headband was adjusted–actually when the current was turned on. Except for headaches on occasions (when they struggled overmuch) there was no after-feeling either.

In the afternoon I was transferred to Dix, one of the "industrial" cottages where all the patients work. A patient who had a ground parole walked me over. She carried my clothes bundled in a sheet with a large record card attached.

A storm was brewing. The sky grew black and the leaves swirled around us in a gale of wind. By the time we reached Dix, rain was beginning to pepper down.

I had lost most of my fear of the hospital inmates. "From here on in it should be easy," I said to myself.

That's what I thought.

It was quiet in the small day room where the attendant directed me. It had an old-fashioned Victorian air with a stuffed-bird wall decoration under glass. There were lots of rockers, pillows on the benches, pink lace curtains—and flypaper on the table. Four or five women were in the room, one of them a grandmother rocking in a corner with a magazine on her lap.

One woman looked as if she had stepped out of a Grant Wood painting. She was fussily shifting a collection of plant stands and plumping up pillows.

The radio was playing and I eased down on a chair to listen. More women came in. One of them sat for a moment and left. Immediately the "Grant Wood" woman pushed her chair in place again.

One of the women suddenly got up and changed the radio program. And the argument was on!

I ducked into the hall. A young girl there was beating her head with her hands and carrying on a jumble of rapid, angry conversation.

I found the clothes room, and in the peace of this retreat I dallied with sorting my belongings until the early (4:30) call for supper.

Meals were served in another building, cafeteria-style. While I waited for my tray to be filled the woman behind me kept mumbling, "I got 11 million bucks and they put me in here."

I had just sat down at a table when I heard an angry voice behind me.

"Get out of here! Get out of here!" it shouted.

I gathered—quickly—that I had taken The Voice's seat. I saw the tray ready to come down on my head and the furious eyes above it. There was no time to call for help—and the attendant was at least 10 feet away. I ducked, scooting to another table.

On one side of me a mumbler was saying: "Johnny get your gun. Johnny get your gun—go nowhere. They'll get Dillinger. Everybody's after him. So am I."

She paused long enough to stick out her tongue at me.

On the other side a woman took a lace-edged collar out of her purse. She placed it on the table, bowed over it and made with a lot of jabbing gestures under my nose.

Dick Griffin tells the agonies of a man who lost everything

When the door closes on a person's life, a newspaper is rarely in a position to know much about the person unless he or she is a public figure. The following obituary, which was published Feb. 5, 1976, was an exception because financial editor Dick Griffin earlier had written a series of articles about how business had closed its doors to this frustrated executive.

William A. Romain was a man who had everything: brains, money, prestige, power, a great job and a great family.

In the 1960s and early 1970s he earned as much as $70,000 a year as a top-level business executive in Chicago. He drove a $10,000 car, lived with his wife and five children in a $100,000 dream house in west suburban Western Springs and had another $100,000-plus in investments.

He had gotten it all on his own. Romain had thrust his own way into the offices with wall-to-wall carpeting and walnut paneling and the heady position where thousands of men and women took orders from him.

He made it to the top despite an education that ended with high school after his father, a factory worker, was killed in a hit-and-run accident.

The Chicago company he worked for, Novo Corp., manufactured complicated heavy equipment and Romain, a self-taught engineer with grease under his fingernails, was right at home as its president.

Then the owners of the company decided the future belonged to the service field—shipping packages and storing things—instead of building overhead cranes and auto parts, businesses Romain knew inside and out.

Romain realized the corporate shift could mean the end of him and he waited for the axe. It fell just before Thanksgiving Day, 1971. He was told his salary was an unnecessary expense and was asked to close the door quietly as he left.

In the next four years he made hundreds of telephone calls, wrote thousands of letters and endured the humiliation of dozens of job interviews with men 20 years younger than he. His hopes were raised thousands of times and dashed as many times. He held half a dozen jobs of one sort or another, none worth remembering, but never again could he find the brass ring that had been his for a dozen years.

Romain died Wednesday in Community Memorial Hospital, La Grange. A physician blamed respiratory failure after a year-long illness.

But friends who had witnessed the agonies of a man who lost almost everything he prized said the cause of death was something else.

He lost the will to live. He never understood why he could climb so high, then fall so far.

He was 56.

Mississippi bean pickers in 1964. Henry Herr Gill / Daily News.

Rights and reform:
Nicholas Von Hoffman
Ray Stannard Baker
Carl Sandburg
Carl T. Rowan
Edwin A. Lahey
L. F. Palmer Jr.
James Bowman
Walter Morrison

Von Hoffman in Mississippi in 1964: 'Every man watches and every man is watched'

Nicholas Von Hoffman, columnist and commentator, was sent to Mississippi in 1964 to write a series of articles for the Daily News *about the civil-rights struggle. "In this summer the stranger is the enemy," he wrote in this article, the first in the series published Aug. 1, 1964.*

Devil's dust, the little wind-stirred geysers of dry earth that blow up between the rows of cotton plants, puff here and there across the fields.

Two Negro women walk by the side of the highway. Their parasols protect them from the sun, which even now in the early morning has laid down its heat over the Mississippi Delta.

The blues and reds of the women's cotton dresses are vivid. The orange umbrella atop the tractor moving down the rows of cotton plants is unfaded in the sun's summer light.

This Mississippi sun does not bleach. It brings out color and magnifies detail so that no man can mistake another.

The lean men of Mississippi are unmistakable. They pause at the gasoline pumps in front of roadside general stores, their lifeless eyes full of suspicion, forcing your own to glance downward as you get out of your car.

In this summer the stranger is the enemy, and the men of Mississippi wait and watch for him. In khaki pants and straw hats they stand their watch against the civil-rights workers across the delta counties . . . Bolivar, Sunflower, Leflore, Tallahatchie.

By night they ride dipping roads in the hill country to the east where that fatal plant, the kudzu vine, grows everywhere, strangling grass and tree. Along Mississippi 19, they drive through Nishoba County's scrub oak and scraggly pine forests without headlights when the moon is bright and the mist is sparse and patchy.

At Natchez cars cross the Mississippi River bridge from Vidalia in Louisiana. The Negroes say they're loaded with guns. Confederate flags fly from their antennas, but no one really knows what they carry.

The little girl whose preacher father heads the Ku Klux Klan around Natchez answers the phone and says, "My daddy ain't here. He's off in town selling Bibles."

Up in Jackson, the state capital, the governor says, "A very great resentment burns inside of me when I consider the distorted picture of my beloved state that is presented to America by our enemies."

For the Negroes, fear makes the night wakeful.

South of Tehula in Holmes County, a mocha-colored old Negro farmer finishes supper and checks to see if his shotgun is where it belongs. Hartman Turnbow knows his delta. There have been many nights since they fire-bombed his farmhouse that the courteous old man has stood watch.

Six miles away to the southeast, Negro farmers in the dirt-road community of Harmony check their guns and count their children as the night comes on. There are no phones in Harmony, and without them the short nights of summer are long, longer than ever now because the white civil-rights workers are living hidden among the Negro farm folk.

Further south, in Laurel, a tough Negro dentist with a reedy voice, Benjamin Murph, must see the straight-up southern sun as it moves toward Louisiana and wonder if this is the night the Klan will make good the promise of death attached to the rock thrown through his window, a few nights ago.

Every man watches and every man is watched.

The whites watch the Negroes. The Negroes watch the whites. The FBI, the State Sovereignty Commission, the newsmen, the White Citizens Council, the Klan, the civil-rights workers watch.

Before the summer and the coming of the hundreds of civil-rights workers, they were watching each other because there is no trust left between the white man and the black man. The "good Mississippi nigger" who played with the white folks' children and cooked the white folks food and labored and loved the white folks and was loyal, if ever he existed, is gone.

Now there is a black stranger in the white man's house.

But even while guarding himself against this new "darkie" who has treasonably and ungratefully turned against him, the white man cannot bring himself to believe it.

The white man is like the volunteer auxiliary policeman in Greenwood who had to take the day off from his business to stand guard while Leflore County Negroes tried, as they have so often before, to register to vote.

"Look at them fool niggers," the man said as he fiddled with his uncomfortable steel helmet. "They can come on down here and register any day they want." Then looking at the line of a hundred or so Negroes standing in the sun, he went on, "There ain't one respectable Greenwood nigger on that line. They're doing it so's they get publicity.

"Why hell, look at that fat old nigger woman. She can't vote 'cause she can't read. There's white people in this county we don't let vote, lots of them.

"We got a lot of good colored people in Leflore County . . . nigger businessmen and nigger preachers. If our good niggers want to vote, why ain't THEY standing up there hollering for their freedom?"

A few feet away an old Negro man, his white straw hat contrasting with the richness of his very dark, almost black, skin, answers a reporter's questions. A small blond boy stands next to his father listening.

The Negro says: "As long as they's only 5 or 6 come to register, it's all right, but when they's 100, they raise hell . . . . Anything that can kill a nigger or a dog—they put a gun on him. There's a law against everything 'round here, excepting it's open season on niggers and snakes all year 'round."

The boy looks up at his father and asks, "Daddy, you hear what that nigger's saying? You hear what that nigger's saying?"

Does the father hear, or is he like the Mississippi father who is supposed to have taken his son to a Klan meeting "so the boy can learn about segregation while he's young"?

Some whites have come to recognize the rebellion welling up in the people they still refer to as "our nigras." They are galled by it, though, like the vindictive Hattiesburg housewife who said, "When I saw that little colored girl of mine waiting in front of the courthouse with those common niggers I couldn't hardly believe it. I would have let her go anyway. She was spending more time eavesdropping than cooking."

They used to say that Negroes knew more about white folks' business than white folks. It didn't matter if they overheard the family's secrets. They were "just niggers."

Long before the "Mississippi Summer Project" brought Northern college kids tumbling into the state, the whites, whether they always admitted it or not, had come to know the Negroes had stopped being "just niggers."

But knowing is not the same as accepting. A white plantation owner can still sit in a Greenwood bar and tell a visiting Yankee about "hoe cake," the corn and water patty that Negro fieldhands used to cook on the blades of their hoes for their noontime meal in the fields. The plantation owner talks as though hoe cakes, "chopping cotton" and pickaninnies having fish fries on the levee were still the life of the delta.

Then came the kids.

They had been recruited off the campuses of the greatest universities in the land—UCLA, Harvard, Stanford, the University of Chicago, Cornell, Yale—but they knew nothing of Mississippi, her mood or her people. Before they had been in the state 48 hours, one of them and two full-time civil-rights workers were dead.

The National Council of Churches had spent a small fortune setting up an orientation program for the students on the campus of Western College for Women at Oxford, Ohio. They brought the full-time civil-rights workers up from Mississippi to train them and warn them about sheriff's posses and the primitive plumbing.

Trained or not, the pious Congregationalist girls, acidic antiwhite Negroes from northern slums, verbose sons of college professors, young romantics, adventurers and idealists were hopelessly alien to Mississippi.

The people from Mississippi at Oxford tried to say "what it is like" but they didn't know how.

George Green who is 21 and has, as someone once said of him, "more bullet holes in his shroud than any other man in Mississippi," knows what it is like, but he hasn't words to convey it. For nearly a year he has been operating in the bad southwest counties where the Klan rides . . . Pike, Amite, Franklin, and Adams. He knows.

George is coffee colored, thin and long, and always pleasant answering questions. He has a bad stomach, but he says it was that way "before," meaning before his leaders began sending him to places like Natchez, where he got four bullets in the rear of his fleeing car one night.

George knows about Mississippi, but he can't tell about it so that it is believable to nice kids from Columbia.

Some are like Peggy Sharp, a round, brown girl from Indianapolis. She went swimming during the training sessions at Oxford, and on the long drive south she giggled and told the other people in the car how frightened she was.

They assigned her to Holmes County where the hills break quickly off just west of Lexington and the delta begins. They told her to find the Negroes living in the shacks with the corrugated iron roofs and persuade them to register.

She thrived. Her only complaint, when she would reappear from time to time in Jackson, smiles on her face, was about the shortage of bathtubs with hot running water up in Holmes County.

They came, as wildly different each from the other as they were from Mississippi itself, and they broke the mood of the state.

Their reactions were Northern and defiantly unsubservient. Phil Moore, the Winnetka boy who was graduated from Harvard this spring, reacted in anger to the beating he got.

Some may have wanted martyrdom, but not the young woman who was liberated after five days in a Greenwood jail. Her Eastern woman's college manners betrayed her when she found out her hunger strike hadn't made the newspapers.

"They should have told us short hunger strikes aren't news.

My god, I starved myself for five days!"

Ultimately more memorable, perhaps, is another young woman volunteer standing in the Vicksburg "Freedom School" showing the first paintings done by her small Negro students.

There are "freedom" schools, libraries and community centers now in many parts of the state. Almost for the first time in this state's history a few of the children are at least in contact with well-educated people.

It is little enough, but amid the passion, the dramatic landscape of heavy foliage and pools of water and ignorance, it is a hope for a new beginning.

Ray Stannard Baker in 1894: Coxey's army of peace ends its campaign in war.

Ray Stannard Baker, later a U.S. ambassador and the distinguished biographer of Woodrow Wilson, was the Daily News *reporter on the scene May 1, 1894, when Jacob S. Coxey's "army" of 500 unemployed men paraded in Washington to demand public-works jobs. The "army" collapsed after Coxey was arrested for walking on the Capitol lawn.*

WASHINGTON—Coxey's eventful march from Massillon, Ohio to the marble steps of the national Capitol closed today in riot and bloodshed. The campaign of the army of peace has ended in war. For the first time in the six weeks during which the Commonweal has been plodding steadily eastward a written law of the land has been willfully violated and for the first time there has been a collision with the authorities.

As a result Carl Browne lies in a cell at the police station tonight and Gen. Coxey, who only escaped arrest because he was less dashing and impetuous than his fellow reformer, is racking his brains for a plan to support the band of penniless wanderers whom he has gathered from all over the country. Furthermore, the good-roads and noninterest-bearing-bonds bills are no nearer passage than they were a month ago.

In today's exciting incidents the army proper took no part. The contest was wholly between 300 armed police officers and the doughty twin reformers. Twenty thousand spectators enjoyed the excitement, and at least a score of them paid for their pleasure with broken heads or black eyes.

A gray-haired member of Congress who watched the riot from a portico of the Capitol said after the mob was dispersed: "The events of this first of May will live in history as the mani-

237

festation of a widespread discontent among the laboring classes of tne country. I think now that the climax has been reached and the furor for industrial armies will gradually subside. This belief that the enactment of new laws by Congress is a panacea for all our national ills is a dangerous symptom. The wise heads of the country have got to give it close and thoughtful attention."

It has been a long day. Early this morning Carl Browne ordered his horse and rode out to Brightwood Park, where the army was encamped. The bugler was just puckering up his lips to blow the assembly for breakfast when the marshal arrived. The men rushed forward, fell into line before the wagons and Commissary Marshal Blinn served each of them with six hardtack crackers, a piece of bread and a cup of coffee. When the breakfast had been swallowed the command to fall in was given.

Commune Marshal Schrum, assisted by several Commonwealers, issued to each man a "war club of peace," consisting of an oak stock 4 feet long with a white banner surmounted by a tiny flag fluttering at the end. Browne made a little speech. "The greatest ordeal of the march is at hand," he said. "The eyes of the world are on you and you must conduct yourselves accordingly." Browne then ordered the commune marshals to form their men for the parade.

Five mounted policemen swung into line at the head of the column. Most of the men had spent hours getting ready for the great occasion. But any improvement in the appearance of the marchers was counterbalanced by the faded and torn banners and battered commissary wagons. Immediately beside the Chicago commune rode Christopher Columbus Jones in a hackney cab. He is a little man with a long nose, and his high hat, ruffled with its experience, comes down over his head.

By the time the procession swung into Pennsylvania Avenue the crowd had grown so great that it was with difficulty that the mounted police escort, now increased to 25, could clear a way for the army.

At last the procession stopped with Coxey's carriage near the B St. entrance to the grounds. Browne dismounted and forced his way back. The general saw him. Rising from his seat, he stooped over and kissed his wife, as if he realized something of the terrible ordeal to follow.

Coxey leaped nimbly to the gound, and in a moment he and Browne were swallowed up in a wild surging mob of men that lifted them from their feet and bore them bodily across the street to the Capitol grounds. More than a hundred mounted policemen who were stationed around the B St. entrance rode into the crowd with the intention of capturing the two Commonwealers, but they might as well have attempted to arrest a cyclone. The mob forced one of them against the stone wall that bounds the Capitol plaza and threw his horse violently to the ground. At this point the man from Calistoga shouted to Coxey to jump over the wall, but the general lost his footing and in a moment he was at the bottom of a pack of writhing, struggling humanity. Browne leaped quickly into the grounds with the mob after him. Here the policemen saw him and forced their horses over the wall. A wild rush through the shrubbery took place, men and women rolling and tumbling over one another in the wild scramble.

The mounted policemen lost their heads and, not being able to see Browne, they drew their clubs and began striking everyone within reach. Women and children were ruthlessly ridden down. A Commonwealer who had some way escaped from the ranks stood behind a tree and struck a policeman a terrific blow in the back with his war club of peace. The next officer that came up saw the attack and clubbed the Commonwealer into insensibility and let him lie where he had fallen.

Just as Browne reached the corner of the steps he was seized by an officer. Without a moment's indecision the man from Calistoga swung his arm quickly around and sent the policeman spinning far out into the crowd. The next moment he was seized from behind, and a clenched fist struck him several blows in the face. In the struggle that followed his clothing was badly torn, and a string of his dead wife's beads, which he always wore around his throat, was scattered. An inoffensive Negro named Johnson crowded up to watch the struggle, and one of the policemen struck him a blow with his club.

Two mounted policemen closed down upon the Negro and

hit him repeatedly until he sank to the ground with his head terribly lacerated. Browne, together with Christopher Columbus Jones, who had been arrested trying to assist his friend in the fight, was taken to the police station.

All this time Coxey had been struggling through the crowd toward the central steps of the Capitol. He had asked a policeman to help him, and the two wormed their way through the mob like sparrows through a wheat field. Before anyone knew it Coxey was bounding up the east front entrance to the Capitol. He was up to the 10th step before he was recognized. Then the officers closed in above him, and his further passage was barred. The great crowd now recognized him, and a shout went up. Coxey turned to the crowd and raised his hat. He was deadly pale. Capt. Garden of the Capitol police stepped to one side of him, and Lt. Kelly of the city police was at his other arm. The other officers formed solidly about him. The crowd below was kept back by menacing clubs.

"What do you want to do here?" asked Garden.

"I wish to make an address," responded Coxey, his voice showing intense emotion.

"But you cannot do that," said Garden, quietly but firmly.

"Then, can I read a protest?" asked Coxey.

There was a moment's hesitation. Coxey drew from his pocket a typewritten manuscript and began to unfold it. There was a movement among the officers. Garden quietly took Coxey by the left arm, and Kelly took him by the right. They moved down the steps, the solid rank of officers following. Coxey thus was impelled downward and forward. He was not pulled or put under arrest, but firmly pushed along until he reached his carriage. Here a big Negro tried to strike an officer and was badly beaten.

The army, which had stood quietly in place under the command of Jesse Coxey during the entire melee, was now ordered to march. The column moved forward like a funeral procession to its new camping place on M St. near the James Creek Canal.

The Senate adjourned today on account of Sen. Stockbridge's death, and many of the Senators watched the riot from the Capitol portico. While the House was nominally in session, most of the members were outside enjoying the excitement.

In his protest this afternoon Coxey said:

"The Constitution of the United States guarantees to all citizens the right to peacefully assemble and petition for redress of grievances, and, furthermore, declares that the right of free speech shall not be abridged. We stand here today to test these guarantees of our Constitution. We chose this place of assemblage because it is the property of the people and if it be true that the right of the people to peacefully assemble upon their own premises and with their petitions has been abridged by the passage of laws in direct violation of the Constitution, we are here to draw the eyes of the nation to this shameful fact."

Coxey talked to a reporter at the new camp. "I was careful to walk on the sidewalk and trespass upon no local regulations when I went up to the steps," he said. "This is the beginning of the movement; that is all."

Carl Sandburg in 1919: Chicago is a receiving station for oppressed Negroes

The Daily News *hired the young Carl Sandburg in 1917 at the suggestion of reporter Ben Hecht, and Sandburg, already considered one of the nation's five finest poets, stayed on the staff for a decade. He worked on his Pulitzer Prize-winning biography of Lincoln and wrote his Pulitzer Prize-winning poems while he was on the paper's staff. For the paper, he wrote movie reviews, reported on the labor movement and was assigned to cover the city's worst race riot in the summer of 1919. Coincidentally, he had written a series of articles about the plight of the blacks two weeks before the riot. This article, which was published July 19, 1919, was part of that series.*

Chicago is a receiving station that connects directly with every town or city where the people conduct a lynching.

"Every time a lynching takes place in a community down South you can depend on it that colored people from that community will arrive in Chicago inside of two weeks," says secretary Arnold Hill of the Chicago Urban League, 3032 S. Wabash. "We have seen it happen so often that now whenever we read newspaper dispatches of a public hanging or burning in Texas or a Mississippi town, we get ready to extend greetings to people from the immediate vicinity of the scene of the lynching. If it is Arkansas or Georgia, where a series of lynchings is going on this week, then you may reckon with certainty that there will be large representations from those states among the colored folks getting off the trains at the Illinois Central station two or three weeks from today."

Better jobs, the right to vote and have the vote counted at elections, no Jim Crow cars, less race discrimination and a more tolerant attitude on the part of the whites, equal rights with white people in education—these are among the attractions that keep up the steady movement of colored people from southern districts to the North.

"Opportunity, not alms," is the slogan of the educated, while the same thought comes over and over again from the illiterate in their letters, saying, "All we want is a chanst," or, as one spells it, "Let me have a chanch, please."

Hundreds of letters written to the *Chicago Defender*, the newspaper, and to the Urban League reflect the causes of the migration. Charles Johnston, an investigator for the Carnegie Foundation, a lieutenant from overseas with the 803d infantry, believes the economic motive is foremost. He says:

"There are several ways of arriving at a conclusion regarding the economic forces behind the movement of the colored race northward. The factors might be determined by the amount of unemployment or the extent of poverty. These facts are important, but may or may not account for individual action.

"Except in a few localities of the South there was no actual misery or starvation. Nor is it evident that those left would have perished from want had they remained. Large numbers of Negroes have frequently moved around from state to state and even within the states of the South in search of more remunerative employment. The migrants to Arkansas and Oklahoma were expressions of the economic force.

"A striking feature of the northern migration was its individualism. Motives prompting the thousands of Negroes were not always the same, not even in the case of close neighbors. The economic motive was foremost, a desire simply to improve their living standards when opportunity beckoned. A movement to the West or even about the South could have proceeded from the same cause.

"Some of the letters reveal a praiseworthy solicitude for their families on the part of the writers. Other letters are an index to poverty and helplessness of home communities.

243

"In this type of migration the old order is strangely reversed. Instead of leaving an overdeveloped and overcrowded country for undeveloped new territory, they have left the South, backward as it is in development of its resources, for the highly industrialized North. Out of letters from the South, we listed 79 different occupations among 1,000 persons asking for information and aid. Property holders, impecunious adventurers, tradesmen, entire labor unions, business and professional men, families, boys and girls—all registered their protests, mildly but determinedly, against their homes and sought to move."

From Pensacola, Fla., in May, 1917, came a letter saying, "Would you please let me know what is the price of boarding and rooming in Chicago and where is the best place to get a job before the draft will work? I would rather join the army 1,000 times up there than to join it down here."

"What I want to say is I am coming north," wrote another, "and thought I would write you and list a few of the things I can do and see if you can find a place for me anywhere north of the Mason-Dixon line, and I will present myself in person at your office as soon as I hear from you. I am now employed in the R.R. shops at Memphis. I am an engine watchman, hostler, rod cup man, pipe fitter, oil house man, shipping clerk, telephone lineman, freight caller, an expert soaking-vat man who can make dope for packing hot boxes on engines. I am capable of giving satisfaction in either of the above-named positions."

"I wish very much to come north," wrote a New Orleans man. "Anywhere in Illinois will do if I am away from the lynchmen's noose and the torchmen's fire. We are foremen, machinist helpers, practical painters and general laborers. And most of all, ministers of the gospel who are not afraid of labor, for it put us where we are."

"I want to ask you for information as to what steps I should take to secure a good position as a first-class automobeal blacksmith of any kind pertaining to such," is an inquiry from a large Georgia city. "I have been operating a first-class white shop here for a quite a number of years and if I must say, the only colored man in the city that does. Any charges, why notify me, but do not publish my name."

"Please don't publish this in any paper," and "I would not like for my name to be published in the paper" are requests that accompanied two letters from communities where lynchings had occurred.

A girl wrote from Natchez:

"I am writing you to oblige me to put my application in the papers for me, please. I am a body servant or a nice house maid. My hair is black and my eyes are black and I have smooth skin, clear and brown. Good teeth and strong and good health. My weight is 136 lbs."

Here is a sample of the kind of letter that is handed around and talked about down South. It was written by a colored workman in East Chicago, June, 1917, to his former pastor at Union Springs, Ala.:

"It is true the colored men are making good. Pay is never less than $3 per day for 10 hours—this not promise. I do not see how they pay such wages the way they work laborers. They do not hurry or drive you. Remember this ($3) is the very lowest wage. Piece work men can make from $6 to $8 a day. They receive their pay every two weeks. I am impressed. My family also. They are doing nicely. I have no right to complain whatever."

"I often think so much of the conversation we used to have concerning this part of the world. I wish many times you could see our people up here, as they are entirely in a different light. I witnessed Decoration Day on May 30, the line of march was four miles, eight brass bands. All business houses were closed. I tell you the people here are patriotic. The chief of police dropped dead Friday. Buried him today, the procession about three miles long. People are coming here every day and find employment. Nothing here but money, and it is not hard to get. Oh, I have children in school every day with the white children."

Enterprise must be the first name of another who wrote back to Georgia:

"You can hardly get a place to live here. I am wide awake on my financial plans. I have rented me a place for boarders. I have 15 sleepers, I began one week ago. I am going into some kind of business here soon.

"The colored people are making good. They are the best

245

workers. I have made a great many white friends. The church is crowded with Baptists from Alabama and Georgia. Ten and 12 join every Sunday. He is planning to build a fine brick church. He takes up 50 and 60 dollars each Sunday."

It must be noted that all the foregoing letters were written with no intent of publication and with no view at all of explaining race migration or factors in housing, employment and education.

Carl T. Rowan: Racism refuses to board the bus

Daily News Washington *columnist Carl T. Rowan wrote this article when violence broke out over forced busing in Boston and Louisville at the beginning of the 1975 school year, more than two decades after the Supreme Court overturned the separate-but-equal doctrine in* Brown vs. Board of Education.

Nothing speaks more eloquently of the depth of racism and the moral deterioration of this society than this ugly ritual Americans tolerate—even encourage—when the schools open each fall.

Far more than our debacle in Indochina, more than the ghastly bungling of our economy, the events in Boston and Louisville these last few days tell the truth about the crisis of morality and leadership that afflicts so much of this society.

Imagine a group of adults in the Charlestown community of Boston chasing a school bus filled with black children, hurling rocks and bottles, shouting that they will "get the niggers next time."

Think of a mob "lynching" a black person in effigy!

Listen to a teen-ager shouting that "All niggers are rapists!" as a rationale for violently opposing the integration of schools.

We ought not kid ourselves. This is part of a racial madness not one whit less venomous than the super-race cries on which Hitler and the Nazis rode to power—and to ultimate tragedy.

The greater danger is not that this kind of mob psychology can get utterly out of control. In this country alone we have had thousands of illustrations that a mob has many heads, but not a single brain. The truly pathetic thing is that Americans who consider themselves decent, law-abiding, free of racism are displaying partial sympathy for the hoodlums who overturn cars, burn buildings, maim innocent children.

247

"Look at what 'forced busing' is doing to this country," they say.

It isn't busing that is wrecking these cities and their public school systems; it is deeply ingrained racism that millions of white Americans can't shuck off—not even in the face of rulings by the most eminent judges in the land.

Busing per se is not the issue and never has been. Vast millions of white children have long been bused to huge consolidated schools in America's countryside because busing is the only way they can enjoy facilities that offer them educational opportunities equal to those enjoyed by the more fortunate children in metropolitan areas.

The busing that has brought violence and terror to our cities is busing designed to give black children that same equality of opportunity. It became a matter of violent emotions after Richard Nixon stuck the word "forced" in front of busing and added "for racial balance."

Now even TV network reporters have embraced the phrase "forced busing" as though they don't realize that the phrase is emotionally loaded and automatically makes their reports biased.

These reports feed a paranoia in which people act as though Russia's Leonid Brezhnev, Uganda's Idi Amin or some sinister alien force has decreed busing to achieve integration without the slightest concern for elements of justice in America.

Doesn't anyone understand that it was a local Irishman in Boston, Judge Arthur Garrity, who held court hearings, listened to weeks of testimony and then decreed that systematic discrimination had been imposed upon the black children of Boston? It was this white judge, part of the local community, who decided that busing was the only effective tool for redressing inequities that have existed for generations. The same has been true in other cities.

These facts don't matter to the haters, the sadists, who are just as eager to "get us a nigger" as any Klan group in Georgia or Alabama ever was. The facts don't matter much to people who have become so emotional, so brainwashed, that they have deluded themselves into believing that "the sanctity of the neighborhood school" transcends everything—which, of course, it never has.

Still, the haters and sadists run wild only when they believe that those in power are at least secretly on their side. President Ford has criticized the judge who ordered busing in Boston although the judge heard the evidence and Ford heard and understood nothing. State and city politicians run scared wherever the issue arises. Some policemen clearly don't want to enforce the law. In such a situation, mob leaders take over.

We can survive an energy crisis, but can we survive this kind of morality crisis? Surely not forever.

Edwin A. Lahey notes the cracking of minority barriers on inauguration eve, 1961

This article by Edwin A. Lahey, distinguished Washington correspondent, was published on the Daily News *editorial page Jan. 19, 1961, the eve of the inauguration of President John F. Kennedy.*

John F. Kennedy's parents can remember when the help-wanted ads in the Boston newspapers carried the line:

"No Irish need apply."

At noon today Kennedy goes up to the Capitol in a plug hat and a long-tailed coat, and utters, with as authentic a Harvard accent as you'll find anywhere, his oath of office as the 35th President of the United States.

Two of Kennedy's cabinet officers, Sec. of Labor Arthur J. Goldberg and HEW Sec. Abraham Ribicoff, are Jewish. Their antecedents as well as their contemporaries know, more keenly than ever the Boston Irish knew, the sound of a door being gently closed.

Several of the new President's appointees are Negroes. These include Andrew Hatcher, the assistant White House press secretary, and the housing administrator, Robert C. Weaver.

I was assigned to Washington 20 years ago this week. At that time, when FDR had been in office eight years, there wasn't a big hotel or restaurant in downtown Washington that would accept the patronage of a Negro.

And a little more than a decade ago, Ralph Bunche felt obliged to turn down President Truman's offer of a job as assistant secretary of state. The Negro diplomat felt that he couldn't live in Washington without subjecting his children to the humiliations of racism.

The point of this discussion is obvious. The United States

in our time has taken giant strides in removing social, economic and political barriers against the traditional "don't belong" groups. The most clearly repudiated groups in the last election were the membership committees of every exclusive club in the United States.

The hard fact is this—in no other country in the world does talent have a better opportunity to express itself than in the United States. And this fact remains in spite of the obvious inequities that still afflict our society.

It is most ironic that the generation of Americans that has taken such great strides in breaking down barriers for the "don't belong" people have been reared on the repetitious complaint that the United States is "losing prestige" abroad.

Are we "losing prestige" with the 15,000 Cubans now looking for entry visas into the United States? Did we "lose prestige" with those millions of Europeans whose desire to come here scared Congress into the inhuman exclusions of the McCarran-Walter immigration act?

The major irony of this is that John Kennedy, more than any other present-day politician, has harped on the "prestige" issue.

As he takes his oath of office, John ought to concede that if the United States is "losing prestige" abroad, maybe the rest of the world is wrong.

And for his text in the inaugural, John could borrow some wise words from Eddie O'Leary, who runs a popular public house at Madison and Austin in Chicago. In his moments of well-being, Eddie always says:

"I'm glad Grandpa didn't miss the boat."

L. F. Palmer Jr. finds the facts don't exactly fit the official version of fatal Black Panther raid

L. F. Palmer Jr. was Chicago's leading black journalist when heavily armed raiders under the direction of State's Atty. Edward V. Hanrahan burst into a Black Panther apartment on Dec. 4, 1969, killing Fred Hampton and Mark Clark. Palmer's story in the next day's Daily News *was the first to cast serious doubt on the official version of the raid. It touched off a furor culminating in Hanrahan's indictment by a special grand jury. Hanrahan was acquitted, but the controversy caused black voters for the first time to rebel en masse against the Chicago political machine and expel Hanrahan from office.*

Bobby Hutton, Huey F. Newton, Eldridge Cleaver, Bobby Seale, David Hilliard.

And now Fred Hampton.

The leadership of the Black Panther Party has been steadily, and some say systematically, skimmed off. The slaying of Illinois party chairman Fred Hampton by police early Thursday led the Panthers to charge once more that there is a national conspiracy to destroy the revolutionary organization.

The national chairman of the Panthers, Bobby Seale, has said that the imprisonment, exile and death of Panther chieftains "is nothing more than Richard M. Nixon attempting to destroy the national- and state-level Black Panther Party leadership."

Seale, himself in prison, has said that U.S. officials are recruiting local law-enforcement agencies across the nation to remove Panther leaders from the streets.

252

They reason, Seale said, that this will kill the movement, which FBI Director J. Edgar Hoover singled out as being "the greatest threat to the internal security of our country" among militant black groups.

Police officials deny any such plot. Yet the death of Hampton, who was being groomed for a high post in the national party, casts a spotlight on the fate of the Panther hierarchy:

• Hutton, national treasurer, was killed by police in Oakland, Calif., April 6, 1968.

• Newton, minister of defense, is in prison, convicted of killing an Oakland policeman.

• Cleaver, minister of information and author of the best-selling *Soul on Ice*, is a fugitive in exile.

• Seale, party chairman, is in prison after contempt-of-court charges growing out of his protests that his constitutional rights were being denied in the Conspiracy 8 (now Conspiracy 7) trial in Chicago.

• Hilliard, party chief of staff, is under arrest, accused of telling an antiwar rally that "we will kill Richard Nixon."

Hampton in the last speech he made in Chicago said:

"This system is out to kill us and we know it. Some say we are not ready to take on this monster. We say that we do not want to, but that is not the question any longer. The monster has taken us on and we have to deal with reality."

Dealing with reality, Panthers say, involves coping with an enormously complex pattern of harassment, including police raids, intimidation of Panthers selling the party newspaper, massive arrests and high bonds followed by dismissal of charges.

Donald Freed of Beverly Hills, Calif., assistant to the provost at the California Institute of the Arts, declared:

"If what is being perpetrated against the Black Panther Party was being done to any white group, the liberal Establishment would absolutely refuse to tolerate it any further.

"Just the matter of Panther arrests, with charges later dropped, and bail in the millions, constitutes an unprecedented national scandal."

Two police raids on Black Panther headquarters at 2350 W. Madison are typical of what Freed describes. Charges of attempted murder were placed against six Panthers following a gun battle with police on Oct. 4.

On Nov. 10, the charges were dropped for lack of evidence.

In an earlier raid on the Panthers' headquarters, the FBI went in on a fugitive-arrest warrant, failed to find the fugitive and wrecked the office in the process.

Eight Panthers were arrested and charged with harboring a fugitive. Sixteen days later, the charges were dropped. George Sams, the fugitive sought by the FBI, was later revealed to be an informer for the FBI and police.

The FBI or police, in rapid succession, conducted raids on Panthers across the country.

In two months, according to Seale, more than 40 Panther leaders and more than 100 members were arrested.

After reviewing incidents of police-Panther strife, the Task Force on Violent Aspects of Protest and Confrontation of the National Commission on the Causes and Prevention of Violence, concluded:

"The confrontations between the Panthers and some elements of the police have become a feud verging on open warfare. This warfare highlights the fact that for the black citizen, the policeman has ceased to be—if indeed he ever was—a neutral symbol of law and order."

The linking of Seale to the defendants in the conspiracy trial here is viewed in some legal circles as indicating similar problems within the nation's judicial system.

The Conspiracy 8 went on trial on a charge of conspiring to cross state lines to incite a riot at the Democratic National Convention.

Those close to this extraordinary chapter in American street politics know that Seale played a marginal role in the clashes.

Jay Miller, director of the Illinois chapter of the American Civil Liberties Union, who said he was mystified by Seale's indictment, attempted to discover the government's motive in charging him. Miller said he finally found one.

"A high-ranking official in the U.S. Justice Department told me that the Panthers are a bunch of hoodlums and we have to get this guy," Miller said.

Seale, bound and gagged after he consistently protested that his constitutional rights had been violated at the trial, was severed from the "8," imprisoned for four years for contempt and ordered tried alone at a later date.

In one of the instances in which charges against a Chicago Panther resulted in a conviction, Hampton earlier this year was found guilty of stealing $71 worth of ice cream from a vendor on a Maywood playground.

He was convicted despite his testimony that he was not on the playground last April when the ice cream was stolen.

Displaying his own kind of humor, Hampton cracked: "I may be a pretty big dude, but I can't eat no 710 ice cream bars."

Seale contends the reason behind the alleged plot to destroy the Panthers is the government's horror of socialist programs the Panthers favor.

The political nature of the party is made clear in what the Panthers refer to as their basic definition: "Black people in America are a colonized people in every sense of the term and white America is an organized imperialist force holding black people in colonial bondage."

Releasing black people from this bondage as seen by the Panthers has developed into the mission of the militant group, a mission most members recognize as suicidal.

Hampton was one of many young blacks who defected from the traditional civil-rights movement after pursuing lawful, peaceful attempts to free "the colonized people."

His commitment to the revolutionary approach showed in the last speech he made in Chicago. It was on Nov. 13 at a memorial service for John and Michael Soto, two black brothers killed by police on the West Side.

On the morning of that same day Spurgeon (Jake) Winters, a young Black Panther and a high-school honor graduate, had been jailed in an early-morning shoot-out that took the lives of two policemen.

Hampton talked that day about the freedom he had sought, but had never known.

"You don't try to articulate or arbitrate with anyone about

what you will be or what you will do at a place that you have never been before, about a person you have never been allowed to be, about a time that you cannot set because of its own uncertainty and dependence on what you decide and do now."

Hampton declared the "only moratorium we want is a moratorium on wanton killing and oppressive tactics."

Then, with tears in his eyes and his voice choked up by emotion, Hampton voiced what turned out to be his benediction:

"I sometimes wonder what I would be doing with my life if I had been born free. I think of it and I say to myself, 'We will be free.' "

'There were a number of times when he literally touched the stars'

This article by Daily News *religion writer James Bowman was published Sept. 17, 1969.*

As a young priest in the early 1920s, Bernard J. Sheil walked to the hangman's chamber at Cook County Jail with an 18-year-old gang member condemned for murder. The youth asked him, "Why do they wait until the rope is around my neck before they do anything for me?"

Sheil never forgot that. And in the 1930s, after a brief chancery career under George Cardinal Mundelein, he put up $112 of his own money (all he had) and secured a sizable gift to start the Catholic Youth Organization, whose initials soon became a household word.

"If things were as bad now as they were then, there'd be a revolution for sure," says the Rt. Rev. Msgr. Edward Kelly, Sheil's successor at CYO.

"When he talked to kids," Msgr. Kelly recalls, "you would watch and ask yourself, 'What's he got?' Kids caught his sincerity. He really believed in them."

He tramped through railroad yards, picking up farm boys coming in on the rods and looking for work. A young attorney, William J. Campbell, who often accompanied Sheil, recalls "poor kids frozen half to death" whom the bishop would take to his home at 1140 W. Jackson for a bath and food.

Campbell, who is now chief judge of the U.S. District Court here, says Sheil helped to motivate the Roosevelt administration to put welfare funds at the disposal of young people through the National Youth Administration and Civilian Conservation Corps.

257

But he saw beyond meeting immediate welfare needs and being a friend of homeless boys.

When radical organizer Saul Alinsky went to work on the Back of the Yards neighborhood, Sheil joined him. Alinsky, a Jew praised by French Catholic philosopher Jacques Maritain as one of the "few really great" men of the 20th Century, says: "Bishop Sheil was tremendously responsible for my doing a good deal of what I have spent my life doing."

Recently, the Back of the Yards community has been notably anti-integrationist, but in the early days of Alinsky's Back of the Yards Council, it was considered a revolutionary liberal force in Chicago.

In the late 1930s, during the CIO organizing days, the United Packinghouse Workers Union turned to Sheil for help. The Chicago stockyards workers, whom Alinsky and Sheil had organized in their neighborhoods. were mostly Catholic.

A banker warned Sheil in 1939 that if he got on a platform with CIO leader John L. Lewis, he never would become archbishop of Chicago. At the time Sheil was thought to be the heir apparent to Mundelein, who had elevated Sheil to bishop in 1928.

Somebody shot a gun into a restaurant where Sheil was eating and he received dozens of threats about what would happen if he showed up.

But Sheil got on the platform anyway. The appearance, according to Ralph Helstein, who was to become president of the United Packinghouse Workers, "had a big impact and unquestionably contributed a great deal to organizing the yards."

Sheil "lent an air of legitimacy to what was considered potentially an illegitimate thing—outside agitators, you know, the usual stuff," Helstein says.

Later the same year, Cardinal Mundelein died, and Pope Pius XII appointed the Most Rev. Samuel Alphonsus Stritch as archbishop of Chicago.

According to a knowledgeable source in the archdiocese, however, Sheil's liberalism had nothing to do with his being passed over. Roman authorities, according to this source, had doubts about Sheil's business acumen, rather than his position on social issues.

"He was the last of the big spenders," said one associate. It was no secret in the archdiocese in later years that both St. Andrew's parish, of which Sheil was pastor, and CYO continually were in financial straits.

One of Sheil's early and longtime financial supporters and highly placed political friends, Democratic national committeeman Jacob Arvey, talked about Sheil's being taken in by ex-convicts and others who didn't deserve his help.

"His own fault was his gullibility," said Arvey. "Perhaps I should call him naive."

Arvey added: "Whatever he did was because of love for his fellow man. No matter who (Protestant, Jew or Catholic) wanted to do that, he was for it. Of all the people outside of my religion (Arvey is a Jew), I have never found a more sympathetic and devoted friend. He never failed to respond in a crisis when we (Jews of the world) needed help."

Shortly before World War II, Sheil walked into a Nazi-front meeting and denounced fascism, anti-Semitism and white supremacy. An old woman spat on him and shouted: "Goddamn you! Nigger lover! Rabbi Sheil!"

The bishop said to her: "Rabbi? That's what they called our Lord." He cleansed himself and left the hall.

"Along with Mundelein, he was an anti-fascist when it wasn't popular to be so," Alinsky says.

After the war, in a speech before the American Veterans' Conference in Des Moines, Sheil pictured the American Medical Assn. as "rising in its musty might to slay the dragon of socialized medicine." He added: "Hippocrates would sure be puzzled."

Of Sheil's many celebrated causes, one of the most memorable was his verbal barrage against Sen. Joseph F. McCarthy in 1954. McCarthy was the darling of many, but Sheil blasted the Wisconsin politician's tactics as "immoral, ineffective, a phony anti-communism."

Only three days before, Francis Cardinal Spellman of New York had feted McCarthy at a communion breakfast.

An appreciative former President, Harry S. Truman, wrote

Bishop Sheil immediately. He had been ready to despair, Truman said, but Sheil left him "very much reassured."

Sheil's action "was a telling blow in helping bring McCarthy down," according to Alinsky.

The uproar Sheil created, however, cost his beloved CYO some of its biggest financial supporters.

But Sheil, on another occasion, summed up his thinking: "Too much respect for the local banker, industrialist or politician has caused . . . (churchmen) to be silent when the teachings of Christ should have been literally shouted from the house tops."

When Bishop Sheil resigned from the CYO a few months later, some jumped to the conclusion he had been fired for his anti-McCarthy remarks. But the fact is that Samuel Cardinal Stritch, then archbishop of Chicago, and Sheil had serious differences over the huge debt (about $3 million) the CYO had built up.

In retrospect, a chancery office official confides that Sheil's resignation came as a surprise to Cardinal Stritch. Sheil wrote personal notes to each employe of CYO, telling them he resigned. The morning they found them, Sheil said good-by to every employe personally. "He cried and everyone else cried," said the CYO office receptionist.

But Stritch, according to a close source, was unaware of the resignation until a newspaper reporter called the chancery office for a comment. Stritch called for his car and rushed to St. Andrew's Church, where he thought Sheil was holding a press conference. But the press conference was at CYO headquarters downtown, and Stritch got there just in time to shake hands with Sheil in front of news cameras.

But that wasn't the last that Chicago would hear from "Benny" Sheil, who was born Feb. 18, 1886, near St. Columbkille Church, Paulina and Grand, to lower-middle-class Irish-American parents.

In May, 1966, John P. Cody, who became archbishop after Stritch's death in 1965, paid a visit to St. Andrew's rectory.

Archbishop Cody already had retired more than 20 pastors.

Sheil was 80, and pastor of one of the wealthiest parishes in the city.

According to Cody, the visit consisted of 40 minutes of "very pleasant conversation."

But Sheil had a different story. "He came and told me I was through," Sheil informed the press. "It came out of the blue."

Cody said Sheil had retired for reasons of health, but Sheil declared: "This is a removal and I want that made clear. I'm in fine health. I'm in perfect health."

But the old man was retired, no matter what anyone said. His health was far from perfect and attacks of asthma finally led him to Arizona where he spent his last three years.

Bishop Sheil, who was named a titular (honorary) archbishop in 1959, died last Saturday in Tucson at age 83. His funeral was held here Wednesday.

Perhaps his old friend Saul Alinsky provided the most fitting epitaph: "There were a number of times when he literally touched the stars."

Walter Morrison sees
in the face of J. H. Jackson
'the look of African kings'

Reporter Walter Morrison wrote this article, published Sept. 5, 1973, about the head of the nation's largest organization of black Americans.

The Rev. Dr. J. H. Jackson rose with out-thrust right hand to greet me. He is a man of big frame, and in his face is the look of African kings. He is dressed in a well-cut, not new but tasteful dark-blue suit. The white pattern in his dark tie cuts a mod swath between his dark jacket and his white shirt.

It is a day whose temperature suggests those regions against which preachers inveigh, but Dr. Jackson's shirt is unwilted.

A fan struggles to overcome the heat in the office at Olivet Baptist Church, where Dr. Jackson has been pastor since 1941. He offers to turn it off if I'm having difficulty hearing.

I am, but I prefer to lean forward to catch, above the whir, the soft-spoken, precise words of one of America's most powerful religious leaders.

Dr. Jackson is president of the National Baptist Convention of the USA Inc., which, with its 6.5 million members, is the largest single organization of black Americans in the country.

He has headed the convention since 1953, and is expected to be re-elected during its convention this week in Los Angeles. Dr. Jackson says he never sought the office, but "I have done the work, and the people have responded."

If there has been tumult over his views on race and on the war in Southeast Asia and his identification as a "conservative," Dr. Jackson shows no sign of being perturbed.

"I am not seeking popularity," he said.

Dr. Jackson's views on appropriate strategies for gaining the rights of black Americans place him at odds with most civil-rights leaders and black intellectuals.

For example, Dr. Jackson objects to the term "black." He says "Negro" is more inclusive, since "black" makes no provision for mulatto or brown-skinned persons. "I know there are those who say 'black' is a matter of philosophy, but 'black' is an adjective, and you cannot through philosophy make white black, red blue."

He adds, "I do not work on any white folks' secret agendas. I am not supported in whole or in part by white folks' money, as some civil-rights workers are. I am not employed by white people."

But Dr. Jackson emphasizes he has no hatred for any race. "I got over all that a long time ago, when I was a boy," he said.

Dr. Jackson opposed the civil-disobedience tactics of the late Rev. Dr. Martin Luther King Jr. "You cannot have civil disobedience in a country such as this without having violence," Dr. Jackson said. "Civil disobedience has never been used to improve a nation, only to destroy a government."

Several years ago, during the time of Dr. King's Chicago campaigns, Dr. Jackson said the implication of "nonviolence" was that the Negro was, by nature, violent.

Dr. Jackson said then: "Using nonviolence as a standard gives the false impression that all a prostitute or dope addict has to do to gain respectability is to subscribe to it. It places the civil-rights struggle on a very low level."

The disagreement between Dr. Jackson and Dr. King over civil-rights strategies, coupled with their differences over the social action role of the National Baptist Convention, has fueled a belief in segments of the black community that there was fierce antagonism between them—even that Dr. Jackson hated the civil-rights martyr.

A new book, scheduled for publication later this month, repeats—with an exclamation point—a story that is supposed to illustrate the depths of Dr. Jackson's hostility to Dr. King.

According to the story, the address of Olivet Baptist Church was 3101 South Park Way before the City Council changed the name of that thoroughfare to Dr. Martin Luther King Jr. Drive. When that change was made, according to the story, Dr. Jackson changed the church's address to 405 E. 31st.

"That is almost too big a lie," Dr. Jackson says.

"You entered from 31st St., didn't you? They were using the 31st St. address when I came here in 1941, but some people were so intrigued by South Park Way that they always thought that was the address."

The story, he said, is "an invention, largely of the white press with an interest in such controversy, that has been seized upon by some unthinking Negroes to prove that I'm some small, petty person, harboring malice and stooping to vindictiveness.

"I disagreed with Dr. King, but I did not hate him," Dr. Jackson said, his fingers tapping his desk to emphasize his words. "Dr. King was a civil-rights worker. I did not choose to be a civil-rights worker. How, then, could I have hated or envied the man, when I did not choose any competition with him."

Dr. Jackson noted that he and his church had aided the Montgomery (Ala.) Improvement Assn., which, led by Dr. King, mounted the Montgomery bus boycott of the 1950s.

Dr. Jackson also pointed to the role played in the early 1960s by the National Baptist Convention, under his leadership, in support of blacks in Tennessee's "Tent City," a makeshift community set up by black tenant farmers who were evicted from their farms when they tried to register to vote.

"We thought if Negroes wanted to vote in Fayette County, they should own some of Fayette County," Dr. Jackson said.

The convention, on Dr. Jackson's recommendation, purchased land and dedicated it as the National Baptist Freedom Farm. Tractors were purchased. Money was deposited in a Tennessee bank to provide crop loans. Houses were built and renovated. "In 1971 and 1972, we sent to the market 110,000 pounds of pork," Dr. Jackson said.

"That sounds like civil-rights activity to me," added Dr. Jackson, who often has said that civil-rights activity should move "from protest to production," and that "civil-rights workers must own something other than the bitter note of protest."

As for his support for U.S. policy in Southeast Asia, Dr. Jackson said: "I took the position that I was not President of the United States, that the President had information that I did not possess. I knew, too, that the war was not the responsibility of any one man, any one President, that there were many intricate factors. Therefore, it was not possible for me to jump to the hasty conclusions some others reached."

In a 1970 speech, Dr. Jackson said: "Support of the President in this issue is not a commitment to all aspects of the problem. It is only recognition that this nation has only one Chief Executive. His leadership at this time seems more to be trusted than those who criticize him without giving a program for peace, strength and security. Any campaign against our President, the highest elected official of our country, strengthens the hand of our enemies."

Dr. Jackson said he had conferred with President Lyndon B. Johnson "in the search for peace" in Southeast Asia.

Dr. Jackson was named Patriot of the Year in 1969 by the ultraconservative organization We, the People! And now he says proudly, "I am pro-America. I am pro-the Constitution of the United States. I am pro-justice. I am pro-that which is constructive."

Once when asked why black Americans should wish to enter America's "polluted stream," Dr. Jackson replied: "All streams are polluted. No government or state is perfect. . . . I would rather swim in this pool than in others I have heard of."

Dr. Jackson believes that those who use "black" are laying "the groundwork for American apartheid, such as exists in South Africa."

The concepts of black separatism and of dual citizenship for black Americans with African countries also are rejected by Dr. Jackson.

The advocates of separatism, he said, "are the chief preachers today of racial segregation. I find that first-class citizenship in the United States is about all I can cover. But there are those, claiming to be civil-rights workers, who are preaching the idea of dual citizenship." Dr. Jackson named no names, but one prominent advocate of dual citizenship is the Rev. Jesse L. Jackson (not related), national president of Operation PUSH.

Dr. Jackson said the presidency of the National Baptist Convention has brought opportunities for "political leadership," which he has rejected.

"I did not want to be restricted by party allegiances. I wanted to be free to criticize any policy or person, even the highest officer in the land," he said.

He has no interest in seeking civil-rights leadership as an outgrowth of his church position, Dr. Jackson said, because "we have too many civil-rights leaders. I am a minister, and I have insisted on being that."

The ministry has been the goal of Joseph Harrison Jackson, the son of a minister, since he was a small boy in Mississippi, reading "The Easy Step," a collection of Bible stories, under the guidance of his mother.

He has been given a lifetime pastorate at Olivet, and says he has plans for what he will do when he retires, but has no plans to retire.

"It's not the job of the batter to say when he's out; that's for the pitcher and the umpire," Dr. Jackson said. "I'm still at bat."

GIs in a Vietnam rice paddy. Henry Herr Gill / Daily News.

Vietnam:

Keyes Beech
Bob Tamarkin
Raymond R. Coffey
Larry Green
Ellen Warren
Betty Washington
Rob Warden
Norman Mark

Keyes Beech tells of terror in Saigon before takeover: 'We clawed for our lives'

Pulitzer Prize winner Keyes Beech was the first of several Daily News *correspondents assigned to cover the war in Vietnam. This is the story of his last hours in Saigon before the Viet Cong takeover. It was written for publication on April 30, 1975.*

ABOARD THE *USS HANCOCK*—Tuesday morning I had breakfast on the ninth floor of the Caravelle Hotel and watched a column of ugly black smoke framed by the tall, twin spires of the Catholic cathedral in Kennedy Square just up the street.

Tan Son Nhut airport was burning; the streets were bare of traffic, unnaturally but pleasantly quiet.

The waiters were nervous and the room boys said I couldn't have my laundry back until "tomorrow."

What tomorrow?

Word was quietly passed among the press corps that the first stage of the American evacuation was due to begin. Correspondents whispered to one another in corridors, just as they always do when things get tense.

The telephone rang monotonously. Vietnamese friends called to ask when they would be evacuated. I told them the truth—that the airlift has been suspended and I don't think they are going to get out. I wondered if I was going to get out.

There was a long, unbelieving silence at the other end of the line. Then an accusatory click of betrayal as they hung up.

But who betrayed whom? It was a question I was to think about later.

Perhaps it was time I got around to writing that 1,500-word "personalized history" of the Vietnam War that the foreign editor asked for last week. I was afraid he was going to ask for that. It's the price you pay for staying out here too long.

I should have written it before, but the words wouldn't come. Sorry 'bout that. I sat down to write when the telephone rang again.

This time it was not a Vietnamese. It was my colleague, Bob Tamarkin, calling.

Bob wanted to stay behind and take his chances. I told him I'd already taken my chances and that I was leaving. But we had been going over that ground for the last two weeks—what to do when the crunch came.

It's your decision, I said. He said he might see me later. I said I hoped so and hung up. It was 11 a.m.

Six hours later, I would be fighting for my life and wishing I had never left that hotel room. But for the moment I was an optimist.

Tamarkin telephoned to say the embassy had ordered a full-scale evacuation—immediately. He said he hoped to see me later.

I joined the others who were leaving and we went to a prearranged assembly point, a U.S. embassy building only a couple of blocks away.

Three buses were quickly filled with a mixed bag of correspondents and Vietnamese. Some of the more dignified among us held back rather than scramble for seats and waited for a fourth bus.

That was a mistake.

The first three buses made it inside Tan Son Nhut airbase and their passengers flew out. Ours never made it inside, and that accounts for one of the longest days of my life.

We heard the bad news over the driver's radio on the way out: "Security conditions are out of control at Tan Son Nhut. Do not go to Tan Son Nhut. Repeat, do not go to Tan Son Nhut."

We went on anyway, the sound of explosions and the rattle of automatic weapons growing louder by the second—incoming mixed with outgoing fire. South Vietnamese soldiers were firing wildly in the air for no apparent reason.

South Vietnamese sentries turned us back at the first checkpoint. For the thousandth time, I made mental note of the billboard legend that departing Americans see as they leave Saigon:

"The noble sacrifices of allied soldiers will never be forgotten."

We tried another approach to the airbase but were again waved back. No way, as the Vietnamese are fond of saying.

The evacuation had broken down.

It was 2 p.m. when we headed back to the city. Nobody on that bus will ever forget the next few hours. We cruised aimlessly about Saigon for at least three hours while our security escorts tried to figure out what to do with us.

We were a busload of fools piloted by a man who had never driven a bus and had to wire the ignition when it stalled because the Vietnamese driver had run away with the keys the night before.

"I'm doing the best I can," said Bill Austin of Miami, Okla., the man at the wheel, as we careened through narrow streets, knocking over sidewalk vendors, sideswiping passing vehicles and sending Vietnamese scattering like leaves in the wind.

When the back-seat driving became too much, Austin, an auditor, stopped the bus and said: "If there is a bus driver aboard, I'll be glad to let him take the wheel."

There were no takers. By now we had been joined by two other buses and half a dozen cars packed with Vietnamese who figured that by staying with us they could get out of the country.

At every stop, Vietnamese beat on the doors and windows pleading to be let inside. We merely looked at them. We already had enough Vietnamese aboard. Every time we opened the door, we had to beat and kick them back.

For no reason, except that we were following another bus, we went to the Saigon port area, one of the toughest parts of the city, where the crowds were uglier than elsewhere. Police fired into the air to part the mob and let us through onto the dock.

I got off the bus and went over to John Moore, the embassy security officer who was sitting in one of those sedans with the flashy blinker on top.

"Do you know why we are here and what you are going to

do with us?" I asked him.

Moore shrugged helplessly. "There are ships," he said, gesturing toward sandbagged Vietnamese vessels lying alongside the dock.

I looked around at the gathering crowd. Small boys were snatching typewriters and bags of film. This, as the Chinese would say, looked like bad joss. I didn't know how or whether I was going to get out of Saigon, but I damned well knew I wasn't going to stay here.

I got back on the bus, which was both our prison and our fortress. And other correspondents, including some of my closest friends—Wendell S. (Bud) Merick of *U.S News & World Report* and Ed White of the *Associated Press*—felt the same way. White's typewriter, his most precious possession at the moment, next to his life, was gone.

Again we had to fight off the Vietnamese. Ed Bradley of CBS, a giant of a man, was pushing, kicking, shoving, his face sad. I found myself pushing a middle-aged Vietnamese woman who had been sitting beside me on the bus and asked me to look after her because she worked for the Americans and the Viet Cong would cut her throat.

That's what they all said, and maybe they are right. But she fought her way back to my side. "Why did you push me?" she asked. I had no answer.

Austin didn't know what to do with us so we drove to the American embassy. There the Vietnamese woman decided to get off.

"I have worked for the U.S. government for 10 years," she said, "but you do not trust me and I do not trust you. Even if we do get to Tan Son Nhut, they wouldn't let me on the plane." She was right, of course.

"I am going home and poison myself," she said. I didn't say anything because there was nothing to say.

For lack of anything better to do, Austin drove us to the embassy parking lot across the street. The embassy was besieged by the Vietnamese that we were abandoning. Every gate was closed. There was no way in.

I went to the parking-lot telephone and called an embassy

friend. Briefly, I stated the situation: "There are about 40 of us —Americans, British and 2 or 3 Japanese. We can't get in."

"Hold it," he said. A few minutes later, he came back on the phone with the following instructions:

"'Take your people to the Mac Dinh Chi police station next to the embassy. They know you are coming. They will help you over the wall."

An uncertain Moses, I led my flock out of the parking lot, across the street and through the police barricades to the police station. They never heard of us. When we tried to talk to them, they told us to move on and fired into the air to make their point.

We dribbled around the corner to the rear of the embassy compound, where several hundred Vietnamese were pounding at the gate or trying to scale the wall. There was only one way inside: through the crowd and over the 10-foot wall.

Once we moved into that seething mass, we ceased to be correspondents. We were only men fighting for their lives, scratching, clawing, pushing ever closer to that wall. We were like animals.

Now, I thought, I know what it's like to be a Vietnamese. I am one of them. But if I could get over that wall I would be an American again.

My attache case accidentally struck a baby in its mother's arms and its father beat at me with his fists. I tried to apologize as he kept on beating me while his wife pleaded with me to take the baby.

Somebody grabbed my sleeve and wouldn't let go. I turned my head and looked into the face of a Vietnamese youth.

"You adopt me and take me with you and I'll help you," he screamed. "If you don't, you don't go."

I said I'd adopt him. I'd have said anything. Could this be happening to me?

Suddenly my arm was free and I edged closer to the wall. There were a pair of marines on the wall. They were trying to help us up and kick the Vietnamese down. One of them looked down at me.

"Help me," I pleaded. "Please help me."

That marine helped me. He reached down with his long, muscular arm and pulled me up as if I were a helpless child.

I lay on a tin roof gasping for breath like a landed fish, then dropped to the ground. God bless the Marines; I was one myself in the last of the just wars.

One American offered me a cup of water and a doctor asked me if I wanted a tranquilizer. I accepted the water and declined the tranquilizer. "Are you sure you're all right?" the doctor said anxiously.

"Sure," I croaked. "I'm just fine. But my friends?"

I looked up and saw a yellow shirt coming over the wall. That was Bud Merick of *U.S. News & World Report*. Minutes later I saw the sweaty red face of big Ed White from the AP come over.

I was very happy to see him. He is not only my friend. He was carrying my typewriter.

A tall, young embassy officer in a pink shirt looked at me and said, "Aren't you Keyes Beech?"

I admitted I was. His name is Brunson McKinley and I last saw him in Peking two years ago. We made our way through the crowd of Vietnamese evacuees gathered around the embassy swimming pool and through to the main embassy building and took the elevator to the sixth floor.

Our embassy friends seemed glad to see us and expressed awe that we had come over the embassy wall. I was pretty awed too, now that I think of it.

A retired American general who has been around here a long time, Charles Timmes, said he had been on the telephone to "Big" Minh, the new president, urging him to ask the North Vietnamese for a cease-fire.

"He said he was trying but they wouldn't listen," Charlie said. "Anyway, they haven't shelled the embassy yet."

"That's nice of them," I said, slumping into a soft chair.

The man I really wanted to see was down on the third floor. His name is Graham Martin and he was our ambassador. In my view, he gambled with American lives, including mine, by dragging his heels on the evacuation.

A few minutes later I was on the embassy roof and inside a

Marine helicopter and on my way to the carrier *Hancock*.

It was exactly 6:30 p.m.

My last view of Saigon was through the tail door of the helicopter. Tan Son Nhut was burning. So was Bien Hoa. Then the door closed—closed on the most humiliating chapter in American history.

I looked at the man next to me. He was a Vietnamese and I moved away from him. Forty-five minutes later we put down on the *Hancock*.

The salt-sea air tasted good.

'Do you know what you saw?' a colonel asked Bob Tamarkin, last reporter to leave Saigon

Daily News correspondent Bob Tamarkin was the last American reporter to leave Saigon. He was evacuated April 29, 1975, and this dispatch was published a week later.

ABOARD THE *USS OKINAWA*—"They lied to us at the very end," said Capt. Stuart Herrington, the tears welling in his eyes. "They promised," he said, biting hard on his lip to hold the tears back.

Shirtless, he sat on the edge of the bunk, shaking his head. He continued:

"I have never received an order in my life to do something I was ashamed of. If I would have known how it was going to end, I would have refused the order."

He was speaking of the evacuation of the Americans and Vietnamese during the frantic day last Tuesday when the Americans pulled out of South Vietnam, leaving hundreds of others who had been promised evacuation working in Saigon and the rest of the country.

Lt. Col. H. G. Summers, a barrel-chested 250-pounder, sitting in the bunk next to Herrington, turned to me and said:

"I asked you to come here because you were the last newsman to see the end. Do you know what you saw? Do you really know what you saw?" he asked.

"I saw the evacuation of the U.S. embassy—the last hours," I answered.

"No," Summers said, pausing. "You saw deceit. You saw how we let this country down to the very end."

Both men hadn't slept for more than 24 hours and both were emotionally drained.

The two had been assigned to the embassy to assist with the evacuation. For nearly 20 hours they organized groups of people, assuring them that they would be evacuated. They used Vietnamese firemen on standby to protect Americans should a helicopter accident occur.

In the end, even the firemen were left behind.

"We had arranged the people in groups of 70. We made them throw away their suitcases. They listened to us and believed us. They waited confidently in those rows, believing their friends would not let them down," Herrington said.

Until a few minutes before they themselves were flown out on the last choppers before the marines left, Herrington and Summers believed those 500 in the compound would be flown out. The two officers said they were told that Ambassador Graham Martin and his key aides would be leaving in the last helicopter, remaining until all evacuees were taken out. They left well before that.

"They didn't have the courtesy to tell us," Summers said. "We learned by accident the ambassador had left earlier. And we knew that those other people would not be going.

"They lied to us at the very end. One thing you don't do is lie to your own people."

There was no indication that the evacuation was going to stop until a security agent told them they would be taking the last chopper out, Summers said.

A total of 70,000 people were evacuated Tuesday. The operation employed 80 helicopters flying 495 sorties.

But as one senior diplomatic official put it:

"The big numbers are irrelevant. The rest of our lives we will be haunted by how we betrayed those people. It made me cry when I got here. There were lots of people who were crying when they got here."

On the second floor of a small annex building just behind the wall, the marines had set up a 50-caliber machine gun ready to strafe the walls should the Vietnamese try storming it.

A three-foot space along the top of the wall, where the barbed wire had been pushed aside, was the only way into the massive embassy compound. The embassy was sealed.

I had gone to the embassy earlier in the day, at noon, about 90 minutes after the evacuation alert was sounded. I was late arriving at a predesignated pickup point, from which I would have been taken by bus to the defense attache office at Tan Son Nhut Airport.

Four other Americans stood with me outside the gate, where only minutes before a portly man dressed in a blue suit had been allowed to enter. He was Gen. Dang Van Quang, the national securities affairs adviser to former President Nguyen Van Thieu.

I now stood with the other Americans, who were waving passports as proof of their citizenship. We were refused entrance.

John Hogan, the embassy press officer, whom I knew, assured me I could get in. But he gave no instructions. As I was walking away, he poked his finger at me from behind the gate and said: "Don't write one word about this evacuation." I returned to my hotel room and filed a story about the initial evacuation alert.

By the time I had returned to the entrance at 25 Hog Thap Tu St., I saw my 61-year-old colleague, Keyes Beech, scrambling to get through the three-foot space. As he was pulled up by the marines, he was pulled back by the Vietnamese clinging to him, hoping that somehow they would be pulled up with him. The marines had orders to grab Americans first, then third-country nationals and then the Vietnamese.

The scene at the wall was brutal. Marines and other embassy personnel threw Vietnamese people off the wall. One official drew his revolver, stuck it point-blank in the face of a young Vietnamese boy and screamed: "Get down, you bastard, or I'll blow your head off. Get down!"

The marines brought the butts of their rifles down on the fingers of those trying to climb the walls. Elderly women and children who were being pushed up by the sheer force of bodies beneath them became enmeshed in the barbed wire, their skin punctured with bloody wounds.

One official who had thrown a young girl from the wall three times finally gave in. "I couldn't take it anymore. I feel sorry for her." said Jeff Kibler, 24, an embassy accountant. "I couldn't play God anymore."

A bus pulled up to the gate jammed with people and with scores more clinging to the top. Under the threat of being machine-gunned, the driver backed away.

One American woman, who had arrived from Honolulu on Saturday to get a family of seven out of the country, arrived at the gate, trailed by the family. She stopped, realizing the futility of the situation.

"I couldn't put them through that," she said, the tears welling in her eyes. She sent the family away and returned to go over the wall herself.

Most of those who were legitimately to be evacuated were ignored as the marines began pulling people up. In some cases, families were separated forever. They were hoisted up and over like sacks of potatoes, dumped wherever they landed. I got in that way.

As the only correspondent who stayed to cover the evacuation of the embassy through the departure of Ambassador Martin (I left 45 minutes after he had), I kept a diary of the events and people I met in those desperate hours.

Following is a chronology of America's last few hours in South Vietnam, as I witnessed them.

3 p.m.—The embassy was surrounded by Vietnamese who wanted to get out of the country. They were screaming, crying, trampling one another, and some clawed at the gates in their futile efforts to get inside the embassy compound.

5:39 p.m.—I was hauled through the gap in the barbed wire. It had taken me more than 1½ hours to inch through the bodies to the marines' grasp, just three yards away.

One marine was pulled off the fence by hands that grabbed his legs. At that point, the mood of the marines turned from bare tolerance into fitful rage. They began pushing back harder and screaming louder.

Security guards in the neighboring French embassy stood on walls of their compound casually watching the pandemonium. Many people ran up to them, waving their papers and cards. The French ignored them.

6 p.m.—The rampage started quietly, and then it snowballed.

A few youngsters wandered into an inconspicuous storeroom filled with 200 or so cases of soft drinks and grabbed a couple of bottles apiece. Within minutes hundreds were storming the storeroom carrying away several bottles at a time. Within minutes the storeroom had been cleaned out. The assault set the mood for what was to follow.

The fever spread into the embassy restaurant, where people began grabbing what they could. They devoured and drank anything they could get their hands on.

The binge spread to the food lockers, where frozen foods were kept. Slabs of ribs and frozen steaks and beef briskets were pounded with hammers and dull-edged knives to soften the meat to be cooked on the stoves and in the ovens, which were in control of the evacuees.

Then they found the storeroom to the restaurant above the main embassy restaurant. Down they came. This time they carried off cases of canned goods, juices, boxes containing cartons of cigarets. Some were stopped by the marines, who began beating looters.

9:40 p.m.—A grim-faced Graham Martin, his hair perfectly combed, followed by four marines, disappeared up a flight of stairs. He surveyed the pillage. The crowd did not recognize the ambassador. He came swiftly down the stairs minutes later, the marines still following closely. He disappeared through the gate that leads to the main embassy courtyard, where the helicopters land on the parking lot.

As the helicopters circled overhead, their red lights blinking off and on, orange flames and thick smoke poured out of the embassy's smokestack. The remaining documents and papers, some collected since 1954, when the United States established its embassy in Saigon, were being burned in the incinerator.

10 p.m.—Only an hour earlier, a marine had threatened to blow the head off a young Vietnamese boy. He pointed his .45 automatic at the youth, forcing him to drop the carton of cigarets he had taken from the storehouse. Then the marines walked the same steps, stuffing cartons into their own knap-sacks.

10:30 p.m.—A 30-year-old American woman named Mari-lyn (she would not give her last name) who came to Vietnam on-ly a few days ago to be with a Vietnamese friend, decided she wanted to go back over the wall. She begged a Marine guard to let her go. There were still thousands at every gate to the em-bassy, but they were quiet, sitting in the darkness, hoping they would be allowed in the next morning.

"In all good conscience, I can't let you go over the wall," the marine said. "You must get permission from the embassy offi-cials in charge of the evacuation."

She was disappointed, but agreed.

The marines began rounding up the last few Americans in the compound. It had been 12 hours since the evacuation began.

11:30 p.m.—The marines were ordered to round up the Americans and let them pass through to the landing-pad door first. The Vietnamese sensed something might be wrong and be-gan to stir. They began to advance toward the gate, but were stopped. The process of getting through the gate is slow. Fifty to 80 people at a time were allowed to pass. A normal helicopter load is 50, but now they were jamming the copters with as many as 80 and 90. The sound of small-arms fire pierced the night along with the muffled sound of artillery.

Midnight—Some of the marines were edgy and a few turned sadistic. One stood before the hundreds of Vietnamese who stared blankly ahead, and said: "All right, now everybody sings." He began waving his hands through the air, conducting them. They didn't understand. He laughed loudly. They just stared in bewilderment, their faces blank. One young Vietnam-ese boy and a man tried to squeeze through the gate.

They were beaten, brutally.

The choppers began landing on the roof of the embassy and on the parking lot. The group I was with was led into the embas-sy to take off from the heliport.

1 a.m.—The inside of the embassy now appeared to have been ransacked. The marines and embassy security officials sys-tematically went through every room tearing up, ripping out and destroying whatever might reveal anything to the enemy.

1:15 a.m.—Ambassador Martin was in the office of Conrad F. LaGueux, a special assistant. A senior diplomatic official, sipping a glass of champagne, was going over last-minute details with Henry Boudreau, counselor of administrative affairs. Martin, still in shirtsleeves, was calm. They were joined by Josiah W. Bennett, head of political affairs. Meanwhile, the deputy ambassador, Wolfgang J. Lemann, roamed throughout the embassy, walkie-talkie in hand, monitoring the evacuation efforts.

2 a.m.—About 200 evacuees had been led to the stairwell of the top floor and were planted there to wait for another chopper to land. The door to the floor was locked. For more than two hours they waited, sealed in the well without water.

One man said that he had been at the embassy since 7 a.m. waiting to leave. An American who worked as a computer analyst had heard on the radio at 8 p.m. that all the Americans had left. He was unaware of the evacuation. At midnight a friend called to let him know the helicopters were still flying. He got to the embassy at 1 a.m. and was pulled over the fence.

3 a.m.—A security official said the evacuation was 12 hours behind schedule.

3:30 a.m.—Marines were stretched out sleeping on the floor of the embassy lobby, machine guns, M-16s, knapsacks, walkie-talkies spread out everywhere. In a back room on the first floor was Maj. J. Keene, commander of the 140-man detail assigned to provide evacuation protection. He was grabbing a few minutes of sleep, his feet propped up on a desk. A young marine in a corridor gathered his gear, stuffing a paperback book into his knapsack. The book: *The Fall of Rome.*

Amid the big plastic bags of shredded paper, a flagless pole stood forlornly, and there were still plaques on the lobby wall. One plaque was in honor of four embassy personnel—an American woman and three Vietnamese—who were killed by a Viet Cong bomb while on duty at the embassy on March 30, 1965.

The other plaque read: "Embassy of the United States of America. Built in time of war. Dedicated to the cause of peace. In memory of those who have served their nation in Vietnam. Ellsworth Bunker Ambassador. September 1967."

4:15 a.m.—Ambassador Martin appeared in the lobby. He was wearing a light-brown suit, and carried a small attache case and a folded clothes bag.

He first walked outside, but several minutes later he and top aides returned. Instead of leaving from the ground-level site, he was instructed to depart from the heliport atop the embassy. He spoke to no one, but stood waiting for the elevator to the sixth floor for the last time. With him were special assistants, Thomas Polgar, LaGueux and George Jacobson. An air of deep depression surrounded them as they walked into the elevator.

About 15 minutes later, a Marine helicopter carried off the ambassador, his aides, two security guards, several personnel from the mission warden's office and a missionary couple, officially ending America's presence in South Vietnam.

They were on their way to the *USS Blue Ridge*, the flagship of the 7th Fleet.

As the Jolly Green Giant CH-53 lifted Martin and the others into the blackness, the lights of Saigon glimmered below and fires could be seen on the city's outskirts. They were from the fighting of the encroaching and overpowering North Vietnamese army, tightening its grip for the kill. Lightning accompanying monsoon rains in the distance lit up the sky periodically.

A stream of lights headed down from the direction of Bien Hoa, 15 miles north of Saigon, where the Communist tanks and troop trucks pushed toward the scared and panicked city. It was just a matter of time before 30 years of war would come to an end.

To the end, Martin maintained the somber aloofness that characterized him. Yet he maintained a certain dignity.

5 a.m.—A sense of panic overtook even the marines. So far there was no actual fighting, just threats and shots fired into the air.

5:15 a.m.—The remaining American civilians—there were three of us—were instructed to go to the sixth floor. One civilian was the young woman who would not give her name. The other civilian was a portly man in his late 30s, who also refused to give his name or even his home in the States. He arrived in Saigon only on Monday to try to help some Vietnamese friends out. It was too late. Now he sulked, turned to an officer and said: "You know, I had ordered $100 worth of tailor-made clothing yesterday when I arrived, and I paid for it in advance." The soldier merely nodded.

The embassy security head appeared, a walkie-talkie in hand. Martin Garrett turned to the group of Army officers, marines and civilians and several other embassy security staff, and said:

"We just got orders from President Ford that the evacuation is to stop immediately. The pilots have been flying for 14 hours, and the President has ordered the commander of the 7th Fleet to halt operations."

He carefully gave instructions to the marines to station themselves on the roof and to leave all their gear behind.

Those marines who were still on the embassy grounds were told to walk back into the embassy casually when the next chopper left, and secure the doors behind them. They, too, would be leaving from the heliport.

5:30 a.m.—The marines took their place on the roof. The helicopter landed, its massive propellers whooshing through the air, creating cyclonic winds, drowning out the sounds of the night.

My chopper lifted off, its red lights blinking, and headed toward the South China Sea. The passengers, including me, sat stoically in the dark, tired and numb. Some were dazed, finding it difficult to believe that the Americans were pulling out in this manner, skulking away in the darkness.

Below in the courtyard, where the big choppers had been loading, the headlights from the cars and trucks surrounding the parking lot were still on to light the way for the choppers.

Hundreds of Vietnamese looked up, waiting for the next one.

It never came.

Raymond R. Coffey witnesses the agony of a Buddhist girl who became a human torch

This is one of the first stories correspondent Raymond R. Coffey filed to the Daily News *after he arrived in Vietnam in 1966. The story was published June 18, 1966.*

SAIGON—Seeing Tuyet Dao Tri writhe in pain and listening to her tortured screams was an ordeal of horror.

Witnessing the callous use that Buddhist leaders made of the 19-year-old girl's agony was even more horrible.

The girl poured gasoline on herself Friday night, lit a match and turned herself into a human torch within the grounds of the Vien Hoa Dao Pagoda, headquarters for the Buddhists' anti-government drive.

She did not use enough gasoline, and, though frightfully burned, she was still alive when she was taken to a hospital.

After six hours of agony, the girl died there.

I was in the offices of United Press International when a phone call from the Vien Hoa Dao advised that a woman was burning herself to death.

Four other newsmen and I drove to the pagoda and we were met at the gate of the darkened compound by several Buddhist youths carrying torches.

Immediately they cleared a path through a crowd of about 100 persons in the compound and escorted us through the muddy grounds to a small room.

Inside, Tuyet Dao Tri, her face and arms blackened and split with fire, was lying on the ground, wrapped in a gray wool blanket.

Three gray-robed monks, several Buddhist Boy Scouts and a few nuns poured spoonfuls of liquid into the burned girl's mouth.

No other effort was being made to comfort or care for her.

But great care was taken to accommodate the reporters and photographers present.

As the girl screamed with pain, one monk and one Buddhist layman pushed the Boy Scouts gathered around the body so that reporters could see and photographers could get a clear view.

Then another young Buddhist escorted us through the muddy grounds to show where the girl had set fire to herself—a spot just inside the pagoda walls and opposite a statue of Buddha.

He flashed a light on the ground to reveal blackened bits of the girl's clothing.

From there the escorts led us off to a small office where a monk, Thich Man Giac, reported details of the burning.

"I am sorry she did not use enough gasoline," he said. "Now she will suffer."

Against everything else that had transpired so far, that seemed a humane remark.

But then he went on to plead with newsmen to "tell the world's newspapers" that the government has shut off light and water service to the pagoda.

"Not good," he said of the government action. Also not very important at the moment, it seemed.

Finally a tiny foreign-made station wagon pulled into the pagoda grounds and Tuyet Dao Tri was lifted into it and driven off to a hospital.

As the vehicle pulled away, scores of young boys and girls in the compound began wailing and pounding on the orange iron gate of the compound.

Then one of the boys, apparently overwhelmed with emotion at the burning, took a dose of what monks said was poison in an attempt to commit suicide.

He too was taken to a hospital.

The publicity exploitation of the horror, however, was still not complete.

Thich Man Giac produced two letters written by the girl before she set herself afire.

One was to Thich Tam Chau, a top Buddhist leader, and

the other to President Johnson. Both protested what the anti-government Buddhists insist on calling oppression of their religion by Prime Minister Nguyen Cao Ky's government.

"She came from a prominent and good Buddhist family," he said.

There was something frighteningly casual about the way he put the life of a 19-year-old girl—at that moment alive—in the past tense.

Pham Van Le's mother cried, 'You used to take me everywhere, why don't you take me with you now?'

Larry Green, who wrote this story for the May 27, 1972, Daily News, *covered the Vietnam War for four years.*

BIEN HOA, South Vietnam—Pham Van Le finished his military training on Sunday, went into battle on Monday, died on Tuesday, was buried on Saturday.

He was 22, married seven months, a porter on the Saigon docks before he was drafted.

He was one of dozens buried this day, buried every day here at the national military cemetery where the wailing never stops and rank knows no special honor.

His wife was there, and his mother, sister, father.

For hours the women mourned, screaming, cursing the government for sending him off to war, begging him to return to life.

"They live in houses and ride in cars. They sit in offices and force my husband to die," his 19-year-old widow yelled above the din of other mourning at other funerals. "Those old men don't die, only the young."

They were poor, Buddhist, a family that has bounced around the country for years trying to escape the fighting.

"My son, my son. I'm here to see you. You used to take me everywhere, why don't you take me with you now?" his mother cried.

A ragtag honor guard marched to the coffin, carried it to a rattling military van painted black, escorted it on the short procession through the fields of fresh graves.

There was one last chance for emotion and both mother and wife threw themselves across the flag-covered box.

As the grave diggers began filling the hole, the black van arrived with the next body and rows of unfilled graves baked in the sun.

"My husband, my husband, they let my husband die."

He was one of more than 8,000 South Vietnamese soldiers killed since the North Vietnamese offensive began March 29.

But there is still room for 25,000 more bodies.

Ellen Warren reports the story of Julie Pearson, whose husband didn't come home from Vietnam

Ellen Warren, a young local reporter on the 4 p.m.-to-midnight shift when she wrote this story for the June 13, 1973, Daily News, *later became a foreign correspondent.*

"This is Richard," announced Julie Pearson. "He is the 'unusual situation.' "

Richard Adamson, 33, rugged and handsome, with a big broad grin and a substantial mustache, came into the room and sat down.

He and Julie, also 33, live in a robin's-egg-blue house on a tree-lined street in quiet west suburban La Grange.

On Tuesday, the Defense Department declared Julie a widow, 5½ years after her husband, Capt. Wayne Pearson, was shot down over Laos and declared missing in action.

But the Defense Department explained Wednesday that it had made an error.

Capt. Ed Robertson, an Air Force information officer in Washington, said Wayne Pearson mistakenly was listed as dead when a sergeant pulled his file card instead of that of another Pearson who had been declared dead Tuesday.

He said the mistake was being corrected and that Wayne Pearson's MIA status definitely hadn't been changed.

"If I had thought there was a chance that Wayne wasn't killed, if he'd been a prisoner, I'd never have done this. I would have waited for him," she declared.

Richard and Julie have a 16-month-old son, Jesse. They have loved each other and lived together more than 2½ years. But they aren't married.

Julie Pearson's story is the tale of a modern war from a very personal point of view.

She and Wayne were high-school sweethearts. Both were nice suburban kids who got married in 1959 after their sophomore year at the University of Illinois.

He was in ROTC and joined the Air Force as a second lieutenant after his graduation. Julie had quit college to be a wife.

"Wayne was going to straighten out the military. He had a lot of plans, bless his heart."

Capt. Pearson volunteered for Vietnam duty and went over in November, 1967, leaving Julie to live with her parents and her two young sons, Greg and Eric.

"I depended on Wayne, but he never really listened to me," she said. "You know, you go from your mother's arms to your husband's arms."

On Feb. 22, 1968, as Julie was sewing a new wardrobe for a rest leave with her husband in Hawaii only two weeks away, the Air Force car pulled up.

Wayne had been shot down over the Plain of Jars. Witnesses said they saw the F-4 Phantom he was piloting crash and explode. They didn't see Capt. Pearson bail out.

"I smoked like a chimney for three days after they told me. I gagged when I ate food. I didn't want to get out of bed. Sleep it away," she recalled.

"Responsibility. All of a sudden, it was laid on me. I bought this house and I just threw myself into working on it. For two years I tried to convince myself he was going to come home!

"Get it over with, please, that's how you feel. This MIA business is a mess.

"Common sense told me, 'You're gonna wait seven years for somebody to tell you he's dead.' Well, it wasn't seven, but it was five.

"I felt as if I should be more than just an appendage to Wayne. I was so involved in myself and my sorrow that I think I neglected my kids."

Julie began to be her own person. It came gradually. Three years ago she opened her own shop, the Calico Mushroom, an arts-and-crafts gift store in Hinsdale. "It's taking off," she said with delight.

Somehow, Richard came along, in June, 1970. "I wasn't looking for someone. But it was just exactly what all of us need," she said.

That September he moved in. Sixteen months later Jesse was born. "We're happy," Julie declared, grinning, looking up from a green-and-blue needlepoint butterfly she was working on.

Sure there were problems. When the Air Force found out about Richard and their new son, it stopped the $1,000 monthly checks, Julie said with a little bitterness. "The Air Force freaked out. They sent me a letter, 'Since you're married, no more money.' I told them I wasn't married, but it didn't matter. They cut me off.

"I had to prove to them that Eric and Greg were Wayne's sons. Now they send me $365-a-month child support, but I haven't heard from them since they found out about Jesse."

And there's Wayne's mother, who lives three blocks away.

"She keeps in touch with the boys, but what I've done, in her mind, is possibly the worst thing anyone could do," Julie said.

"You know, I went to Washington for a POW-MIA thing. I wish I knew why. I felt as if I was nothing more than one of a herd of cattle. They paraded us around. To me, we were pawns. We had been used. We were propaganda."

The blue house is a happy place now. Julie feels self-sufficient. Richard works hard as a carpenter and poet (his book will be out soon). He has been a husband to Julie and it has been rough sometimes. He has been a father to the Pearson boys. They adore him.

Some neighbors think Julie's and Richard's relationship is, well, illicit. But they don't make a big deal of it. Julie and Richard exchanged "wedding" rings to keep the rumors down.

Maybe they'll make it official someday, "if she'll have me," Richard jokes. Maybe they won't. Julie is determined to be very independent.

"I'm different now," she proclaims. "We're two separate people, you know."

Three years after this story appeared, Ellen Warren telephoned Julie Pearson, who reported that she and Richard Adamson were living happily together, still unmarried.

Betty Washington describes the tragedy of a Vietnam hero turned deserter

This story by reporter Betty Washington appeared in the Daily News *of Dec. 29, 1972.*

Nearly five years ago, Army Staff Sgt. Larry M. Osche braved enemy fire in Vietnam to rescue a wounded comrade.

Now Osche, who wanted to be a career soldier, is in an Army stockade because he deserted to care for his ailing family in Chicago.

Osche, 25, had been absent without leave from his post in Aschaffenburg, Germany, since May 5. The FBI arrested him Tuesday at his wife's apartment, 3825 S. Emerald, and turned him over to military police.

Osche is being held at Fort Riley, Kan., hundreds of miles from the family he sought to protect, and a nightmare's distance from the military career he'd hoped for.

"It's unfair," said Osche's 25-year-old wife, Linda, who fears that she is partly to blame for his plight.

Linda sits at home now, reading letters from Army officials that praise her husband's performance. She weeps, and she wonders if the words have any meaning.

One letter details how Osche was awarded the Bronze Star for "outstanding leadership" and "exemplary courage" during a Jan. 15, 1967, battle when Osche was on a search-and-destroy mission near Phu Loi, South Vietnam.

In the foray, the company's lead man was wounded and lay unconscious within 20 meters of a Viet Cong base camp.

Osche, the letter states, "unhesitatingly exposed himself to insurgent fire as he crawled to the wounded man." As the heavy firing continued, Osche tossed a grenade into the Viet Cong bunker and then "carried the wounded man to safety." He also is credited with forcing the Viet Cong to flee and bringing credit to the "the entire U.S. Army."

294

Osche's troubles began after he was reassigned to Germany in 1971 and took his wife and infant son, Larry Jr., with him.

Linda became pregnant and was frightened because she previously had had two miscarriages. When she fainted one day in her Army quarters and awoke to find young Larry perched on the windowsill in their seventh-floor apartment, she decided it was time to come home.

Larry was frequently assigned to temporary duty elsewhere, and Linda's mother, Lois Rychlock, was in Chicago.

Linda arrived last February to find her mother hospitalized and unable to assist her. Mrs. Rychlock, Linda said, is still "very ill."

Brandy Lynn, the Osche's second child, was born July 24, but Linda continued in poor health and in need of assistance.

After several requests, Osche was granted a 30-day leave, later extended 10 days. However, his request for compassionate reassignment to a base near home was denied. Osche refused to return to the Army and took odd jobs "where people wouldn't ask questions" to support his family, his wife said.

"We even called the commander in Germany hoping to convince someone of our crises. But we failed," she said.

"Larry wanted a career in the Army. He was dedicated and took pride in his uniform. It was the first time he asked for anything. Now he's bitter. He doesn't even want to talk."

Mrs. Osche said that at one point her husband was told, "If the Army wanted you to have a wife and child they would have issued you one."

Sen. Charles Percy (R-Ill.) has tried to help the family, Linda said. And the American Red Cross here verified the family's condition.

"Larry has just given up. He knew he had a duty to the Army. But he also had a duty to us. We need him.

"My God," she said, her voice breaking, "you'd think they'd make an exception. Larry says he won't go back to Germany, that they'd have to kill him."

Col. Albert Steffen, commander of the personnel control facility at Fort Riley, said he'd had no opportunity to look at Osche's records. But he said the length of the desertion (seven months), the family condition and Osche's commendations would be considered before it is determined whether the sergeant will receive a summary court-martial or company punishment.

"We're pretty flexible in these matters. It just depends on the individual case," Steffen said. Compassionate reassignment still may be a possibility.

Later, perhaps as a result of Betty Washington's story, the Army decided not to prosecute Staff Sgt. Larry Osche. On Jan. 16, 1973—the fifth anniversary of the heroic rescue for which Osche was awarded the Bronze Star—he was granted a general discharge.

For Bobby Frakes
the Vietnam truce
came one day too late,
Rob Warden reports

This article by Rob Warden, a local reporter
who later became a foreign correspondent, was
published in the Jan. 30, 1973, Daily News.

MACOMB, Ill.—The last present Bobby gave his mother was a Bible.

With it she will keep the formal picture of him in uniform, his letters from Vietnam and the telegram that came this weekend from the Defense Department.

Her blue-eyed Bobby will not be coming home.

Army Specialist 4 Robert L. Frakes, 20, of Macomb, was the last soldier from Illinois killed in Vietnam before the ceasefire began.

At 6:30 a.m. Saturday the headlights of an official limousine pierced the morning darkness in Macomb while Eva Irene Frakes and her two other children, Gene, 18, and Nava, 16, slept.

Bobby's father, Ira, who doesn't live with the family, was in the car with Maj. William Patterson of the Western Illinois University Army ROTC unit.

To Maj. Patterson had fallen the grim duty of notifying the family that Bobby's helicopter—Bobby always called it "my ship"—had been shot down in Vietnam. Ira Frakes was notified first because he was listed first among the next of kin.

Tears filled the aging father's eyes when he rapped on the front-door glass of the little green house at 332 N. Dudley St. to awaken his wife and children.

At that time, Bobby was still officially listed as missing in action. The telegram that arrived held out hope because "posi-

297

tive individual identification had not been established."

They prayed for a miracle in Macomb for the next 48 hours, until Bobby's death was officially confirmed by the Army Monday morning.

"One more day, just one more day," Ira Frakes anguished, "and all the boys would be coming home."

Bobby was born in Macomb on New Year's Day, 1953. When he was in grade school his dad won a bicycle in a local contest. One of the tires went flat and Bobby took it to a bike store run by a grandfatherly man named Art Justus and his wife, Helen, on N. MacArthur St.

Art Justus choked back tears when he talked about that Saturday afternoon: "Bobby looked around and asked if he could go to work, so I put him to work. He was the most perfect boy always. He never done anything that wasn't nice. He was just one kid that was always right there willing to do anything without you having to ask."

Bobby worked for Art and Helen until he was graduated from Macomb High School in 1971. "He wasn't what you'd call bright in school," Art said, "but we got on him and he made the honor roll his senior year, the last semester."

For graduation Art and Helen gave him gift certificates for a suit and a pair of shoes with the amounts of the certificates left blank.

"We told the stores to give him what he wanted. Didn't matter what it cost," Helen sobbed. "Now how many boys could you trust like that? That was the kind of boy he was. He went down to the store and he didn't pick out a pair of $40 shoes. He just got the ones that fit."

Growing up, Bobby's main interest was mechanics. "He'd get that bicycle apart all over the yard," Ira Frakes said. In high school he excelled in the auto mechanics course.

Bobby and his brother Gene shared the hobby of coin collecting. The prize of the collection is a 1914 gold piece bequeathed when their grandmother died recently.

"He was a good boy, never in any trouble," Mrs. Frakes said. "He wanted to make something out of his life, maybe go to college and be an accountant."

After graduation he got a job in a factory. His parents both worked in factories, but Bobby wanted something better. By the end of the summer he was bored.

Art and Helen gave Bobby the money to pay for a first quarter's tuition at Western Illinois University, which is in Macomb, 250 miles southwest of Chicago. "He took it at first," Art said, "but I guess he was just too proud to let us do that. He gave back the money and said he was going to enlist in the Army instead."

By the time he reported for basic training at Fort Lewis, Wash., on Oct. 15, 1971, Bobby was beginning to get serious about Janet Hickman, whom he had taken to the school prom his senior year.

After basic, Bobby went to Fort Rucker, Ala., to train as a helicopter mechanic. Then he came home in June to see his family, Janet and Art and Helen before beginning a one-year tour of duty in Vietnam.

Before he left Macomb the last time, Janet said, he asked her to wait for him and promised, "I'll be back."

Tears streamed down Janet's cheeks as she told how a few weeks after that she had met Doug Willey. Only a week ago, Janet said, she wrote Bobby a long letter explaining that she planned to marry Doug in February. She doesn't know if Bobby got the letter.

"He wanted to go to college," cried the 17-year-old bride-to-be. "He went in the Army because he thought they would help him get to study accounting when he got out. I tried to talk him out of it. I didn't want him to go in."

Bobby, according to his family and friends, had no feeling about whether the war was right or wrong, but he was skeptical about the prospect of ending it soon.

"It doesn't look like it (will end) no matter what you hear," he said in the last letter to his family, received the day he was killed. "They can say anything they want, but it's the actual doing that I want to see."

Art and Helen also received a letter the same day, expressing the same thought. Helen noted that Bobby had written the letter before President Nixon announced the peace agreement last week and wrote in reply: "Didn't I tell you it would be over in January?"

Art went out Saturday morning to mail the letter before he knew that Bobby had died the day before.

Norman Mark writes that public TV's Vietnam history came years too late to help

Television critic Norman Mark wrote this column for the June 4, 1975, Daily News *after previewing the Public Broadcasting System's Documentary "The End of the Ho Chi Minh Trail."*

I'm sick of Vietnam.

I was sick of it while we were there and I'm sicker of it now that we're out.

I voted for one President who said he wouldn't make American boys fight there, and I watched another President take five years to unveil his nonplan for getting us out.

The night we finally left that bloody, sorry country, I watched CBS spend 3 hours to eulogize our involvement, with NBC offering an hour and ABC 90 minutes of about the same thing. It was an awful war, the networks seemed to say, and we shouldn't have been there, but boy did we get some great film footage of the fighting.

Now public television weighs in with its analysis, a 90-minute effort to be seen at 8 p.m. Wednesday on Channel 11 (PBS). It uses hindsight as a club to tell us over and over again that we were wrong, wrong, wrong.

It is something that many of us knew years ago but that public TV didn't discover until recently.

"The End of the Ho Chi Minh Trail" is an American-British co-production. Three correspondents, representing the United States and North and South Vietnam, offer a history of the war.

Jim Lehrer, the American reporter, says we entered the war with a "benevolent arrogance." Olivier Todd, a French journalist who covered the war from Hanoi, accuses us of "innocence with soiled hands." And Julian Pettifer, a BBC reporter, shows us some film he took in South Vietnam.

We hear all the stock phrases ("body count," "Vietnamization," "limited war" and so on). And we see some shocking film —a legless woman whose stumps are being measured for wooden legs, a child emasculated by American weaponry in 1967. We see the boy painfully attempting to urinate.

Awful sights, but then all wars are hell (the most applicable cliche) and they've never been healthy for women and children.

The documentary does make the viewer angry, only this time the futile rage is not directed at the leaders who dragged us into that Southeast Asian swamp and kept us there. I've been angry at them for too long to sustain the emotion.

No, this time I'm angry at the messengers, those smug people of the BBC and PBS who conclude that it was the "wrong war with the wrong leaders and the wrong allies" for the South Vietnamese. They sit there, in their nice suits under the antiseptic glare of the TV lights, and ponder, "What has the war done to our sense of benevolence?"

That's bunk.

Where were these people in 1966, 1967, 1968, 1969, 1970 and even later when messages like that might have affected events?

In those years, public television was avoiding broadcasting a film made in North Vietnam and it was bending over backwards to cover Support America rallies in an effort to gain congressional and White House support for permanent funding. It was beginning its trendy steps towards its current hidebound sycophancy.

Because it was too cowardly to tell us five years ago what it smugly reveals today, PBS' hands are also bloody. And its message is corrupt.

About the last program I need today is one that rehashes what happened yesterday. I'm worried about tomorrow.

I want shows that ask: Can America stand another $150 billion adventure that costs 50,000 lives and divides our country? What will we do in the next war? Prove our might again or retreat? Is there such a thing as a good war?

How could the Constitution, a beautiful document, become so subverted that we could elect two Presidents who were peace candidates but who fought the war anyway?

PBS and the BBC and Lehrer conclude that "the people will decide from this point on what burdens we will bear and what price we will pay." It's a smarmy, oversimplified conclusion, unjustified by the facts presented in the film. It's typical of an effort that is too late.

Where were you, PBS, when the killing time was with us?

World War II MPs oust Montgomery Ward & Co. chairman Sewell L. Avery from company premises after he refused to obey an order from the National War Labor Board in 1944. Hartland Klotz / Daily News.

Money:
Mike Royko
Raymond R. Coffey
Finley Peter Dunne
Betty Flynn
Joe Cappo
Steve Yahn
George Harmon
Anthony Campbell
Sandra Pesmen
Alan D. Mutter
Dick Griffin
Marge McElheney

Mike Royko: Would you want Lester Crown to walk with you to the OK Corral?

Mike Royko offered some observations in this June 7, 1976, column about multimillionaire businessman Lester Crown, who bribed several state legislators. Crown was given immunity from prosecution for his testimony but six of the men he testified against were found guilty of taking Crown's bribes.

You just couldn't find two individuals who are less alike than Louis Capuzi, the ward heeler politician, and Lester Crown, the millionaire executive.

Using any standard—professional, social, cultural, educational or financial—they are of different worlds. I'm sure Mr. Crown and his friends would agree, if they ever took notice of someone like Louis Capuzi, which is unlikely.

In politics, Capuzi is what they call a follower. He is an outstanding follower. He is one of the great followers of our time.

When he first got a chance to warm a seat in Springfield, he followed Pete Granata, one of the most prominent gray fedoras on the West Side.

Somebody once observed that, in complete defiance of the laws of probability, Capuzi and Granata always served on exactly the same committees, subcommittees and state commissions. It might have been the first time that happened in the history of the Legislature.

That was easily explained. Granata didn't know how to drive. He didn't like cars, because some of his best friends had died in accidents, like when they turned on the ignition and a bomb went off.

So he had it arranged for Capuzi always to be around to turn on the ignition, and if nothing happened, to drive him around.

Granata is gone now, but Capuzi is still here. And until recently he was considered a success by the standards of any reasonable precinct captain.

He has managed to get on not one, but two payrolls. When he is not in Springfield, he is a deputy coroner. This job permits him to carry a badge, conduct meaningless inquests and impress funeral directors and widows.

Before getting that prized job, he was with the Sanitary District, the county treasurer's office and other agencies where a good afternoon's sleep is seldom interrupted.

Capuzi has enjoyed a long career as a payroller and legislator because he has the qualities of reliability and loyalty. As one of his acquaintances said:

"When there is a vote in the House, you never have to worry about Capuzi being somewhere else. He keeps that chair warm. And he always votes the right way. When he's not sure, he's not too proud to ask. And he never says anything foolish on the floor of the House. He never says anything."

In contrast to Capuzi, the follower, we have Lester Crown, the leader.

He is a leader in business, running the giant Material Service Corp., the nation's biggest supplier of ready-mix concrete.

He is a leader in civic affairs, serving on the boards of universities, hospitals and the kind of charities that make the society pages when they help the lowly.

Even his wife is a leader, a member of the Lyric Opera board. That's no Tupperware party.

When the Crowns want to get away for a few days—even a mansion in Wilmette with an indoor swimming pool can be confining—they fly up to Sun Valley to ski.

Capuzi's idea of a big evening is playing gin rummy.

Crown lunches in sedate, private clubs. Capuzi belongs to a club, too. American Legion Post something or other.

When he wants to golf, Crown goes to the exclusive Northmoor Country Club. Capuzi always buys a mittful of tickets for the assessor's annual golf outing.

When Crown was a lad, his father, Henry, the superrich industrialist who once owned the Empire State Building, prepared him for his leadership role by sending him to Harvard's School of Business. People fortunate enough to go there end up clipping their coupons. He made Tau Beta Pi, Pi Mu Epsilon and Phi Eta Sigma.

Capuzi, as a young man, went to chiropodist school to learn to clip toenails. He hasn't touched a corn in years, but some friends still call him "Doc."

I could go on, but it's obvious. They have little in common.

But there is one thing.

Not long ago, Crown sat in the witness box in the U.S. District Court and testified how he and other powerful men in the ready-mix concrete business tossed together a bundle of money to bribe state legislators. They wanted the state law changed to permit their trucks to carry heavier loads. This crumples highways, but what the hell, their limos glide over bumps.

For someone like Crown, the court appearance was distasteful business. But he handled it with his usual dignity and poise. You get that at Harvard.

A few days ago, Capuzi sat in the same courtroom, same chair. But Louis looked sweaty and nervous.

You can't blame him. The government says Louis got a piece of that bribe money. A tiny piece. A lousy 200 bucks, in fact. Crown pays chauffeurs and maids more than that.

Louis admitted he took some money. Somebody just handed it to him. But he says he didn't know it was a bribe. He thought it was a campaign contribution.

Of all the legislators accused of sharing the wealth, nobody got less than Louis. That shows where he stands, even among his peers.

But if the jury doesn't believe him, he's had it. That $200 will get him a chance to say "Hi" to Tom Keane in a prison workshop.

But not Lester Crown, business and civic leader. Once again, he and ward heeler Capuzi are different.

When Crown finished testifying, he would walk away. His lawyer, the brilliant Albert Jenner (remember how Jenner felt about Nixon's immunity?), had worked out immunity for Crown.

Just like Daisy and Tom in *The Great Gatsby*, Crown and the other concrete fat cats could walk away from the shambles their greed created.

It should be said for Capuzi that while he is a political sheep, he did not bleat about somebody else to save his own hide. He might be only a ward heeler, and it was only $200, but whatever happens to him, he didn't point at someone else.

I have a friend who has a funny way of judging character. He boils it down to this question: "Would you want him to walk down to the OK Corral with you?"

Of the two, I'd take Capuzi.

Besides, why would Lester Crown want to walk down to the OK Corral? He'd probably hire someone to go.

Raymond R. Coffey interviews an inventor who runs his car on 127-octane manure

Shortly after the average American discovered the energy crisis in 1973, Daily News *London correspondent Raymond R. Coffey interviewed a British inventor who ran his car on pollution-free methane gas distilled from manure. Here is Coffey's story.*

TOTNES, Devon, England—For Harold Bate this whole noisy business about the energy crisis and automobile pollution is a lot of unnecessary nonsense.

He has been running his car for nearly 17 years now on pollution-free and exceedingly high-octane pig manure.

Furthermore, for $33 including postage he will send you a converter device and full instructions on how you too can run your car on manure—pig, cattle, chicken, dog or almost any other variety.

Bate is not a nut. He is an inventor, and his system works.

He distills methane gas from the manure, puts the gas into small steel cylinders that fit in the trunk of his car and runs a small hose from the cylinder to the engine.

The heart of the system is a small sort of suction valve, which operates on suction created by the carburetor and feeds the methane gas into the engine.

He calculates that about 100 pounds of pig manure produces a volume of methane gas equivalent to about eight gallons of regular gasoline.

And, he says, "it's very high-performance stuff, about 127 octane. You can't get an engine to knock on it; you can even start off in high gear. Coming back from London the other week I got up to 78 miles per hour on the motorway." Which is not bad going, especially for Bate's superannuated 1955 Hillman.

Bate, an extraordinary character, lives with his wife in an isolated 400-year-old stone cottage about seven miles from this west-country Devon town.

He is 65 years old, has one wooden leg, great shocks of wild white hair that makes him look a bit like Israel's David Ben-Gurion, gets about with the help of a cane, wears glasses with broken brown rims and dresses memorably in ballooning straw-colored corduroy trousers, yellow shirt and bow tie, heavy-duty suspenders, tan jacket.

He has always been interested in invention, he said, and his tiny house, his tool shed and the self-built garage where he does his work are crammed with wheels, nuts, bolts, hoses, gears, switches, old motors and incredible piles of what looks to others like assorted junk.

He is also mainly self-taught, as his books—*The Boy Electrician, The Amateur Mechanic, How to Build a Dynamo* and so on —suggest.

The idea of running his car on methane gas first occurred to Bate at the time of the Suez crisis in 1956 when a shortage of gasoline developed.

"Everyone was talking about alternative sources of fuel," he said, and he decided to do something about the manure-methane process that none other than Louis Pasteur had written a paper about way back in 1884.

Bate now has two methane "digesters" bubbling away in his garage-workshop and he gets the pig manure to keep them going from a nearby farmer.

There is no pollution, no smell at all, from the methane fuel and a further benefit, according to Bate, is that the residue of manure from which the gas is produced makes excellent fertilizer.

There is one problem, Bate concedes, and that is that "not everyone has easy access to manure . . . . If you live in a flat in the city your neighbors probably wouldn't want you running in and out with buckets of manure."

While accessibility may be a problem, Bate thinks manure (and human excreta) and the methane gas that can be produced from it should be considered an important energy source.

"It's the only alternative," he said. "Oil is drying up, the world's running out (of other fuel) but as long as we have humans and animals there'll be methane gas."

One human being, Bate calculates, produces enough waste each day to make "one cubic foot of methane." It also takes, by his calculations, about 30 cubic feet of methane to equal 1 gallon of gasoline.

He figures he has sold well over a thousand of his patented converter devices. He figures the cost of his methane gas works out at less than 3 (U.S.) cents for the equivalent of a gallon of gasoline.

And, he said, it will work on any horsepower engine so it can be used on anything from a power mower to a Rolls-Royce.

He thinks the world is passing up a big thing. Only recently, he recalled, "two professors from up in London" told him that in Britain alone there is produced each year 200 million tons of assorted manure.

"Just think, 200 million tons," he said. "Imagine what it must be for the whole world."

Finley Peter Dunne marvels at the wonders of the Masheen Age

Humorist Finley Peter Dunne, the Daily News
*writer who created 'Misther Dooley,' delighted
readers with his Irish brogue and observations
like the following.*

Th' shoes that Corrigan th' cobbler wanst wurruked on f'r a
week hammerin' away like a woodpecker, is now tossed out be
th' dozens fr'm th' mouth iv a masheen.

A cow goes lowin' softly into Armour's an' comes out glue,
beef, gelatine, fertylizer, celooloid, joolry, sofy cushions, hair
restorer, soap, littrachoor, an' bed springs so quick that while
aft she's still cow, for'ard she may be annything fr'm buttons to
Pannyma hats.

Lammot du Pont Copeland Jr. was just an heir who couldn't say, 'No,' Betty Flynn reports

When reporter Betty Flynn was assigned to try to interview a Du Pont heir who went bankrupt, she protested that she didn't have a background in financial reporting. "Financial reporting is also about people," her editor said. "Write a people story." This story, which resulted from that assignment, was published Nov. 23, 1970.

WILMINGTON, Del.—Lammot du Pont Copeland Jr. is the kind of guy who just can't say, "No."

Ever since he was forced to declare bankruptcy in a Delaware courtroom last Oct. 20, owing $59 million to at least 121 creditors, he has been politely declining interviews with persistent reporters who want to know the details of his amazing riches-to-rags story.

The financial world was shocked to learn of the situation of Copeland, the older son of the board chairman of Du Pont Co., the world's largest chemical company, with sales last year of more than $3.6 billion.

Copeland Jr., 38, has been a Du Pont employee for more than 16 years, but never rose past the rank of security analyst, a lower-level job with no supervisory capacity.

In 1963, he initiated his outside financial interests, which have since included a chain of newspapers, three colleges, a toy company and assorted loans and investments.

That private effort at the kind of financial wizardry for which his father is noted apparently now has caved in.

He is reported to have assets of only $25.7 million against liabilities of $59.1 million, making his one of the biggest personal-bankruptcy cases in U.S. history.

There have been intimations that Copeland is "naive" and

315

"reticent" and "too kind" in pursuing the private business deals that landed him in his monumentally tangled financial straits.

"He got himself in deeper and deeper," said one financial associate, "because apparently he just can't say, 'No'."

My experience with Copeland, when I arrived at his huge tree-shaded estate in the Du Pont dynasty's "Chateau country" northwest of Wilmington, bore out that judgment.

He drove up in a gray Camaro just as I was about to knock at his door.

I introduced myself and, to my surprise, he agreed rather quickly to my interviewing him on some "biographical aspects" —rather than financial—of his life.

But when we entered the cheerful, sunny-yellow kitchen next to the four-car garage, his long-legged slender wife, Deborah, a 1950 New York-Boston debutante, nodded coolly when we were introduced, then nearly hissed through clenched teeth:

"Motsey, don't you think you should call Norman?"

"Norman" is E. Norman Veasey, the Du Pont attorney who has been fending off reporters as Copeland's spokesman.

Two of the Copelands' five children—four girls and a boy ranging in age from 1 to 12—peered around the kitchen door and were shooed away by their mother.

"Motsey," Copeland's family nickname, looked mildly confused and a little sad. He stands about 5 feet 11 inches, with slightly wavy dark hair, blue eyes, the famous Du Pont cleft chin and, in this circumstance, a kind of Dagwood Bumstead bewildered manner.

Three dogs—a shiny black named Shadow, a giant poodle named Holmes and an unnamed old spotted creature—yapped and scampered around the kitchen as we three stood in awkward silence.

Then, Mrs. Copeland wheeled around and burst into tears. "It's all so nauseating. If our name were Smith, nobody would care. It wouldn't make any difference to anybody at all."

There is a certain calm surrounding the red-brick home, in front of which lies a huge grass-covered circle. Nearby stands an empty swimming pool and diving board, some glass-paned greenhouses, a set of children's swings, a placid pond. The spa-

cious grounds are dotted with near-leafless trees, white ash, sycamore and the willow, used by his ancestors in the manufacture
of the lucrative black powder.

The serenity doesn't extend to the financial world he has
greatly shaken up.

There are those who believe that Copeland's middle name
made all the difference.

As a Du Pont, his signature had an extraordinary credibili-
ty. His willingness to sign guarantees and commitments was also
extraordinary, associates say.

According to a number of persons, including his mother-in-
law, Mrs. Charles T. Lovering of New York City, his financial
entanglements resulted from a series of bleak encounters with
sharp "con artists." Of two close associates, one went bankrupt,
and another had been in prison.

Copeland's entrepreneurship began in 1963 with the purchase of the *Valley Times*, North Hollywood, Calif., from the
Minneapolis Star & Tribune Co. In 1964, he picked up the
Hollywood Citizen-News, a daily once owned by humorist Will
Rogers, and 27 weeklies. By 1967, his newspaper holdings included three Florida weeklies and a chain of northern California
papers.

He formed Winthrop Lawrence Corp. in 1967, in partner-
ship with Thomas A. Shaheen Jr., who had gone bankrupt in
1966, and a third man. Together, they launched the "security
investment and venture capital concern," which dabbled in everything from toys to trade schools, from superstore chain to a
moving-van company.

Apparently, they made mistake after mistake, compound-
ing interest with increasing despair, overextending at every
turn. Copeland was too quick to make decisions, too proud to
rescind them.

Even help from his father, who as a director of the Chemical Bank New York Trust Co. helped arrange for a $3 million
loan in late 1969, was to no avail.

In early 1970, he sold out his interest in the *Hollywood
Citizen-News*, the assets of which had plunged from more than
$9 million to about $5 million and from which he drew a $13,000

monthly consulting fee. But that paper went under in August.

Two of his schools, the Bates Business College, Mobile, Ala., and the College of the South, a Pascagoula (Miss.) trade school, went bankrupt. A third, Massey Junior College, Atlanta, is seriously threatened with the same fate.

He owes money to many banks, including $400,000 to the University National Bank of Chicago.

And a Chicago federal grand jury is now investigating an unpaid loan, in excess of $2.5 million with interest, made by the Journeyman Barber, Hairdresser and Cosmetician International Union, Indianapolis, to Copeland and his associates.

He said he was "unable to pay his debts as they matured and intends to propose an arrangement." He is scheduled to meet with his creditors in an open meeting Tuesday in the Wilmington federal building.

How did Copeland get himself into such a money mess? There is no easy answer. The Du Ponts are notoriously close, and closemouthed, when it comes to family affairs. The French Huguenot baronial family that arrived in America on New Year's Day, 1800, has grown to some 1,600 clan members today.

Copeland definitely is not considered among the up-and-comers in the company ranks, despite his father's status. "There are enough Du Ponts around so that outgoing executives can pick and choose really brilliant men to lead the company and still keep it in the family hands," a close watcher of the Delaware scene said.

Young Copeland, he added, "never made much of a stir. He is a nobody among a group of several very bright young Du Ponts of his generation."

Pierre S. Du Pont IV, 35, for example, was just elected to Congress as a Republican. Irenee du Pont Jr., 50, is likely to be the next company president.

Neither is "Motsey" a colorful personality, like John Du Pont, who recently built himself a pentathlon course in his back yard just to practice, or Richard Du Pont, who likes airplanes and so built himself a small airport to run.

Motsey's father is a great-great-grandson of Eleuthere Irenee du Pont, who founded a black-powder company and the family dynasty, on the banks of the Brandywine River in 1802.

Lammot Jr. was raised in almost feudal splendor and isolation with his sister, Louisa, now married to one of the Philadelphia Main Line Biddles, and their brother, Gerret van Sweringen, now a stockbroker with the Du Pont family firm of Laird, Bissell & Meeds.

Their childhood home was the fabulous Mount Cuba, a Queen Anne-style plantation mansion in red brick built by the Copelands in 1937 on their 3,000-acre estate outside Wilmington.

One complete Colonial house in the Wilmington area was purchased and dismantled by the Copelands for the interior wood paneling, which was then transferred to the Mount Cuba home. Paneling from several other houses was also used.

The Copelands of Mount Cuba loved to entertain in the formal manner of their splendid home.

Fresh green beans and tomatoes grown in estate hothouses appeared on the family's supper table year-round, along with fresh flowers daily.

There were the fishing trips with Dad—salmon and trout were favorite sport—to Norway, Ireland, Canada and the Catskills. And target practice in the home's basement pistol range, another favorite sport of the elder Copeland.

For Lammot Jr. there was the ultrafashionable Brooks Prep School, North Andover, Mass.; Harvard University (B.A., applied science, 1954); two years in the Army in Kansas and Germany, and various low-level jobs in the family-controlled chemical complex.

Like some of his forebears, Copeland evinced an interest in politics, conservative-style. He was an early Goldwater supporter and in 1964 took a leave of absence to work for a month as an advance man for vice presidential candidate William Miller.

He tried for the chairmanship of the 2d GOP District in Delaware earlier this year, but was defeated by a narrow margin.

Now, with political and financial ambitions at least temporarily thwarted, Copeland is spending his days in the quiet of the Delaware countryside, awaiting the Tuesday confrontation and its aftermath, almost certain to be painful.

Joe Cappo looks at the faded majesty of Bart Lytton

Daily News *writer Joe Cappo wrote this strik-*
ing profile of a wealthy businessman whose
star burned out. The story was published Feb.
7, 1969.

LOS ANGELES—Bart Lytton strides over the plush, tanger-
ine-colored carpeting and steps out onto the balcony of his 20th-
floor penthouse apartment.

He flicks an ash from his cigar and waves an arm over the
scenery spread out in front of him—the UCLA campus, Los Angeles Country Club and rolling Beverly Hills.

"I don't have to work. I can live an upper-middle-class life.
It's a pretty nice way to live, with a valet, a chauffeur, a secretary. That's a pretty nice way to live.

"I take a couple of trips to Europe a year, wear clean shirts
and all that, eat bread and meat.

"I don't have to work. I can't live the way I used to live. I
used to spend several hundred thousand dollars a year. I can
now spend $75,000 a year, maybe even a little bit more, and still
not pinch into capital. You can live pretty nicely. You and I
know that, both having lived for a lot less."

There is a look of faded majesty in Bart Lytton as he sits
easily in a lounge chair in his living room. His white hair is plen-
tiful, and the barber has done a fine job of giving it a casual
sculptured look.

He resembles an aging movie star who has lost the title role
in an epic—too poised to cry, too hurt to ignore it.

For nearly 10 years, his name was in lights—as chief executive officer of an adventure drama called Lytton Financial Corp.
He was the star.

Two months ago, Bart's name was taken off the marquee.
The company name was changed quite unsubtly to LFC Financial Corp., and the star was plucked from Bart Lytton's door.

It was a symbolic action, the crowning blow to a corporate

crisis that forced Lytton last April to bow out of the leadership of the company he had founded.

Bart Lytton was born Oct. 4, 1912, in New Castle, Pa., near the Ohio border. His father, a lawyer, died when Bart was 3, and his mother subsequently married a physician.

Bart attended the University of Virginia, and almost defensively admits he didn't have to work his way through college.

"But I didn't get anything from them after that," he said, pointing the cigar.

Lytton did some magazine writing, and then switched to radio, producing scripts for several popular shows of the 1930s and 1940s—*Gangbusters, Date with Judy, Skyblazers* and others.

When radio started drying up in the '40s, Lytton took on screen-writing. He wrote five screenplays, none of them above the mediocre class.

"I was prouder of some of the mortgages I wrote," he said.

About 1947, Lytton said he "went dry. I developed a writer's block. I couldn't write."

He underwent psychoanalysis, moved to Pennsylvania, then back to Hollywood, where he started doing promotion and advertising work for a mortgage company.

"I'm a quick study. So I studied the mortgage business, and I found out that I thought it was being done very archaically. All little mortgage companies out here then—in 1948."

Eleven months later, Lytton left the company and with borrowed capital of $351,000 he started the predecessor of Lytton Financial Corp.

In four years, the company had 11 offices and was the biggest mortgage brokerage house on the West Coast.

An important element was Lytton Savings & Loan Assn., which grew from nothing to fifth-largest in the nation in 10 years.

In 1959, the institution had resources of $72,068,000. By 1966, they had grown to $729,562,000.

Lytton bought several other savings-and-loan associations in the Los Angeles area, consolidated operations and continued growing.

He advertised at a record rate, with his picture in newspaper ads and his voice on television commercials.

But in early 1968, the Lytton empire started to crumble. The company couldn't meet a $1.6 million note due April 25, and an $800,000 sinking fund installment on May 1.

The crises followed three successive years in which the company was not able to turn a profit. The creditors moved in for reorganization, and Lytton was the first to go.

Respecting his potential, they agreed to keep him on as a "consultant" for seven years at $50,000 a year. He agreed not to enter the savings-and-loan business in California during that time.

The roller-coaster ride was over. Lytton stock, which had reached a peak of $42.25 a share in 1963, plunged to $5.50 a share in 1968.

At the height of his financial power, Lytton's personal wealth was estimated to be in the $30 million range, although he admits he never knew exactly what he was worth.

Today, including his stock holding in LFC and real estate, his wealth approaches $1 million.

Even if his contract allowed, Lytton said, he wouldn't go back into the savings-and-loan business.

There is the "time of the tycoon" in every business, he said, and "that business will never again create a tycoon."

Lately, Lytton has talked freely about going into the advertising business, but one can't help feeling that he would rather talk about it than go into it.

But he does discuss it at length, about how he has three choices: buy a small West Coast agency, start his own agency or establish an office for a big agency that does not have a West Coast office.

"The advantage of starting an agency is that it is all mine," he said. "The concept I have is to try to have it more than an advertising agency, to make it a technological, advisory service for total merchandising."

He is considering advertising because he had a "superb track record" of advertising in the financial world and also because he can "get the big accounts.

"I can open doors. It's no problem for me to open doors. There are very few doors in the United States and in most places in the world—but certainly in the United States—there are very few doors I can't have opened to me. If I don't know the person, I know somebody who knows him, and I can see the top man.

"I don't have to see the chief advertising officer. I go in and see the chairman of the board, the chief executive officer, whoever it is. So I have the leads toward the accounts."

But there is the feeling that Bart Lytton's advertising career is a long way off, the feeling that he is comfortable and content.

"I've enjoyed myself in the last few months very, very much. Because it's the first time I have been without pressures since I can remember, really since I can remember, since college."

So he does without working. He lectures on urban planning and architecture at colleges, referring to himself as a "full visiting professor" at Stanford University, where he holds a once-a-month seminar.

He still meets with the old movie crowd and is active in civic affairs, particularly working with the Los Angeles Museum of Art.

He recently acquired a Henry Moore sculpture for $15,000. He has loaned it to the museum.

Since he was forced to sell his $500,000 home in fashionable Holmby Hills, Lytton spends a good deal of time in the small, but posh apartment, surrounded by many objets d'art.

He has a little office, where a secretary can produce Xerox copies of his press clippings at a moment's notice. The walls are filled with pictures of Lytton with people like John F. Kennedy and Mrs. Jacqueline Onassis.

There are also a dozen or so certificates of merit, including the one he displays most proudly: a framed document of appreciation signed by all of his former employees at Lytton Financial.

His time is taken up by minor details, a good number of interviews, and the charitable work.

He recently spent $2,960 to have his 1957 Mark II Continental rebuilt for his wife, Beth. The Lyttons have one daughter, Timi, now Mrs. Herbert Stewart.

And now Lytton says he feels pressure from the business community to start work again.

"I'm telling you a story I haven't told anybody, Joe. I do feel it. It's the damndest thing. It's the subtlest thing.

"I don't understand it psychically. I don't know what the psychic mechanisms are that go to work, but I'll tell you this, no man is an island unto himself. It's true.

"The fact is that so many people ask me what I'm going to do next, and so many people have faith that I'm going to conquer worlds, that I begin to get the feeling like I owe it to them.

"But I felt like, 'Oh, hell, I don't owe the world a living. I don't have to go back now and make another living. The hell with it. I've had my bumps. I've worked my tail off enough years."

So Bart Lytton fights and becomes defensive because he is a "poor millionaire" instead of a "rich millionaire."

"We all have our insecurities and all that. I am particularly fortunate in that in my personality, for good or for bad, I have less than most people. I seem to have a very low quotient of insecurity and a very high quotient of security.

"I didn't feel insecure when I lost control of Lytton. Looking back, it apparently was remarkable because of the acceptance I've had since. It's been fabulous because I didn't feel insecure.

"I felt unlucky. That's all. I fell into some bad luck, more than I could handle.

"See, I didn't get one day's grace. Not one day. The very first day the debt was due and we couldn't meet it, they were in.

"And I couldn't blame them. It was a prize. They took a hell of a prize, the biggest company of its kind in the United States."

Movin' on: 26-year-old Kenny Brown on the Great American Superhighway

Financial reporter Steve Yahn captured the mood of a young motorcycle millionaire in this extraordinary profile, which was published May 30, 1972.

Twenty-six-year-old motorycle tycoon Kenny Brown is sitting in the dark at R. J. Grunts Restaurant ordering another martini and forgetting about his Evel Knievel shows and his huge motorcycle-mechanics training school and his nationwide motorcycle-repair-and-rental franchises.

Brown is motorcycling his mind out on the Great American Superhighway.

"I used to love to go out on the interstate and get going 80, 90 miles an hour, and then as I was passing a car, lift up my front wheel and do a wheely. It really freaked them out to see you coming by on one wheel. One wheel, man!"

He was the dark, long-haired biker from Chicago. Mary was the beautiful, built blond from Danville, Ill. She was on Greenleaf Beach. He had been dating a rich girl, but she kept him waiting on his cycle in front of one of her father's hotels, so he roared off to the lake, scattering the bleached beach boys lolling around Mary.

BARAPPP! BARAPPP! Don't loll around. Mary didn't. She got on the big, orange Triumph and years later, when he pulled a $13,000 ring out of a pocket in his Levis, they were married and Mary moved into his condominium in Skokie.

"When I was in high school I had what was considered long hair," Brown says. "If you didn't have a crewcut and pegged pants—the college look—people judged you. The guys that were my friends drove motorcycles. If you had long hair and drove a motorcycle, you were really a greaser.

"Some of my friends even quit high school," he says, letting a slight smile slip out.

Strange things that boy was doing. Turning down a scholarship from Francis Parker High School to take machine-shop courses at Lane Tech. Rejecting a General Motors design-school award to work nights on diesel engines at International Harvester. Leaving home at 17. His parents were having trouble. His father was a dentist but didn't want to be. Moving in with a friend's family and opening a bicycle, lawn mower and motorcycle repair shop on Ashland Av.

The first year the wiry, bowlegged kid makes $14,000. Then he buys a Bridgestone motorcycle franchise. Then, at 19, he rents an alley in Old Town for $125 a month and wheels down the first two Bridgestones to what will be . . . .

Ken Brown's Cycle World!

Old Town going WILD—300,000 people a weekend jamming the only place where it is—go-go girls, sawdust floors, funky fudge, head shops, big hamburgers, psychedelic posters, boutiques.

And Kenny Brown the only one with wheels on Wells St.!

"I knew motorcycles would go over big," Brown says. "They couldn't miss. Sales were picking up. Honda was doing it with its advertising campaign: 'You meet the nicest people on a Honda.' The image changed from black-leather jackets to meeting the nicest people. I knew there were millions of people who had never ridden who wanted to. We taught them right there. God knows how many people we taught to ride.

"I made it fast. I didn't think there was any end to it. I went out and did crazy things. I bought a Corvette and two Cadillacs and then I got a limousine. I got a big kick out of taking all the mechanics into McDonald's in a chauffeur-driven limousine."

Old Town going WILD! Putting people on motorcycles and letting them ride, 17 hours a day, 7 days a week. Running at night with the Wells St. clan. Drinking at the Crystal Pistol go-go bar. Racing horses at the Dundee dude ranch. Partying all night in his Skokie condominium, not knowing who is staying and not caring, welcoming everybody. And driving off to the gambling casinos in Biloxi, Miss., because somebody whom nobody could remember said the casinos spin and flash and go all night; blasting down hot, steamy-night roads deep into the heart of the country, searching for the neon casinos that never stop.

"Yeah, I miss it," Brown says, ordering another martini in R. J. Grunts. "I miss it because the responsibilities weren't so great. When I first started in Old Town and had only $125-a-month rent in the alley, I was running around in Levis and a T-shirt.

"I was making a lot of money. I had 15 mechanics and 5 salesmen working for me when I was in the garage on Wells, and every night I'd take them out and blow $200 or $300 just on dinner. We went into the Tap Root Pub so much that the guy who owned it named a steak after me—'The KB Double-Steak.' "

High flyin'.

Until the Old Town murders began. And the shootings, knifings and muggings.

"You didn't hear about a lot of the stuff because there was heavy money sunk into the street. But you'd walk a block and maybe get mugged, stabbed, shot. They tried to keep it quiet, but when people were killed, the crowds stopped coming."

So back in 1969, after a petty thief swung a hatchet at his head and almost got it, Kenny Brown said good-by to Old Town.

He moved on, promoting rock concerts and a Mod Expo Show and "Cycle-Rama" Evel Knievel shows in Chicago and Detroit. But that was a vacation. Soon he was renting a big, blackened-brick warehouse at 2840 N. Halsted St. for . . . .

Ken Brown's American Motorcycle Mechanics Training School!

The first cycle-repair school in Chicago. One of the three biggest in the country.

Kenny Brown going again! Setting up in New Town, working 17 hours a day, training bikers and long-haired dropouts and hundreds of very different dudes wheeling into the warehouse from all over America.

But was somebody saying that from this warehouse Ken Brown is going—nationwide?

Yup, says George Hurstak, a young bony blond who is giving his master's degree in mechanical engineering a regular workout operating one of Brown's Electro-Cycle repair centers at 2036 N. Clark St.

Can't miss, Hurstak says, because of "the machine." The motorcycle-testing machine Brown designed with Sun Electric Corp., the largest automobile-testing equipment maker in the country.

Take two red wires, clamp them to motorcycle spark plugs and, zingo, a whole wall of gauges bleep on and George is rocking and squinting and reading almost any cycle problem in minutes: That's the Electro-Cycle.

Beating olden times by about 150 m.p.h., George says. You can do repairs in 24 hours, not 2 weeks. And the only way you can get one is to buy a franchise.

When Evel Knievel saw the gleaming, gray-metal machine, he believed. In April, Knievel signed a contract to make it the Evel Knievel Electro-Cycle performance tester.

Knievel and Brown as partners, Knievel promoting the Electro-Cycle at his shows and signing autographs at grand openings and Ken running the business and improving the machine. He also will keep expanding his AAA Motorcycle Leasing franchises. In Chicago, St. Louis and Florida soon you will be able to lease a motorcycle from Brown like renting a car from Hertz.

Just go into a Spanish-stucco AAA shop, lease a cycle and ride away for three months or six months or whatever. Then when it's time to ride back, if you can't face giving up your machine, well, take those rental payments, throw in some cash or promises and buy the cycle.

R. J. Grunts, in the meantime, is filling up. The place is growing mighty dark.

"Party time at Lori's! Wow! Bring EVERYBODY! I can't wait!"

Lori the dark-haired waitress talking up her Friday night party, shimmering right there in front of Brown in her watery-red blouse and tight blue jeans.

He looks at her with his big brown Omar Sharif eyes (older

movie fans say Errol Flynn), but he doesn't say anything.

"Now LOOK, man," Lori says, "I really want you to come to my party. Bring whatever it takes to get you off."

And Lori is off, inviting EVERYBODY to come to her party.

"Sure I've had some business failures," says Brown, who is pushing past his first million dollars.

Like New Year's two years ago when he threw a three-day Mod Expo Show at the Amphitheatre and the hassles stacked up to heaven.

"They thought every hippie in the country was going to show up and smoke dope. We heard that word came down from the mayor not to let it go. They closed the doors early, they screwed up traffic, they did everything.

"I lost my shirt—$70,000.

"Some people really thrive on you being down. The stories that get back—if I have a problem in business, or make an investment in something and lose a chunk of money, some people think it's the greatest thing. And these guys are supposed to be my friends. We grew up together. It's unbelievable the way people are about money.

"Sometimes I think about giving it all up and building my ranch in Arizona, but then I wonder if I wouldn't be missing something."

He would be missing hustling 20 hours a day during the "Cycle-Rama" production, losing 20 pounds in two weeks making sure the Amphitheatre is full when Knievel kicks on his motorcycle and jumps 13, 14, 15 cars—or kills himself.

And he would be missing driving up to Lori's party in his shiny black limousine, stepping out into the damp and drizzle and following the noise in the night on W. Belmont St.

Ken and Mary crowding up the old, dark stairway with hundreds of people off the New Town streets; Kenny Brown jamming into Lori's party, dark eyes flashing, in there doing it, keeping it going.

Moving on . . . .

'It's just like you
were in the pumpkin business
and they did away with
Halloween'

When the Arab oil embargo almost wiped out the recreational-vehicle industry, financial reporter George Harmon was sent to Forest City, Iowa, to report on how the king of the industry was surviving. He filed this report Dec. 22, 1973.

FOREST CITY, Iowa—There has been no shortage of things happening here. A deer jumped through two windows of the gas company's office downtown. An expert pronounced large sections of the school building beyond repair. The Indianettes, a girls' high-school basketball team, are winning.

But nothing much is happening to the most closely watched figure in town, the price of the common stock of Winnebago Industries. It just lies there like stale Christmas gingerbread.

Winnebago and Forest City have been prominent in the news since the national passion for recreational vehicles (RVs) pushed the stock above $48 a share and made instant millionaires (on paper, at least) of several dozen of the many local folks who invested.

In recent months the $3 billion RV industry has been shuddering through a shakeout. Winnebago, the Henry Aaron of the business, is laying off workers and piling up inventory among the swirling snowdrifts on its vast lots. Its common stock, impaled on fears of a gasoline squeeze, nosedived from a 1973 high of 27½ to a low of 3.

"It's just like you were in the pumpkin business and they did away with Halloween," jokes stockholder Joe Macrill between waiting on customers at Coast to Coast Stores.

330

The index board in the front hall of Winnebago County's handsome stone courthouse says, "Contrary to the old belief, oil seems to be one of the main causes of troubled waters."

Yet Forest City is optimistic about the future. Despite huge layoffs at Winnebago, unemployment is low because neighboring factories are hiring. Farm crops are good. Christmas sales are booming. And there is confidence in the ability of John K. Hanson, Winnebago's founder and Forest City's financial guru, to adapt to change.

It's not pleasant to lose $1 million, even on paper, and the Forest City natives hate being portrayed as a bunch of hayseeds fooled by the stock market. The new ex-millionaires no longer talk about their investing careers.

Even with stock selling at $3 a share, they've got a hefty paper profit (Winnebago has gone through seven splits, making an investment of $25 for 10 shares in 1965 worth $24,000 today). They hang onto their stock, partly because they don't relish paying capital-gains taxes and partly because, like everyone else here, they are confident that Winnebago has the ability to shrug off its latest crisis.

It was able to battle back from total destruction by fire in 1964 and from recession in 1970. Oil shortages, however, present Winnebago with its worst crisis yet.

From peak employment of 3,900 last fall (Forest City has less than 4,000 residents), only about 1,500 workers are on the job today. In Big Bertha, a cavernous factory building where motor homes are assembled and emblazoned with the Flying W trademark, production has fallen from 600 to 200 vehicles a week.

"The world believes Winnebago is rolling over and dying. It just isn't true," says Larry Crail, a company spokesman. "It's true we're scrambling.

"But this is a temporary setback. If there is one word that characterizes Winnebago's management, it is flexibility, the ability to adjust to meet conditions."

The company is looking aggressively at diversification. Crail says its new agricultural division already is off and running, turning out such products as 5th-wheel grain-hauling trailers, hog chutes and hog houses. Hanson, in releasing Friday's report showing that Winnebago ran $250,000 in the red during the third quarter (it earned $13 million in the same quarter last year), said the company is studying mass-transportation vehicles and equipment-component manufacturing.

The importance of hog houses is well-known to the farmers who drop in to check stock prices at the branch office of M. Wittenstein & Co., a Des Moines brokerage firm. The back room, where stock prices move across a lightened panel above a dart board, used to be jammed at lunchtime with excited townspeople munching sandwiches from a buffet tray and watching the numbers from New York.

The other day, a single farmer in dungarees was there punching stock symbols as branch manager Norman Stromer observed that his business is good even though things around the office aren't as glamorous as they once were.

Stromer said 85 per cent of his customers are farmers who are just as surprised to be receiving this year's high prices for corn, beans and hogs as they were when their Winnebago stock took off like a moonshot. Very few of them have dumped their stock in Winnebago or Kayot, a small RV maker in Forest City.

"Three years ago Winnebago went down to 10, the same as it is now without the splits and nobody ever thought they'd come out of it then. But they did," said Stromer. He believes that Winnebago's strength lies in its capitalization: The long-term debt it carries is low by comparison with other RV makers.

The argument goes in Forest City that if any company makes it through the RV depression, it will be Winnebago. Wall Street just doesn't understand, the residents say, and neither did the television correspondents who passed through town.

To the driver passing through at this time of year, with the wind spitting snow like a shotgun and the radio's "party line" selling Girl Scout calendars or used Christmas lights, northern Iowa might seem cut off from the world.

But it isn't. Forest City knows what's going on and it's fighting back. They're even turning to their own advantage the argument that patriotism means setting down the thermostat and unscrewing light bulbs.

An RV, they want to convince visitors, uses 20 per cent as much energy as a home. A patriot, therefore, should hop in his RV and go camping.

Anthony Campbell meets a young swinger who makes hundred-million-dollar decisions

Banking isn't a gray world where old men make boring decisions, as financial reporter Anthony Campbell shows in this profile of a young bachelor who can invest up to $200 million on his own say-so.

At 27, James G. McCormick thinks he has got the best job at Continental Bank.

Up there in the big fifth-floor room, high above the din of La Salle Street, there are hundred-million-dollar decisions to be made. And young Jim McCormick, a blond-haired, North Side bachelor, makes them.

No stodgy mortgages or trust funds for him. He's where the action is, at the heart of the world's money and banking industry.

Each day from his command post in a far corner of the big, richly paneled room, McCormick, surrounded by desks and hysterically blinking telephones, directs his harried troops toward one goal—making a profit for the bank in the wildly volatile arena known as the money market.

As a newly appointed second vice president, McCormick is the bank's sole broker in this widespread market, a position he shares with only a handful of brokers in the country.

He makes decisions that mean thousands of dollars of profit—or loss—each day for his employer.

He has authority to invest $200 million of the bank's assets on his own say-so. He shifts around between $50 million and $100 million of the bank's assets each business day.

For his efforts—and the sweaty moments and restless nights they sometimes lead to—he is paid a modest $20,000 or so a year, plus a bonus. But that bonus and the bonuses of his subordinates depend on his decisions.

Unlike a stockbroker who sells investors stocks and bonds in such companies as General Motors and IBM, McCormick deals in a wide range of fixed-income, short-term promissory notes, or IOUs.

These IOUs, called money-market instruments, are issued by the Treasury, states, cities, other government units, banks, other financial institutions and big corporations. They include:

• Treasury bills and notes.
• Bank certificates of deposit.
• Commercial paper.
• Municipal bonds.

Since the same institutions that sell the IOUs also are the biggest buyers, the market is primarily designed to help them find a place to put huge chunks of extra cash to work for short periods of time. Life spans of the IOUs range from a day to a year, with most less than 90 days.

And while the individual investor is free to participate in the money market, the staggering amounts of money that change hands (any trade less than $5 million is considered small potatoes, an "odd lot") keep it out of the reach of all but the supperrich.

We get used to throwing around such incredible sums that a deal for $100,000 makes us shudder," says McCormick, a native of West Lafayette, Ind. "You forget that's a hell of a lot of money for one person."

Like bonds, the prices on the IOUs are expressed in terms of interest rates. If a certificate of deposit is bought by the bank at 10 per cent, for instance, it must be sold by the bank at a lesser rate of interest—letting the bank keep the difference—for the bank to make a profit.

A typical trade might unfold as follows:

A Continental Bank money-market salesman calls Ford Motor Co. to find out what the giant auto maker's needs are that day.

The Ford man, usually an assistant treasurer, says the company has $25 million that it needs to put to work until September when it will be needed to pay a tax bill.

Looking through his portfolio, the bank's salesman says he has a $10 million secondary certificate of deposit (CD) from a West Coast bank that it will offer at 11.05 per cent for the maturity Sept. 16.

After talking with perhaps 50 money-market dealers in other parts of the country, Ford calls Continental back and says it will take the CD, but only at a slightly higher rate, 11.10 per cent.

At this point it's up to McCormick. He must decide quickly whether to wait for a better deal or sell.

If the bank had bought the CD at 11.55 per cent, the sale to Ford at 11.10 would mean a profit of about $1,200 to the bank. By waiting, McCormick might be able to sell at 11.05 per cent for a $2,400 profit. But he also might find the next offer is 11.20 per cent, resulting in a $1,200 loss.

Sitting on the edge of his desk, phone jammed to his ear, McCormick makes dozens of these decisions daily.

The decisions are nerve-racking under good conditions, and the recent interest-rate spiral has piled further pressure on McCormick and others like him.

"This spring has been absolute carnage for people like ourselves," says McCormick, running a hand through his disheveled hair. "That's the only way of putting it. There have been days when the (nation's investment banking) community has lost $50 million to $100 million because yields have gone up and prices down."

Despite the frantic pace, emotional wear and tear and continuous threat of disaster, McCormick thrives on the job. He says it's exciting, "a good trip." More exciting than he'd ever imagined it would be when he was studying banking at Ohio's Miami University.

"There's no question it's a strenuous life," he explains, waving his arm toward the hubbub at the center of the room. "If you look around you won't see many 50-year-olds. But I like to be in the middle of the action and this is where it is in the banking business."

Coping with the tension is a "personality thing," he maintains. Some people can learn to live with "disaster looking over their shoulder." Others can't.

"You've got to learn that you can't control the thing," he says. "If you don't swing with the punches you're in trouble."

Nevertheless, he admits to lying awake in bed many nights "wondering what the hell is going on" in the market.

He says the biggest stumbling block to successful money-market trading is the herd instinct.

"It's tough to be a gambler and go off on your own away from the herd, even if your experience tells you it's the thing to do," he says. "It's easier to sit back and say, 'Well, I lost, but so did the others.' "

Sandra Pesmen writes
a tale of man's
humanity to man

Feature writer Sandra Pesmen told a story
about money, mankind—and God, in this arti-
cle published July 16, 1974.

God must wake up each morning, look down at the world with
disgust—then glance over at the Lambs Pet Farm in Libertyville and say, "Well, at least SOMETHING'S going right down
there!"

For the 48-acre tribute to man's humanity to man has been
going right, getting better and growing bigger ever since small,
sweet-faced Corinne Owen and her co-founder, big, burly—but
very gentle—Bob Terese, decided to create a work-living shelter
for the retarded 13 years ago.

Mrs. Owen and Terese believe the Lambs Pet Farm is successful because they never kept any of their plans, dreams or
worries a secret from the Lord.

"And we've never lost sight of our original objective—to
create a place where retarded young adults can work under su-
pervision, meet the public and earn enough to support a living
shelter here on the farm. Our dream is to build an entire community where young retarded adults can work and also enjoy a
happy, social, spiritual family life. In the meantime, they com-
mute from Chicago and the suburbs," Terese explained.

He squinted into the sunlight that came over the big barn
into his tiny office. "Each of our projects here on the farm—the
pet shop, the bakery, the silk-screening shop, the gift shop, Her-
itage House, the market, the tearoom—developed and grew and
became financially successful right after we told the Lord about
them," he said.

And lately, the two have been chatting pretty regularly with
God about their long-awaited home residence on the farm.

"Look over at that foundation," Terese said, pointing with

pride—and some disappointment—to the concrete hole just beyond the Lambs' new small-animal barnyard zoo.

"We had hoped to complete it in 1972, then we thought this was the year—but we couldn't get a building permit until we put in an entire sewage-treatment plant. What you see over there is $225,000 worth of work underground. Now we need $350,000 to build, furnish and landscape our home for 17 young women, 17 young men and 2 house parents. The original plans called for a social-recreation center, as well as sleeping quarters. But the way costs are rising, the price will go up another 25 per cent if we have to wait much longer."

When Terese and Mrs. Owen explain all this to the Lord, they add, "And remember, God, a lot of our kids are just hanging on by their fingernails. There's one young woman whose parents have died. She lives with a sister, but her brother-in-law would certainly like it better if she could move out. And listen, Lord, there's another young boy whose parents are dead. His sister is understanding, but she has a young family to attend to, and it's just too much for her to care for him, too."

It's possible that when Terese and Mrs. Owen catch the Good Shepherd's attention he also hears Patty Horgan, 30, a pretty, pleasant and very efficient waitress in the tearoom, say, "I was one of the 12 original lambs. My mother went to live with the Lord in heaven in 1972. Ever since then I've lived with my sister, but someday I'm going to live at the Lambs. I have my roommates all picked out—Theresa and Libby."

Patty, Mrs. Owen and Terese are all confident that action will be taken soon because it always has been, ever since the Lambs became a realistic dream in January, 1961.

Mrs. Owen, a housewife and mother of three, was a teacher of the retarded in a small school in Glen Ellyn. Terese, a Milwaukee Road fireman, took a job driving the school bus to supplement his income. Pretty soon he began conducting physical-education classes, and both teachers began to worry because no preparations were being made for their young students' futures.

"We felt that more had to be done than just keep them busy. We wanted to give them a purpose in life, and to help them do really meaningful, productive work," Terese said.

Done In A Day

Mrs. Owen added, "And we, like their parents, began to worry about who would take care of them when their parents couldn't later on."

After deciding that a pet shop was the answer, the pair found the name "Lambs" while reading the Bible together.

In John 21:15, Jesus asked Peter if he really loved Him. Peter said he did. Then Jesus said, "Feed my lambs." And it is to little lambs—child-innocents in adult bodies—that Terese and Mrs. Owen have dedicated their lives.

When their first Lambs Pet Shop, at 913 N. State St., was bursting with almost 30 retarded employes, the directors decided they had to expand. They heard of a farm in Libertyville and went out to look at it.

"We knew the moment we saw it that this was to be the Lambs Pet Farm," Mrs. Owen recalled. "We stood in the barn and prayed. Bob explained to the Lord that we simply had to have this farm if we were to tend his flock properly, and we gave the owners $1, in good-faith money, to hold it for us 90 days."

On the last day God—and millionaire W. Clement Stone—lent them some hope and some money. (The former the hope, the latter the money.)

"We were rescued in the nick of time, which happened so many times in the Lambs' history. The farm cost $186,000. We were to pay back $35,000 by the end of 10 years. There was no interest on the money and Mr. Stone was paying property taxes. In 10 years, the deal was to be renegotiated. In 1970, however, Mr. Stone donated the land," Terese reported.

The Lambs Inc. is a private, nonprofit organization providing semiprotective activities for about 60 moderately mentally retarded adults from 18 to 35, who have completed available public school education, and who, because of mental handicaps, have difficulty succeeding in today's working society.

"Many of our young people try to work outside the farm, but if we can't intervene and teach employers how to help them, they often fail," Mrs. Owen explained, with a motherly, worried frown.

"One of our boys is an excellent worker here because we've made it very clear to him exactly what is expected of him, and

340

he has learned to do these jobs well. But outside, employers often talk too quickly, give too many orders and confuse him. That's the biggest problem we face once our people have gained skills and confidence and are really ready to work outside."

Visitors to the farm are often surprised by the bright, happy gleam in the eyes of these young retarded adults.

"Everyone expects them to look dull. But that only happens when they're left alone with no one to talk to and nothing to do. Our people lead active, productive and social lives, so they look bright," Mrs. Owen said proudly.

Everyone at the farm remembers the day a woman walked into the pet shop and demanded, "Where are the retarded boys and girls?"

And Patty walked up to her and answered, "I'm one of them!"

"I could have hugged Patty when she did that," Terese recalled. "It meant she was able to be candid and honest about the fact that she isn't as smart as some people. And she couldn't have done that unless she knew that we think she's very special."

Well, God. That's it. And now they need a home residence.

The residence hall opened two years later, and was dedicated by First Lady Betty Ford.

Alan D. Mutter tells how Johnnie C. Ellis got squeezed by the big guys

When business comes down to the big guys vs. the little guys, guess who usually loses. Financial reporter Alan D. Mutter related the story of one such situation in this story, which appeared on Dec. 11, 1975.

The high-powered lawyers had their say about the Kassuba bankruptcy as they stood clustered about the judge in a spartan courtroom at the Federal Building.

But one of the little guys had to wait to have his say Tuesday until the lawyers filed into the long gray corridor outside the court. The little guy was big Johnnie C. Ellis of Durham, N.C.

He was one of more than 1,500 unsecured creditors who are being asked to approve a plan to end the 2-year-old reorganization of the real-estate empire of Walter J. Kassuba, the man who was hailed as the No. 1 landlord in the nation.

Ellis had flown all the way to Chicago for a hearing on the reorganization Tuesday—only to see the case continued until Jan. 29. It was the second time he had made the trip. And the second time the proceedings were continued.

This time, Ellis wanted some answers.

To get them, he approached Richard F. Levy, one of the lawyers representing Kassuba. Moments earlier, Levy had announced in court that 684 unsecured creditors had approved a plan that would consolidate the vast Kassuba operations into a single entity in which Kassuba and his creditors would share ownership.

Levy had told U.S. District Court Judge Charles McCormick that a little more time was needed to get the required majority of the creditors to agree to the reorganization plan, and the judge granted the request.

342

But Ellis, a general contractor back in Durham, didn't want any more delays. He wanted his money—about $30,000 plus $11,000 in interest.

"Can't you help me make some arrangements to get my money?" he asked Levy.

Levy explained that the success of the reorganization hinged on the creditors' acting in unison to support Kassuba as he tries to steer his empire back into the black.

"Remember, the creditors will own half the company," said Levy. "And there never was any misfeasance. In two years of handling this bankruptcy case, I have never heard any evidence that anything wrong was done.

"No, the problem wasn't Kassuba. It was the beginning of a sickness in the country in real estate. The problem was with the economy and it was inevitable. I'm sorry it happened."

"It looks like the little guys are being hurt the most," said Ellis. "After all, the big guys got their money."

Levy explained that the big guys were the secured creditors whose claims against Kassuba had first priority. "That's the law," he added.

Levy also said Ellis might as well forget about collecting interest on the money owed him, since unsecured creditors aren't entitled to interest as of the day a company files for bankruptcy protection. That, too, is the law.

But there's little consolation in the law for Johnnie C. Ellis.

He says he saw the crunch coming months before Kassuba actually filed the bankruptcy papers four days before Christmas in 1973. Ellis said he was repeatedly—and rudely—rebuffed as he sought through the better part of 1973 to get the money owed him for work already completed on two Kassuba apartment complexes in Durham.

Ellis' business was divided among five small companies back in 1973. Of three that worked on the Kassuba jobs, only one is operating today. His work force has been reduced from 45 men to 6 (including himself), and he says he was forced to sell his concrete drainage-pipe manufacturing plant for 20 per cent of what he paid for it.

"My business was grossing between three-quarters of a million and half a million dollars a year then," said Ellis. "Now, I'll be lucky to gross $50,000."

As he watched his little empire crumble, Ellis says he always felt obliged to pay his bills. He lost about $70,000 on the sale of his pipe plant for only $18,000 rather than let his debts go unpaid.

"I wanted to treat my creditors as I would like to be treated myself," he said.

But the experience has forced him to change his method of doing business.

"Now, I am subcontracting the work I get," he said. "Instead of doing the work myself and waiting to get paid, I let the subcontractor earn his money first.

"I guess you could say I'm operating more like Kassuba now."

Green-eyed, red-headed pipesmokers need not apply, Dick Griffin discovers

Despite the enormous sophistication of the corporate world in the last third of the 20th Century, idiosyncrasies and prejudices still play a surprisingly-large role in the hiring process, as financial editor Dick Griffin learned when he reported this story. It was published March 23, 1974.

The personnel director of a major Kansas City company won't hire any executive with green eyes. He says he doesn't trust people with green eyes. Another boss won't have a redhead around.

A big Chicago company wants only Ivy League graduates, preferably from Princeton, in its executive suite. The same company also refuses to rehire anybody who once worked there but had the judgment to quit for a job someplace else.

That company also recently turned down an apparently well-qualified woman executive for an important quality-control job because she would have to spend a lot of time in the company's factory.

"The factory's dirty," the personnel man told her, "and it's no place for a woman."

He wasn't precisely right, since about half of the dirty production-line jobs were being done by women.

A Minnesota company refuses to hire anybody from east of Chicago. Years back it had an East Coast man in a key job, and he didn't work out.

Some companies seek out college athletic stars for their management-training programs. Other companies refuse to hire athletes. One top executive, who likes to have ex-athletes on his management team, prefers quarterbacks over tackles.

Despite the rising sophistication of corporate management

and spreading use of scientific testing methods to help identify good executive prospects, subjective judgment still is an overriding factor in the decisions of hiring managers.

And judgment still is distorted in some cases by idiosyncrasies and prejudices. Purely irrational standards are still set by some hiring managers, the experts say.

The *Daily News* interviewed a number of experts on management: Gardner W. Heidrick of Heidrick & Struggles; James R. Arnold, William J. Guyton and Marvin Schiller of A. T. Kearney & Co.; Richard D. Gleason of Man-Marketing Services; John Paisios and John Leach of John Paisios & Associates, and Allen Penman and Bill T. Meyer of Rohrer, Hibler & Replogle.

They agree to a man that companies still hire executives for irrational reasons—and also reject qualified candidates for irrational reasons.

"Irrational standards? We're trying to convince people that kind of thing doesn't exist as a significant factor any more," said Arnold. "But the fact is, it probably does."

"We sit down with a hiring executive for several hours to get the specifications for the job," said one of the group. "Then we get down to the hidden specifications, and sometimes they take months to discover."

Small companies and family-owned concerns are more likely to set irrational specifications than the big publicly owned firms, they said.

"Heads of some small companies have highly opinionated views of what it takes to be successful in their business," said one of the experts. "They're usually dead wrong, too."

But big companies also have made some personnel decisions that don't make sense, they pointed out.

Heidrick recalled the case of the chairman of a big broadcasting company who refused to hire an eminently qualified man as president because the man's socks drooped.

Guyton remembers a top executive who wouldn't hire anybody who drove a Cadillac. He assumed this meant the person was ostentatious, and he wouldn't listen to arguments that it might also mean the job candidate was success-oriented.

Pipe smoking is a fixation among some hiring executives.

Penman knows a businessman who won't have a pipe smoker on his staff. He says they burn holes in desks.

Heidrick tells of a client who won't hire a pipe smoker because "anybody willing to spend all that time trying to keep the damned thing lit" would be "insufficiently action-oriented."

Arnold said the president of a Midwest food company believes that men who smoke pipes are financial types and cigaret smokers belong in sales.

He refused to hire a cigaret-smoking certified public accountant with seven years' experience in financial operations—but offered him a job as a salesman, even though he had never sold a thing in his life.

Height hang-ups also appear to be common.

A Chicago manufacturing company was looking for a labor-relations director who was at least 6 feet 2 inches tall. Schiller said the company's president thought a tall man could dominate the union's representatives.

An electrical-equipment maker had a chairman who was 6 feet 4, and he required that all management and sales personnel be at least 6 feet tall so they could look him in the eye, recalls Guyton.

But Gleason knew a 5-foot-5 high-school dropout who was a self-made millionaire. He hired only 6-footers with college degrees because he enjoyed giving hell to big men.

"There's no law that says you have to hire without regard to height," said Schiller. "Qualifications are whatever is acceptable to the buyer."

"Some companies won't hire short men because they're wary of the 'little-man complex,' " said Heidrick. "Tall men tend to hire tall men. Many want a certain height-weight ratio."

Paisios says some sales managers try to hire fat salesmen in the belief they can use their bulk as a selling advantage.

Some personnel executives say prejudices against women in executive posts are fading away, but Darlene Stille of Women Employed, a nonprofit Chicago group, thinks hiring executives still have a long way to go.

"They frequently tell a woman she can't have a certain promotion because she'd have to work some evenings and 'we can't have our girls out after dark,' " Ms. Stille said. "But they don't mind the cleaning women working nights.

"They reject women because promotions might mean transferring to another city and they don't think women are free to move as men are.

"And they can't picture a woman taking a customer out to lunch and picking up the tab. It's common for a woman executive in such a situation to have the man ask her, 'You sure you can afford it, honey?' "

Many times, careers are made or aborted because of a minor habit or a small mistake.

"A man who sits on the edge of his chair looks enthusiastic," said Gleason. "I know a man who got a job because of that."

He also tells of a businessman who walks all candidates to the door of his office so he can watch them walk down the hall and see if they have "spring in their step."

Heidrick knows an industrialist who took a candidate for a top job to a French restaurant. The industrialist ordered a meal and the candidate said he'd have the same only "medium rare." He didn't get the job. It was a fish dish.

Religion can't be considered, according to the law, but it sometimes is.

A Wisconsin heavy-equipment manufacturer hired only members of a small religious sect, said Schiller. When the company needed a production superintendent, it gave a list of the church membership to Schiller and told him to find an acceptable candidate from that group.

A North Carolina furniture maker met a candidate at the train station and took him directly to church, said Gleason, where they could "pray for a good relationship between us." The man fled north.

Some firms favor candidates who have worked for a number of other companies, figuring their experience is broader. Others consider such people unreliable job-hoppers.

Stress tests are uncommon today, the experts say, but a few executives still practice them.

Penman knows an executive who seats interviewees in an

uncomfortable bamboo chair and sees how much they squirm. (He also checks their horoscope.)

He also knows a manager who leaves crumpled pieces of paper on the floor of his office and in the hall. If a man picks them up, he's neat and a good soldier. This manager, says Penman, is a "lightswitch snapper" himself.

The classic stress tester, says Arnold, is an Ohio manufacturing company with a complex screening procedure for prospective executives. A candidate navigates through 10 levels of interviews plus psychological and aptitude tests before he's finally interviewed by the director of personnel.

The personnel director tells the candidate that the president makes the final decision and the director leads the man to the president's office, a brisk climb up three flights of stairs without a handrail.

The president meets them immediately and shakes hands. One of those sincere types, he grasps the candidate's hand with both of his for a long time, gazing into his eyes and telling him how pleased he is to meet him.

Then, said Arnold:

"He asks one of those impossible questions like 'Tell me the story of your life. I have five minutes to spare.' The poor guy has to talk nonstop, then suddenly the interview is over.

"What the president really was doing was taking the guy's pulse after he climbed the stairs, then seeing how long he took to recover his breath before he could talk normally again.

"If the candidate didn't meet his standards he won't hire him no matter what everybody else thought of him. He'd just say his energy level was too low."

Steve Yahn meets 'the men with the golden arms'

Financial reporter Steve Yahn captured the drama of a steel plant in this report published Aug. 17, 1972.

The legend of "The Man with the Golden Arm' is being talked up by management at U.S. Steel Corp.'s massive plant in South Chicago.

It's a new type of productivity incentive.

For 28 years, Stanley (Bart) Bartniczak was simply a shambling, smiling steel pourer. Now management calls him "The Man with the Golden Arm." They say Bart tells his wife he won't paint their house in Calumet City for fear he'll hurt his arm. They say he won't paint until he misses a pour, even if Eva isn't happy with the chipped white trim, which she isn't.

Bartniczak, shades of Joe DiMaggio in his legendary 56-game hitting streak, has poured hot steel into 9,286 cast-iron ingot molds since late February without a single dribbly pour. And his streak goes on.

Seven of the last 11 months, Bart has been honored as South Works' "Steel Pourer of the Month." Seven wins, seven awards like his blue warmup jacket, seven pictures with his boss.

And at least $1,000 a month of hot steel not spilled.

The legend of "The Man with the Golden Arm" is a showcase example of a big productivity-boosting program U.S. Steel started at South Works two years ago. Called QW-DOT (Quality Workmanship-Delivery on Time), the program was created in the summer of 1970 because South Works was in trouble. The flush days of the mid-1960s had disappeared, the recession was not going away and problems were everywhere.

Big problems were:

• An alarmingly high worker turnover rate—more than 40

per cent of South Works' 8,000 wage earners in 1970. At a cost of about $325 to train an employee, that's a loss of $1 million in one year.

• Substantial alcoholism and absenteeism.

• A history of distrust between management and labor, causing a growing number of complaints and grievances.

But perhaps the most embarrassing problem was the on-time delivery performance. It was at only 82 per cent, far below the company goal of 95 per cent.

"Morale was low everywhere in the plant," says Victor Lindberg, South Works' No. 2 man. "There was a real communications gap between management and workers. To turn this around, we held a series of gutsy meetings with our people. We let them cut loose, and we listened to them."

It made sense to listen—labor costs make up at least 40 per cent of a steel company's expenses.

Out of the talks came QW-DOT and the rise of aggressive, ambitious managers like 36-year-old Bob Alberts. Alberts, who heads a 400-man Basic Oxygen Processing (BOP) shop, is the kind of boss steelworkers like to perform for: educated but earthy, Alberts does Boys Club volunteer work, enjoys a good steak in a good restaurant and loves his job ("I'd go anywhere to talk about steel," he says).

"Our answer to low worker morale in the past was always discipline, more discipline," Alberts says. "But that won't work any more. We've tried to minimize it."

Alberts saw the QW-DOT program as a chance to search for different ways to improve productivity. His BOP shop was a crucial test area. New technology in the BOP had created what plant officials termed a "hotbed of complaints." Workers were grumbling about speedups, unsafe conditions, lack of manpower and schedules that were insensitive to individual needs.

The unhappiness was costing money. The defective-pour rate was running at an extremely expensive 2.8-per cent level at the critical point: where liquid steel is passed from huge ladles into ingot molds, through a narrow nozzle system controlled by a steel pourer standing on a nearby platform. In fact, when Alberts decided to take on the challenge of QW-DOT in December, 1970, the 2.8-per cent defective-pour rate was costing South Works about $120,000 a year in wasted molten steel.

Alberts' first move under QW-DOT was to study and redesign his shop's machines and routines—the technology phase.

"We wanted to make our processes as 'people-proof' as possible," he says.

A push button used by steel pourers to open and close the nozzle system inside the ladle was replaced by a steering wheel that gives the pourer more control. BOP workers helped change job descriptions, the nozzle system was altered and the search for better ways was on.

In four months, the defective-pour rate was cut to 2 per cent.

"At this point, we felt we had done as much as possible with materials, and further improvement would have to come from people," Alberts says.

A competitive man himself, Alberts began by dividing his men into four rival teams built around the BOP's four crews. Each crew works a different shift on the 24-hour-a-day schedule and includes all shop functions, from loading iron and other raw materials into the furnaces to pouring hot steel to sweeping clean the pits.

In April, 1971, Alberts publicized his first contest. He said awards should be given to members of the first team to knock the defective pour level below 1 per cent in a one-month period.

By June, Alberts had a winner. The team led by pourers Benny Nowaczyk, Van Marciniak and Eddie Nagler pulled down its defective-pour rate to seven-tenths of 1 per cent. The championship crew's reward was a golf cap for every man and dinner on the corporation at Marquette Gardens, a local beer and banquet hall.

"We had an open bar and a family-style spread of roast beef, chicken and plenty of Polish sausage," Alberts says. "We had a great evening together. It was a way of saying, 'We recognize you guys.' "

In the shop, the golf caps became a symbol of excellence. With most of the men wanting a cup and other prizes, the contests rolled on, and by the end of 1971 all of Alberts' teams had cut the number of defective pours to less than 1 per cent.

So he roughened the goal to one-half of 1 per cent and prepared for the biggest challenge of all—how to further increase the productivity of the individual worker.

His answer was individual "all-star" awards. He set up contests for all types of jobs in the shop, and soon Bob Alberts' all-stars were winning cuff links, tie clasps, tape measures, money clips, "USS" T-shirts, sweatshirts, warmup jackets, decks of steel-colored playing cards and a Rand McNally road atlas of the United States.

By April of this year, the combined team and individual all-star competitions had reduced the defective-pour rate to a record low level of less than five-tenths of 1 per cent.

Then came May, the grandest month. All of the teams were pouring along so close to perfection that it took a while to notice that the team led by pourers Clem Czaja, Chester Cherry and Frank Dolan was making history: They were working, turn by turn, toward the first perfect-pour month.

Shortly after midnight on May 31, BOP pit foreman Paul Bentley made a series of excited telephone calls—the team of Czaja, Cherry and Dolan has poured a perfect game! Besides the pourers on the perfect team, there were four other perfect pourers in May, one of whom was smiling Bart Bartniczak.

So back they went to Marquette Gardens. Back to the thick mahogany bar with the Cubs schedule on the wall and the juke box loaded with the latest rock songs; another open bar, more roast beef, chicken and plenty of Polish sausage. No speeches, though, said Bob Alberts.

But Frank Dolan pushed his chair back anyway. He said he didn't know if it was a speech, but he just wanted to stand and say, "This is the first time in 20 years that this big corporation has recognized me."

Bob Alberts said, simply, "I've lived side by side with this union for two years."

Joe Cappo tells how
Zoecon Corp. bugged out

*Daily News marketing columnist Joe Cappo
had a word March 8, 1971, for the people who
chose the name for a new insect product.*

Last September, Zoecon Corp. ran a full-page ad in *Scientific American,* asking readers to suggest names for an insect-controlling substance it was researching.

"We're still several years away from developing the product, so we wanted to generate public intest in it," said Daniel Lazare, vice president of the Palo Alto (Calif.) company that specializes in hormone biology research.

The product, intended to take the place of insecticide, works on insect reproduction. I guess you would call it birth control for bugs.

Attracted by an offer of $500 for the best entry, "well over 2,000" persons sent proposed names to Zoecon. The readers outdid themselves submitting such zingers as: Bugabate, Bugoff, Zu-I-Cide, Harmocide, Celibug, Cella-Bait, Mate-Abate, Catch-284, Contrapestive, Croakaroach, Emascu-Mate, Insectisick, Insexicide, Nile-8, Nitless Wonder, Pest Arrest, Slug-A-Bug, Stalemate, Stud-Dud, Terminit and Zero Bug Growth.

Confronted with an array of sparkling nominations like these, what do you think Zoecon chose? Entocon.

Pfffft.

'Thank you very much for staying at the Oxford House . . .'

By the mid-1970s computer goofs had become legendary, but the one described by Daily News *reporter Marge McElheny in this story tops them all.*

Bob and Carol and Ted and Alice all received the Oxford House letters, thanking them and 4,000 other persons for staying at the Loop hotel sometime during the last six months.

The only problem was that the 4,000 letters went to the wrong addresses.

Thanks to a computer goof, letters intended for Oxford House clients across the nation were sent to 4,000 persons in Chicago's suburbs and some community areas on the Southwest Side.

And in that phony, friendly way computers have, each letter addressed the recipient by his or her first name, then began: "Thank you very much for staying at the Oxford House . . . ."

"The phone hasn't stopped ringing all day," said a weary and red-faced Jerry Belanger, general manager of the hotel.

"I've had four people just answering phones since early morning," he said.

"One woman who received the letter is expecting her fourth child. Now she says her husband doesn't believe it's his," Belanger moaned.

"Another woman who is suing her husband for divorce thought she might have some incriminating evidence to use. She was very upset when she found that the letter was a mistake," he added. "Some men called and demanded a retraction while their wives listened in on extension phones.

"The husbands were really the most irate. They got the letters but their wives opened them. Some couples said it was destroying their home life."

More than a few callers threatened lawsuits.

Belanger said he isn't positive how the whole mess started, but it had something to do with a mixup in computer tapes by a large letter-mailing firm that had purchased address lists of department-store credit-card holders.

Belanger, 37, who has managed the Oxford House at 225 N. Wabash for eight years, said the computer is composing a letter of apology.

"If it were any other business but a hotel it would be forgotten," Belanger said.

"It's things like this that make you wish you were selling aluminum siding," he said.

Chicago White Sox shortstop Bee-Bee Richard after double play throw in 1974. Fred Stein / Daily News.

Sport:

John P. Carmichael
Ray Sons
George Vass
Lloyd Lewis
Dave Nightingale
Harvey Duck
Robert Signer
Sydney J. Harris

John P. Carmichael tells what Joe Louis did to Billy Conn

John P. Carmichael, one of the best sportswriters in the business, filed this report on the second Louis-Conn fight June 20, 1946.

One minute there was Billy Conn under the hot lights, sidestepping Joe Louis and trying to grin through his mouthpiece like a small boy saying: "Yah, yah, can't catch me."

Then, before the throng in Yankee Stadium could fathom the challenger's futile endeavors, there was Conn on his back, holding both gloved hands to his head, the blood running down his left cheek, the mouthpiece protruding from crippled lips ... and the cry of "Ten ... and out" echoing around the ringside.

And Louis was still the world's heavyweight champion.

The last time Billy fought Louis he was something to watch. He got in there and pitched, back in 1941, and when he was finally punched down to the resin in the 13th round he had done so well that on the official cards he was ahead on points through 12 unpredictable rounds.

But not this time; this was a pathetic Conn ... a guy who might have left off the extra "n" as far as his followers were concerned ... because he looked the part of a con man. On our score card he was given an even break in only one round ... the third.

It was Louis all the way, including the fatal eighth stanza when Joe first painted Billy's face red and then pushed it in for him, with two terrific right hands sandwiched around a left hook.

Conn still was standing, if bleeding from a right to the face, when the Brown Bomber caught him just off center ring. One right landed flush and Billy's spindly legs buckled. A smashing left hook took the last bit of resistance out of the black-haired

Irishman and then the champion seemed actually to hold the boy up and push him away before delivering the coup de grace, one last paralyzing right.

The man who once trod the threshold of fistic fame knew he was all through. His eyes were open, but there was a roaring in his head and he knew he couldn't make it. They had to help him to his corner, and even then he was trying to smile, but it was a pitiful effort.

Little Johnny Ray, his happy-go-lucky manager, had no excuses. "He got beat by a better man," said Johnny. "That guy is a terrific puncher . . . just terrific."

So that's about all there is to it, as is usually the case when Louis takes charge. After five years away from the ring, the champ came back as sharp as a razor, as unruffled as a robot.

He deliberately went out to outbox Conn, to beat the will-o'-the-wisp challenger at his own game, and he did it.

"I wasn't careful," said Louis afterwards. "I went out to box him and show him up. He isn't fast anymore. When I got back to the corner at the end of the seventh round, I told Mannie (trainer Mannie Seamon) that I was gonna fight him 'two-fisted now' . . . and I did. I was trained for a 15-round fight, if it had to go that long, and I knew Conn never would make me look bad again."

The first round probably was as bad a championship heat as ever was fought. Conn looked worse than Lou Nova, backing away and making only two vague motions with either hand in the full three minutes.

From there on Joe's left stung Billy's face at will and drew only occasional counterattempts. When Billy did swing his left, he was landing inches above the titleholder's purple trunks. He didn't touch Joe with six blows to the head all night.

By the fourth round, Louis was moving steadily along, forcing the fight and staring his adversary out of countenance.

Then he started the Pittsburgh hopeful on the downgrade in the fifth with two smashes to the face. Billy wavered but swung back straight and got out of the way.

Slowly but surely Louis was stalking Conn around the ring, stealthily slipping in closer, shortening the circle of the kid's safety arc and gradually stepping up his timing.

He had Conn all set for the last roundup, which came at 2: 19 of No. 8 . . . while 45,266 cash customers finally got a break for the $1,925,564 they had paid into promoter Mike Jacobs' coffers.

It was the kid's last fight, he said so himself. At no stage of the fight did he look as if he belonged in the same ring with Louis, a Louis who had brought himself to a 207-pound peak with solemn efficiency, a Louis who was ready to fight it out along any line Conn chose . . . only Conn didn't choose to fight.

He was 4-1 going into his corner and he never once looked the part.

Ray Sons says
good-by to the beloved
Gale Sayers

*Sports editor Ray Sons wrote this affectionate
farewell to the Chicago Bears' brilliant and beloved Gale Sayers Sept. 11, 1972. The writer
got a bonus some months later when he was
stopped for a traffic violation. When the policeman looked at Sons' driver's license, he said
he remembered this column and liked it so
much that he let Sons go without a ticket.*

He has limped off his last playing field. Gale Sayers. The most
exciting athlete I've ever seen. Through at 29.

And it's a damn shame.

As I write this, Joe Moore lies on an operating table and the
knife slices into another football knee and the endless toll cries
out for a remedy.

Somehow, the solution must be found, for the sport is devouring its best young men, the quicksilver running backs who
kindle the excitement.

Gale was somber when I talked to him late Sunday night
after the day that had rung down the curtain. In the morning he
had told George Halas he was retiring.

"It made me very unhappy to tell him," he said.

Halas, the old curmudgeon of football, has been like a second father to this quiet, withdrawn young man since Gale came
out of a poor neighborhood in Omaha, Neb., only seven years
ago.

Halas, in fact, was the reason Gale tried to come back this
year, on knees that had taken too many hits and would never be
the same again.

"I owed the old man one more year," Gale said. "He's been
very good to me, and I haven't been able to do much for him the
last two seasons."

So he went into Busch Stadium in St. Louis Saturday night, and carried the ball three times. Once he tripped over Don Shy's feet. Twice he fumbled and gave the Cardinals cheap touchdowns.

What a sad curtain call for a legend!

Had he really felt that he could come back this year?

"Yes, I'd always had the feeling I could do it," he replied. "I thought I ran well, but the pounding from the AstroTurf and from getting hit were too much. My knee was so sore."

So he came to realize Sunday morning that it could only be another season in which he'd be "in and out of the training room all the time, and not able to play every game."

A few minutes earlier, he had told his friend, Johnny Morris, on television: "I know I can't go on . . . I'm just getting myself into condition to walk right, not run."

This is a man who once could run like a wind-swept ghost.

I covered every league game he played as a Bear, except the first two, and I don't expect ever to see his equal.

There is no runner in football today who can approach him. In his prime, he could flit through a whole team with hardly a hand being laid on him.

He had the grace of a ballerina, the unpredictable moves of a tumbleweed in a tornado.

This was the man who was now looking me in the eye and saying: "I walk with a limp. I want to work that out. I was pressing too hard to get ready to play. Now I don't have to press. I can take my time."

And he moves on, at 29, to do something else.

Some day they'll put him on a pedestal in the Hall of Fame, with Thorpe and Grange and Jim Brown.

In that company, he'll run forever—without a limp.

George Vass writes about
the tension and despair
in a goalie's life

George Vass, author of six popular books on sports and one historical novel, Tiberius *(Regnery), has covered professional hockey a dozen years for the* Daily News. *This Vass story was published March 5, 1970.*

So beautiful the dream, so soothing the balm to a bruised spirit that a pleasing thought comes often to Glenn Hall.

It comes in those frantic moments when the hockey rink reverberates with the animal cries of fans delighted by the sight of a puck eluding Hall, the goalie supreme.

"All I want to do is stand in the middle of that farm I've got near Edmonton and holler until I'm good and hoarse and hear the echo come back across the field."

Echoes of despair:

Echoes of the heart from the ever-hunted, the always-victim, the recurrent-sacrifice in the not-always-bloodless rites of hockey.

For that is what he is, the man in pads, this awkward skating, scrambling, lunging, feinting, diving web of nerves that crouches stick in hand and heart in mouth before a net 4 feet high and 6 feet wide.

He is like no other man in sports, including the players who skate in front of him trying to prevent the shots from being directed toward the net. He is a sacrifice, doomed several times a night, each time mocked by the red light that flashes on behind him to signal a goal.

It does not matter whether he or someone else is to blame for that goal because it will be marked against him. There are no "earned runs" and "unearned runs," as in baseball. There are only goals-against, and each one is marked in lights in full view of the mocking crowd.

"Every time a goal is scored against me, that's a mistake I

made," said one of them. "And every time I look up, I can count my mistakes on the scoreboard."

The mistakes have to be his. No excuses suffice. The blame may more properly belong to the defensemen who let him down, but in the final analysis the puck went past the goalie. He is all-important.

"A goalie represents 65 per cent of a team's effectiveness, while the other five players put together represent only 35 per cent," said Emile Francis, New York Ranger coach, who has one of the best in Eddie Giacomin.

"A pitcher in baseball probably has the same level of responsibility, but he pitches only once in four days."

It is this that makes the goalie a man apart, not the considerable physical danger presented by a puck that flies at him sometimes at the speed of 120 m.p.h. Fear of physical injury is secondary to the well-padded goalie—consciousness of being a living wall, the last stop, comes first.

"A goalie has the best job of all," said Jacques Plante, like Hall now working for the St. Louis Blues. "The only place you can get hurt is in the face. A defenseman or forward can get hurt in many ways, by a stick for instance, and in other parts of the body. He can even break a leg."

The face mask, the padding, the glove protect the goalie's body. But nothing can protect him from the pressure, the tension that tears at his confidence, nurtures self-doubt and eventually robs him of his usefulness to the team.

It is said tension caused the early deaths of such legendary goalies as Charlie Gardiner of the Black Hawks and George Vezina of the Montreal Canadiens—whose name lives on in the trophy-given goaltenders.

It is certain tension caused Roger Crozier, Detroit Red Wing goalie, to retire briefly from the game two seasons ago.

It is known tension still causes Hall, 17 years a big-leaguer, to vomit before, after and between periods of a game.

And it grips even Plante, 41, who admitted to virtually hypnotizing himself before every game.

"In the dressing room I like to stay to myself before the game," said Plante. "Even if I feel like talking to somebody, I don't. I want to feel half groggy when I go out on the ice. That way I won't feel nervous. The sleepy feeling keeps me relaxed until the game starts."

When the game starts it's another matter. Most goalies give the appearance of being relaxed, at ease, even if they snap to position with a certain elaborate precision.

It's not like that, of course. They are on edge.

Muzz Patrick, who once coached the New York Rangers, said: "A goalie just stands there, seemingly impassive, but boiling inside."

Denis DeJordy, traded by the Black Hawks to Los Angeles this season, admitted he's tense during a game.

"But it is good to be nervous," said DeJordy. "You are more alert, you move better when you're a little edgy. If you're not nervous, not keyed up, you don't play well. Your reactions are slower. I worry if I am not nervous."

A goalie worries either way. And he worries whether ahead or behind.

"There's more pressure when the other goalie is going well," said Hall. "Then if you let a cheap one go in, you start thinking. It all narrows down to that thinking. If you think, you worry. But if the other goalie is having a bad night, then you don't look so bad."

It's looking bad that worries a goalie. The feeling that he has let down his team, failed his mates. It is a feeling that can destroy a goalie as it almost did Crozier two years ago. After a string of bad games, he announced his retirement. He feared a nervous breakdown.

"I'd be a nut within three weeks if I continued," he said, adding that he was sorry Brian Conacher of Toronto had not jolted him harder in a collision.

"I wish he had hit me even harder between the eyes," said Crozier, "and put me out of my misery."

Self-pity! It is the bane of goalies, a curse of the profession, one that afflicts them all from time to time. Crozier, like others, overcame it and returned. So has Hall, a reluctant performer, who customarily reports to his team after the season starts.

"There have been times I've wished I didn't have to go out

on the ice," he said. "I ask myself sometimes what the hell I am doing in hockey. If I could support my four kids some other way you could bet I wouldn't be playing hockey."

A couple of seasons ago, in despair at what he considered his poor play, Hall resolved to quit but was persuaded by Blues coach Scotty Bowman to see the team physician, Dr. J. G. Probstein. Hall moaned that hockey was destroying him emotionally.

"So no job's perfect," the doctor told him. "Suppose you go back to the farm. You'd still worry there. You'd worry that the barn was going to burn down. You'd worry that the tractor was going to run over your kids."

"You make farming sound worse than hockey," said Hall.

"All I'm saying is that you're a born worrier," replied the doctor.

Perhaps it is worry that makes a good goalie. All admit to worry, if not fear, that they will fail, that the puck will get past them more often than it should.

When it starts to do that, even if they are not largely at fault, they go to pieces. Not only on the ice, but off as well.

Wilf Cude, a goalie of three decades ago, described vividly the moment he decided it would be better to quit.

"I was having an afternoon steak before a game," said Cude. "I poured a hell of a lot of ketchup on it. I'd just started to eat the steak when my wife, Beulah, made some casual remark about a trivial subject.

"For no good reason, I picked up my steak and threw it at her."

"She ducked and the steak hit the wall. The ketchup splattered and the steak hung there on the wall. Slowly, it began to peel and I stared at it. Between the time that steak hit the wall and then hit the floor, I decided I'd been a touchy goalkeeper long enough."

"By the time it landed, I'd retired."

Cude's retirement was no more sudden than that of Bill Durnan, goalie of the Montreal Canadiens two decades ago. Durnan was only in his eighth season and had won the Vezina Trophy seven times when he quit right in the middle of the Stanley Cup playoffs.

He was replaced by Gerry McNeil, who had been sidelined by a nervous stomach before the playoffs.

"I could never stand another season," said Durnan. "My nerves are all shot and I know it."

At least Cude and Durnan had the option of playing or retiring. Gardiner and Vezina never had a choice, dying almost with their skates on.

Johnny Gottselig, a teammate of Gardiner with the Black Hawks in the early 1930s, has told the story of the goalie.

"Chuck was only in his prime when he died in 1934," said Gottselig. "It was only his sixth season in the league. I think his whole life was shortened by goaltending. He was always alone. He worried a lot and he was the nervous type."

In the next-to-last game of the 1934 Stanley Cup playoffs, the Hawks and Gardiner lost 5 to 2 to the Detroit Red Wings. It was the only game Gardiner had lost in the playoffs but he was shattered by the defeat.

"They sent him to Milwaukee for two days' rest," said Gottselig, "and then he came back for the last game, which we won 1-0 after 30 minutes of overtime to take the Stanley Cup."

In appreciation of the goalie's play, teammate Roger Jenkins wheeled Gardiner in a wheelbarrow through the Loop. Eight weeks later Gardiner collapsed in Winnipeg and died three days later of a brain hemorrhage.

Old-timers insist Vezina was the victim of an overactive nervous system. He collapsed during a game in 1925 and died four months later. A post-mortem disclosed huge ulcers but also tuberculosis, the real killer.

There can be little doubt that many goalies—like Vezina or Hall—have queasy stomachs. Davey Kerr, a New York Ranger goalie, tried to settle his with a glass of red wine with his dinner on game days.

Hall's efforts to settle his stomach have been less drastic. When he suffers an attack of nausea on the ice he tries to control it by deep breathing:

"I learned that by watching basketball players on the foul line."

Yet this delicately tuned man set an endurance record that

may be even more remarkable than that of Lou Gehrig, who played 2,130 consecutive baseball games for the New York Yankees.

On Nov. 7, 1962, after 10 minutes and 21 seconds of a game against the Boston Bruins, Hall, then with the Hawks, was forced off the ice because of a painful back injury. It was the first time he had been relieved during either a regular season or Stanley Cup game in more than seven seasons and a string of 552 consecutive games.

Hall had played at the most demanding position in sports without a substitute. He had played despite occasional severe injuries and constant tensions.

In the last two decades the three outstanding goalies have been Hall, Plante and Terry Sawchuk, who at 40 occasionally fills in for Giacomin.

Sawchuk's 20-year career as a big-leaguer should be chronicled in a medical journal. He has had back surgery, eye surgery, shoulder surgery, broken ribs and torn muscles, and psychologists once found a persecution complex.

He has retired almost annually, pleading the pressures of the game, yet has been overawed by the large sums of money impressed on him by hockey impresarios.

The reason was never more clear than on April 15, 1967, in a playoff game in which Sawchuk worked and worried for the Toronto Maple Leafs against the Black Hawks at Chicago Stadium. It was a game that illustrated perfectly the goalie's plight, his value and his attitude toward it all.

Johnny Bower started in goal for the Leafs, but begged off in the second period with the score tied 2 to 2. His stomach was just too jumpy, said Bower; his nerves were shot.

Leaf coach Punch Imlach sent in Sawchuk, who was greeted almost immediately by a shot from Bobby Hull at close range. The puck struck Sawchuk's left shoulder and knocked him down and out.

As Sawchuk lay on the ice, Pierre Pilote, Hawk captain, skated by.

"How do you feel, Terry?" asked Pilote. "You should have let it go, Terry. Might have been a goal."

Bob Haggert, Toronto trainer, came out on the ice to help Sawchuk.

"Where'd you get it?"

"On my bad shoulder."

"Think you're all right?"

Sawchuk pulled himself to his feet, and snapped: "I stopped the damn shot, didn't I?"

He did, and stopped 16 more in that period and 22 in the final period in what Hawk coach Billy Reay, an admiring foe, called the greatest exhibition of goaltending he had ever seen.

It was and no goalie, once his quivering nerves and carousel stomach are laid to final rest, could ever have a finer epitaph than that provided by Sawchuk's words:

"I stopped the damn shot, didn't I?"

Lloyd Lewis: A bitter brew for a fan of Christy Mathewson

Lloyd Lewis was a man of many talents: sportswriter and editor, critic, historian, managing editor and a war correspondent who covered the Nazi surrender in 1945. He wrote this paean to one of his favorite sports figures soon afterwards.

When the bleacher gates at Shibe Park in Philadelphia were thrown open on the morning of Oct. 24, 1911, I was in the mob that went whooping toward the front seats. I got one, partly because the right-field crowd was smaller than the one in left, partly because most Philadelphians wanted to sit close to their worshiped Athletics, for the World Series at that moment stood two games to one for Connie Mack against John McGraw, and Philadelphia was loud and passionate in the confidence that now they would get revenge for the bitter dose—four games to one, three shutouts—the Giants had given them six years before.

Me, I wanted to get as close to the Giants as possible, and found a place at the rail close to the empty chairs that would that afternoon become the Giants' bullpen. My whole adolescence had been devoted, so far as baseball went—and it went a long way to an Indiana farm boy—to the Giants and to their kingly pitcher, "Big Six," the great incomparable Christy Mathewson. I hadn't had the courage to cut classes in the nearby college and go to the first game of the series at Shibe Park. But today I had. Things were desperate. Up in New York's Polo Grounds to start this, the World Series, Mathewson had won—2 to 1—giving but five hits and demonstrating that with 12 years of herculean toil behind him he was practically as invincible as when in 1905 he had shut out these same Athletics three times.

It had looked like 1905 over again: Then, in the second game, the A's long, lean yokel third baseman J. Franklin Baker had suddenly and incredibly knocked a homer off Rube Marquard, the Giants' amazing young pitcher. Baker, who had hit only nine homers all season, had tagged the 22-year-old Giant and two runs had come in—and the final had stood 3 to 1.

In the syndicate newspaper article signed by Mathewson the day after Marquard's disaster it had been said that Rube had lost the game by throwing Baker the high outside pitch he liked instead of the low fast one he didn't like and which McGraw had ordered.

The rebuke had been a sensation that grew in the third game, Oct. 17, when Baker had hit another homer off Mathewson himself, and had been the main wrecker of the great man's long sway over the A's. Up to the ninth inning of that third game Matty had kept command. Always when the Athletics had got men on bases he had turned on his magic. As he went to the bench at the end of the eighth, New York had risen and given him a tremendous ovation, for in 44 innings of World Series play, 1905 and 1911, he had allowed the Mackmen exactly one run—and the A's were hitters, indeed. Their season's average for 1911 had been .297.

Then in the ninth, Eddie Collins had gone out, and only two men had stood between Matty and his fifth series victory over his victims. Up had come Baker with the American League fans begging him to do to Matty what he had done to Marquard —and, incredible as it seemed, he had done this.

As home runs go, it hadn't been much more than a long fly that sailed into the convenient right-field stand at the Polo Grounds, but it had gone far enough to tie the score and give Baker a nickname for life—"Home Run" Baker.

All that was in everybody's mind—and mine—as on Oct. 24 the fourth game came up at Shibe Park.

Onto the field came the Giants with their immemorial swagger, chips still on their shoulders—the cocky, ornery, defiant men of Muggsy McGraw.

As the Giants began to toss the ball around, I couldn't see my hero, Mathewson. Then, suddenly, there he was. He held his head high, and his eye with slow, lordly contempt swept the Athletics as they warmed up across the field. He was 31, all bone and muscle and princely poise. Surely he would get those Athletics today.

Up came the Athletics. Matty, as though in princely disdain, fanned the first two men. The third man, Eddie Collins, singled. Here came Baker, his suntanned face tense, his bat flailing—the air thick with one word from 25,000 throats, "Homer! Homer!"

Matty studied him as a scientist contemplates a beetle, then struck him out! What I yelled, I don't know. All I remember is standing there bellowing and paying no heed to the wadded newspapers the Athletic fans around me threw. It was wonderful.

In the fourth, Baker came up to start it and doubled. Dannie Murphy doubled, Harry Davis doubled. Ira Thomas hit a sacrifice fly—three runs. It couldn't be. Up came Baker again in the fifth with Collins on first and another double boomed across the diamond. I saw Snodgrass eventually stop it, but he didn't really have it in his glove at all. It had stuck in my gullet.

The eighth. A pinch hitter went up for Mathewson. I was sorry I hadn't died in the seventh.

Finally it was all over: Athletics 4, Giants 2.

I walked out through 25,000 of the most loathsome individuals ever created—all jeering at Mathewson, all howling Baker's virtues. I dragged my feet this way and that trying to escape the currents of fans. At the end of a dolorous mile I stopped at a saloon. I had never had a drink. Now was the time.

But what I started out to tell was about my greatest day in baseball. That came three years later, Oct. 9, 1914, when the lowly, despised Boston Braves wallowed, humbled, trampled, laughed at the lofty Athletics to the tune of 7 to 1. Hoarse and happy, I came out of Shibe Park, spent hours hunting that same saloon, but I couldn't find it. It had to be that one. What I wanted to do was to walk in all alone—find nobody else in there—order two beers, and, when the bartender looked inquiringly at the extra one, say to him in a condescending voice, "Oh, that? That's for Mathewson."

Dave Nightingale watches
the Chicago Fire
flicker out

Daily News sports columnist Dave Nightingale
tells of the pathetic end of the doomed World
Football League's Chicago franchise in this story, published Nov. 15, 1974.

In the beginning, there was hope. And opulence. In the end?
Well, in the end, really, there was nothing.

It all started in a posh office building out in Park Ridge . . .
done in Spanish modern, with plush furniture, roaring fireplaces
and deep-pile carpeting. The official birth of the Chicago Fire.

The coach was presented. Dozens of newly signed players
dripped from the rafters, brimming with optimism. Even two
pedigreed Dalmatians, the team mascots, were introduced to a
waiting world.

The dogs promptly messed on the deep-pile carpeting. It
was a portent of things to come.

It all came to an end on Thursday. The Fire was extin-
guished. Symbolically, if not officially.

It came to an end at a post-season "awards luncheon." A
luncheon tossed by the brewing company that sponsored the
team's telecasts. Not by the team's management.

It came to an end in half of a motel dining room—in a section of town where you don't walk alone after dark.

It's a long way from Park Ridge to W. Madison St.

A sign in the dining room said: "Occupation by more than
400 persons is dangerous." Which is understandable. Because
the room was 45 feet long and 30 feet wide. Which meant that
each of the 400 would have exactly 3½ square feet.

But the room was large enough. Because only 45 people
showed up. And one was not Tom Origer, the owner.

At least, Tom Origer thinks he's the owner. But if he
doesn't pay off a 150-grand loan by Jan. 2, he'll find three men

who would disagree vehemently with him.

"I don't know where Tom is. I guess he's lying low. I don't talk with him much anymore," said Jim Walker.

Jim Walker is the Fire's public-relations director. He quit a good job to take that position. Now, he has no idea what he'll be doing for a living, come 1975.

Even with his future in doubt, Jim Walker can't stop talking like a PR man. "Do you know that we finished third in the league in offense," he said. "Even though we lost the last 10 games we played . . . and didn't play the final game."

In a corner of the room, up on a platform, stood the valuable hardware. Sixteen "Player of the Game" trophies, donated by the brewery, crowned by a gold plaque for the team's most valuable player.

Fortunately, none of the players stepped onto the platform to accept their awards. The thin plywood flooring was incapable of holding 200-pound bodies.

Bill Berg, one of the Fire's TV voices, was delegated to pass out the awards. "First, we're going to give the trophies," he said. "Then, the second part of the program is lunch. I understand the second part is scheduled to take place in either Toronto or Philadelphia."

It was graveyard humor. And the "corpses" laughed.

Berg passed out the awards: Four for Virgil Carter, three for Rudy Kuechenberg, two each for Mark Kellar and Harry Howard and one apiece for Ron Porter, Cyril Pinder and LeRoy Kelly.

Oh, yes, also two engraved, pewter-tankard trophies for Joe Womack.

"Joe Womack? Hey, that's outtasight! Really outtasight!" roared Mike Sikich, the offensive guard.

His teammates tittered appreciatively. Joe Womack, you may recall, was cut from the Fire in midseason.

Finally, the crowning achievement of the luncheon: the presentation of the MVP plaque, and its attendant $1,000.

The most valuable player on the Fire was a man who played every offensive minute of 19 consecutive games. If not the most talented, he was the hardiest. Or bravest.

On the "glamour" teams, the MVP award usually goes to a player from a "glamour" position. The most valuable player on the Chicago Fire in 1974 was Barrington's own—Guy Murdock.

Who plays offensive center.

Now, it was time for Murdock to step to the microphone and accept his plaque and thousand bucks.

Except he wasn't there. (Military obligations.)

Beautiful!

His wife, Linda, took the money. And a guy from the brewery said: "We hope to get lunch on the table in the next half an hour. In the meantime, why doesn't everybody have another beer."

The Chicago Fire went out Thursday afternoon.

It did not go out in style.

Harvey Duck: Requiem for a charger

A stock-car racer was killed in a crash when his throttle stuck, and the accident got two paragraphs in the next day's paper. But sportswriter Harvey Duck sensed a story worth telling and his reporting efforts resulted in this article, which appeared Oct. 13, 1973.

Whitey Gerken was a "charger" . . . a race driver with a compulsion to be first. He must run as hard and as fast for as long as his car holds together.

Some drivers are called "strokers," fellows who are content to back off the pace, stay in the middle of the pack while hoping that the leaders will run into trouble and fall out. Occasionally they win a race but they seldom have as much fun as the chargers.

Whitey Gerken was a charger and that's the way he died when the throttle of his stock car stuck and it crashed at full speed last Sunday during a qualifying run at Illiana Speedway, near Schererville, Ind. Whitey, 43, of Villa Park, suffered a broken neck and smashed spine and died the next day.

"He wouldn't have had it any other way. He always said that the best way to go would be when he was racing."—Patricia Gerken, Whitey's widow.

The front pages this past week were devoted to stories of a war in the Middle East and of Vice President Spiro Agnew's resignation. Sports sections were crammed with reports of baseball playoffs and football and hockey and basketball openings. Whitey's death rated only a two-paragraph mention.

Yet the funeral home in Melrose Park was packed Wednesday and Thursday with hundreds of friends and fans who had followed his 25-year racing career.

A photograph of his race car rested behind the casket and the helmet that he had worn Sunday covered his head. He was dressed in a black and white checked sport shirt made by his mother. She had given him a new shirt before the start of every racing season—always a black and white checked design.

"I'm glad they didn't put a suit on him. He never was a formal guy and he wouldn't have looked right all dressed up."—Hugh Deere, Rockford Speedway owner.

Whitey's name isn't easily found in the U.S. Auto Club's official record book although he had been a professional driver for almost 25 years.

"He did win a couple of big races, I guess, but he lost a lot more than he won. Still, racing was the absolute end as far as Whitey was concerned. There was nothing else in life that interested him except his family."—Gene Marmor, professional race driver.

His greatest triumph came in September, 1961, when he won a 250-mile race at the Wisconsin Speedway in Milwaukee, picking up $4,500 in prize money—the biggest purse he would ever earn. Driving a patched-up, under-powered car, he outran such well-known drivers as Rodger Ward, Paul Goldsmith, Eddie Sachs and Dick Rathman.

"It was a remarkable win. His regular car had been wrecked shortly before and we put his engine into one of my old cars for the race. Nobody thought that car would hold up. I still meet people who were there who say that it was the greatest race they ever saw."—Gene Marmor.

But such exhilarating moments were a rarity, even though Whitey always drove a full schedule, mostly on the small, "short" Midwestern tracks.

"He had to run as hard as he could. There was something in his makeup that prevented him from laying back. He had to get in front and stay there as long as his equipment held up. But, something always seemed to go wrong. I guess he was what you'd call a hard-luck driver."—Norm Nelson, professional race driver.

His luck seemed ready to improve in 1963 when he signed with the Mercury Racing Team. Obtaining a factory ride is the dream of every independent driver who has his fill of scrounging for money to buy used parts and who never seems to have enough time to get his car ready for the next race.

Eager to take a fling at big-time stock-car racing, Whitey went to Daytona Beach, Fla., outfitted in a new Merc, with a competent pit crew and more spare parts on hand than he'd ever seen.

But his free-spirited approach to racing couldn't be shackled. Despite all the fancy equipment, he was soon back home again looking for another ride.

"He didn't like the way one of the other Merc drivers ran him into a guard rail during a practice run so he told some of the front office brass what he thought about it. They didn't like it and dropped him from the team"—Former member of the Gerken crew.

Whitey couldn't have cared less about loss of the factory ride. He returned to the Midwest and promptly won 1963 driving championships at Soldier Field and Rockford, winning every feature race that he entered.

"That might have been one of his failings. He could have gone far in racing if he wanted to leave the Chicago area. But he liked his friends and didn't want to uproot his family. So he was content to stay there, work his butt off on his cars and race as often as he could."—Bob Stroud, USAC [United States Auto Club] stock-car supervisor.

The seasons rolled by and Whitey kept on racing. He married a second time, a divorcee named Patricia Paulsen with four children who cheerfully welcomed Whitey's first son, Tom, into her brood.

"I knew from the start that racing would always come first, because my first husband was also a driver. But he was never as good as Whitey, nor as dedicated. Racing was always a seven-day-a-week thing with Whitey. If he wasn't driving, he'd be up all night working on his cars. He never seemed to be able to find time to attend graduations or birthday parties, but I never minded. That was the way he was."—Patricia Gerken.

A son, Richard, was born seven years ago and, although his racing schedule remained demanding, Whitey appeared happier than ever.

He made several halfhearted attempts to develop a taste for

the business world but each time another racing season approached, the shop doors were rolled shut and Whitey would go racing. Again. The Gerken home was bustling. Again.

He had dreamed for years about building the world's finest stock car and in 1968 the dream almost came true. With a group of partners, he devoted four months to creating a mechanical masterpiece valued at $100,000 that he called "a classic race car."

But the car was stolen from his west suburban garage the night before he planned to take it to Indianapolis for pre-race testing. It was never seen again.

"Disappointments like that never got him down, though. He just kept on with what he liked to do and helping everybody when he could. He'd get mad sometimes when another driver bumped him or cut him off, but he'd get over it and make up in a few minutes. He even got mad at me once in a while and we were always good friends."—Sal Tovella, professional race driver.

The inflation of the 1970s began to crimp the already lean budgets of the independents and it became increasingly difficult to field a respectable race car. Even so, in 1970, when running at the Indianapolis Fairgrounds with a chance to finish among the leaders and pick up some much-needed prize money, Whitey dropped out of the race to aid a fellow driver whose car had flipped.

"He was trapped in the wreckage so I stopped and helped him get out," Whitey said later. "No one seemed to be around to give him a hand, so I thought that I'd better do something."

Prize money became skimpier and two years ago he decided to sell his "big-track" car and keep only the "small-track" car. He got an occasional ride from another owner and usually, with little or no practice, he would be out and "charging" again.

His short-track car was demolished in a 15-car pile-up at the Grundy County Speedway at Morris three weeks ago, but once again, Whitey walked away without a scratch.

It looked as though Whitey would sit out the rest of the season until another one of his many friends offered to lend him a car for the final two races at Illiana.

Enthused and eager as always, Whitey worked 18 to 20 hours a day to get the car ready. It ran well in practice and when his turn came to qualify last Sunday Whitey was off and charging.

"You could always tell when he was driving. He never backed off going into the turns and he had a style all his own."
—Bay Darnell, professional race driver.

Whitey picked up speed on the warmup lap and came barreling down the main stretch to take the green flag and begin his qualifying attempt.

Then came the crash.

"I can't say that I hate racing now, because Whitey loved it so. But I don't know if I'll ever be able to watch a race again."—Patricia Gerken, the widow.

Jackie Robinson said, 'Pray for the whole team, Ma'

Robert Signer wrote this obituary of Jackie Robinson Oct. 24, 1972. Signer wasn't a sportswriter, but he grew up in New York City and worshiped the Dodgers and Robinson. Knowing this, the city editor asked Signer to write a crash obit with less than an hour to deadline. He did it—so fast and so well that his peers gave him a loud round of applause when he finished.

Somewhere in Brooklyn there's a drab housing project where the winds sweep in off Bedford Av., the soulful sound of Gladys Goodings' "Dodger Symphony" wafts over the streets, and, if you listen carefully, the echoes of cheers and roars still sound.

Ebbets Field it once was, a tiny, miserable ballpark where the fielders couldn't roam, the pitchers got claustrophobia and the crowds couldn't find seats.

A legend grew there, like Betty Smith's tree, the legend of a team of heroes, the boys of summer, skillful artisans who could do no wrong—except that they couldn't win the World Series from the hated Yankees.

The legend died in 1957, when the Brooklyn Dodgers, the finest group of bums ever to play baseball, moved west to Los Angeles, and something in the city they left behind died a little, too.

Jackie Robinson didn't go west with the team. He stayed back home in retirement, a ballplayer who once could hit and run and field and drive the fans crazy with the little dance he would do on the base paths.

Try me, he would taunt the pitcher. Just try me. I'll outrun you every time. And he usually did.

Jackie Robinson, who died Tuesday morning in Stamford, Conn., at the age of 53, was the first black man to play major-league baseball.

He broke the ground for the scores of black men who now are the mainstays of every major-league team, the winners of numerous top awards, the unquestioned superstars who draw the fans to the ballparks in record numbers.

It was not easy. There were times when it seemed that Jackie wouldn't make it, not because he didn't have the ability or the inner strength, but because he was fighting a nearly unbroken wall of racial prejudice that permeated the world he was trying to move into.

He was born in Cairo, Ga., and christened Jack Roosevelt Robinson. He was one of four boys and a girl, and they never knew their father. To support the family, his mother took in washing and ironing. Soon afterward, the Robinsons moved to Pasadena, Calif.

Young Jackie played softball on a corner lot with the other members of his childhood group, the Pepper St. gang, and they occasionally earned pocket change by sneaking onto nearby golf courses to retrieve lost balls.

Ma Robinson, a fervent Methodist, kept him in line with stern talks about how to live a proper life. (Once, in later years, when the Dodgers weren't doing so well, Jackie wrote to his mother: "Quit praying just for me alone, Ma, and pray for the whole team.")

His mother told him it was a sin for a 12-year-old to be playing baseball on Sundays while the pews at nearby Preacher Scott's church were empty.

"The devil is sending the people to watch you play, and he's also sending you to play," she told him.

He was a natural athlete, and when he went on later to the University of California at Los Angeles, he gained national notice in football, basketball and track. He won an All-American honorable mention in football, set a Pacific Coast Conference broad-jump record and led the league in basketball scoring.

After service in the Army, Robinson made history Oct. 23, 1945—just 27 years ago Monday—when he was signed by the Brooklyn Dodger baseball organization to a contract with their Montreal farm club.

He had first come to the attention of Branch Rickey, the

owner and undisputed boss of the Dodgers, through Wendell Smith, now a sportscaster here for WGN-TV. Smith, at that time a columnist for the *Pittsburgh Courier*, a black newspaper, had seen Robinson play for the Kansas City Monarchs, a Negro team.

From the start, Rickey intended to watch Robinson and, if possible, bring him into the major leagues. The time was ending, Rickey believed, when white men and black men could be segregated in American life.

"I need more than a great ballplayer," Rickey told Robinson when he said he was planning to bring him to the Dodgers. "I need a man who can fly the flag for his race, who can turn the other cheek. If I get a firebrand who blows his top and comes up swinging after a collision at second base, it could set the case back 20 years."

There was no question about Robinson's ability on the baseball field. After watching Jackie in action during spring training of 1946, Clay Hopper, a Mississippian who became Robinson's first minor-league manager, said: "Mr. Rickey, do you think he is human?"

Robinson got a $3,500 bonus and a $600 monthly salary to play with Montreal. By the time he left the Dodgers a decade later, he was one of the big-money boys, earning $42,000 a year and six World Series purses.

He won a minor-league batting title with a .349 average his rookie year in professional ball, earning a chance with the Dodgers. Rickey warned him, "I want a man with guts enough not to fight back."

Robinson broke into the major leagues in 1947. He batted .297, led the league in stolen bases and kept his mouth shut. The next year, he batted .296 and clearly established himself as the best second baseman and baserunner in the major leagues.

In his third year, Robinson put together enough credentials to take the gag off. He won the National League batting title with a .342 average and was named most valuable player. He felt he now could speak out, like any other ballplayer.

"I'm a human being," he said. "I have a right to talk, haven't I?"

Most Dodger players, notably shortstop Pee Wee Reese, treated Robinson as one of the boys. Enemy pitchers, quickly learning of his abilities, treated him with respect.

Acceptance quickly set in among the fans and the ballplayers. Robinson could do everything better than most ballplayers. He deserved to be there.

In 1956, the Dodger organization stunned the Brooklyn fans and the baseball world. Robinson, then 37, was traded to the archrival New York Giants. But he wouldn't go. If he couldn't play for Brooklyn, he wouldn't play for anybody. He came up as a Dodger; he would quit as a Dodger. And he did.

With his retirement, an era closed in a sense, although he had opened the way for the others of his race who otherwise might have languished in the Negro leagues, unheralded legends and forgotten names.

Protection and persecution
—the story of a prizefight
and a cello performance

Sydney J. Harris pondered the obscenity of one sporting event in the context of current affairs, in this editorial-page column.

A few days after the Clay-Terrell fight, I was having a cup of coffee with a friend, when he pointed to the front page of the paper. A lady cellist in New York had just been arrested for performing with a bare bosom during an avant-garde concert.

"I wish you'd explain to me," he said, "why this event is considered 'obscene conduct,' and the Clay-Terrell fight isn't. Why are we so repressive about sex, and so permissive about violence?

"I watched the Clay-Terrell fight," he went on, "and by my definition, it was an obscene performance. After the seventh round, Terrell was just a punching bag. And Clay was as ugly and vicious as a man could be. Yet the public pays millions to watch such spectacles, and feels cheated when one of the fighters doesn't end in a bloody pulp on the floor."

It wasn't hard for me to agree with him that we have a perverted sense of values in Western society, insofar as sex and violence are concerned. It seems absurd that a bare bosom is considered in any way "lewd," while the brutal batterings of two anthropoids are applauded and approved as a great sporting event.

Neither a prizefight nor a cello concert cum nipples would attract me as a customer, but I fail utterly to see why one is given police protection while the other is subjected to police persecution. The lady cellist wasn't hurting anybody, or doing anything intrinsically wrong, and her bosom is certainly no more offensive than Terrell's blood-streaked chest.

I am almost convinced that this curious inversion of values

—where violence is condoned if not actually sanctified, while sex is still shrouded in shame—explains in large part the shifting sexual morality of young people today. A society that is so willing to send them out to be killed, that is so indifferent to human life, and yet at the same time that places so many safeguards against sexual activity, seems unworthy and hypocritical in the eyes of many youngsters.

Unnecessary pain of any kind is what is "obscene" in human conduct, while pleasure may be good, bad or indifferent, depending upon the other values involved in it. Surely the display of the body is not lewd by and of itself, with or without a cello; nor is there anything lewd about the mutual enjoyment of sex by two consenting adults. It may not be prudent, but that is quite another matter.

Is it possible that our strictures against sex are the way we buy off our collective conscience for our obscene addiction to violence?

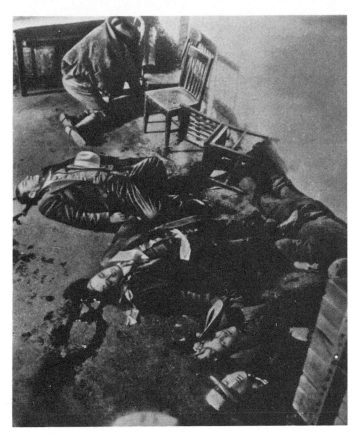

St. Valentine's Day massacre. / United Press International.

Crime:

Van Gordon Sauter
Donald Zochert
Edmund J. Rooney
Rob Warden
Wade Nelson
Bob Schenet
Ben Hecht
Marge McElheny
George Harmon

Van Gordon Sauter writes the saga of Sheer Folly, a bank robber's girl

Van Gordon Sauter, A Daily News *local reporter who later became CBS' vice president in charge of program practices, wrote this Nov. 2, 1967, article after a dramatic suburban bank robbery during which two policemen were slain.*

The swarthy man with the pudgy lips and long, thick black hair stood at the rear of the 606 Club and watched the stripper on stage auditioning for the new vacancy in the show. The management isn't expecting Mary Cook back.

She was in La Porte, Ind., Wednesday, playing to a larger crowd than the one in the 606. In the club at 606 S. Wabash, she was Sheer Folly, a lanky, peroxide blond, who thrashed about onstage before the silent stares of Chicago conventioneers.

In La Porte, she was a real celebrity.

The drugstore clerks and shoe salesman peered out around the Halloween displays in their windows as the matrons led Mary Cook from the two-story limestone jailhouse across the street through the rain to the courthouse in the square.

On Tuesday night the FBI closed in on a shabby shack on a lake outside La Porte where Mary Cook and another girl were hiding with two men accused of holding up a Northlake bank Friday and killing two policemen.

Now she is charged with harboring a criminal and being an accessory after the fact in a bank holdup. She was dressed in skin-tight brown slacks and a gaudy pullover; her spirits seemed to sink as she was led into the austere, intimidating courtroom for arraignment.

It was the wrong scene for Mary Cook. It was distant from the familiar bright spotlight and sequined gowns with instant zippers and throbbing music and the men with name badges on their suits who applauded and stomped their feet after her dance.

It was even further from the secure tranquility of Denton, Tex., where she was raised. As a teen-age bride, she left there years ago with her husband for the bright lights of Washington, D.C., where they planned to find prosperity and happiness.

It didn't work out. In spite of their two children, they got a divorce. She went downtown and asked a club owner for a job as a waitress. There were plenty of waitresses, he said, but if she was willing to dance, there was a job. She was willing.

About eight years ago, she came to Chicago and worked around the clubs, including the notorious Club 19 at 19 E. Chestnut. She married a Chicago man who leased filling stations, but that marriage, too, went on the rocks.

She then ended up at the 606. As clubs go, it's not bad. The girls are more attractive and supple than those in the burlesque houses on S. State, and while the prices are high (a bottle of beer: $1.50), a shot of booze is a shot of booze.

"I went with Mary to visit her children in Washington this summer," said a girl friend from one of the clubs. "She loves those kids. She'd send them money, and we were always going out to buy them presents."

The children—a girl, 13, and a boy, 11—still live with their father in Washington.

Mary Cook lived in a studio apartment at 60 E. Bellevue. The manager there, a blind man, also was surprised to learn Mary was in jail.

"She's not a gun moll," he said. "I can tell you that."

He also said that one of Mary Cook's visitors at the apartment was Henry M. Gargano, one of the men arrested in the fishing shack. Police say Gargano was badly wounded in the holdup, and may lose an arm.

"I don't know anything about him," the manager said. "I can't see. Besides I have 32 girls living in this building and each one of them seems to have five boy friends. How am I to know anything?"

Friends say Mary Cook was very fond of Gargano, though when they first dated he didn't mention he had served time for robbing a bank. He was released on parole from the high-security federal prison in Marion, Ill., on March 20.

"A boy friend asked me if Mary knew about Henry's being an ex-con," the girl friend said. "When I asked her she said, 'I don't believe it.' "

Mary Cook questioned Gargano about the prison. He admitted everything and promised everything. Mary Cook went back and told her girl friend, "Henry said he is going to change his ways."

Mary Cook was planning some changes, too.

"I'm too old to be dancing," she said. "I'm 30. It's time to get out. When you're 30 it's time to quit this business."

She started going to a beautician school five days a week. Backstage, while some other girl was dancing in front of the red curtains to "Temptation" or Art Blakey's "Drum Suite," Mary Cook was backstage with her books.

It was that way Friday night, and as she left the 606 early Saturday, she was carrying a load of homework.

The FBI contends she joined Gargano, his sister and Clifton O. Daniels, the other accused bank robber, at an apartment in Bellwood. She also, according to the FBI, tried to bribe a South Side doctor into treating her boy friend, who was in great pain and bleeding profusely.

"Mary called me Saturday," the girl friend said, "and said she would be off for a few days. She asked me to get someone at the 606 the watch her stuff in the dressing room.

"She said she was going to Denton to visit her mother."

On Sunday, the FBI visited the girl friend's house and asked for information about Mary Cook. The girl friend knew then that Mary Cook had not gone to Denton.

When Mary Cook left the 606 Friday, a picture of her in a skimpy two-piece bathing suit was posted in a display window outside. They removed the picture Tuesday, and stored it away at the rear of the cloakroom.

And Wednesday night they hired a replacement for Mary Cook.

'All according to Emily Post: terror on a first-name basis'

Donald Zochert, one of the best newspaper writers in America, and Edmund J. Rooney, one of the best police reporters, teamed up to write this story for the Dec. 7, 1968, Daily News.

It was 6:50 p.m. on Thursday, Nov. 14, when they knocked at the front door.

Bernard Politte got up from his easy chair and swung the door open. Two men stood outside. One of them, the older one, raised his hand.

In it he held a shiny gold badge.

"Would you step outside a moment? he asked.

Bernie did and the man raised his other hand.

In it he held a snub-nose revolver.

"We need shelter," he said. "Let's go inside."

Bernie Politte backed into his living room.

The older man, square-jawed and soft-spoken, introduced himself. Patrick Kane. Then the younger man, his eyes intense despite their lightness. Dale Wilson. What's your name? Where's your wife? In the bedroom? Call her. Her name is Odetta? OK, Bernie. OK, Odetta. No one will get hurt.

It was all according to Emily Post: terror on a first-name basis.

Patrick Donald Kane, white male, age 43, brown eyes, hair graying at the temples. Bank robbery.

Dale Glennon Wilson, white male, age 24, hazel eyes, pock-marked face. On his right forearm, tattooed, "love and hate." Kidnaping. Murder in prison.

They were strangers to each other.

Four hours earlier, near Warrenton, Mo., they had overpowered the deputy U.S. marshal and special-duty St. Louis police officer who were transferring them from Leavenworth Penitentiary to St. Louis.

Kane was to attend an appeal hearing, Wilson to stand trial for murdering a fellow inmate. They couldn't wait.

They handcuffed the guards, drove toward Pacific, Mo., and put the lawmen in a shack in the woods.

From Officer Robert Gentry, of the St. Louis police department, Kane took $240 and a revolver. "I'll see that you get this back," he said, "but I need it now."

From Vernon Whitlock, deputy U.S. marshal, Kane took a gold badge and a ring.

Then he and young Wilson got in the car and headed for St. Louis. In Bridgeton, a suburb west of the city, Wilson spotted a red and black 1968 Malibu parked in a driveway. Not bad.

It was getting dark and they were hungry.

Patrick Donald Kane and Dale Glennon Wilson decided to pay Mr. and Mrs. Bernard K. Politte a visit.

They stood around in the living room, four people and a gun, and Kane said sit down and nobody will get hurt. Wilson didn't say anything.

At 7:30 p.m., Ronnie Politte, 13, came home, through the garage and family room and into the living room. Now there were five.

Two were still hungry.

Kane took the Malibu and drove to the shopping center, a few blocks away. Wilson waited. He paced back and forth in the living room, seemed nervous, but said nothing.

In half an hour, Kane came back. He brought two big steaks, a bag of potato chips, a couple of onions, some beer, whiskey and a bottle of champagne. He also brought paper plates.

"I don't want to mess your kitchen up," he told Odetta Politte.

Kane tossed one steak in the refrigerator and cooked the other—medium. Then they ate, he and Wilson. He had a beer and two glasses of champagne; Wilson sipped the whisky.

The hostages watched.

After dinner, Kane and the Polittes went into the living room. They sat down and talked.

Kane was a good talker. He put his gun in the holster and

stretched his legs and talked. He talked about prison.

Ronnie Politte was only 13 and no one was going to spoil his evening. He went into his bedroom and began to play rock-'n'-roll records.

Wilson, tight-mouthed and a little wobbly, went with him. Kane watched him go.

"I don't know this boy too well," he said to the Polittes. "If you don't want him back there with your son, just tell me."

Three times, Kane got up and walked over to the boy's bedroom to see that everything was ok. It was.

At 10 p.m., they were still counting the hours. Wilson wandered out of the bedroom, saying nothing, and they all sat down to watch the news on television.

Two convicts had escaped, the newscaster said, and one of them—Patrick Donald Kane—was a bank robber and murderer.

"That's a lie!" Kane snapped at the television. "There's your murderer right there!"

He pointed at Wilson.

There wasn't much more to talk about.

At 3 a.m., Wilson took Ronnie Politte into the boy's bedroom. He tied Ronnie's hands and feet with hosiery. But first he gave the boy a $5 bill.

"Be nice," he said. "Don't turn out like me."

Kane took Bernard and Mrs. Politte into the master bedroom, tied their hands with hosiery, and lashed them to the bed with drapery cords.

"Is that too tight?" he asked. It wasn't.

"I want you two to stay here for a couple of hours," Kane said. Then he left.

From the bedroom, the Polittes heard the radio go on— loud. They heard the sound of the shower.

Kane and Wilson were cleaning up. It was time to move out. They found about $800 in cash. They took some clothes: a blue suit, five sport shirts, two black windbreakers. They took Bernie Politte's billfold and his credit cards.

And then there was only the sound of the radio.

It was 9:30 a.m. Friday, Nov.15.

At a table in the North Grand Club, 1024 N. Grand E.,

Springfield, Ill., two men sat looking at the morning's edition of the *Springfield State Journal.*

One of the men was getting gray at the temples. The other looked young enough to be his son.

Eight blocks away, near Springfield Junior College, a red and black 1968 Malibu with Missouri license plates was parked. It was empty.

The waitress in the North Grand Club walked over to the men and asked for their orders. For the older gentleman, a fish sandwich and a mug of draft beer. For the younger man, a fish sandwich and a Pepsi.

While they ate, they thumbed through the paper. They were looking for used-car ads.

At 10 a.m. the older man got up and went to the pay telephone. Name's Ben Johnson, he said. Want to buy a car for my son. Got anything for around $100?

A few blocks across town, at Jack's Auto Sales, 704 N. Ninth St., Jack Means sat in his office and told the man on the telephone sure, he had some junkers.

The caller said he and his son were at the North Grand Club having breakfast. Could they get picked up in about an hour? It was a deal.

Patrick Donald Kane put down the phone and walked back to the table. The waitress came over and they chatted. They seemed like average Joes.

The boy had an accident with his car, Kane explained, and they were going to pick him up another one.

"Don't be too hard on him," the waitress chided. "All kids have accidents."

Dale Glennon Wilson didn't say anything.

Jack Means finally showed up at 11:30 a.m., in a 1957 Pontiac he had just swapped for, and the waitress in the North Grand Club lost her two customers.

They didn't leave her a tip.

Jack showed the two men around the lot. There seemed to be no hurry.

Finally the older man, Ben Johnson he said his name was, decided maybe he liked the '57 Pontiac best, so they went into the office to close the deal. Ben pulled a fresh fifth of whiskey from his pocket and offered it around.

No takers.

They sat there for 15 minutes, gabbing—"trying to beat me down on the price," Jack Means said. And then they closed the deal. The men gave Jack two $100 bills, and Jack gave them $50 change.

At 1 p.m., the two men headed downtown in the Pontiac to buy 1968 Illinois license plates. But 15 minutes later they were back.

"You forgot your dealer's plates," friendly Ben said to Means, "so we brought them back."

A nice touch. The world's not full of bums after all.

Patrick Donald Kane and Dale Glennon Wilson drove across the street to a gas station. They fastened the 1968 license plates, SM 7363, to the car, and pulled out into Ninth St.

Up the road was U.S. 66.

It was 1:30 p.m. and four hours to Chicago.

At 6 p.m. on Friday, Nov. 15, Kane and Wilson checked into the Villa Motel, 5952 N. Lincoln, Chicago. They gave their names as Ben and James Johnson, father and son, Springfield, Mo.

The clerk gave them Room 9.

Now, for about 48 hours, Kane and Wilson dropped from sight. Perhaps they slept.

They had been busy.

After dark on Sunday evening, Nov. 17, a powder-blue Volkswagen drove past the Villa Motel.

In the car were a 23-year-old Air Force veteran from Michigan and his blond bride. They had been married in Michigan Saturday, and had come to Chicago for their honeymoon.

A sign advertising color television caught the bride's eye. They decided to stop.

The clerk gave them Room 11.

The newlyweds had been in their room 20 minutes when there was a knock at the door. They ignored it. Ten minutes later there was a metallic tapping on the picture window.

The bridegroom went to the window and pushed back the

drapes. A man peered in the window. He had a key in his hand.

"Hey!" the man shouted. "You left your key in the door!"

The bridegroom went to the door and opened it.

Two men stood there. One was middle-aged, graying at the temples. In one hand he held a shiny gold badge. In the other he held a snub-nose revolver.

Kane and Wilson pushed themselves into the room and shut the door behind them.

This time, they didn't introduce themselves.

It was 9 p.m.

"We're not police officers," Wilson said. "We're here to rob you."

"Where's the girl?" Kane said.

This was no pleasant conversation. Nothing was according to Emily Post.

The two men bound the hands and feet of the honeymooners with adhesive tape. They ransacked the couple's personal effects, pocketed $400 in cash and took the bridegroom's identification papers.

Then they unwound the tape from around the ankles of the bride.

Kane raped her first.

The room was quiet.

Wilson left and came back in a few moments with an armful of sheets and pillow cases.

Then he raped the girl.

Kane and Wilson worked quickly.

They ripped the sheets and pillow cases into shreds and tightly bound the newlyweds.

Earlier, they had moved the old Pontiac from the motel parking lot and left it parked a block and a half away, in front of 5828 N. Whipple St.

They didn't need it anymore.

Now they had a powder-blue 1967 Volkswagen, with wedding gifts and a sun roof.

But there was no sun.

It was midnight, Sunday, Nov. 17. Patrick Donald Kane and Dale Glennon Wilson really had reason to run.

Three days later, Mrs. Odetta Politte of Bridgeton, Mo., had her red and black 1968 Malibu back. The police had found it parked in Springfield, Ill.

The car had been driven 211 miles and something was wrong with the ignition.

Mrs. Politte drove the car to a garage in St. Charles, Mo., to have it worked on. It was almost 1:30 p.m., on Wednesday, Nov. 20.

And she heard sirens.

A few minutes earlier, two men had walked into the First State Bank of St. Charles at 121 N. Main St., a block from the Missouri River and three doors from the St. Charles police station.

One of the men carried a carbine. The other, graying around the temples, carried a snub-nose revolver.

They forced 15 bank employees and customers into a rear room.

"I want everyone to be careful," the man with the revolver said. "I'm Kane."

The young man with the carbine stood guard over the employees while Kane prodded cashier Russell Kanseiner around the bank, ordering him to open cash drawers and the big bank vault.

He stuffed the cash, an estimated $50,000, in a white laundry bag.

Then he and Wilson fled.

Two days after the robbery, a letter arrived at the St. Louis police station. It was addressed to Robert Gentry, the officer who was with Vernon Whitlock when Kane and Wilson escaped.

The letter bore a St. Louis postmark, dated Nov. 21. But Gentry was off.

On Monday, Nov. 25, he returned to work. His sergeant handed him the letter and he opened it.

Inside were 100 $20 bills—2,000—and a note. The note said: "Take care of Whitlock."

The note wasn't signed. It didn't have to be.

It was only three days before Thanksgiving.

Since then, there have been steady developments in the

manhunt for Kane and Wilson.

Area 6 homicide Lt. John Glas, of the Chicago police department, said the newlywed couple from Michigan has positively identified photographs of the two fugitives as their assailants.

The $2,000 in cash sent to Robert Gentry is being checked to determine whether it came from the bank robbery.

The Volkswagen stolen from the honeymooners in Chicago was found this week abandoned on Eads Street in St. Louis.

And the FBI says it has identified a South St. Louis residence where Kane and Wilson stayed the week of the bank holdup.

They are hunted. The Chicago police seek them on charges of rape and robbery.

St. Louis-area authorities seek them for holding the Politte family hostage the night of their escape.

The Federal Bureau of Investigation, with positive identifications from bank employees, seeks them on a warrant charging them with the robbery of the First State Bank of St. Charles.

A report that one of the men was involved in a bank robbery in Shreveport, La., the same day of the St. Charles holdup has been discredited by police.

Day by day, the fugitives run their race, but the snare tightens.

And Mrs. Odetta Politte remembers the words of a "houseguest" who bore the name of Kane:

"We will never go back."

Patrick Donald Kane and Dale Glennon Wilson were arrested separately by the FBI near Long Beach, Calif., 37 days after this article was published.

The Daily News tells
of the horror of the infamous
St. Valentine's Day Massacre

Bugs Moran and his gang of bootleggers con-
trolled much of the North Side of Chicago dur-
ing Prohibition. A South Sider named Al Ca-
pone wanted some of that territory but the
Moran gang fought him. They hijacked his
whiskey and beat up his men. Moran taunted
Capone, calling him "the Beast." The Beast
caught up with Moran's gang (but not Moran)
on Feb. 14, 1929, when Capone hoodlums wear-
ing policemen's uniforms lined up seven of
Moran's boys in a warehouse and gunned them
down. A Daily News *circulation driver hap-*
pened on the scene moments after the real po-
lice arrived and he alerted the city editor, who
locked the city room so nobody could get in or
out and cut off all the telephones except the
rewrite men's. The Daily News *scored a stun-*
ning beat on its competitors on the infamous
St. Valentine's Day Massacre, and an anony-
mous rewrite man working under fierce pres-
sure produced this graphic sidebar, which was
published only hours after the killings. Six
were first thought to have been killed, but the
total was seven. Nobody was tried for the mur-
ders and Capone, who was in Florida, said he
couldn't imagine who would commit such a
dastardly crime.

It's too much to tell. You go into the door marked "S-M-C Cart-
age Company." You see a bunch of big men talking with
restrained excitement in the cigaret smoke. You go through an-

other door back of the front office. You go between two close-parked trucks in the garage.

Then you almost stumble over the head of the first man, with a clean gray felt hat still placed at the precise angle of gangster toughness.

The dull yellow light of a lamp—daytime shows dark rivulets of blood heading down to the drain that was meant for the water from washed cars. There are six of the red streams from six heads. The bodies—four of them well dressed in civilian clothes—two of them with their legs crossed as they whirled to fall.

It's too much, so you crowd on past the roadster with bullet holes in it to the big truck behind.

You look at the truck. It is something to look at because the men were fixing it. It's jacked up, with one wheel off. You look and the big man called "Commissioner" looks and a crowd gathers, and then it gets too much for the police dog you had failed to notice lying under the truck, tied to it by a cheap yellow rope.

It gets too much for the big brown and gray police dog and he goes crazy. He barks, he howls, he snarls, showing wicked white teeth in bright-red gums.

The crowd backs away. The dog yowls once more and subsides.

Your thoughts snap with a crack back to the circle of yellow lamplight where six things that were men are sprawled.

It's still too much. You push out into the fresh air.

You find that traffic was quiet in front of 2122 N. Clark St. at 10:30 this morning. A streetcar rattled down the narrow way left by parked cars. Across from the high garage, two windows of one of those old-fashioned gray-stone apartment houses were open. Two women were exchanging gossip despite the cold.

A blue and black sedan stopped in front of the garage. The women exchanged their curiosities about it and then went back to gossip.

They jumped as a muffled roar reached them. The blue and black car sped away and turned the corner.

Out of nowhere the crowd came pouring in from the rooming houses, the little stores, the automobiles, the street cars.

They set up a hum. A policeman arrived—another. A police siren sounded—the clang of a patrol wagon.

The two women ran down and joined the buzzing in the street.

By this time people from the big apartment hotels on Lincoln Park West, half a block away, had heard and had come. The crowd was a cross-section. Gold Coast and Clark St. merged in the gathering.

"What is it? Who were they? What did they do? Were they in the know? Double-crossers. Them guys had the pull and pulled it too strong—"

Inside six pairs of lips failed to answer.

Loeb-Leopold case: A baffling type, more agile than bandits and bootleggers

Every few years, there's a "crime of the century," but the original one for this century was the world-famous case in which two brilliant and wealthy university students kidnaped and murdered little Bobby Franks for the thrill of trying to commit a perfect crime. The killers: Nathan Leopold and Richard Loeb. They were undeniably connected with the murder and they confessed after two Daily News *cub reporters, Alvin Goldstein and Jim Mulroy, discovered the typewriter Leopold and Loeb used to write a ransom note to the victim's parents. The efforts of Goldstein and Mulroy in 1924 brought the* Daily News *its first Pulitzer Prize. The following story, a front page sidebar, carried no byline but likely was written by Goldstein or Mulroy, or a third reporter who helped cover the case, Meyer Levin. Later, Levin wrote the best-selling novel* Compulsion, *based on the case. The book was made into a popular movie in 1959. The killers were saved from death row by the eloquent Chicago barrister Clarence Darrow. Loeb was killed in prison in 1936 after making a homosexual pass at a fellow prisoner. Fabled* Daily News *writer Edwin A. Lahey, then a crime reporter, wrote a classic lead for that story: "Richard Loeb, who was a master of the English language, today ended a sentence with a proposition."*

In Nathan Leopold and Richard Loeb, the University of Chicago students on whom the shadow of the Franks murder mystery

405

fell today, the police and the state's attorney's staff have a type entirely new to them—a baffling type, too agile intellectually to be handled as bootleggers and bandits and confidence men are handled.

Off the hard surface of their sophistication the best questions the state's attorney and his men could contrive glanced harmlessly.

Inquisitors skilled at talking secrets out of sharp gangsters couldn't dent the bland assurance of Leopold, a PhD at 19, and Loeb, his little less prodigious chum.

The type they represent is a new neighborhood development, which has puzzled faculty and students alike. It has grown out of the financial independence, the intellectual alertness, the ambition and the clannishness of the sons and daughters of wealthy persons living in the university section.

The men with whom Leopold and Loeb have been associated are keener mentally than the average—they get better grades, but they also keep later hours. They are more brilliant to debate than the average, but they go in more strenuously also for gin and "petting."

This type calls itself "intellectually emancipated." Their conduct, like their thinking, is independent of conventions and taboos. They scorn the judgment of other students, glorying in their superior wealth, their sharper wits, their greater capacity for forbidden pleasures.

Some of them are poets—"new" poets, you may be sure. Some of them are political radicals, though their radicalism rarely falls into patterns so conventional and unexciting as socialism or communism. Some, like Leopold, are specialists in extraordinary forms of research.

Leopold's specialty, strangely enough, is emotional perversion as described in obscure medieval books—sexual perversion particularly.

He admitted his interest readily enough, under the questioning of the state's attorney's aides, but insisted that it was scientific, not morbid. The field is a legitimate one, he said, and his study of it has the beauty of any purely scientific research. He is interested, not in the practices described, but in the amazing divagations of the mind that those practices reveal.

Fellow students grew long ago to know Leopold as a dealer in racy stories of medieval perversion. The subject was likely to bob up in any conversation with him, they say. "He was proud of his knowledge."

Other boys' classification of Leopold as "queer" and perhaps perverted may have been due to racial prejudice but it was given serious consideration by the state's attorney's investigators. The possibility that Franks was killed as a "laboratory experiment" in perversion or even cruelty, a perversion itself, was added to the many other possibilities that are under consideration.

But that is as far as the state's attorney got. When he and detectives and assistants—all versed in the difficult art of "conversational third degree"—tried their stuff on Leopold and Loeb, they were helpless. The amazing erudition of the young PhD (he boasts of ability to write in many languages) staggered the questioners, and his self-possession turned all their thrusts.

Leopold knocked them flat with a discussion of perversion in scientific terms that they didn't understand. Turning to ornithology, his other hobby, he left them breathless by a brilliant exposition of knowledge.

They sought to trap him with questions about the swamp country in which Franks' body was found. He confounded them with answers revealing the most thorough knowledge.

He knew every inch of the section where the body was hidden—not the culvert grave alone, but every other topographical accident as well. He was more familiar with the district than were detectives who have been over and over it daily since the murder.

Northwestern University students, witnesses in the Leighton Mount mystery, gave the state's attorney's staff a rather difficult experience, but nothing so startling as this.

Two reporters describe the last troubled hours of Al Keller's life

This story by Rob Warden and Wade Nelson was published in the Daily News *on July 28, 1976, the day after a 33-year-old toy designer went on a violent rampage at work.*

After dinner Monday night, Al Keller sat alone at the picnic table in the neat yard behind his modest brick home.

A neighbor, John Stefanich, saw Keller there and invited him over for a beer.

"I better not sit over there," Keller told Stefanich. "Somebody's trying to kill me."

Shrugging off Keller's remark, Stefanich was politely insistent. "Sit down and have a beer," he coaxed.

Keller agreed. As they slowly sipped beer for the next two hours, Stefanich realized that his neighbor was deeply troubled. When Keller left about midnight, Stefanich told his wife: "He's been talking crazy—just talking kind of wavy. Keller's not himself."

It was not because he feared somebody was trying to kill him but because of general rising crime in his troubled Southwest Side neighborhood that Al Keller had bought a Smith & Wesson Model 39—a handgun designed to stop human beings at close range with one pull of the trigger.

Just nine hours after Keller left Stefanich's home, he was on his way across Chicago from the Chicago Lawn neighborhood to the Near North Side with the 9-mm. weapon stuck in his belt.

Twice a day, five times a week, for four years and three months, Keller had punctually traversed Chicago between his happy home and his high-paying job at the swank Marvin Glass & Associates.

The ultramodern white stone Marvin Glass headquarters on N. La Salle St. houses what innumerable financial writers in

408

this town have unabashedly called genius. Marvin Glass, named after the man who founded it on $80 in 1939, is the world's largest toy-design company.

Al Keller was, in the opinion of most of his 75 co-workers, a valued designer of toys you might buy from companies like Mattel and Playskool.

Nobody knows why, at age 33, Al Keller's once sharp, creative mind would suddenly snap. His wife, Joanne, says she knows of no traumas, emotional or otherwise, that he might have suffered recently.

Yet it is clear that by yesterday morning Al Keller was tortured unbearably by paranoia.

He had made a list of a dozen persons he suspected were trying to get him—including neighbors and his boss, Anson Isaacson, managing partner at Marvin Glass.

He had written down the license numbers of cars he thought were following him.

He was convinced he was being exploited and plotted against by fellow employees.

Perhaps thinking to himself on paper, he had scrawled a note: "Paranoia? No."

He arrived at work just before 10—uncharacteristically, about an hour late.

He went to his tiny, glassed-in office on the second floor of the bastille-like building where you may go only after you've been perused, approved and buzzed through security barriers by guards.

A few minutes later, he emerged from the cubicle waving the Smith & Wesson.

In a nearby cubicle Donald F. Nix, 32, a toy designer, was talking to another Glass employee, John Spilone.

Keller shot Nix once in the back, but ignored Spilone. Surgery at Northwestern Memorial Hospital saved Nix' life.

In the corridor, Keller then encountered Kathy Dunn, 33, another designer.

He shot her in the head at point-blank range, and she died a few minutes later at Henrotin Hospital.

Next, Keller walked into the executive office where Anson

Isaacson, 56, was talking business with Joseph Callan, 54, a supersalesman and partner in the firm. He fired several shots at both executives.

Callan, a collector of Rolls-Royces, pre-Columbian art and quarter horses, died at Henrotin.

Isaacson, top man in the firm and guiding creative force since the death of Marvin Glass in 1974, was dead on arrival at Northwestern Memorial.

Next, Keller started back through the corridor toward his own office.

On the way he met Douglas P. Montague, 45, a designer. Keller shot Montague in the belly and chest. After surgery at Henrotin, Montague remained in critical condition today.

Then Keller stood in front of his own office, observed by near-hysterical employees who had escaped the barrage of bullets, and poked the blue barrel of the Smith & Wesson into his neck. He pulled the trigger and fell onto the blood-stained red carpet, still conscious.

As determined as the assassins of Rasputin, Keller struggled to his feet and turned the gun he had been using like a garden hose to his temple. He fired the 12th and final bullet in the magazine through his brain.

He probably died before he hit the floor.

The episode—four dead or dying, two wounded—was over in three minutes or less; so fast that several employees didn't realize what was happening until the shooting stopped.

"I thought someone was popping balloons," said Burton Meyer, a partner who may have been the target of one or two wild shots. "It sounded like he was joking. We thought it was in fun."

When the shooting stopped, a different kind of pandemonium began—the one that always accompanies the police, stretchers, reporters, minicams and microphones.

Distraught relatives of employees, who had heard radio bulletins about the tragedy, pushed their way through the sea of curious onlookers.

One of them was Marjorie Isaacson, wife of the managing partner, who was rushed there by police from the family home, nine blocks away from the scene of the tragedy. "I have to give him some medicine," she cried repeatedly as she passed through the crowd that was blocking traffic on La Salle St.

A policeman who escorted her explained later that she wasn't aware that her husband had been slain, but was worried about medicine he needed for a chronic illness.

At Northwestern Hospital, Jeannie Nix arrived just as her husband came successfully through surgery.

"My husband was very good friends with Keller," she told a reporter. "There must have been something awful happening to him."

The 'Yellow Kid' turns 99 without a conning touch, Bob Schenet reports

Bob Schenet, a local reporter who later became
night city editor, wrote this story for the June
24, 1974, Daily News.

Surrounded by well-wishers helping him celebrate his 99th birthday, the old man blinked into the television lights and said he had a suggestion.

"Let's take up a collection for me," he said, explaining that a pile of money in front of him would illustrate that he has been a man of wealth.

But the celebrants and members of the news media knew better than to put a plateful of money in front of this particular old man.

It was a birthday party for Joe (Yellow Kid) Weil, the self-acclaimed con man of the century, the man who swindled, and spent, millions during his career.

At his party Sunday at the Lake Front Convalescent Center, 7618 N. Sheridan, Weil said he had no regrets about his life, which has included more than 30 arrests and a few prison sentences. He would have changed nothing.

But Weil, who "retired" from his profession about 40 years ago, would not advise the youth of today to go into his line of work.

"It's not a life to live. It has its troubles. A penitentiary term is not fun," he said.

"But to grow wealthy you have to do something. I had to steal. No man grows wealthy by his efforts unless they are false and fraudulent," he said.

Small, thin and in failing health, Weil still was as dapper as always in his blue suit, refusing the friendly arm of a nurse when he would move about.

He always has maintained those he fleeced had larceny in their own hearts, and that his victims always could stand the loss anyway.

"The best moment of my entire life was when I met the girl I married," he said. "She was a blond, a natural blond, very, very beautiful and very well structured.

"When she died, my world died with her."

Weil shoved aside the crumbs from his birthday cake, lit a cigaret, took a sip of champagne and stared into space.

Then, very casually, the old con man picked up a small box of birthday candles from the table, and when he thought no one was looking, they were quickly stuffed into the pocket of the Yellow Kid.

Ben Hecht tells the story of Carl Wanderer and the 'ragged stranger'

Ben Hecht, famed novelist, playwright (co-author of The Front Page*) and screenwriter, was a jack-of-all-trades for the* Daily News *for 16 years. He covered World War I, local news and the arts. But he's best remembered for his streetwise stories of the tough side of Chicago, including this murder story.*

Carl Wanderer, freshly shaved and his brown suit neatly pressed, stood looking over the back porch of his home at 4732 N. Campbell Av. His wife, who was murdered last night by a holdup man in the doorway downstairs, lay in their bedroom.

Wanderer looked at his gold watch, and his hand was steady. He smiled blankly at the back porches in front of him and, with his eyes grown cold, repeated, "Well, I got him. I got him anyway."

At two o'clock this afternoon there are scheduled two inquests, one over the body of Mrs. Carl Wanderer and the other over the body of the stickup man. Wanderer, standing two feet away from the man who had killed his wife, opened fire with his .45.

Last October Wanderer was discharged from service as a first lieutenant. He came back from France with a Croix de Guerre and a DSC [Distinguished Service Cross]. He had for a year been the best pistol shot in his battalion—the 17th machine-gun battalion.

Campbell Av. is a quiet, snug neighborhood, and in the morning children play under the trees in the back yards. Wanderer, putting his gold watch back in his pocket, went on talking in a quiet, tense voice.

"The first shot blew him across the hallway," he said.

414

"Then I couldn't see him. But I knew where he'd landed and I let him have three more. I got him but—."

The machine gunner and owner of a Croix de Guerre stopped talking, and a young husband in a brown suit with eyes reddened from tears finished the sentence. "If I'd only gotten him sooner. Just a nickel's worth sooner."

Later the husband said, "There isn't much to tell. We'd been to a movie and this man followed us, I suppose. I was going to turn on the light in the vestibule so as to see the keyhole, when I heard a voice, 'Don't turn on the light.' I reached for my gun. I knew what the fellow was up to. But he got cold feet. He never asked us to put our hands up, but began shooting right off the bat. I was a few seconds late. I don't know why. But I got him. He got what was coming to him."

Outside, neighbors sat on their sunny porch steps and stared at the house at 4732. The street was again quiet and peaceful, as if tragedy had never visited it. A gray hearse motored up in front of the address, and the neighbors discussed the life of the couple as it had been before last night. One of them said, "She told me only yesterday she was going to be a mother, and was so happy."

Through a card found in the clothes of the assailant he was tentatively identified at the hospital as Edward Masters, who, the police say, is a well-known slugger and gunman. The card bore the name of the John Robinson circus and indicated that he had at one time been an employe of the commissary department of the circus. He also wore a newspaper driver's badge, which bore the number 706.

Capt. Michael Evans of the Bureau of Identification made an effort to identify the dead slayer of Mrs. Wanderer through fingerprints. He said later, however, that the prints did not correspond with any on record. It is thought that the man was an ex-convict, but that he came here from another city. The manager of the circulation department of a morning paper viewed the man and said that he believed he had formerly been employed on a wagon driven by one of the newspaper's employees.
This was the first part of the story. Here's the
rest: Hecht developed an instant dislike for

Wanderer, who seemed to be unconcerned about his wife's murder. The police shared his feelings and they soon discovered that the "ragged stranger's" gun had been in Wanderer's possession the day before the murder, and one gun had been used in both killings.

Wanderer soon confessed that he hired the stranger to kill his wife, then killed both. He was sentenced to death and Hecht visited him a few hours before he was to hang. Hecht persuaded Wanderer to give a speech from the gallows in which he roundly and obscenely condemned the editors of the Daily News. Hecht had written the speech about his bosses and gave it to Wanderer, who put it in his pocket. Unfortunately, his jailers tied his hands behind him and he couldn't reach Hecht's speech so he sang a religious song as the hood was placed over his head. The song prompted the humorist Alexander Woollcott to write: "From one of the crowd of reporters watching the execution came the audible comment that Wanderer deserved hanging for his voice alone."

Marge McElheny reveals how the penal system tortured an innocent man

This story by Marge McElheny, a local reporter, was published Aug. 14, 1975.

For more than three months, Ronald Mayes lived what he called a "nightmare" in Cook County Jail.

Mayes says he was raped repeatedly by another inmate, choked into unconsciousness and beaten so severely that he may require ear surgery.

And the torment was worsened by the fact that Mayes was innocent of the crime for which he had been jailed—a fact discovered belatedly by law-enforcement authorities when the real criminal confessed.

Mayes, 33, a Berwyn construction worker, entered the jail on March 29, after two employees identified him as the armed man who two days earlier had robbed the Walgreen's drugstore at Cermak and Harlem in Berwyn of $2,985.

He was released July 14, 107 days later, after Richard A. Beasley, 44, of 3026 S. Cicero, in Cicero, confessed to the crime.

"I just don't feel right anymore," Mayes said Wednesday after his appearance before Criminal Court Judge John Hechinger, where the state's attorney officially dropped charges.

"I'm just not the same. I'm going to leave Chicago. I want to go back to my family in Indiana," he said.

Mayes said he "never even went into that drugstore" he was accused of robbing, and that the man who confessed to the robbery "doesn't even come close to looking like me."

"You could stand him next to me and people would laugh if you tried to compare us," Mayes said. "He's 10 years older, taller, heavier, with a lot of gray hair. I've got red hair."

Mayes said he was "in a daze" after he was arrested.

"I kept hoping someone would come to the jail and set them straight," he said.

417

"I had never even been in a police car before in my life."

Mayes says he is absolutely mystified why he was arrested. He said he was sitting in The King and I tavern in Cicero when two policemen came in to tell him they had a warrant for his arrest.

Berwyn police said a Walgreen's employe who witnessed the robbery spotted Mayes in the tavern, thought he was the robber and notified them.

Henry Schmid, then assistant manager of the drugstore where the robbery occurred, later picked Mayes out of a lineup at the Berwyn police station.

Berwyn investigator Tony Adolf said that while Beasley and Mayes do not look at all alike today, witnesses said that the robber at Walgreen's wore a hat and that Mayes wore a hat in the lineup.

And, Adolf said, Mayes and Beasley do look remarkably similar when wearing hats.

Mayes said he was "treated like an animal" in jail and repeatedly raped by an inmate "built like Charles Atlas."

"He was on me from the minute I got in there till the day I left," Mayes said.

"He told me he would do everything in the world to me and he did everything in the world. I don't even want to talk about what happened. People wouldn't believe it."

Mayes said he "tried to talk to the guards but they wouldn't help."

Acting jail warden Robert E. Glotz said in response to Mayes' charges: "We have no record that he ever complained of mistreatment."

Glotz said jail records show that Mayes was treated for an ear infection and an upper respiratory problem while confined.

"He was placed on Tier D-1 with fellows 30 years of age and upward," Glotz said. "He slept in the dayroom area. It's one of the most trouble-free areas of the jail."

Mayes' attorney, Irwin Field, failed to win bond reduction from the original $25,000 ($2,500 cash).

Mayes said that while he was in jail, his car was stolen and he lost his job, his apartment and his girl friend.

"The first week I was out I just didn't care anymore," he said.

Attorney Field said a lawsuit may be filed against the county Department of Corrections and other parties.

"I think someone should pay a price," Mayes said. "I didn't do anything. I just can't believe that something like this could happen to a human being."

Two reporters tell how the quiet peace was shattered in a wealthy, folksy suburb

On the night of Aug. 4, 1972, retired insurance executive Paul M. Corbett and three members of his family were brutally murdered in their secluded suburban home. Three members of what State's Atty. Edward V. Hanrahan described as a terrorist gang were convicted of the murders two years later. Reporters George Harmon and Edmund J. Rooney wrote this story as a sidebar to the main story on the murders in the next day's Daily News.

It's a perfect summer day in Barrington Hills. Young girls, their hair streaming, ride along the 55 miles of bridle paths.

Their kid brothers float a flat-bottomed boat out onto a man-made lake in someone's front yard.

Dad, who probably runs or helps run a company, is downtown at the office. Mom is at the Barrington Hills Country Club, trying to improve her 18 handicap.

Dusk rolls across the hills and the families are back together. It may be Chicago's wealthiest suburb, but it's still a folksy place where Friday night parties include all three generations of the families.

The dining room of the country club is filled with parents and kids laughing together Friday night.

But at one table, Chuck Boand eats alone.

A couple of miles away, in a hilltop house that overlooks a pastel countryside of manors and farmsteads, Boand's ex-wife and his daughter sit down at a small family supper.

And minutes later the haven of Barrington Hills is shredded.

It is a tale of butchery straight from the annals of the Sharon Tate massacre. Or maybe it recalls the Friday night ghetto brawls in which a wife cuts her husband's throat with a paring knife from the kitchen.

But somehow it's different from all the rest, because this is Barrington Hills.

This is the wealthiest suburb of Chicago, if one judges suburbs by their property values. It is 42 miles northwest of the Loop in what was once lush pasture. The median home value is $82,200 and no house is built on less than five acres.

The Kempers, the Bards, the Smiths live there. They and the Corbetts are what the New York magazine writers like to call captains of industry and country gentlefolk.

And yet they are not really grist for the society columns. They like the simple things in life: the family, the outdoor life, the garden.

The Boands and the Corbetts have lived in the Barrington area a long time and they are liked and respected by their neighbors.

"The Corbetts are a terrific family and Paul was very successful," said Thomas Z. Hayward, who stepped down May 1 as village president.

"I just played golf with him this week."

Saturday a rising sun washed scarlet onto the foot-high marker that read "Paul M. Corbett" in white letters on a black background. Dogs barked in the distance.

Edward Putta, 81, of Cary, drove by to poke a morning paper into the cylinder standing at the end of the circular drive that leads to the gray French provincial home.

Putta noticed the commotion and, as the sky lightened, saw the police cars.

"Oh, this is terrible," he said after asking what had happened.

"Corbett was such a wonderful nan, such a good man. Was it robbers? Just terrible, just terrible."

Beyond the manicured lawn and shrubs, the shadows of detectives flickered past the windows as they moved through the home's large rooms lined with expensive paintings and books, dusting for fingerprints and picking up evidence.

Paul Corbett and his wife had lived alone in the 14-room

house, which has a patio overlooking a small lake. Its value is estimated at more than $100,000.

They and their guests had left fresh coffee cups in the dining room when they were herded into an 8-by-12-foot serving pantry.

Chicago police crime-lab technicians took one door off that room, spread newspapers on the floor to soak up the blood and scattered fingerprint dust all over the room.

In the pantry are beautiful wooden wall cabinets, a refrigerator, a washer and dryer. It is connected to the dining room by a hall.

Bullet holes riddled the walls and some of the blood was tracked onto the front walk by those who removed the bodies.

The Corbetts, who had installed outdoor lighting and had a burglar alarm they turned on at night, obviously lived in elegance.

In an attached garage were a 1933 Rolls-Royce, a Renault, a Ferrari, a Mercedes-Benz and a golf cart.

"Look at all this and look at the way he died," said one investigator. "Much too early."

Protesters at 1968 Democratic National Convention in Chicago.
Perry Riddle / Daily News.

Challenges:

Peter Lisagor
Robert Gruenberg
Georgie Anne Geyer
M. W. Newman
William J. Eaton
Finley Peter Dunne
Larry S. Finley
Harlan Draeger
Paul Ghali
Nicholas Shuman

JFK tribute: 'And he will make the face of Heaven so fine'

Peter Lisagor, distinguished Washington Bureau chief of the Daily News, *wrote this story on the last day of the 1964 Democratic National Convention.*

ATLANTIC CITY—The Democrats told Bobby Kennedy they remember . . . and it brought him to grateful tears.

The man they call ruthless stood alone on the giant dais swallowing his Adam's apple. This was a hurrah that nobody organized. Nobody had to. It sometimes happens that a genuine emotion can be felt even at a political convention.

The memorial to the late John F. Kennedy followed a film of Lyndon B. Johnson titled *Road to Leadership,* reviewing the President's career from his days as a young Texas congressman to the highlights of his nine months in the White House.

Sen. Henry (Scoop) Jackson of Washington, who served as Democratic national chairman during the 1960 campaign and who had been under consideration as a possible vice presidential candidate by John Kennedy, touched off the first affectionate outburst for the late President by asking the convention to join in the Kennedy tribute.

The delegates responded with measured applause, and presently they were rising, joined by the galleryites. For seven minutes they stood clapping.

Jackson finally got to the point where he would introduce Robert F. Kennedy, brother of the martyred President, as simply the man who was closest to him.

The sight of the attorney general moving to the dais, solemn, gaunt, looking not unlike a youthful choir leader, broke the dam. He stood there nodding his head in appreciation for the wave of applause that crashed in on him, and his lips formed

425

the words. "Thank you, thank you, thank you."

The ovation now begins to swell, a boiling mixture of memory and regret, reverence and grief recalled. Bobby Kennedy lowers his head, his jaw set, his lips pressed tightly together, his eyes alight with gratitude.

It is a tradition of these affairs to manufacture enthusiam and emotion. But this is a rare thing, not unexpected but real. The convention managers had expected it, and so had Lyndon B. Johnson, who ordered the Kennedy tribute to be staged on the last day of the convention lest it interfere with the main business.

But nobody had been sure what form it would take, what depths of emotionalism it might tap.

Now the delegates are standing on their chairs, cheering, whistling, waving prematurely the pennants they held for a later event, red-and-blue "Hello Lyndon" pennants. Men holding aloft placards saying "New York Welcomes Bobby" yell out "Go, go, go."

The solemn wistful face of Bobby Kennedy creases in a quick smile, and he raises his hand in a short, sharp wave, now uncertain about the nature of the ovation, aware that a note of gaiety has crept in and that maybe the message being powerfully dispatched now is for him as well as for a memory.

Spotlights wash the vast hall. One light bathes the presidential box, where Ethel Kennedy, Bobby's wife, and his brother-in-law, Stephen Smith, stand to the left of the First Lady, Mrs. Lyndon B. Johnson. Behind them are James Roosevelt and his brother, Franklin D. Jr., who campaigned at John F. Kennedy's side in the West Virginia hills in 1960.

Cheers, whistles, applause, yells, and roars now ricochet off the walls and skip along the domed ceiling, not yet a frenetic force but increasingly evocative.

Was this a message of sympathy to Bobby for being ruled off the vice presidential course? At least one delegate thinks so, a man from Montana, who says: "That Johnson knew what he was doing when he got rid of him."

Massachusetts is now screaming in unison, creating a chant for Bobby. And New York looks a bit smug, pleased that a frequent visitor has decided to cancel his hotel reservation and buy a house in town.

After 10 minutes, Kennedy steps back from the podium. He is unwilling to use the gavel to intrude into this meaningful tumult. Chairman John McCormack, speaker of the House, picks up the gavel.

"The attorney general," begins McCormack, and a fresh outburst of cheers rolls through the hall. It roars and reverberates yet a while, until every cheering delegate has made sure that the lone, slight figure on the dais understands that nothing has faded or been forgotten, that his brother's image has lost no luster.

Bobby Kennedy finally got to say his modest piece. He thanked the Democrats for supporting his brother, sharing in his joys, comforting him in times of sorrow, sustaining him.

He quoted from Shakespeare:

When he shall die take him and cut him out in little stars,
And he will make the face of Heaven so fine
That all the world will be in love with
Night and pay no worship to the garish sun.

A girl knelt in the aisles, and Bobby Kennedy choked back his own tears.

Came then the lines from Robert Frost which JFK loved to quote, about "promises to keep . . . and miles to go before I sleep."

All Bobby had come to do was to introduce the film, *A Thousand Days,* a vivid remembrance of crisis and crowds, of President Kennedy at home and on the water he loved, with his wife, Jacqueline, and his children, Caroline and John, of moments of wit and moments of solemnity.

But when the youthful, slight figure turned away from the podium, it was almost as certain that he would return to future Democratic conventions, in his own behalf perhaps, as anything can be in politics.

'The lights of television crews brought a false light to the real darkness'

Robert Gruenberg, one of America's most sensitive newspaper writers, made the last trip home with Robert F. Kennedy. His moving story of June 6, 1968, captured the sadness and despair shared by millions for the man who assured his supporters, "No martyr's cause has ever been stilled by his assassin's bullet."

NEW YORK—It is about 2,500 miles across the country as the presidential jet flies—from the gray-brown desert of Southern California to the dazzling spires of this American metropolis.

The proud bird, blue and white, soared at 35,000 feet or more, its silver wings glinting as it fled the setting sun, bearing the heavy burden of a man who sought to lead his country.

Robert Francis Kennedy has come back to the state he adopted and which adopted him.

In a box covered with a soft, purple velvet he came, his skull shattered, as was the dream of thousands of people who placed their faith in his youth and his willingness to break the patterns of old.

Over Southern California, parched and dry in the Mojave but green and fertile in the rest of the state, the bird flew.

This was the California that gave him victory, seconds before death, victory from the stubby, dark Mexican workers in the grapeyards and victory from the black people in Los Angeles.

"He paid attention to us before anyone else did," a union organizer among the grapeworkers said in Chicago last week, and they shouted, "Viva Kennedy!" And it echoed in the ghetto, too, and they handed him their votes.

They had cheered because he spoke their language.

In the plane, his widow, Ethel, with 3 of their 10 children, and another man's widow, named Jacqueline, sat together and talked, sometimes in low tones. Grief had never been a stranger to either over the years.

The white-capped Rockies clawed upward through the clouds. Out the window Ethel Kennedy could gaze; off to the south lay New Mexico, the Sun State.

It was in March, wasn't it, that they had both stopped in Snowball, N.M., a little town that hardly anyone knew? It was only supposed to be a four-or five-hour pause for a much-needed rest in the strenuous campaigning that had begun too late. And during the rest she had made six difficult ski runs over the snow-covered slopes, and they had all laughed about it and gone on campaigning.

The war had been terrible. It had grown from a small flame to a great blaze, and somehow none could run from it, but instead only became more deeply drawn into it.

Many were drawn, and among them were black boys from the ghettos of the big cities, unschooled, unknown. There was no college deferment for them when the Army called, and he talked about it across the country in the campaign.

The white-topped mountains had given way to green-clad slopes and these, in turn, to the prairies. Across Nebraska, the bird flew, and there was Omaha, and Creighton University.

"Isn't drafting young Negroes into the Army at least a partial solution to the problem of the ghetto?" a student had asked him at a political meeting.

"How can you speak like that?" he asked, his voice rising. "How can you talk like that, particularly you kids on a campus who are so comfortable? Look around you. How many black students do you see in your class, how many Mexicans? They go off to war while you sit there. What does the American dream mean to them?"

They didn't like it, but he had said it. And Nebraska, too, gave him a primary victory.

The monotonous prairies soon gave way to the small patchwork quilt of farms in the Mississippi Valley. Across the great river of America, over its Lincoln land of Illinois and Indiana, now the melting pot and the bleaching pot of its whites and blacks, its "100-per cent Americans" and its Eastern European sons and their sons.

It had been only a few days since President Johnson had declared on March 31 that he would not seek the Presidency again.

There had been a triumphal reception in Gary, where Richard Hatcher, the first black mayor of a major American city, had introduced him.

Then he had gone on to South Bend, where Poles were celebrating a holiday that some called Dyngus Day, and he had introduced a real, live prince named Stanislaus Radziwill, husband of Jacqueline Kennedy's younger sister, Lee.

"Stash won the election in 1960 by going all over the country," he told his audiences, recalling his brother Jack's victory, and now Stash would do it all over again. And in a Polish hall in South Bend Robert Kennedy sang a Polish song with three Polish kids.

Over the neat farms and orchards of central Ohio the big bird was flying. To the north lay Cleveland, on the shores of rotting Lake Erie. How could he ever forget Ohio and Cleveland?

It was on April 5, a day after the Rev. Dr. Martin Luther King Jr. was slain by an assassin in Memphis, and it was a time not to politick, but he went to Cleveland anyway and talked before the well-heeled Cleveland City Club.

"No martyr's cause has ever been stilled by his assassin's bullet," he told them. 'This is a time of shame and sorrow . . . what has violence ever accomplished? What has it ever created?

"A sniper is only a coward, not a hero, and an uncontrolled, uncontrollable mob is only the voice of madness.

"We don't want guns in the hands of people who shouldn't have them," he said.

Pennsylvania and its green carpet of low Appalachian mountains lay below. The sun was almost on the horizon in the west and the long shadows of the mountains mottled the valleys, in which the little twisting mountain roads disappeared only to reappear again.

Pittsburgh and steel slipped behind, Phildadelphia and a challenge to the old party stalwarts lay ahead.

It was a great fund-raising dinner, a gala, as they had taken to calling these things, at $100 a plate, and all the party bosses had turned out a couple of months ago.

There he was, behind the big banquet table, starting his speech, and for all the proud Kennedy tradition, those cigar-chewing, vote-counting party realists heard him say, trying to bring it off lightly:

"Every once in a while I look down the table hoping Mayor (James) Tate will smile at me."

Tate, like all the others, smiled. Indeed, he laughed, but his allegiance at the time was to another man named Hubert Humphrey.

But it didn't matter any more.

The big bird lowered itself gracefully on Long Island in the evening, with only the lights of the television crews bringing a false light to the real darkness.

For now he lay in the purple-covered box, forever.

Georgie Anne Geyer interviews an ex-Nazi SS officer in exile at Earth's end

Correspondent and columnist Georgie Anne Geyer's first assignment for the Daily News *Foreign Service was Latin America. She built a national reputation with exclusives like this one from the* Daily News *of March 12, 1966.*

The cold, gray waters from Antarctica slap at the black, rocky beaches of Porvenir, and the wind wails day after day.

Black-necked swans fly overhead, white salt beds freckle the land like liver spots, and the camel-like guanacos race in packs of thousands across the unrelieved loneliness of Tierra del Fuego, the island that is the last place on Earth.

For two days I had traveled from Santiago to get to Porvenir, first by jet to Punta Arenas, then by plane to the island and overland by truck. In Porvenir I asked the carabiniero (police): "Can you tell me where Walter Rauff lives?"

A carabiniero climbed into the truck and offered to take us there. "We had a scare that somebody might attack him some time ago," he said, "and we try to watch his house."

We knocked at the door of the office of the Pirata crabmeat factory. It opened, and there he stood, a short man with fine, chiseled Prussian features, dressed in a handsome brown tweed jacket with a tan neck scarf.

"Yes, come in," said Walter Rauff. "It's nice to have company. But, no, I cannot give any interview. I am not news any more, and I don't want any publicity."

But in the day I was to spend with Rauff, it seemed that he didn't want to talk, but he did want to talk. He said, for example, "I think the Americans will come to understand Germany better in the next couple of years. Now you too are involved in a dirty war in Vietnam. And your soldiers must fight it, no matter what."

Just below us, on the cold bay of Porvenir, stood the German-owned crabmeat factory Rauff manages. Above us was the neat wooden house, where he lives with only his police dog, Bobby.

Rauff has a big blue truck, which he drives around town on business, with Bobby in the back, barking at the other dogs, but Rauff does not go out much. He stays home at night, listening to German shortwave programs.

He is known in Porvenir as a quiet, friendly man, well liked by everyone and protected by them. And the simple Yugoslav fishing folk of the town do not understand why their neighbor, who is invited to town functions and gives his worn-out clothes to an old Czech fisherman, should be accused of killing 100,000 persons.

It was 5 p.m. Rauff stood by his radio set, trying to call the main office in Punta Arenas. Then it was 5:05, and 5:10. He paced. "One thing I cannot stand," he said, "is when people are not punctual. I am always punctual. I cannot bear it."

He took me for a ride in his truck. We drove in five minutes all around the little town, whose name inexplicably means "Future." Once there was a future in gold here; now there is fishing, sheep and oil. The town, all of colored frame houses and empty streets, is the capital of the 10,000 residents of the island, who stay close to their stoves.

We drove out the five miles to the Straits of Magellan, the historic passage that divides the island from the mainland. This evening, the straits, through which Magellan and Darwin passed, were wild, with stormy whitecaps.

Along the way, Rauff showed me the fishermen's camps, bits of shacks of wood and window huddled along the beaches. "And I, who loved big cities, have to live here."

"Why do you stay now?" I asked.

"There are many people who'd like to get me," he answered. "Here—they see everyone who comes and goes."

"Do you really think someone would try to get you?"

"No, of course not." Now he changed. "Israel suffered too

much in public opinion with its kidnaping of Eichmann. They would not do that again.

"We had a scare in November, 1964, though. The police got a note that some Jews would kidnap me, and one night I was lying in bed reading when I heard a tap on the window. It was a carabiniero.

"I invited him in and he said they were going to give me a guard, and the next morning there were, not two, but three carabiniero here." He smiled. "My neighbors moved out. I asked them. 'Why do this? You're safer now. All they can do that could hurt you would be to bomb me.' "

He chuckled. "I asked the carabiniero if they couldn't be a little more discreet, so the next day they, whom any child in the town knows, were here, but in their plainclothes."

A visit with Walter Rauff is a strange experience. You know he is wanted by West Germany as the second-most-wanted Nazi war criminal. Martin Bormann, whom Rauff says is dead, is first. Yet he can be a charming and cultured man, and you feel safe with him because, if the evidence against him is correct, he was what the Germans call a "schreibtisch" murderer—a man who kills by signing papers.

"I had been here before," Rauff said. "In 1925, when I came to the straits with the German Navy, and so I knew the area."

Now it was 7 p.m., and he was sitting in his little living room drinking coffee, which he served in a neat setting. The hot water for the powdered coffee was in a pitcher. His napkin was in a special holder. Everything was perfectly in order in the warm, wood-paneled living room with its simple furniture.

Outside, the bay was getting darker, and it was getting colder. "I like the house cold at night," Rauff was saying. "I have an automatic switch that turns the heat on at 7:30 in the morning, when I get up."

Then, in a conversation that kept changing from minute to minute, I asked him of what he is accused, and his face tightened.

"They say I killed 96,000 Jews. They know I never killed one man, except in battle. I was in North Africa for a long time, and we never killed one Jew there." He paused. "That was a gentleman's war."

Again the conversation changed. "I usually make package soup in the evening," he went on, "but that is not good enough for a guest. So let us go downtown and have dinner at the hotel. I will show you the 'nightlife' of Porvenir."

First, since it was still partially light, we drove out in the truck to "Useless Bay," a new moon of lonely sand. By now the sunset was breaking over the water, and the yellow light was exploding behind the clouds.

By the time we got to the Hotel Tierra del Fuego, a little low place in simple but comfortable style, it was after 10 p.m. A small band of men, all very Yugoslav-looking, were sitting in the bar, talking politics. We had a drink, a mixture of Chilean Pisco and vermouth, before retiring into the dining room, a little room warmed by a stove.

And now Walter Rauff, the silent recluse of Tierra del Fuego, began to talk slowly, hesitantly, about his past.

"There is no brief way to explain it all, " he said, as we drank a white Chilean wine. "Nobody can explain simply what happened in Germany. You have to understand what Germany went through in the '20s and '30s. It was a proud country, humiliated. No people can stand that.

"There were terrible things done, after the beginning—I don't say there weren't terrible things. I'm not one who says he didn't know. I knew. But I was a soldier—right or wrong, my country. A soldier obeys. That's what he is."

I pressed him, because I did not, then, know all the details of his case. "What exactly are you accused of?"

"They say I was in charge of technical things," he said, his voice getting lower. "What did I know of technical things? I was the organizer. Organization— that was my power."

Later I would go back over Rauff's trial in Chile two years ago and learn more about the "technical things." He had started as a career navy officer in the German navy and was a commander when Hitler came to power. Then he joined the SS and, when Hitler began eliminating the Jews, Rauff was head of that section of the national security office in charge of all the trucks,

435

of dispatching and of transportation.

Someone invented an efficient way of killing more people: the exhaust from the trucks carrying the victims to concentration camps was piped into the trucks, and the victims were dead when they arrived.

It was part of Rauff's job to approve these orders, to dispatch the trucks and to approve the method. More than 100,000 died in the trucks.

After the war, he escaped from the Allied prison camps and eventually came to South America with his wife, who died four years ago, and his two sons, both educated in Chilean military academies ("a boy should have a military education").

Although he returned to Germany for visits in 1960 and 1962, he was not arrested then. No one knows why. Then, in 1963, Germany attempted to extradite him to stand trial.

Because Chilean law provides that 15 years after the crime was committed a man cannot be extradited, and possibly because Rauff has influential friends in Chile, he was tried and set free.

"In the jail, I was so calm, so peaceful," he was saying, "as I have never been before. Once, some of the jailers came to me and asked, 'Now, tell us how it really was.' "

As the fat, dark-haired hotelkeeper's wife served us some of the lamb from Tierra del Fuego, I asked him, "If you could go back, would you do the same thing over again?"

"Yes," he said slowly. "I would have to say I would do the same things again. There was nothing else to do."

Now he was beginning to look drawn and depressed. Outside the cold had set in, and we said goodnight.

When I met him for breakfast, he looked different. His face was strained, his eyes bloodshot.

"I didn't sleep," he explained. "I don't know why." He smiled, but it was strained. "Old things. . . ."

He drove me to the little runway he calls the "international airport," and before I left, said, "I know you will write something, but please don't say anything too bad about me."

And so, Walter Rauff is left alone at the end of the world.

"I don't know how much longer I can stand it here," he had

said, "but I still owe money for the trial. It cost me $10,000." He talks about going back to Germany to testify for his old SS friends, now on trial for his same crime. But this is not the time.

"I don't know about Germany today. They just seem to care about making money. They don't work any more."

In Chile, Rauff is still a curiosity, but most people seem to think he should be allowed to live in peace. "He is a quiet man, cultured and kind. He's not a problem for anybody, and neither will we permit anybody to create problems in this place," says Porvenir's mayor, Leopoldo Fernandez.

No one really thinks he will be kidnaped or even extradited—the only incident he has ever had was once in Punta Arenas, when a Jewish businessman, in a fit of anger, struck him on the street.

But peace for Walter Rauff does not seem possible. I recall standing with him by the bay, with its incredible loneliness and grayness, and he said to me, playing on the meaning of the town's name, "This is Porvenir, where there is no future."

'Hubert Humphrey pulled down the window, cleared his throat and spat on Michigan Avenue'

Wednesday, Aug. 28, 1968, was a day the press could hardly forget. It was a day of violence for police and antiwar protesters, and it was the day the Democrats nominated Hubert H. Humphrey for President of the United States. M. W. Newman spent the day as close as he could get to the candidate and wrote this classic story for the Aug. 29 Daily News.

On the biggest day of his life—Wednesday, Aug. 28, 1968—Hubert H. Humphrey arose at 8 a.m. and saw that the morning was fair.

Twenty-five floors downstairs in the lobby of the Conrad Hilton Hotel, the remnants of a stench bomb still fouled the air.

But there was no trace of tear gas in the streets—not yet. The sun glinted on blue Lake Michigan. There had been head-bopping during the night far below the vice president's windows, but he had not gotten out of bed to look.

Quickly, he dressed in a TV-blue ensemble—dark suit, pastel blue shirt, dark tie. He was a little tired, but he looked very good, his skin pink and smooth.

Within 30 minutes, Chicago's thickset boss, Mayor Richard J. Daley, hustled into the security-ringed suite marked 2525A. And Ted Kennedy was on the phone.

The young senator wanted to explain just where he stood; by ruling out a last-ditch "draft-Kennedy" move, he in effect wrapped up the nomination for Humphrey. The men in suite 2525A were elated, but they already knew it was just about a sure thing.

Although not quite.

"I have been in politics long enough to know its uncertainties," Humphrey assured a caucus of Connecticut delegates.

It was 10:30 a.m. in a cramped, sweaty room at the Pick-Congress Hotel.

Already the vice president was a little hoarse. Under the heavy lights, sweat glistened around his blue eyes. He thumped his hand on the lectern.

"I've won a lot of elections and I don't intend to lose this one to Richard Nixon," he told the cheering delegates.

He handshook his way out of the room, and sped back to the Hilton in a late-model Cadillac. On the way, he did a surprising thing—he pulled down the window, cleared his throat and spat on Michigan Avenue.

Young McCarthy demonstrators standing on the crowded sidewalk gasped and laughed. And they shouted, "We want Gene—we want Gene."

Back in the smelly Hilton lobby, Humphrey began pumping several hundred eager hands. "Nice to see you, hello there," he told the packed throng. He was relaxed, calm and genial, but the Secret Service men around him were not. For not all of the people in the crowd were friendly.

"You used to be our hero," a man wearing a McCarthy button told Humphrey. The vice president did a double take.

One blond lad, 5 feet tall at most, wormed in next to Humphrey and said slowly, "Mr. Vice President, you're a warmonger."

The vice president replied calmly, "You know better than that."

He edged ahead and a security man carrying a walkie-talkie shouted at the boy:

"You're a disgrace to your parents. Is that the way you talk to your vice president?"

He grabbed the boy by the shoulders and shoved him several feet.

Another teen-ager shouted "Dump the Hump" in the vice president's face. Strong arms reached out and propelled the boy away.

Humphrey made it to the elevators as the lobby swelled to

439

throaty roars of "We Want Gene," "We Want Humphrey" and "Dump the Hump."

And then began the wait in 2525A. Mayor Daley announced that Illinois was going for HHH. Jackie Robinson, the ex-Republican, dropped in for lunch. The vice president already was working on his acceptance speech.

But no, said his press secretary, Norman Sherman, Humphrey had not offered the vice presidency to Ted Kennedy. Nor to anybody, in fact. It was still open. He wouldn't decide until Thursday.

Sherman has a fast, witty style. A reporter asked him an angled question and he replied, "Can't answer that. I'm not George Christian (President Johnson's press secretary), I'm Norman Jewish."

It was good for a laugh on a day not exactly full of laughs.

Downstairs in Grant Park, the police had resumed a skull session with visiting hippies. The gas fumes swept westward and some penetrated Humphrey's suite slightly.

"He's relaxing in there," Sherman told newsmen sweating in the 25th-floor lobby.

"Relaxing? While police are clubbing kids?"one reporter cried.

Had Humphrey seen the fighting? "He did look out the window," Sherman conceded.

The repartee ended after Sherman announced that he was "not the public-relations man for Mayor Daley's police."

The day wore on, and beneath the big windows of 2525A there was roaring and swirling and more bloodshed in the urban war of Michigan Avenue.

Like many Americans, Hubert Humphrey—on the biggest day of his life—sat and watched it on color television.

He dined at about 9 p.m. on ham and eggs and cottage cheese and peaches, in a paneled two-bedroom suite graced with figured wallpaper.

On two TV screens a few feet away, the urban war flickered. Humphrey sat in a beige armchair with about a dozen friends around him, including LBJ's old aide, Jack Valenti. They all looked glum.

"They (the demonstrators) are muttering, 'Get out of Vietnam,' " the vice president said.

"I don't feel so good tonight—what's going on down there?" he added later.

And suddenly it was time for the first ballot at the convention.

Friends kept piling in, and the vice president's normally buoyant spirits seemed to revive.

He had changed to a striped shirt and a maroon tie and he began to chuckle occasionally. He heard and saw himself being placed in nomination and remarked: "I'm sure getting recommended tonight."

When the balloting began, the vice president was ready. On his crossed knees were two sheets. On one he had a projection of the votes he expected; on the second, he kept count.

It was clear that at this late date he wasn't expecting any upsets. He was the coolest man in the room, now crowded with seated reporters and cameramen.

Booing sounded through the television set when Illinois cast 112 votes for HHH. His face betrayed nothing.

And as the voting developed, it turned out that the man from Minnesota had called the shots with astounding precision.

He predicted he would get only two votes from Massachusetts and that's all he got. He grinned because he was right.

His New Hampshire projection showed six votes—right on the head.

He had 61 for New Jersey, and got 62. And he leaned forward when big, divided New York came up. "Ninety-six," the vice president said. The vote for him was 96½.

"I had 96," he repeated with a big grin. It was by now a very winning game.

When Pennsylvania's turn came, the vice president suddenly leaned forward. His aplomb had gone and he was excited, because this was the state that would put him over.

"Ah," he said happily when the vote was announced.

Everyone stood and applauded and so did Hubert Horatio Humphrey.

He kissed the graying woman on his left and a brunet on his

right. The television screen showed his happy wife, Muriel, at the International Amphitheatre and he ran over to it, saying:

"There she is. See how pretty she looks."

Joyfully, the Democratic nominee for President blew a kiss to Muriel Humphrey and patted the screen. Then he bent down and kissed that screen, twice.

It was a few minutes before midnight on this great day for Hubert Humphrey. He beamed, his blue eyes sparkled, and he hurried to an anteroom to take a phone call from President Johnson, back at the ranch.

"Bless your heart, thank you," Humphrey told him. Mrs. Johnson and the two Johnson daughters also got on the phone.

And when that five-minute conversation ended, the next caller was a political figure named Richard M. Nixon.

It was a courtesy call. Humphrey had done the same for Nixon after the Republican candidate was chosen in Miami Beach.

In this second installment of Dick and Hube on the telephone, the two men exchanged what was officially described as "banter." It isn't likely to happen again.

Meanwhile, the roaring and confrontations continued where Grant Park meets Michigan Avenue. And Hubert Humphrey knew it. Amid the happiness in 2525A, his feelings were very mixed. A night of terror and tear gas wasn't the perfect way to start a campaign.

But it was interesting to note, he remarked, that the demonstrations and violence had been forecast by both sides. The affair was unfolding almost like a script, he said.

A couple of hours later, he came into a jammed Waldorf Room on the hotel's third floor. He was beaming, and his wife smiled and so did three sons and a daughter.

Among those with him were San Francisco's Mayor Joseph Alioto, Lawrence O'Brien, Agriculture Sec. Orville Freeman and Senators Fred Harris (Okla.) and Walter Mondale (Minn.).

There were many young people in the room. The vice president talked to them and thus to all young people in America including Sen. McCarthy's backers and the battered demonstrators as well.

"Tonight my happiness is mixed with sadness," he said. "It makes me feel very bad when there's trouble—violent things that injure others.

"In a sense it puts a bad mark on what could be a beautiful picture. When there is trouble on the streets, no one profits.

"Democracy does not require force, brutality or violence," Humphrey continued. "It requires reason, tolerance and forebearance.

"Dissent is a legitimate function of a democratic society but it must be carried out within the rules of that society. My heart goes out to the injured."

And, he noted, "Life is not always a story of success. There are times when our hopes seem dashed—but there are very few dashed hopes if you have the will to carry on."

HHH, beaming, chin jutting firmly, strode out. The young people cheered and the band played "Up, Up and Away."

It was the end of a very big day, but HHH did not seem a bit tired.

The President's Supreme Court choice relied on the recommendation of Atty. Gen. Mitchell

William J. Eaton of the Daily News *Washington Bureau won a Pulitzer Prize for disclosures that led to the Senate rejection of Richard M. Nixon's nomination of Clement F. Haynsworth Jr. to the Supreme Court. This story by Eaton was published Nov. 8, 1969.*

WASHINGTON—The President, thinking he had a perfect Supreme Court nominee who came from a traditionally Democratic Southern state, made only a cursory background investigation and did not consult members of the Senate on the choice.

Instead, the President relied almost exclusively on the recommendation of Atty. Gen. Mitchell, who praised the nominee's "high legal competence."

Much of the initial reaction was favorable but there were disquieting rumbles from organized labor and the National Assn. for the Advancement of Colored People. Eventually, Senate leaders from the President's own Republican Party urged him to withdraw the nomination rather than risk rejection.

The American Bar Assn. rallied in support of the nominee, who sat on the 4th Circuit Court of Appeals, and the President determined to make it a fight to the finish.

The nominee in this historic confrontation between the White House and the Senate was Judge John J. Parker. The President was Herbert C. Hoover, his attorney general was William Mitchell and the year was 1930. The Senate rejected Parker by a two-vote margin.

The sequence of events bears almost an uncanny resemblance to Richard M. Nixon's nomination of Clement F. Haynsworth Jr. to the Supreme Court.

The Haynsworth nomination is in serious jeopardy in the Senate. A variety of surveys show senators almost evenly divided over the selection of the 57-year-old South Carolina judge for the high bench. Opponents say they have the votes to block his elevation, while White House sources insist he will win confirmation by an eyelash. A vote may come in the week starting Nov. 17.

Parker's judicial ethics never were questioned, while Haynsworth's business dealings have been a constant target for his critics. But other circumstances are nearly identical.

Parker, like Haynsworth, came from a Southern state that had voted for the victorious Republican presidential candidate.

Parker, a North Carolinian, also came from a distinguished family whose ancestors fought for the Confederacy in the Civil War. Both men won academic honors in college and became widely known attorneys in their state.

Both Parker and Haynsworth were appointed to the U.S. Court of Appeals for the 4th Circuit by Republican presidents—Calvin Coolidge and Dwight D. Eisenhower, respectively.

Both judges were regarded as amiable and charming and both were strict constructionists of the law when on the bench.

Both men were criticized for their decisions in controversial labor cases and both were accused of being unfriendly to the aspirations of Negroes.

Liberal Republicans said—in 1930 and 1969—that the President's nominee was obscure and mediocre in his legal scholarship.

In 1930 and 1969, the opponents included liberals, moderates and conservatives from both Democratic and Republican blocs.

Labor spearheaded the opposition to Parker, who ruled in favor of the antiunion "yellow-dog contracts," and Haynsworth, who ruled that a textile chain could shut down a mill because the workers wanted union representation.

In 1930, Senate hearings opened with the nominee under sharp attack from William Green, president of the American Federation of Labor, and Walter White, acting secretary of the NAACP. In 1969, leading critics included George Meany, head of the AFL-CIO, and Roy Wilkins, executive director of the NAACP.

President Hoover—and President Nixon—were unyielding despite the rising opposition to their nominees.

Many Republicans, especially those from large Northern states with significant numbers of Negro voters, urged withdrawal of the nomination, without success.

In the drive to round up votes for Parker, the White House was accused of trying to persuade wavering senators with patronage, including judgeships and ambassadorships. In the pro-Haynsworth effort, some senators have complained of heavy pressure from big Republican contributors, bar associations and business groups in their home states.

The vote against Parker was 41 to 39, with both liberal and regular Republicans deserting the President on the issue.

Will history repeat itself in 1969? Only the Senate can say.

Of sausages and Presidents— a few well-directed wurruds from Finley Peter Dunne

Humorist Finley Peter Dunne authored the few wurruds below after Upton Sinclair's devastating novel The Jungle *shocked the nation.*

Tiddy was toying with a light breakfast and idly turnin' over th' pages if th' new book with both hands. Suddenly he rose fr'm th' table, an' cryin'; "I'm pizened," begun throwin' sausages out iv th' window.

Th' ninth wan sthruck Sinitor Biv'ridge on th' head an' made him a blond. It bounced off, exploded, an' blew a leg off a secret-service agent, an' th' scattered fragmints desthroyed a handsome row iv' ol' oak-trees.

Sinitor Biv'ridge rushed in, thinkin' that th' President was bein' assassynated by his devoted followers in th' Sinit, an' discovered Tiddy engaged in hand-to-hand conflict with a potted ham. Th' Sinitor fr'm Injyanny, with a few well-directed wurruds, put out th' fuse an' rendered the missile harmless.

Since thin th' Presidint, like th' rest iv us, has become a viggytaryan.

Larry S. Finley chronicles one man's train of thought on an America 'going to hell'

Larry S. Finley was returning to Chicago from a weekend in Wisconsin when he stumbled into this story that a less perceptive reporter doubtless would have missed. The story appeared in the Daily News *of Oct. 7, 1970.*

The old man definitely had a message. "Wake Up, America!" he said.

The woman with the silver blue hair raised her head from her husband's shoulder and looked around, toward the voice.

"Dummies, a whole country filled with dummies and foreigners. What's happening to you, America?" someone was saying.

She whispered something into her husband's ear and he answered her without turning his stare from the rain and darkness that moved past the train window.

The old man with the fishing rods had boarded the train somewhere south of Madison, in one of those little towns surrounded by Wisconsin lakes.

In his right hand, he carried two fishing rods tied together with the reels taken off. In the same hand, he carried a green metal tackle box. In the left hand, he carried a white plastic-foam bucket filled with ice and cans of Hamm's beer.

He was 55, maybe 60; his eyes were squinty, his face sprouted a silver coating of whiskers through the tanned skin.

He took the last seat in the car. He could have had seats anywhere in the car. Only five others were taken. But he took the last seat.

After the conductor picked up his ticket and left, the fisherman reached into the bucket, pooshed open the pop-top ring on the beer can and quickly emptied it.

He began talking, very loudly, as though he were talking with someone in the seat across the aisle, someone who wasn't answering or only nodding without listening.

Soon his voice rose and filled the car. He spoke quickly.

"The only thing I caught was some damn perch. I used to come up here and catch walleyes and pike and bass. Now only perch can live in that filth. It's not the same.

"Dummies, what are you doing to this country? What's happening to you, America?" he repeated.

America didn't answer.

After the first few minutes, no one looked around at the fisherman.

"They think I'm going to take $40 or $50 out of my check every week so that some damn dummy can sit around and have babies."

Then, in a passable Irish tenor, he began to sing.

"A-mare-e-ca, A-mare-e-ca," He stopped.

"A World War II hero with medals. Big deal. What good does it do me? This Lindsay in New York, big man, big deal:

" 'You're a brave man to stay out of the war and go to Canada.' "

"This is just the start. Listen to me. What happened in Madison can happen all over the world. Give these students a real liberal education. Kick them out. Close the colleges in America and put them to work.

"The educated dummies. If their brains was dynamite they couldn't blow their noses.

"Saran Saran. There's another foreign-born dummy. He didn't kill Bobby Kennedy. The labor unions did. They've got more power than the government.

"Those prisoners on the hijacked planes. Anybody who can afford to fly all over the world like that deserves whatever they get.

"Now the price of my plane tickets will go up too."

He whistled a stanza of "America," ending it with the clink of an empty beer can against the metal side of the train. The train jogged sideways at a turn and a bump sent the can rolling between the seats.

"Now they are going to have U.S. marshals on every flight. Imagine getting shot at 50,000 feet. Boom. Boom.

"If you didn't make a dollar, the FBI couldn't find you. The couldn't find first base unless you put $20 bills along the baseline. 'FBI'—Foreign Born Idiots.

"Oh, Beautiful verboten skies.

"42 out of every check goes for some dummies. That leaves me with one hundred dollars and nine cents.

"Whatever happened to the Constitution? Wake up, America. You're going to hell."

Before each speech, the old man announced his subject with a word or a sentence, explaining his topic, like a sixth-grader reading the title of a theme.

His range was wide, as wide as the world, or the night through which the train rushed.

"I see the Cubs lost a couple more in the 8th.

"I see Cassius Clay or Muhammad whatever is going to fight on Oct. 26 in Atlanta.

"He won't fight in the army, but he wants to fight in the ring. When you don't want to fight anymore in the ring, you can just lay down and quit and you aren't dead.

"And bless thy good with brotherhood.

"Brotherhood? I've never seen so much hate in all my life. Even bartenders hate me. Remember Joe's Friendly Bar? Joe ain't friendly no more.

"Agnew has a very good choice of words. They're so good they ain't even in the dictionary. I tried to look them up.

"And bless thy good with brotherhood.

"Green, white, yellow, black. It doesn't seem to make any difference anymore. Dummies.

"Damn all the dummies and the long-hair punks. They're dirty and use vulgar language, and there ain't no sonofabitch that is man enough to stand up to them."

Clink, another can under the seat. Poosh, another can open.

"Lincoln-Rockwell had the right idea. The major leagues. That's a farce too."

He coughed deeply and repeatedly, cutting the first cough with the gurgle of a mouthful of beer.

"There's a cough that tears you off.

"Listen. Damn it listen. I'm going to Australia. America, you've shot your load. Just a bunch of stupid foreigners. We feed 'em. We pay 'em. If we need something, get lost.

"Doesn't anyone know the facts of life any more? Don't they use their brains? Overpaid, oversexed and over here. Get lost. Get lost.

"Over here, over here. Send the word, send the word. I'm over here.

"And bless thy good with barrenhood. And bless thy good with . . . Robin Hood? He steals from the rich to give to the poor. No more. It's the other way around now. Vote for the Democrats. Vote for the Republicans. George Wallace had the right idea. I hope you get in. No busing: states' rights.

"America, you're gone. I said so. According to the Constitution, which we don't have, only the Congress shall have the power to declare war. Ha.

"Social Security. When I get old enough to collect, they'll be broke. They're broke already. Everybody's broke.

"We put a dime in, and somehow the politicians figure out how to pocket a quarter.

"Good old Uncle. Uncle Sugar. Uncle Sam will take you from the cradle to the grave. Do we abide by the Constitution now?

"America, wake up. They're laughing at you. Wake up."

He ran his hand through the ice and water in the bucket. Then wiped it dry on his trousers.

For a few minutes he just sat there with his eyes closed. Then he slumped back into the seat. Asleep.

"Chicago. End of the line. Chicago. End of the line."

He didn't wake up. The conductor shook him gently. "Wake up," the conductor said.

"What? Yeah, wake up. We've all got to wake up."

Thirty minutes of sleep had refreshed the fisherman, and he was off, telling the troubles of the world at high voice, off the train and into Union Station.

"Damn it," he said, walking down the platform. "It used to be a good neighborhood, out there. People would sit around on the porches at night and talk and drink. Now you can't even go outside.

"Wake up. You're going to hell, America. Listen to me. Listen to me."

The heads among the benches in the waiting room turned toward the echoing voice, then turned away. Finally a policeman walked over, firmly took the fisherman's arm, and walked him through a doorway.

America had finally listened.

Reporter on the road finds American spirit alive, but stunned by events of the '60s

In 1972, Daily News *reporter Harlan Draeger was assigned to report on the mood of an America obviously afflicted with a severe morale problem. He talked to typical Americans and wrote an unusual series. This was the first installment, published June 17.*

Tom Bryant, if anybody, has a right to be cynical.

For 24 years, he has swallowed the dust and heat that go with the hardest, dirtiest job in a Chicago steel mill. His spit comes out black.

Bryant survived four major battles in Europe during World War II. Two decades later, his son and only child came back from Vietnam badly crippled.

Income taxes and inflation are cutting deeply into his paychecks. His property taxes have tripled in 13 years. Economically, he's "just not getting nowhere." On top of all this, he has the added pressures of being black.

Life has been one long, tough grind for Tom Bryant.

He should be screaming at the system—and, to a certain extent, he is. But this 240-pound steelworker with the callous-crusted hands is no cynic.

Along with most Americans, he shares a spark of hope.

It comes out, not as reliance on the big institutions of society, but as a stubborn faith in his fellow man: "We've got a whole lot of good, sound-thinking people. I think the great majority are really decent. They just got to the point where they're complacent and don't fight City Hall. Nobody's willing to take the lead."

Tom Bryant's message is that the American spirit is not

453

dead—just temporarily stunned by events, waiting to be revived.

Over the past several weeks, I discovered this same core of belief in talks with scores of people across the nation.

True, skepticism may run deeper than before. Americans are being pushed around by changes they dimly understand and can't seem to control. For many, life has turned sour, empty, unrewarding.

But the central, inescapable fact is that we have not given up, nor have we thought of surrender.

This pebble of truth is easily overlooked. It is, after all, a presidential election year. Pollsters, reporters and other professional pulse-takers are swarming over the landscape like grasshoppers.

People feel almost compelled to spit out their frustrations and resentments. Why not? Bitch a little ("Since you asked, Mac") and something might change.

So the man on the street talks like a loser, partly for effect. It is fashionable in 1972. And he is merely catching up to the social critics who have produced a steady stream of pessimism over the last decade.

The easy analysis that usually follows is that America is in a hopeless state that can only become worse.

It pays, I learned, to spend a little more time with people. Examine the whole person, watch how he lives, sift out what he says from how he acts. You rarely find genuine despair.

The essential fabric of trust still remains—largely intact, largely unnoticed, clearly our greatest national asset.

It is something on which to build a better life in this country if we only can regain the will and a sense of direction. We have at least a fair chance.

My assignment was to take a close look at what's happening to Americans in 1972—and especially at our obvious morale problem.

I found most of us floundering, groping awkwardly for some meaning to a world, that, like bakery products, seems to be remade fresh every day.

More than anything else, our national mood resembles the

stage of life that Tom Bryant has reached at 49: middle age, with all its fears and doubts.

New pressures are bearing down from all sides, and we can't respond the way we once did. The scenery shifts constantly. The pace and complexity of change are too much.

"If you go down a street for years and suddenly it's ripped up, you're shook," said Nat Pressman, a former New York lawyer who now sells hardware in Maryland. "Life is hitting a detour these days."

Pressmen, like many others, resists. An outspoken conservative in his 50s, he talks in political terms, and his villains are predictable:

"The liberals want to do it differently. If it's black, make it white. They got to live in a world of change. Why change everything? All these landmarks and beliefs we entertained are being attacked. We buck it. We're on the defensive. The average man just mutters to himself. He's wondering why."

Pressmen is quick to condemn irritants that he associates with younger people—sloppy dress, violent demonstrations, the push to legalize abortion and marijuana.

Even in his outrage, Pressman, the supreme realist, has not given up on human values.

"My goal is happiness and love and respect," he said, softening his tone. "I find it in my family and the people I know. The warmth, the human element is fading out, but not completely. People are basically good."

If life today is a "detour" for Nat Pressman, it is a sea disaster for 22-year-old Milo Mason—as apostle of change.

"We're shipwrecked," he said in the midst of repairing a tractor to get back to planting 60 acres of soybeans. "But only when you're shipwrecked can you reach for a more meaningful life."

Milo runs his father's 250-acre farm near the Wabash River that separates Indiana and Illinois. He uses the profits to attend Cornell University. And he typifies the 180-degree shift in the attitudes of many young people.

In 1968, Milo was co-chairman of Illinois Youth for Nixon. This year, he said, "I will probably be working for George

McGovern when I get the soybeans planted."

Milo's creed developed slowly. It began taking shape when he was 17 and wrote a pessimistic poem about man's humanity to man.

"I had a feeling then that something wasn't right, but I really didn't know the answers or ultimate causes," he recalls. "I was sickened by the hypocrisy of so many adults. They could go to church on Sunday and all that. Yet, when someone speaks of low-cost housing for low-income people and them paying taxes for that, it gets them upset."

Milo's search for answers provided him with another familiar catalog of devils—the Vietnam War, materialism, corporate pollution, deceitful politicians, racial bigotry, "the iron menagerie running a very inhumane system."

Lately, Milo hasn't seen much of his old high-school pals, who don't feel quite as strongly as he does.

"The majority of them really see something wrong, but they are still following in the footsteps of the consumer society," he says. "Their ideal is a 472-cubic-inch GM car. They have much more social responsibility in many ways, but they still haven't admitted blood on their hands."

Milo's personal ambition is "experiencing and creating beautiful things, whether planting a soybean field or rewriting an analysis of American history."

He believes his country can create such opportunities for all its people if fundamental changes are made—first in government, then in the economic system:

"Mass technology, if properly channeled, can elevate man from his total economic struggle. We have the power to make over meaningless, dehumanizing jobs so we can sit on the corner and play a banjo. We just can't turn off technology, but we can't go on with the only motive being profit.

"Just sweet Christian words won't do a damned bit of good."

Nat Pressman and Milo Mason. Two different generations. Two very different outlooks. Yet both critical of what's happening in society. Both wanting something better for their country. Both somehow hopeful that decent people can work it all out.

And there stands Tom Bryant, balancing his hopes and frustrations daily in the U.S. Steel Corp. mill on Chicago's Southeast Side.

Every working day, Bryant puts on a respirator and crawls inside big ingot molds. With an air hammer and 12-pound sledge, he chips off the rough spots so another cast can be made.

"It's a lousy job," says Bryant. He's the only one left out of 45 who were chipping molds when he started. He says about half a dozen are on pensions and the rest are dead, many of silicosis, a lung disease.

Bryant earns about $9,000 a year. He lays out $750 for house taxes and another $110 every two weeks for federal and state income taxes.

"I think the whole tax structure is wrong," he said. "The little guy is being squeezed. I have nothing against taxation, but we're not getting a dollar's worth.

"Police protection is lousy. They should put the cops back walking beats. I pay for mosquito abatement, but the last time they came was about 1960."

What's needed, according to Bryant and many others, is someone to "grab the ball"—political leadership:

"I think it all depends on who we elect to run the country. We need to do some thinking, get some new faces more representative of the people as a whole.

"We could probably start in our cities and communities. We tend to elect people who get in office and think they own the whole town. They are not responsive to the needs of the people."

Then he picks up enthusiasm:

"Maybe we should get a new kind of election system where the party bosses don't pick the guy to run. I think there's enough good people to make it work."

Paul Ghali sees Mussolini
swing by the feet from
a gasoline-station roof

*Paul Ghali was one of a legion of World War II
stars of the* Daily News *Foreign Service. This
dispatch of his from Italy was published April
29, 1945.*

MILAN—I have just seen Europe's first and longest-lived dictator hanging by the feet in Milan's Piazzo Loretto, his black
shirt, half covering the once famous Roman features, stained
with blood.

The body of Il Duce hung among a gruesome court of ca-
davers. On his left was that of his mistress, Claretta Petacci,
clad in a brown suit and barely soiled white blouse. Petacci had
been a happy refugee in Spain, but she had had the unfortunate
idea of rejoining her lover at Lago di Garda.

Morgue attendants found pinned to her underclothing a
diamond-studded gold locket, a gift from Il Duce.

It bore this prophetic inscription: "I am thee, thou art me,
Ben."

Then came the body of Alessendro Pavolini, the last secretary of the Fascist Party and Achille Starace, former secretary
general of the party.

On Il Duce's right swung Interior Minister Paolo Zerbini,
Undersec. of the Interior Ministry Francesco Barracu and Atti-
lio Terruzi, former minister to Italian Africa. All except Mussolini wore civilian garb.

When I arrived in Milan after crossing from Switzerland into Italy and motoring to Como to visit Partisan friends whose
acquaintance I made at Domodosola last October, the people
were demonstrating their joy at being rid of the tyrant.

The body of the late ex-dictator, whose last appearance in
public was mute but more eloquent than any of his speeches
458

from the famous Piazza Venezia, along with those of his closest followers, had first been laid on the ground after they were shot.

When the people shouted they could not see them they were hanged to the roof of a gasoline station, where they were on exhibition from 8 Sunday morning until 2 in the afternoon.

I was driven here by Silvio Baridon of the Partisan division's "Fiamme Verde" (green flame) and now head of Como's troops. On the famous autostrada from Como to Milan there was plenty of evidence that only 24 hours before, heavy fighting had taken place there between the Partisans and Germans. Burned-out tanks lay on the road and planes circled overhead.

Silvio was worried by the planes, fearing we might be taken for Germans. He insisted on our taking cover at each plane swoop. Finally I persuaded him to risk proceeding.

On the way he filled in the background of the capture and shooting of the Italian dictator. A section of the Garibaldini partisans, commanded by one "Bill," was responsible, according to Silvio.

"Bill," it seems, had spotted a convoy of eight cars hastening eastward toward Valetellina. He ordered the cars stopped. Mussolini, wearing a German cap, was discovered hiding under a pile of coats. He immediately raised his hands, begging for mercy.

After a brief trial, presided over by Cino Moscatelli, popular Communist partisan leader, Mussolini and those accompanying him were condemned and shot in the backs like traitors. The shooting took place at Giulino de Messegre.

According to "Bill's" story, Il Duce appeared dazed, and indulged in no heroics. In fact, he was the only one of the party who did not cry "Long live Italy."

Remnants of the Nazi occupation were still visible. At crossroads a poster welcoming the Allies was affixed just under a big placard showing Hitler's thumb over London.

American and British troops waited at Milan's gates until the bodies of Mussolini and his followers had been taken down and transported to the Milan cemetery. Then, late this afternoon they entered.

As for the way in which Mussolini and the others died, not

a single Italian with whom I have talked had any criticism to offer, though perhaps to Anglo-Saxon minds the exhibition of a former dictator hanging by the heels may be shocking. The Italians seem to feel that it was more humane to shoot Mussolini on the spot than to move him from prisons to tribunals for public debates.

In fact, the only indulgent remark I heard all the while I was in this city was that of a woman standing next to me in Piazza Loretto.

"It would have been better for him had he remained a schoolmaster at Predappio," said this good soul.

Traveling with Khrushchev: 'Like holding a stick of dynamite with a sputtering fuse'

Washington Bureau chief Peter Lisagor wrote this story for the Sept. 21, 1959, Daily News.

SAN FRANCISCO—Soviet Premier Khrushchev's fantastic confrontation with America has reached the midway point—and both give evidence of surviving each other.

It hasn't been easy.

American officials accompanying the Communist guest, their fingers still crossed, hope their worst moment has passed.

But no one can safely predict what this volatile visitor may do next in an Odyssey as strange perhaps as any in the history of the republic.

Traveling with Khrushchev is like holding a stick of dynamite with a sputtering fuse.

This man has an endless repertoire of moods. He can flit from a touching recital of his life as a soiled coal miner dreaming of a Communist paradise to a fist-clenching menace threatening to grab the first plane back to Moscow—almost in mid-sentence.

He can quote from the Bible in one breath and Joe Stalin in the next.

He is by turns indulgent, wrathful, comical, earnest, contemptuous and solicitous.

Aboard a plush Southern Pacific train from Los Angeles, he walked among reporters, red-eyed with fatigue, and told in moving tones how a little girl waved at him from the countryside.

"A little girl waving at a Communist," he said. "Her mother probably told her I am one of the men on whom war or peace depends."

A few minutes later, he said of his threat to leave the country in Los Angeles: "When you have needles punched in you, you retaliate." The remark seemed innocuous enough, but he punctuated it with a sharp gesture of his fist directed at a reporter's belt.

At an angry, roughhouse debate with labor-union leaders, according to Walter Reuther, AFL-CIO vice president, he got up from his chair and demonstrated the "immoral" dance of the cancan he had seen on a Hollywood movie lot.

This chameleon-like man told Frank Sinatra that he hoped to see *Cancan,* the movie, when it was completed. But afterwards he expressed disgust at what he saw, calling it pornographic.

He cried out that he was being prevented from visiting Disneyland by American security arrangements when it was his own Soviet security police who originally vetoed the plan as too risky.

And when he finally chose to walk among Americans gathered at San Luis Obispo on his route to this bay city, he announced that he had been liberated from "house arrest."

Again it was his own Soviet security boys who fought against such stops up to the moment the train pulled to a halt.

"I have seen some real-live Americans," he exulted later, "and they are as kind and gentle as the Soviet people."

He has called United Nations Ambassador Henry Cabot Lodge, his official escort, "my exploiter," in a laughing, childish manner.

He meant that Lodge was putting him through a strenuous schedule—but one that had been arranged largely by his own ambassador, Mikhail Menshikov.

He blows hot and cold, and when he's hot, he's very hot—which worries his official hosts.

His verbal tantrums have been sandwiched between passionate appeals for peace and contrite apologies. Sometimes these angry outbursts seem contrived and sometimes genuine.

When anyone at lunch or dinner meetings mentions a subject about which he is sensitive, he builds up a head of steam slowly and then lets go like Chinese firecrackers.

For a time he apparently thought the questions he considered embarrassing were part of a plot hatched in Washington to ridicule or demean him. This is the way it would be done in Russia.

But it is now felt he has been reassured that they are not, but nobody can be certain.

Lodge has made efforts to get local officials, many of them candidates for re-election, to soft-pedal any references to sensitive topics.

For a great concern is that Khrushchev will approach his meetings with President Eisenhower at Camp David, Md., Sept, 25, in a temper that would rob the talks of the slim hope they have of producing some kind of understanding.

Khrushchev is showing himself to be a man of immense self-confidence and a massive vanity who likes to refer to himself in the third person when emphasizing that he is the head of the powerful Soviet Union.

He doesn't like the gibes of a movie studio or a mayor, for in his organization they are minor functionaries who ought to be seen working and not heard, especially in the presence of an august figure such as himself.

He has proved himself devastating in debate, ripping off fresh aphorisms and proverbs to illustrate every point, with no particular attention paid to the facts as related by competent historians.

President Eisenhower invited Khrushchev here to learn something about the United States and its people. It will be a good time before one can know, if he ever knows, whether America to the world's top Communist becomes more than the faces of Walter Reuther and Frank Sinatra, top business leaders and a little girl waving to a train.

It will take time to learn, if ever possible, whether his three-hour discussion with the labor leaders, described as angry, unruly, insulting at various points, made a dent.

But of one thing you can be sure—this country is learning a good deal about Khrushchev as they watch him range over his emotions like a xylophonist playing *The Flight of the Bumblebee.*

Americans can see for themselves that, variable and unpredictable as he is, he remains nevertheless a formidable antagonist, shrewd, tough, proud, defiant, obstinate.

And as one reporter on the trip has said, "Khrushchev's jokes are no laughing matter."

It said a lot for the performance at midpoint.

'It recurs on grave markers with anguishing monotony: Aug. 6, 1945 . . . Aug. 6, 1945'

Nicholas Shuman, Daily News *Foreign editor, visited Hiroshima as the 30th anniversary of the holocaust approached. He filed this memorable article, published July 29, 1975.*

HIROSHIMA—Unlike other Japanese cities, this one is laid out in grids. The boulevards are broad, and the vistas often are grand. Though it stands amid the relics of a 2,000-year-old-civilization, Hiroshima is new. Glass and aluminum high-rises sparkle in the sun, unsullied by time.

Urban renewal—the hard way.

The Bomb was dropped 30 years ago. The date is easy to remember here. It recurs on the markers in Hiroshima's cemeteries with anguishing monotony: Aug. 6, 1945 . . . Aug. 6, 1945 . . . Aug. 6, 1945 . . . .

Today, 1,850 feet below where the fireball burst, lies a plain cleared by its blast. Thirty years ago this was Nakajima-cho, the hub of the city, jammed as only Oriental cities can be with stores, restaurants, temples and homes. Now it is Peace Memorial Park.

In the park's center stands a simple stone arch, a cenotaph, on which is inscribed: "Rest in peace, for the error shall not be repeated." Error? That's Japanese understatement.

The ambiguity also is typically Japanese. Who made the error? Was it the people who brought you the rape of Nanking, the attack on Pearl Harbor and the Bataan Death March? Or the people who created The Bomb and delivered it to Hiroshima and Nagasaki? Or was it man at large who, alone among God's creatures, slaughters his own?

Never mind. There was sin enough for all, and Americans wear it heavily as they move from monument to monument.

(And never mind, either, the promise that the error shall not be repeated. Six nations at least now have The Bomb and the experts estimate that at least 10 others have or will have the capability to make it. Thus, the Japanese are entitled only to hope, not to promise.)

Hiroshima is a delta city, sitting on six arms of the Ota River that fan out into the serenely lovely, island-dotted Inland Sea. A crescent of mountains binds it to its shores.

Today, with its suburbs consolidated, it has a population of 750,000. The city is thriving, in spite of the recession, and the people hustle about their business—and even their recreation—with determination. The pace, however, seems a shade easier than the frenzy of Tokyo, 555 miles to the east.

On Aug. 6, 1945, an estimated 420,000 persons were in the city, including substantial numbers of soldiers, for Hiroshima was a major army base of western Honshu, the main island of the Japanese archipelago.

There had been an air of foreboding among the people, some recalled later, because Tokyo and other major cities by then had been devastated by American bombers, yet Hiroshima had been spared, as if for a special fate.

It came in an American B-29, the Enola Gay, at 8:15 on a hot and cloudless morning. A few survivors saw the bomb drift downward, slowly, like a spider descending on its thread.

Only later were they to give it a name, "Pikadon" (flash bang), and still later to know what it was.

First it blossomed silently into a blinding, bluish-white ball, incinerating man, metal and masonry. The blast wave followed, leveling almost everything that stood before it. Ground Zero was Shima Hospital—which vanished—though the target was said to be a bridge nearby. Every building within a radius of more than a mile was demolished and, beyond that, most of what little was left was consumed by the fires that burned for two days thereafter.

More than 70,000 persons were killed instantly, and the total, by Japanese count, was to rise to more than 200,000—nearly half of the city's inhabitants.

They still are dying, according to the authorities here.

Next Wednesday, as on every Aug. 6, there will be a ceremony at the cenotaph. Prayers will be said, the mayor will read a "peace declaration" calling for nuclear disarmament, and a stone vault beneath the cenotaph will be opened to receive the names of the newly dead. There are 84,803 names of known dead in the vault now.

Critics of Hiroshima charge the city with obsession (When did you last hear of Nagasaki and its bomb?) and say that this part of the ceremony—the sealing of the names—taints it. They say that deaths directly attributable to the bomb are presumed to have ceased long since and that the new "victims" are A-bomb survivors who died of any illness that conceivably might have been induced by radiation—such as leukemia and other blood diseases.

But if any city has paid for the right to be obsessed, it is Hiroshima. And if any man lived to carry the memory of the holocaust for 30 years, rather than died in it, let him, too, rest in peace.

One visits Peace Memorial Park on this pleasant Sunday and is torn by contrasts. Death is here—but resurrection, too.

Memorials abound, but a new generation of tremendously vital Japanese frolics among them in holiday mood.

Ahead, across the river, stands the ruin of what had been the Industrial Promotion Hall, its masonry shredded, the steel framework of its dome stark against the sky. It is the only remnant of the bombing that has been allowed to stand. But beyond it are the modern high-rise apartments, the handsome department store and office buildings, the new factories of a city reborn.

At the cenotaph flares an eternal flame, but below, in the river, the living shout and splash in a fleet of rowboats.

To the left looms the towering, bomb-shaped monument to the children who perished under the A-bomb. Inside its hollow hang hundreds of multicolored strands of paper cranes—birds of good wishes here—each strand 1,000 cranes long, laboriously folded by schoolchildren of today's generation in memory of those of another.

At the cenotaph, an old woman in blue-gray kimono places

467

a bouquet in a rack of them, claps her hands twice to summon Buddha and bows her head in meditation. Behind her, on the broad lawn, pink-cheeked children play amid their picnics, pestering parents for the price of a "French dogu" (hot dog) or a helium balloon.

A museum in rectangular, contemporary style, floating on concrete piers, seals off the end of the park. Inside, solemnity has replaced holiday festivity. The foreign visitors move along shoulder to shoulder with the Japanese, who with inbred courtesy do not make eye contact, leaving us alone to our American thoughts.

The first exhibit is a panoramic reconstruction of the city, perhaps 15 feet in diameter, showing what was left after The Bomb—a plain of rubble broken only by the clean lines of the winding rivers.

In the exhibit cases are samples of The Bomb's refuse—a watch stopped at 8:15, glass fused to metal, shattered roof tiles, a photo of a man's figure silhouetted on stone by the flash, molten buttons of a schoolchild's tattered uniform . . . .

And most startling of all, a life-size diorama of two women and a child in mad flight from the unknown terror, clothing torn from their bodies, flesh shorn from their faces, arms and exposed breasts.

At the exit is a visitor's book, a registry of names, addresses and impressions. Among the impressions written in English, most with American addresses, are these:

"A very great lesson." . . . "May God and history forgive us." . . . "Embarrassment." . . . "War is foolish." . . . . "Disgust." . . . "The innocent suffer with the guilty." . . . "Tragedy and hope." . . . "Horrifying." . . . "We are ashamed."

The visitors return to the tour bus in silence. Aboard, rock music blares from the radio, and someone asks the driver to turn it off, please.

Yet, as the days that followed showed, if there is any residual anger left among the Japanese, it is not apparent or uttered.

"There is no feeling against Americans here," we were assured by Toranosuke Takeshita, vice governor of Hiroshima Prefecture.

On the streets teen-agers wear T-shirts emblazoned with the names of American universities, and younger children are eager to try their English on you.

In a recent survey, Hiroshima schoolchildren were asked who, among foreigners, were their favorite people. "Americans," a majority replied.

Tekeshita reported that "the younger generation has no interest in the past (The Bomb)," and this is concern enough to the administration so that it has put out a special 30th-anniversary pamphlet to remind them of it. "We don't want them to be angry," he said. "But we do want them to remember those who suffered . . . to realize how much tragedy there was."

One evening we had dinner with two students from the University of Hiroshima—Takafume Sato, 25, a graduate law student, and Hitomi Okuda, 22, a third-year law student. Their view on Americans and The Bomb:

Sato—"Certainly the use of the atomic bomb should not be sanctioned, but because of The Bomb, Japan was emancipated from militarism."

Miss Okuda—"I can't agree with the use of the atomic bomb, but if Japan had it before you, they would have used it against you."

True, but not entirely absolving. We did not get to speak to any eyewitnesses of the bombing, like one of those whose statements are on exhibit at the Peace Memorial Museum:

"Around me lay people with reddish-white skin peeled off and hanging down, people with swollen bodies, people scorched all black . . . lying all about . . . and everywhere people were groaning, and everywhere it smelled very bad, the stink of death . . . . One after another they passed away . . . silently all. The invaluable human life was as worthless as that of a nameless insect."

Robert Gruenberg tells how a nurse helped keep a spark of life from dying

In 1952, a live birth was recorded at Chicago's Michael Reese Hospital, thanks in large part to the valiant efforts of one nurse. Six years later, Robert Gruenberg told about it in this touching story published Oct. 16, 1958.

He was nothing more than a tiny spark of life on that cold January night nearly six years ago.

He weighed a trifle over 3 pounds. You could cradle him between your elbow and your hand.

He was pink, almost red, and his hair—hair that covered his whole, tiny, fragile body—was orange.

A tiny postage stamp of a face peeped out from the mass of hair. He didn't cry. He didn't turn. He lay still.

He was a "preemie," one of thousands of premature babies born in Chicago each year.

"Maybe he'll make it," said the intern as they rushed him in the Board of Health ambulance to the world-famous premature center at Michael Reese Hospital.

"Maybe . . . maybe . . . maybe . . . ."

The man in the white gown was clinically cold.

At Reese he was placed in an "Isolette," a special kind of incubator. He lay still.

Nurses spun wheels and turned handles. They made it warm and moist for him inside. But he was motionless.

Then passed the longest days. His parents telephoned the nursery again and again, night and morning and afternoon.

They came to see if there was a change. There was none.

"Don't be too hopeful," the nurses said as gently as they could.

"He has lost 4 ounces, he is down to 2¾ pounds."

They fed him. Eight times a day, around the clock. They

used a medicine dropper, filled with milk—and a little whisky! But he didn't respond very much.

Then his parents got the news: "He has sclerema. You ought to talk to the doctors."

The specialists gathered and shook their heads. One said:

"Sclerema neonatorum. It is a hardening of the skin and of the feet and the legs because of a lack of fatty acids in the tissue. It is almost always fatal.

"He is in the hands of the gods."

But nobody told that to the little wisp of life.

And Evelyn Lundeen—with her 29 years of life-sustaining experience—did not give up. She started when the doctors gave up.

Up—up—went the temperature in the "Isolette," to 101 degrees. Up went the humidity to 90 per cent.

She was literally "melting" him down, melting the hard tissue! Around the clock nurses under her direction exercised his tiny legs and arms.

An eon seemed to pass. It was really only three or four days.

Finally—he moved. He struggled out of the apathy.

He was to live.

Then half ounce followed half ounce each day. Soon it was an ounce a day—then two.

The medicine dropper was abandoned in favor of a bottle.

At the end of two months he weighed a miraculous 4½ pounds. And home he went, to sleep in a basket and be bathed in a dishpan.

Today he is healthy and alert and even "ornery," sometimes, thanks to Evelyn Lundeen and her staff.

His name is Mark Gruenberg. He is my son.

Index To Reporters

A

Ade, George   18, 43

B

Baker, Ray Stannard   237
Beech, Keyes   87, 269
Bell, Edward Scott,   67
Bowman, James   257

C

Campbell, Anthony   334
Cappo, Joe   320, 354
Carmichael, John P.   359
Casey, Robert J.   23, 84
Christiansen, Richard   151
Coffey, Raymond   285, 311

D

Draeger, Harlan   453
Duck, Harvey   377
Dunne, Finley Peter   314, 447

E

Eaton, William J.   444
Eulenberg, Ed   101

F

Field, Eugene   182
Finley, Larry S.   448
Flynn, Betty   315

G

Geyer, Georgie Anne   432
Ghali, Paul   458
Goldstein, Alvin   405
Gorlick, Arthur   212
Green, Larry   288
Griffin, Dick   227, 345
Gruenberg, Robert   428, 470
Gunther, John   67
Gysel, Dean   56

H

Haas, Joseph   99
Hanson, Henry   147
Harmon, George   330, 420
Harris, Sydney J.   118, 155, 386
Hecht, Ben   67, 414
Herguth, Robert J.   110

J

Jackson, David   215

K

Kisor, Henry   162
Kloss, James   58

L

Lahey, Edwin A.   250, 405
Levin, Meyer   405
Lewis, Lloyd   371
Lisagor, Peter   425, 461
Long, Hwa-Shu   138

M

McElheny, Marge   355, 417
McMullen, Jay   157
Mark, Norman   301
Miller, Dan   177
Monk, Diane   60
Mooney, William F.   201
Morrison, Walter   262
Mowrer, Edgar   67
Mowrer, Paul Scott   67
Mulroy, Jim   405
Mutter, Alan D.   342

N

Nelson, Wade   408
Newman, M. W.   35, 126, 131, 438
Nicodemus, Charles   199
Nightingale, Dave   374

O

O'Brien, Howard Vincent   192

P

Palmer, L. F. Jr.   252
Pesman, Sandra   338

R

Rooney, Edmund J.   123, 394, 420
Rowan, Carl T.   247
Royko, Mike   40, 107, 307

S

Sandburg, Carl   242
Saperstein, Saundra   218
Sauter, Van Gordon   391
Schaudt, Harry   220
Schenet, Bob   113, 412
Schnedler, Jack   169
Schultz, Robert G.   97, 123
Sellers, Thomas E.   103
Shuman, Nicholas   123, 465
Signer, Robert   382
Smith, John Justin   62, 91
Snider, Arthur J.   123, 204
Sons, Ray   362
Steele, A. T.   73

Stowe, Leland   77, 80
Swing, Raymond   67

T

Tamarkin, Bob   276

V

Vass, George   364
Von Hoffman, Nicholas   231

W

Warden, Rob   297, 408
Warren, Ellen   93, 290
Washington, Betty   294
Weller, George   11
Wille, Lois   45, 185
Wright, Edan   222

Y

Yahn, Steve   325, 350

Z

Zochert, Donald   26, 394